Information and Notification Duties

Editors:
Ilse Samoy
Marco B.M. Loos

Information and Notification Duties

intersentia

METRO

Ius Commune Europaeum

Intersentia Ltd
Sheraton House | Castle Park
Cambridge | CB3 0AX | United Kingdom
Tel.: +44 1223 370 170 | Fax: +44 1223 370 169
Email: mail@intersentia.co.uk
www.intersentia.com | www.intersentia.co.uk

Distribution for the UK and Ireland:
NBN International
Airport Business Centre, 10 Thornbury Road
Plymouth, PL6 7 PP
United Kingdom
Tel.: +44 1752 202 301 | Fax: +44 1752 202 331
Email: orders@nbninternational.com

Distribution for Europe and all other countries:
Intersentia Publishing nv
Groenstraat 31
2640 Mortsel
Belgium
Tel.: +32 3 680 15 50 | Fax: +32 3 658 71 21
Email: mail@intersentia.be

Distribution for the USA and Canada:
International Specialized Book Services
920 NE 58th Ave. Suite 300
Portland, OR 97213
USA
Tel.: +1 800 944 6190 (toll free) | Fax: +1 503 280 8832
Email: info@isbs.com

Information and Notification Duties

ISBN 978-1-78068-353-9
D/2015/7849/130
NUR 822

British Library Cataloguing in Publication Data. A catalogue record for this book is available from the British Library.

Ilse Samoy and
Marco B.M. Loos

INFORMATION AND NOTIFICATION DUTIES – AN INTRODUCTION

Technological and economical developments require contracting parties to be informed and advised: informed about the characteristics of the services or the goods they order; well advised about their choices and options; informed about the remedies that may be used against them; and well protected from the consequences of a lack of information or notification. It is only through the gathering and the supply of information that one can obtain knowledge. In sum, information and notification duties are designed to facilitate a well-informed behaviour.

Information and notification duties can be found in different varieties. Traditionally they have been associated with doctrines such as mistake and misrepresentation and have been brought in relation with conformity issues. These duties to warn play an important role in various domains and especially in construction law, financial services and tort law. An important question in this regard is: *who is responsible to supply or to acquire the information*? This problem is indissolubly intertwined with the tension between autonomy (getting informed is each person's own responsibility) and solidarity (informing another person in order to protect that person from harm that the informing person is aware of, but the other person is likely not to be aware of). More recently, this question has been linked with the upcoming concept of the "duty of care". This seems to mark an era where there is a shift from autonomy towards solidarity and protection of the weaker party. These considerations are in line with legislative action, for example information obligations have been introduced through (European) consumer law legislation. In particular, the introduction of information obligations in consumer legislation aims at restoring the balance of negotiating power between traders (that have information) and consumers (that lack information) and thus creating a level playing field for participants on the internal market.[1] In the above, the emphasis lies on the duty to inform and to notify the other party. This does not, however, completely wipe out the

1 See for instance recital (5) to the Consumer Rights Directive (Directive 2011/83/EU of the European Parliament and of the Council of 25 October 2011 on consumer rights, amending Council Directive 93/13/EEC and Directive 1999/44/EC of the European Parliament and of the Council and repealing Council Directive 85/577/EEC and Directive 97/7/EC of the European Parliament and of the Council, *OJ* 2011, L 304/64). On the effectiveness thereof, see *infra*, nos. 8 and 9 and the contributions to this book referred to in those numbers,.

responsibility of any party to gather information herself:[2] a failure to gather information may, for instance, lead to the loss of a claim for damages on the basis of contributory negligence.

In the first contribution of this book, **Sanne Jansen** focuses on the notification duties with regard to contractual parties. She discerns three different types of duties, namely: (1) the duty to put someone in delay in case of a breach of contract; (2) the notification of (partial) non-performance or breach of contract; (3) the notification of remedies. Indissolubly intertwined with this matter are the consequences of a lack of such a notification. It is clear that the notification of a (partial) non-performance and the notification of the consequential remedies are classical examples of "information and notification duties" and are indispensable. First of all, it is important that the debtor is notified of the shortcoming, so that he is offered a second chance and enabled to remedy his shortcoming. Secondly, these notifications also secure the possibility for the creditor to invoke the shortcoming and, in principle, the consequential remedies. When the creditor refrains from these actions this could have an impact on the interests and on the transfer of risk. The author conducts a profound study of the different notification obligations and searches for a balance between the rights and duties of the debtor on the one hand and those of the creditor on the other hand by studying the Belgian law of obligations and consumer law, European soft-law instruments and EU consumer law legislation (Principles of European Contract Law (PECL), Draft Common Frame of Reference (DCFR), the former proposal for a Common European Sales Law (CESL), Consumer Sales Directive).[3] Through this comparison some divergences are revealed between Belgian law *vis-à-vis* European law and suggestions are made to how the balance can be achieved.

As has been pointed out legislation concerning information and notification duties tends to put more emphasis on the protection of the weaker party and shifts away from the basic principle of autonomy and contracting freedom. This protection is mainly offered to consumers, but it is arguable that also small and medium enterprises (SME's) should benefit from these rules.[4] Most recently the information obligations have been

2 K.J.O. Jansen, "Informatieplichten. Over kennis en verantwoordelijkheid in contractenrecht en buitencontractueel aansprakelijkheidsrecht", Dissertation Leiden University, 2012, 1–3.

3 In the Communication from the Commission to the European Parliament, the Council, the European Economic and Social Committee and the Committee of the Regions of 16 December 2014, Commission Work Programme 2015: A New Start, COM(2014) 910 final, the new European Commission announced the withdrawal of a number of legislative proposals. CESL was listed as one of these, but a '(m)odified proposal in order to fully unleash the potential of e-commerce in the Digital Single Market' was announced together with the withdrawal of CESL (see Annex II, no. 60). The proposal for this instrument is expected to be published by the end of 2015. At the time when this book is being finalised for printing, it was thought that the provisions of the modified proposal would to a large extent resemble the provisions of CESL, but be restricted to contracts concluded online.

4 This matter is not dealt with in this book, see M.B.M. Loos and I. Samoy (eds.), *The position of small and medium-sized enterprises in European contract law*, Ius Commune Europaeum 121, Cambridge/Antwerp, Intersentia, 2014.

introduced on the basis of the implemented Consumer Rights Directive.[5] These information obligations have also been included in the proposal for a Common European Sales Law (CESL).[6] Amongst other things, two important interests have to be balanced against one and another when such consumer law legislation is adopted. On the one hand the functioning of the internal market must be further stimulated and distortions must be avoided as much as possible. On the other hand weaker contracting parties must be protected against a shortage of information or against a lack of knowledge about the exact content of the agreement.

Standard terms may also lead to an imbalance to the detriment of the weaker party. This contracting party will often be in the situation where he can't negotiate the conditions of the contract and is therefore confronted with a "*take it, or leave it*"-situation. In order to remedy this asymmetry, rules have been developed to protect weak contracting parties. Some of these rules were adopted at the European level so that pre-existing distortions of competition between the Member States are tackled. The provision of standard terms used by one party aims to inform the other party of the terms for the proposed contract. On the basis thereof the other party should be able to decide whether it wishes to be bound by the contract. For this reason, the Court of Justice regards the timely supply of standard terms in a consumer contract to be of fundamental importance to a consumer.[7]

In her contribution to this book, **Johanna Waelkens** elaborates on article 5 Unfair Terms Directive[8] that introduces a transparency and interpretation rule in business-to-consumer contracts (*B2C*). The author evaluates two systems of implementation of the Directive, namely by means of a separate statute (e.g. in the United Kingdom) or by integration in existing legislation (e.g. in Belgium, France, and the Netherlands). Article 5 stipulates, *i.a.*, that when a seller or supplier fails to draft a consumer contract in transparent, plain and intelligible language an interpretation at his disadvantage could be triggered. So, the interpretation most favourable for the consumer actually functions as one of the possible sanctions for not complying with the transparency and information requirement for terms that have not been individually negotiated.[9] The author deals with the reference person, in relation to which the judge has to ascertain the clearness of a consumer contract. She deciphers that the "average consumer"-test is differently construed depending on the subject matter (e.g. the "*notional, typical*

5 Directive 2011/83/EU of the European Parliament and of the Council of 25 October 2011 on consumer rights, amending Council Directive 93/13/EEC and Directive 1999/44/EC of the European Parliament and of the Council and repealing Council Directive 85/577/EEC and Directive 97/7/EC of the European Parliament and of the Council, *OJ* 2011, L 304/64.

6 On these instruments, see A.L.M. Keirse and M.B.M. Loos (eds.), *Alternative ways to Ius Commune: the Europeanisation of private law*, Ius Commune Europaeum 105, Cambridge/Antwerp, Intersentia, 2012.

7 See CJEU 21 March 2013, case C-92/11, ECLI:EU:C:2013:180 (RWE Vertrieb), point 44; CJEU 30 April 2014, case C-26/13, ECLI:EU:C:2014:282 (Kásler), point 70.

8 Council Directive 93/13/EEC of 5 April 1993 on unfair terms in consumer contracts, *OJ* 1993, L 95/29.

9 Another possible sanction is that the standard term itself is found to be unfair.

consumer" in the European Unfair Commercial Practices Directive as regard to a more flexible variant for the Unfair Terms Directive). She concludes with the possible outcomes of an interpretation by a judge and points out that the transparency and interpretation requirements are important, yet often unrecognised, rules that result in a wide consumer protection.

The question whether or not parties may be under an information obligation, is much more controversial in commercial law. The most debated issue is whether or not standard terms are incorporated into the contract if they have not been provided to the other party before the contract was concluded. In this respect, the jurisprudence of the Austrian *Oberster Gerichtshof* contradicts the jurisprudence of the German *Bundesgerichtshof* with regard to the Vienna Sales Convention (CISG). The highest Austrian court ruled that the CISG does not provide a specific rule, so that the general rules on the formation of contracts apply.[10] In short this means that standard terms are valid and can be relied upon by the party whenever the other party has accepted them. As opposed to this finding, the highest German court deducts an obligation from the CISG. According to the German court the CISG requires that the party wishing to rely on its standard terms has provided its counterpart with the opportunity to take note of these terms in an appropriate way and that this is only guaranteed where the first party provides the other with the standard terms.[11] Nevertheless, there is no provision in the CISG that explicitly requires providing the standard terms to the counterparty.[12] The European Commission seems to have followed an 'in-between' solution for B2B-contracts in the proposal for the CESL. Article 70(1) CESL provides that standard terms may only be invoked against the other party if the other party was aware of the terms or where the party supplying them has taken reasonable steps to draw the other party's attention to them before or at the time when the contract was concluded. With respect to consumers, Article 70(2) stipulates that: "*For the purposes of this Article, in relations between a trader and a consumer contract terms are not sufficiently brought to the consumer's attention by a mere reference to them in a contract document, even if the consumer signs the document.*" This paragraph implies that a mere reference to the existence and the applicability of standard terms suffices in commercial contracts (*B2B*). It will be interesting to see whether the European Commission will continue with this approach in the upcoming modified proposal for contracts concluded online.[13]

10 OGH 6 February 1996, 10 Ob 518/95, *Recht der Wirtschaft* 1996, 203–205, available at www.unilex.info/case.cfm?id=202 *(last visited on 23 September 2015).*

11 BGH 31 October 2001, VIII ZR 60/01, *NJW* 2002, 370, *BGHZ* 149, 113, available at www.unilex.info/case.cfm?pid=1&id=736&do=case *(last visited on 23 September 2015).*

12 M.B.M. Loos en H.N. Schelhaas, "Commercial Sales: The Common European Sales Law Compared to the Vienna Sales Convention", *European Review of Private Law*, 2013, 111–114. See also M.B.M. Loos, 'Art. 70–71: Incorporation and making available of standard contract terms', in: A.L.B. Colombi Ciacchi (ed.), *Contents and effects of contracts. Lessons to Learn from the CESL*, Cham/Heidelberg/Dordrecht/London, Springer, 2015 (forthcoming).

13 See *supra*, footnote 3.

As mentioned before, European legislation to protect consumers mainly focuses on the adequate and obligatory supply of information by the professional to the weaker party. This line of action has become the object of more and more criticism. Therefore, in this book not only the information and notification obligations as such are dealt with, but also their (in)effectiveness. Information obligations may remedy market failures according to law & economics theories, but consumer behavioural studies frequently criticise information obligations for being ineffective. **Johan Vannerom** critically scrutinises the shortcomings of the present European Consumer (Credit) Regulation by studying the behavioural abnormalities of consumers and the double consumer image that has surfaced in the case law of the European Court of Justice. It is however clear that the market systems themselves are insufficient to remedy the information asymmetry. Therefore, the author analyses, in a second step, alternative consumer policy methods. In this respect he develops the innovative notion of the "Multi-Layered Consumer", as consumers cannot be confined to a homogeneous group of people. Three different categories of consumers are distinguished, each requiring another level of protection. Subsequently the author applies this new criterion to the consumer credit legislation. He concludes by encouraging economists and European (and national) legislators to further explore the alternative policy choices and to come to a legal framework that achieves a high standard of consumer protection at minimal cost to businesses.

Carien de Jager approaches this gap between theory (i.e. information disclosure leads to optimal decision-making by the consumer) and reality (i.e. there are behavioural abnormalities that corrupt this link) in the light of investment products. The European Union stresses the importance of information disclosure by financial institutions. Recently a mandatory Key Information Document (KID) for investment products was proposed. The main purposes of this document are to improve the comprehensibility of financial products and to improve the comparability of financial products. The author evaluates the KID in light of insights from behavioural finance by comparing the behaviour of the rational investor with the conduct of an actual person. Psychological factors such as framing, heuristics, biases, emotions, self-deception, limited self-control and social influences make the rational investor a utopian image. However, little attention has been paid to these factors while drafting the KID. In the last part of her contribution, the author suggests some improvements to fine-tune and to improve the effectiveness of the KID by taking into account the actual behaviour of investors.

Finally, **Joasia Luzak** discusses the question *how* online traders must inform consumers under the disclosure rules of the Consumer Rights Directive. She starts from the assumption that – as is demonstrated in behavioural sciences – most information that is provided before the contract is concluded is probably not read by consumers at that stage. However, she argues that information obligations could be effective in another sense, that is: they could ensure that consumers possess the relevant information contained in the disclosures when they need that information at a later stage, e.g. when a lack of conformity in the goods delivered manifests. If consumers would then be able to find the information who to contact, than in this sense the duty to inform actually is relevant for consumers. With that starting point in mind, she searches what efforts traders must undertake to ascertain that the disclosure reaches consumers and whether they could rely on an, at least partially, active behaviour of consumers in obtaining this information, *e.g.* by requiring the consumer to click on hyperlinks leading to the relevant information. In this respect, the case-law of the Court of Justice on the information obligations of the former Distance Selling Directive[14] becomes relevant. In the Content Services case[15] the Court of Justice made clear that under that Directive, traders had to ensure that the information actually *reaches* the consumer. Merely providing evidence that information was *made available* to the consumer (so the consumer herself could then obtain the information via the hyperlink provided) does not suffice for the obligation to be met. She concludes that although the new Article 8 Consumer Rights Directive uses different wording than the Distance Selling Directive did, the implementation of the Consumer Rights Directive in the Netherlands and the United Kingdom may very well signal that the new legislation will not lead to a different decision by the Court of Justice. The author therefore concludes that although theoretical arguments could support a somewhat more lenient approach for complying with information obligations in the online environment through hyperlinks, traders would be wise not to hide mandatory disclosures behind hyperlinks.

Next to the problem of effectiveness, this book touches upon the question of compatibility of the European legislation with national and pre-existing EU-law. In his contribution, **Gerard de Vries** addresses the question whether the pre-contractual information duties for traders in the Draft Common Frame of Reference, the Consumer Rights Directive and the proposal for a Common European Sales Law are in line with the systems of national law of the Member States of the European Union and with the existing EU-law (the *acquis communautaire*). Firstly, the author examines the different European information duties of traders to provide the other party with information with respect to the main characteristics of the goods or services to be supplied. Secondly, he investigates how the systems of private law in France, Germany, the Netherlands, and the United Kingdom regulate these pre-contractual information requirements (e.g. the right to invoke vices of consent like mistake and fraud). He then concludes that, with the exception of French law, these systems of law reject a general pre-contractual information duty as put forward in the European instruments (DCFR, CRD, CESL). Moreover, the author puts question marks next to the compatibility of such a general duty with other existing EU-law.

In the last contribution of the book, **Mark Kawakami** and **Catalina Goanta** come with an innovative approach to discover which level of consumer protection is actually offered in internet contracts. Most literature – also in this book – is based on the interpretation of applicable rules and of available case-law, or consists of doctrinal critique on the basis of, for instance, the insights law & economics or behavioural

[14] Directive 97/7/EC of the European Parliament and of the Council of 20 May 1997 on the protection of consumers in respect of distance contracts, *OJ* 1997, L 144/19.

[15] CJEU 5 July 2012, case C-49/11, ECLI:EU:C:2012:419 (Content Services Ltd).

sciences offer. Instead, the authors of this final contribution have put theory into practice by conducting a personal experiment based on five jurisdictions (the Netherlands, Romania, the United Kingdom, Japan and the United States). They have determined the e-store with the largest market share for each jurisdiction and have ordered the same product in each e-store. They have then exercised their withdrawal right. In their contribution the authors link their findings with the discussions and method of implementation of the Consumer Rights Directive in the different jurisdictions and with the case law of the Court of Justice on the Distance Selling Directive. With their paper, the authors argue that the existing literature may mislead readers to believe that the interests of consumers have thoroughly been discussed, considered, and incorporated into the existing conversation. They conclude that in fact the existence of mandatory withdrawal rights in the EU does not offer much additional protection to what at least most major companies would offer their customers anyway, and that awarding such mandatory protection is not the only way to ensure consumer protection, and nor is it 'the best way' of doing. We remark, however, that whereas it may be true that major companies offer comparable or even better protection to consumers than mandatory consumer law does, this does not mean that the same is true for smaller companies. In this respect, we note that major companies have a reputation to loose. The fear for reputational damage may bring companies to offer more rights to consumers than they would otherwise be entitled to on the basis of the law. However, it seems doubtful whether the same is true, or to the same extent, with regard to smaller companies: we would think that for some it is, but for others it is not. The implied suggestion to 'just leave it all to the market', therefore, is not one we would recommend to be introduced in the European Union.

CONTENTS

CONTENTS

Sanne Jansen*

NOTIFICATION, SHORTCOMINGS, REMEDIES, AND DEFENCES: A COMPLEX RELATIONSHIP

A Comparison between Belgian Law and European Legal Instruments

"Obviously, a man's judgment cannot be better than the information on which he has based it."
Arthur Hays Sulzberger

I. Introduction

Jan rents an apartment from the company 'Rentanoffice'. No problems occur up until the day Jan notices that the heating and air-conditioning system has broken down. He wants Rentanoffice to fix it. At the same time he also wants the rent to be reduced for loss of enjoyment of his apartment and to withhold the future rent as to stimulate Rentanoffice to carry out the repairs as quickly as possible. The first initiative Jan should undertake is to inform Rentanoffice about the shortcoming in the heating and air-conditioning system and about the steps he intends to take.

Informing the debtor of a shortcoming and the steps the creditor wants to take (the remedies or the defences) are the central problems to this contribution. It focuses on the notification duties of contractual parties with regard to shortcomings and the desired remedies (or defences). Three different notification duties can be discerned: (1) '*the duty to put someone in delay*' in case of a breach of contract (i.e. 'a default notice'); (2) the *notification of* (partial) *non-performance* or breach of contract (*i.e.* a shortcoming); and (3) the *notification of remedies* (or defences) which can be analysed with regard to different remedies (and defences) such as termination, dissolution, price reduction, damages, suspension and specific performance.

Various questions will arise from this study and will be addressed in this contribution: What are the different ways to inform the debtor about a shortcoming and/or the remedies that can be used against him? What are the consequences of a lack of notification of a shortcoming, remedies, or defences? Do the notification duties differ if the temporary

* PhD., fellow of the Research Foundation – Flanders (FWO), KU Leuven, Institute for the Law of Obligations.

defence of suspension is relied on rather than any of the other remedies? Is it necessary to notify the debtor in the event of an excused shortcoming due to *force majeure*? What is the interplay between the duty to notify a shortcoming and the duty to give notice of remedies/defences to be relied on?

This study will be conducted according to the classical legal method, that is through a thorough study of regulations, recent case law and doctrinal studies. In addition, this research will not only be conducted for the Belgian law of obligations. Also, an in-depth comparison with EU soft law and consumer law instruments (such as the PECL[1], the DCFR[2], the CESL[3], and the Consumer Sales Directive[4]) will be carried out. Whereas Belgian law contains a general principle of 'putting the debtor in delay', some of the European instruments are more lenient towards this requirement, especially for consumers. This comparative legal research can question and challenge the classical Belgian solution.

In sum, this paper aims to clarify the ways in which the debtor is to be informed about a shortcoming and about the remedies that can be used against him. On the one hand, this information is crucial for a *debtor* to determine which actions he can undertake. On the other hand, the notification of a shortcoming or a remedy also provides legal certainty for the *creditor*. The notification will clarify the position of the creditor (e.g. in case of suspension or in applying a unilateral remedy) and it can have implications on the transfer of risk and on the interest. We will also examine the consequences of a lack of such notification. An interesting question is whether or not such a duty to notify can be qualified as an *Obliegenheit*, which cannot lead to a performance in kind in case of breach.[5] Unfortunately, the scope of our contribution does not allow us to go more deeply into this last matter.

Of course, in examining the described problems and questions we must strike a balance between the rights and duties of the debtor and the creditor in the contractual relationship. A possible answer lies in the comparison with the new European soft law instruments and the 'consumer *acquis*'.

1 Principles of European Contract Law (hereafter: PECL).

2 Draft Common Frame of Reference (hereafter: DCFR). C. Von Bar and E. Clive, *Draft Common Frame of Reference (DCFR)*, Munich, Sellier, 2009.

3 Proposal of the European Commission of 11 October 2011 for a regulation of the European Parliament and the Council on a Common European Sales Law, COM(2011) 635 final: http://ec.europa.eu/justice/contract/files/common_sales_law/regulation_sales_law_en.pdf. Hereafter the Annex of the Proposal for a regulation on a 'Common European Sales Law' will be referred to as the 'CESL'; the Proposal of the regulation will be referred to as the 'CESL-proposal'. It has to be noted that the CESL-proposal is on the List of withdrawals or modification of pending proposals of the Commission, issued the 16th of December 2014. In this document the Commission makes clear that it wants to issue a "Modified proposal in order to fully unleash the potential of ecommerce in the Digital Single Market": http://ec.europa.eu/atwork/pdf/cwp_2015_withdrawals_en.pdf. The European Commission intends to issue a new project with regard to the e-commerce sector: http://data.consilium.europa.eu/doc/document/ST-8672-2015-INIT/nl/pdf.

4 Directive 1999/44/EC of 25 May 1999 on certain aspects of the sale of consumer goods and associated guarantees, *OJ L*. 1999, 171/12 (hereafter: Consumer Sales Directive).

5 M. Fontaine, "Obliegenheit, incombance?" in X (ed.), *Liber Amicorum Hubert Claassens*, 1998, (151) 151–163.

II. Notifying a shortcoming

The duty of the creditor to notify a shortcoming is important for both parties, debtor and creditor. On the one hand, the duty to notify a shortcoming informs the debtor of the non-performance.[6] This information can be crucial for the debtor to determine which action he can undertake, such as to remedy the shortcomings. On the other hand, important repercussions exist for the creditor, such as the transfer of risk, the interests that start to run and the possibility to invoke a remedy.

In this part of the contribution a distinction is made between the duty to notify an *unexcused* shortcoming (breach of contract) (2.1) and an *excused* shortcoming (*force majeure*) (1.2). This distinction is made because Belgian law distinguishes between the remedies of *unexcused* and *excused* shortcomings. However, note that this distinction is not made in the DCFR, the PECL, the CESL and the Consumer Sales Directive.

2.1. Notifying an unexcused shortcoming

Under Belgian contract law, *two different mechanisms* interfere with each other with regard to the duty to notify an unexcused shortcoming. On the one hand, a creditor has '*a duty to put his debtor in delay*'. On the other hand, some specific contracts require a general '*duty to notify*' a shortcoming. Consequently, I will examine 'the formal requisition of putting the debtor in delay' (2.1.1) apart from the 'other notification duties' (e.g. in sale and tenancy contracts) (2.1.2) without omitting to scrutinise the interplay between both mechanisms. Finally, the notification duties under European contract law (2.1.3) will be addressed and compared with those under Belgian contract law.

2.1.1. The formal requisition of putting the debtor in delay under Belgian contract law[7]

2.1.1.1. General principle and exceptions

i. General principle for contractual sanctions

When a debtor fails to perform his contractual obligations, the creditor has 'to put the debtor in delay' before being able to enforce his contractual rights by way of a contractual sanction.[8] Under Belgian law this has to be done by a 'default notice' (*ingebrekestelling/*

6 See for the same opinion about the default notice in French law: D. Allix, "Réflexions sur la mise en demeure", *JCP G* 1977, (2844) No. 6.

7 See also the contribution: S. Stijns, S. Jansen and K. Vanhove, "Contractual liability by non-performance and termination by fault" in I. Samoy and B. Lambrecht (eds.), *Consortium Agreements for Research Projects. Multiparty Agreements under Belgian Contract Law*, Cambridge, Intersentia, 2011, (163) 163 *et seq.*

8 In Belgian law the word 'sanction' is usually used for remedies in case of an *unexcused* non-performance such as termination, damages and performance (in kind).

mise en demeure).[9] The default notice has to convey the intention of the creditor to demand performance of the obligations by the debtor.[10] An important ruling of the Court of Cassation established a 'general principle' of putting the debtor in delay.[11] Some French authors specify that the duty to put a debtor in delay results from the duty to perform the contract in good faith.[12]

First of all, it is necessary to put the debtor in delay before any of the judicial sanctions for unexcused (partial) non-performance or breach of contract can be applied: performance in kind, performance by equivalent (damages), price reduction in special contracts (such as Article 1644 CC) and judicial termination for reciprocal contracts. Secondly, a default notice is also needed when calling upon a contractual clause that provides for a sanction in the case of breach,[13] for example, the use of a penalty clause.[14] Finally, it is also necessary to put the debtor in delay when applying a unilateral/extrajudicial sanction such as an extrajudicial termination (e.g. by means of an express resolutive clause)[15], an extrajudicial price reduction (Article 50 CISG)[16] or an extrajudicial replacement.[17]

9 Both the terms 'to put in delay' as 'default notice' will be used to indicate the requisition of putting the debtor in delay under Belgian contract law. In Dutch law Article 6:82 of the Dutch Civil Code (DCC) prescribes a similar duty of putting the debtor in delay. See also about this "ingebrekestelling": C. Asser, A.S. Hartkamp and C.H. Sieburgh, *v° Verbintenis in het algemeen, eerste gedeelte, Asser-serie*, 6-I, 2011, 387.

10 L. Demeyere and M. Visser, "Ingebrekestellingsclausules" in G.-L. Ballon, H. De Decker, V. Sagaert *et al.* (eds.), *Contractuele Clausules*, II, Antwerp, Intersentia, 2013, (997) 1004. Compare with France: B. Gimonprez, *v° Mise en demeure, Rép. civ. Dalloz*, 2009, No. 1.

11 Cass. 9 April 1976, *Arr.Cass.* 1976, 921, *Pas.* 1976, 887 and *RW* 1976–77, 921, note.

12 B. Gimonprez, *v° Mise en demeure, Rép. civ. Dalloz*, 2009, No. 4. Compare with: Y. Picod, "L'obligation de coopération dans l'exécution du contrat", *JCP G* 1988, I, (3318) No. 16 ("*tout changement dans l'exécution devra être signalé par celui qui attend une prestation certaine ou éventuelle de l'autre afin que ce dernier exécute en connaissance de cause*").

13 S. Stijns, *Leerboek Verbintenissenrecht*, vol. 1, Bruges, die Keure, 2005, 168; W. Van Gerven and S. Covemaeker, *Verbintenissenrecht*, Leuven, Acco, 2006, 594–595; P. Wéry, "La mise en demeure en matière d'obligations contractuelles" in P.A. Foriers (ed.), *Les obligations contractuelles*, Brussels, JBB, 2000, (285) 325–327; P. Wéry, *Droit des obligations*, I, Brussels, Larcier, 2011, No. 469–472.

14 Article 1230 CC.

15 See, for example, Article 1656 CC (sales) and Cass. 24 March 1995, *Arr.Cass.* 1995, 346, *Pas.* 1995, 358, *TBBR* 1997, 98, note K. Creyf, *T.Not.* 1996, 140 and *R.Cass.* 1995, 267, note S. Stijns. See also for France: C. Paulin, *La clause résolutoire*, Paris, LGDJ, 1996, No. 153. Seems *contra* for France (certainly for urgent situations): C. Pelletier, "Rôle de la mise en demeure dans le mécanisme de la résolution unilatérale aux risques et périls du créancier" (case note under Cass. Fr. civ. 24 September 2009, No. 08–14524), *RDCO* 2010, (690) No. 2–4 (see also: Cass. 24 September 2009, No. 08–14524, *not published in Bull. Civ.*).

16 United Nations Convention on Contracts for the International Sale of Goods, 1980.

17 H. Geens, "Ingebrekestellingsbedingen" in S. Stijns and K. Vanderschot (eds.), *Contractuele clausules rond de (niet-)uitvoering en beëindiging van contracten*, Antwerp, Intersentia, 2006, (157) 158–159; S. Stijns, *Leerboek Verbintenissenrecht*, vol. 1, Bruges, die Keure, 2005, 168; W. Van Gerven and S. Covemaeker, *Verbintenissenrecht*, Leuven, Acco, 2006, 594–595; P. Wéry, "La mise en demeure en matière d'obligations contractuelles" in P.A. Foriers (ed.), *Les obligations contractuelles*, Brussels, JBB, 2000, (285) 327. See e.g. also for France: C. Popineau-Dehaullon, *Les remèdes de justice privée à l'inexécution du contrat*, Paris, LGDJ, 2008, No. 863 and 865.

ii. Exceptions

Although there is a general rule to put the debtor in delay, several exceptions exist to this rule.

First of all, there are *provisions* of the Civil Code[18] and special laws[19] that provide for (one of) the effect(s) of a default notice, without actually serving such a notice (see about the effects *infra*, 2.1.1.4).[20] Article 1378 CC is especially of interest: '*if a party has received* (an undue payment), *in bad faith, he does not have to return solely the capital, but also the interest and other rewards (vruchten) as from the day of the payment.*' Secondly, an explicit legal provision can 'exempt' the creditor of the obligation to put the debtor in delay. Such provisions can be found in the Civil Code. Article 1146 CC states for example: '*it is not necessary to serve notice to the debtor when the debtor could not fulfil its obligation within a certain time limit, fixed beforehand.*'[21] Article 1145 CC states that when a debtor has promised not to act/to abstain, but he does act, there is no need to put him in delay in order to benefit in the same effect as if there was a default notice.[22]

Besides the exceptions in legal provisions, the *Court of Cassation* has ruled that no default notice is needed when (in line with Articles 1145 and 1146 CC) performance has become impossible,[23] or when it becomes evident that performance has lost all usefulness[24] for the creditor.[25] A ruling of the Court of Cassation – which falls outside the scope of this article – held that when a creditor wants *extra-contractual* or *quasi-contractual* repair, no default notice is required.[26] It is indeed useless, because this situation is similar to the situation in Article 1145 CC: a debtor has acted but should not have acted in the first place. Another ruling of the Court of Cassation also stated that any useful *contractual*

18 E.g. Arts. 1378, 1436, 1652, 1657, 1996 and 2001 CC.

19 Article 102, Law of 3 July 1978 on employment contracts, *Belgian Official Gazette* 22 August 1978, *err.* 30 August 1978; Article 10, Law of 12 April 1965 on the protection of wages of employees, *Belgian Official Gazette* 30 April 1965; Article 5, Law of 2 August 2002 on combating late payment in commercial transactions, *Belgian Official Gazette* 7 August 2002, *etc.*

20 See also for legal exceptions in French law: R. Libchaber, "Demeure et mise en demeure en droit français" in M. Fontaine and G. Viney (eds.), *Les sanctions de l'inexécution des obligations contractuelles*, Brussels, Bruylant, 2001, (113) No. 15 (no default notice needed so that the effects of it take place) and 16 (no default notice because the debtor cannot be in 'default').

21 See e.g.: Cass. 14 March 1991, *Arr.Cass.* 1990–91, 734, *Pas.* 1991, 651 and *RW* 1993–94, 1276. See detailed: L. Demeyere and M. Visser, "Ingebrekestellingsclausules" in G.-L. Ballon, H. De Decker, V. Sagaert, *et al.* (eds.), *Contractuele Clausules*, II, Antwerp, Intersentia, 2013, (997) 1011.

22 See e.g.: Cass. 23 September 1994, *Arr.Cass.* 1994, 777 and *Pas.* 1994, 759. See for France e.g.: Cass. Fr. civ. 26 February 2002, No. 99-19053, *Bull. Civ.* 2002, I, No. 68.

23 Cass. 23 September 1994, *Arr.Cass.* 1994, 777 and *Pas.* 1994, 759 (breach of an obligation not to act). See also for France: B. Fages, "Nul besoin de mise en demeure lorsque l'exécution est devenue impossible" (case note under Cass. Fr. com. 17 February 2009, No. 08-13.896), *RTD Civ.* 2009, (322) 322.

24 Cass. 26 September 1996, *Arr.Cass.* 1996, 810 and *Pas.* 1996, 868.

25 Cass. 29 November 1984, *Arr.Cass.* 1984–85, 1011, *Pas.* 1985, 399 and *RW* 1986–87, 542; Cass. 22 March 1985, *Arr.Cass.* 1984–85, 1011, *Pas.* 1985, 929, *RW* 1986–87, 851 and *RCJB* 1989, 7, note R. Kruithof.

26 See, for example, Cass. 26 September 1996, *Arr.Cass.* 1996, 810, *Pas.* 1996, I, 868 and *RW* 1996–97, 1030.

performance becomes impossible when all the trust between parties is lost.[27] The most far-reaching ruling of the Court is that there is no need for a default notice when the debtor announces, unambiguously, that he has no intention to perform his obligations.[28]

The contracting parties can also stipulate a *contractual exemption* from the obligation to put the debtor in delay.[29] Parties must be careful while drawing up these exemption clauses. Only very specific and precise clauses can exempt the creditor: the clauses are submitted to restrictive interpretation, because they are an exception to the general rule.[30] There are some laws that forbid the contractual exemption of a default notice.[31]

iii. The *enac* and the requisition of putting the debtor in delay

There is a controversy in Belgian law about the need for a default notice before exercising the *exceptio non adimpleti contractus*[32] (hereafter, '*enac*'). The majority of legal doctrine[33] and jurisprudence[34] argues that a default notice is not required. The *enac* does not require

27 Cass. 24 March 1972, *Arr.Cass.* 1972, 707 and *Pas.* 1972, 693.

28 Cass. 17 January 1992, *Arr.Cass.* 1991–92, 436, *Pas.* 1992, 421 and *TBH* 1993, 237, note M.E. Storme. See also for France: Cass. Fr. com. 14 February 1967, *Bull. Civ.* 1967, III, No. 73; Cass. Fr. civ. 3 April 1973, No. 72–10247, *Bull. Civ.* 1973, III, No. 254. See about this exception for French law: C. Popineau-Dehaullon, *Les remèdes de justice privée à l'inexécution du contrat*, Paris, LGDJ, 2008, No. 886.

29 Article 1139 CC. Cass. 4 September 1975, *Arr.Cass.* 1976, 20, *RW* 1975–76, 1561, note H. Van Houtte, *JT* 1976, 243 and *Pas.* 1976, I, 16; Cass. 9 April 1976, *Arr.Cass.* 1976, 921, *Pas.* 1976, 887 and *RW* 1976–77, 921, note; see especially H. Geens, "Ingebrekestellingsbedingen" in S. Stijns and K. Vanderschot (eds.), *Contractuele clausules rond de (niet-)uitvoering en beëindiging van contracten*, Antwerp, Intersentia, 2006, (157) 166–170. See also for France: B. Gimonprez, *v° Mise en demeure, Rép. civ. Dalloz*, 2009, No. 28–29; R. Libchaber, "Demeure et mise en demeure en droit français" in M. Fontaine and G. Viney (eds.), *Les sanctions de l'inexécution des obligations contractuelles*, Brussels, Bruylant, 2001, (113) No. 15; C. Popineau-Dehaullon, *Les remèdes de justice privée à l'inexécution du contrat*, Paris, LGDJ, 2008, No. 893.

30 A restrictive interpretation means that the application of the clause is reduced to a minimum.

31 See, for example, Article 45 of the law on mortgage loans, Article VII.105 WER ("*Wetboek van economisch recht*" or Code on Economic Law, with regard to consumer loans), and Arts. 69–70 of the new law on insurance contracts of 4 April 2014.

32 The plea of suspension ("*exceptie van niet-uitvoering*"/"*exception d'inexécution*"), or *exceptio non adimpleti contractus* (*enac*), is a temporary defence that allows a party to a reciprocal contract not to perform / to withhold his performance, as long as the other party fails to perform his own obligations.

33 A. De Bersaques, note under Cass. 27 April 1947, *RCJB* 1949, (127) 134, No. 9 and 11; J. Herbots, "De exceptie van niet-nakoming", *TPR* 1991, (379) 394, No. 29; L. Lamine, *Het retentierecht*, Deurne, Kluwer, 1993, No. 133; M.E. Storme, "De exceptio non adimpleti contractus als uitleggingsvraag", *RW* 1989–90, (313) 323, No. 22; H. Van Gompel, "Vereist de toepassing van de exceptie van niet-uitvoering een voorafgaande ingebrekestelling?" (case note under Antwerp 9 December 2009), *Limb. Rechtsl.* 2010, (116) No. 4–6 (The application of the *enac* does not require any prior default notice; nevertheless a default notice is recommended in good faith if it is not clear which party has to perform first). See also for France: B. Gimonprez, *v° Mise en demeure, Rép. civ. Dalloz*, 2009, No. 53; R. Libchaber, "Demeure et mise en demeure en droit français" in M. Fontaine and G. Viney (eds.), *Les sanctions de l'inexécution des obligations contractuelles*, Brussels, Bruylant, 2001, (113) No. 20; C. Popineau-Dehaullon, *Les remèdes de justice privée à l'inexécution du contrat*, Paris, LGDJ, 2008, No. 898.

34 Cass. 16 March 1846, *Pas.* 1846, I, 368. Antwerp 30 September 2013, *Limb.Rechtsl.* 2014, 131, note I. Samoy and S. Jansen. See for France: Cass. Fr. com. 27 January 1970, No. 67–13764, *JCP* 1970, II, 16554 and *RTD civ.* 1971, 136.

a prior default notice because it is a mere 'defence' and not a 'sanction' or a 'remedy' for breach of contract.

Nevertheless, this point of view has recently been refined in two ways. Firstly, the creditor has the obligation to act in good faith, and consequently the *enac* will require in some situations a prior default notice.[35] Secondly, the *enac* has been considered a real *sanction* against breach of contract[36, 37] Consequently, some doctrine seems to accept that the *enac* is a real *sanction* or a remedy and not a mere defence which implies the use of a default notice.

The following paragraphs will demonstrate that in most cases, the first (majority) opinion is to be preferred. Nevertheless, the first opinion must be nuanced somewhat. It is important to stress that the *enac* must be considered a *temporary defence*. It allows the creditor of an unexcused shortcoming to suspend its own obligation(s) until the debtor performs.[38] In the meanwhile, both the suspending party and the debtor must refrain

35 Ghent, 27 June 1996, *AJT* 1996–97, note B. Wylleman.

36 See extensively about this topic (without taking stance): S. Stijns, C. Goethals and S. Jansen, "De ontbinding en de exceptie van niet-uitvoering bij meerpartijenovereenkomsten" in I. Samoy and P. Wéry (eds.), *Meerpartijenovereenkomsten*, Bruges – Brussels, die Keure – la Charte, 2013, (113) No. 76 and 88. Defending that the *enac* is a sanction and requires a perior default notice: C. Cauffman, "Opschortingsrechten bij niet-nakoming" in J. Smits and S. Stijns (eds.), *Remedies in het Belgisch en Nederlands contractenrecht*, Antwerp, Intersentia, 2000, (141) 161, No. 39; B. Dubuisson and J.-M. Trigaux, "L'exception d'inexécution en droit belge" in G. Viney and P. Jourdain (eds.), *Les sanctions de l'inexécution des obligations contractuelles*, Brussels – Paris, Bruylant – LGDJ, 2001, (57) 84, No. 35; S. Stijns, W. Van Gerven and P. Wéry, "Chronique de jurisprudence (1985–1995)", *JT* 1996, (689) 718, No. 86; P. Wéry, *Droit des obligations*, I, Brussels, Larcier, 2011, No. 474. *Contra*: D. Decloedt, "Enac-clausules of opschortingsclausules" in G.-L. Ballon, H. De Decker, V. Sagaert, *et al.* (eds.), *Gemeenrechtelijke clausules*, II, Antwerp, Intersentia, 2013, (1035) 1102.

37 Every sanction requires a prior default notice (general): Cass. 9 April 1976, *Arr.Cass.* 1976, 921, *Pas.* 1976, 887 and *RW* 1976–77, 921, note.

38 P.H. Delvaux, "Les clauses résolutoires expresses et les clauses aménagent l'exception d'inexécution" in X (ed.), *La rédaction des conditions générales contractuelles*, Ghent, Story-Scientia, 1985, (87) 91; I. Demuynck, "De exceptio non adimpleti contractus als deel van de algemene contractvoorwaarden", *TBBR* 1992, (328) 328, No. 1; H. De Page, *Traité*, II, Brussels, Bruylant, 1964, No. 859; B. Dubuisson and J.-M. Trigaux, "L'exception d'inexécution en droit belge" in G. Viney and P. Jourdain (eds.), *Les sanctions de l'inexécution des obligations contractuelles*, Brussels – Paris, Bruylant – LGDJ, 2001, (57) No. 1; C. Goux, "Les clauses relatives à l'exception d'inexécution" in P. Wéry (ed.), *Les clauses applicables en cas d'inexécution des obligations contractuelles*, Bruges, die Keure, 2001, (147) 149, No. 4; J. Herbots, "De exceptie van niet-nakoming", *TPR* 1991, (379) 380, No. 2; I. Samoy and S. Van Loock, "Actuele ontwikkelingen inzake uitvoering en beëindiging van contracten" in S. Stijns, V. Sagaert, I. Samoy, *et al.* (eds.), *Verbintenissenrecht, Themis*, Bruges, die Keure, 2012, (101) No. 32; S. Stijns, *Leerboek verbintenissenrecht*, Boek 1, Bruges, die Keure, 2005, No. 291; E. Swaenepoel, "Bedingen over de exceptie van niet-uitvoering" in S. Stijns and K. Vanderschot (eds.), *Contractuele clausules rond de (niet-)uitvoering en de beëindiging van contracten*, Antwerp, Intersentia, 2006, (133) No. 4; W. van Gerven and S. Covemaeker, *Verbintenissenrecht*, Leuven, Acco, 2006, 209; A. Van Oevelen, "Schorsing van verbintenissen en overeenkomsten krachtens de exceptie van niet-uitvoering en het retentierecht" in A. De Boeck, S. Stijns and R. Van Ransbeeck (eds.), *Schorsing van verbintenissen en overeenkomsten*, Bruges, die Keure, 2010, (15) No. 2–3; B. Wylleman, "Het verband van wederkerigheid tussen

from any act which could render performance of the contract definitively impossible.[39] To put it in other words: delay may not lead to denial.[40] This 'temporary' character is often underestimated in Belgian law. The application of the *enac* implies that, if suspension ends, the performance of the whole contract must still be possible in the future. If this is not the case, this concept cannot be qualified as the temporary defence '*enac*', but as a real sanction.[41] Furthermore, the question arises as to whether the *enac* has to be restricted to situations where the *excipiens* invokes it in a stage in which he can still perform *in kind*.[42] It seems defensible that if a party brings an action in performance by equivalent (damages) because performance of in kind became impossible, the other party cannot invoke the *enac* as a *temporary* defence.

> The facts of a case before the appellate court of Antwerp can give an illustration.[43] In this case an employer goes bankrupt and an employee still has the right on his wage in arrears. The employee orders a lawyer to the necessary actions to recover her wage from the bankrupt's assets. The lawyer starts with the procedure but fails to fulfil all the necessary actions in time. In the meanwhile, the lawyer asked the employee two times to pay him the retaining fee by means of sending her a letter. The competent authorities inform the employee that she cannot recover her wage from the bankrupt's assets because the necessary

verbintenissen als toepassingsvoorwaarde voor de exceptio non adimpleti contractus" (case note under Cass. 8 September 1995), *R. Cass.* 1996, (86) No. 2.

39 Liège 12 March 1998, *TBBR* 1999, 204; Ghent 14 September 1999, *AJT* 2001–02, 408, note F. Coryn. See e.g.: C. Cauffman, "Opschortingsrechten bij niet-nakoming" in J. Smits and S. Stijns (eds.), *Remedies in het Belgisch en Nederlands contractenrecht*, Antwerp, Intersentia, 2000, (141) 168, No. 52; F. Coryn, "Exceptio non adimpleti contractus: bezint, vooraleer U – voorlopig – niet begint!" (case note under Ghent 14 September 1999), *AJT* 2001–02, (411) 412, No. 4; I. Demuynck, "De exceptio non adimpleti contractus als deel van de algemene contractvoorwaarden", *TBBR* 1992, (328) 330, No. 2; C. Goux, "Les clauses relatives à l'exception d'inexécution" in P. Wéry (ed.), *Les clauses applicables en cas d'inexécution des obligations contractuelles*, Bruges, die Keure, 2001, (147) 153, No. 5, e); J. Herbots, "De exceptie van niet-nakoming", *TPR* 1991, (379) 393–394, No. 28; S. Stijns, C. Goethals and S. Jansen, "De ontbinding en de exceptie van niet-uitvoering bij meerpartijenovereenkomsten" in I. Samoy and P. Wéry (eds.), *Meerpartijenovereenkomsten*, Bruges – Brussels, die Keure – la Charte, 2013, (113) No. 91; M.E. Storme, "De exceptio non adimpleti contractus als uitleggingsvraag", *RW* 1989–90, (313) 321, No. 19; P. Van Der Putten, "Toepassing van de exceptio non adimpleti contractus bij huur" (case note under Cass. 2 November 1995), *AJT* 1996–97, (70) 72, No. 4; A. Van Oevelen, "Schorsing van verbintenissen en overeenkomsten krachtens de exceptie van niet-uitvoering en het retentierecht" in A. De Boeck, S. Stijns and R. Van Ransbeeck (eds.), *Schorsing van verbintenissen en overeenkomsten*, Bruges, die Keure, 2010, (15) No. 13; P. Van Ommeslaghe, *Traité de droit civil belge – Tome II: les obligations*, I, Brussels, Bruylant, 2013, No. 576.

40 I. Samoy and S. Jansen, "Uitstel is geen afstel: *enac* als tijdelijk verweermiddel en de noodzaak tot ingebrekestelling (neen) en kennisgeving (soms)" (case note under Antwerp 30 September 2013), *Limb. Rechtsl.* 2014, (135) No. 4.

41 See for a similar reasoning concerning insurance contracts (contracts with continuing obligations) in the Netherlands: G.J.P. de Vries, "It takes two to tango: exceptio non adimpleti contractus en ontbinding van overeenkomsten op grond van niet-nakoming", *Praktisch Procederen* 2004, (18) 19.

42 I. Samoy and S. Jansen, "Uitstel is geen afstel: *enac* als tijdelijk verweermiddel en de noodzaak tot ingebrekestelling (neen) en kennisgeving (soms)" (case note under Antwerp 30 September 2013), *Limb. Rechtsl.* 2014, (135) No. 4 *in fine*.

43 Antwerp 30 September 2013, *Limb.Rechtsl.* 2014, 131, note I. Samoy and S. Jansen.

declaration was not complied with in time. The employee filed an action against his lawyer and asked for contractual damages. The lawyer invokes, amongst other arguments, that he could suspend his obligations towards the employee as long as she had not paid the retaining fee.

The court of first instance of Tongeren rejects this reasoning because the lawyer has nor put his client in delay to pay this retaining fee, neither warned his client that he would suspend his contractual obligations.

In contrast, the court of appeal of Antwerp agrees with this reasoning of the lawyer because the general principle of *enac* allows that a contracting party, without prior intervention of a judge, suspends his own obligations. The court stresses that the *enac* does not require a warning and that the lawyer can suspend his obligations as long as the employee does not pay the retaining fee. According to the court it has no relevance that the possibility to recover debts in case of bankruptcy is limited in time. Moreover, according to the court, the lawyer is in good faith because the husband of the employee is known as a defaulter and the employee has never asked any information concerning her case.

This case illustrates that the lawyer puts the performance of the contract at risk by not fulfilling the required actions in time, and even made performance impossible. According to me, the lawyer has not invoked a 'temporary' defence such as the *enac*, but has invoked a definitive remedy such as termination.[44] Indeed, the action of the employee has been brought in a stage in which performance in kind became impossible and the employee requested performance by equivalent in the form of damages.

Because of the qualification of the *enac* as a temporary defence, and not as a definitive sanction or remedy, a prior default notice seems not necessary. A default notice is meant to express clearly and unambiguously the will of the creditor to obtain the main performance (see *infra*, 2.1.1.3), before coming into action. The default notice is the last 'warning shot' before the 'attack'.[45] However, the *enac* is not a means to attack but a means to defend (against an attack of the other party) and cannot be considered a precursor of an attack. It is illogical to fire a warning shot, before defending against an attack. This is the reason why the *enac* does not require a prior default notice. This does not preclude that in some specific circumstances good faith will require that the party invoking the *enac* has to notify the other party of his intention to invoke the *enac*. This brings us to the subject matter of part 2 'notification of a remedy or a defence', where we will treat this question (see *infra*, 3.1.3).

44 See for the same reasoning: I. Samoy and S. Jansen, "Uitstel is geen afstel: *enac* als tijdelijk verweermiddel en de noodzaak tot ingebrekestelling (neen) en kennisgeving (soms)" (case note under Antwerp 30 September 2013), *Limb. Rechtsl.* 2014, (135) No. 4.

45 See for the same expression: I. Samoy and S. Jansen, "Uitstel is geen afstel: *enac* als tijdelijk verweermiddel en de noodzaak tot ingebrekestelling (neen) en kennisgeving (soms)" (case note under Antwerp 30 September 2013), *Limb. Rechtsl.* 2014, (135) No. 6.

2.1.1.2. Timing of the default notice

The default notice has to be addressed to the debtor from the moment performance can be claimed by the creditor.[46] In 1989, the Court of Cassation[47] also accepted the principle of 'putting in delay *ad futurum*': the default notice can be addressed to the debtor even before performance can be claimed by the creditor, when the claim is not contested. The effects (see *infra*, 2.1.1.4) of such a default notice – the interests and the allocation of risk – will only take place from the moment that performance can be claimed by the creditor. Thus, the creditor can safely put the debtor in delay beforehand. Nevertheless, good faith requires for this moment to be chosen closely enough to the moment that performance can be claimed.[48]

2.1.1.3. Form and content of the default notice

Article 1139 CC states that a 'judicial demand' or any act with an equal status is needed to put the debtor in delay. Traditionally, a 'judicial demand' is an official summons (*deurwaardersexploot/exploit d'huissier)* by means of a so-called 'bailiff' (*gerechtsdeurwaarder/huissier de Justice).* Acts with an equal status to this '*exploit d'huissier*' are: serving a party with a writ of attachment (*beslag/saisie)*; a summons (*dagvaarding/citation en justice)*; a writ/petition for an amicable settlement; a statement/ brief; an appeal, *etc.*[49]

However, an important ruling of 28 March 1994 of the Court of Cassation[50] interpreted Article 1139 CC[51] in a very broad way. A default notice is, according to the Court, 'any

46 H. Geens, "Ingebrekestellingsbedingen" in S. Stijns and K. Vanderschot (eds.), *Contractuele clausules rond de (niet-)uitvoering en beëindiging van contracten,* Antwerp, Intersentia, 2006, (157) 162.

47 Cass. 19 June 1989, *Arr.Cass.* 1988–89, 1249, *Pas.* 1989, 1132, concl. Adv. Gen. Liekendael and *JLMB* 1989, 1186. Confirmed in Cass. 20 November 1989, *Arr.Cass.* 1989–90, 383, adv. Adv. Gen. Lenaerts, *Pas.* 1990, 342 and *RW* 1989–90, 957; Cass. 25 February 1993, *Pas.* 1993, 210, *RW* 1993–94, 126, note A. Van Oevelen and *TBH* 1994, 141, note M.E. Storme; Cass. 27 March 2000, *Arr.Cass.* 2000, 652, *Pas.* 2000, 643 and *RW* 2000–01, 773; Cass. 16 April 2009, AR C.07.0604, concl. Adv. Gen. Werquin, *JLMB* 2010, 1304.

48 B. De Coninck, "La mise en demeure. Rapport Belge" in M. Fontaine and G. Viney (eds.), *Les sanctions de l'inexécution des obligations contractuelles. Etudes de droit comparé,* Brussels-Paris, Bruylant-LGDJ, 2001, (113) 153; H. Geens, "Ingebrekestellingsbedingen" in S. Stijns and K. Vanderschot (eds.), *Contractuele clausules rond de (niet-)uitvoering en beëindiging van contracten,* Antwerp, Intersentia, 2006, (157) 163; S. Stijns, D. Van Gerven and P. Wéry, "Chronique de jurisprudence. Les obligations: les sources (1985–1995)", *JT* 1996, (689) 719.

49 W. Van Gerven and S. Covemaeker, *Verbintenissenrecht,* Leuven, Acco, 2006, 597–598; R. Van Ransbeeck, "Sancties bij niet nakoming. Ingebrekestelling" in L. De Keyser, E. Dirix, C. Sluyts and A. Van Gelder (eds.), *Bijzondere overeenkomsten: commentaar met overzicht van rechtspraak en rechtsleer,* Antwerp, Kluwer, 2010, losbl., (1) 4.

50 Cass. 28 March 1994, *Arr.Cass.* 1994, 319, *RW* 1994–95, 499, *Soc. Kron.* 1994, 163 and *JTT* 1994, 323. This has been accepted for longer in business-to-business (B2B) relations: Cass. 7 May 1880, *Pas.* 1880, 138, concl. first Adv. Gen. Mesdach de ter Kiele.

51 Which states that a default notice must take the form of a 'notice or an equivalent act'.

act that contains an injunction that makes it clear for the debtor that he is ordered to perform his obligation.' The form is thus less important than the content.[52] Practically speaking, it is enough – in civil and in commercial relations – to send a registered letter, but also a normal letter (with acknowledgement of receipt), a telegram, or an e-mail... will suffice.[53] Some authors[54] also claim that an 'oral' notice would be valid.[55] In commercial business-to-business relations (B2B), a recent ruling of the Court of Cassation of 20 November 2008[56] held that a written default notice is not necessary. For the sake of completeness, it should be mentioned that there are some laws that prescribe a compelling form for the default notice.[57]

The importance of the content of the default notice has already been highlighted in the preceding paragraph. The Court of Cassation stated in 1983 that the creditor must demand, in a compelling way, the performance of the obligations by the debtor – it must be a '*clear and unambiguous expression of the will of the creditor to obtain the main performance.*'[58] It is not necessary to use the specific wording,[59] but it is not enough to specify that you 'hope for' performance of the debtor.[60] Here, too, for the sake of completeness, it is worth mentioning that there are some laws that prescribe a specific content for the default notice.[61]

52 B. De Coninck, "La mise en demeure. Rapport Belge" in M. Fontaine and G. Viney (eds.), *Les sanctions de l'inexécution des obligations contractuelles. Etudes de droit comparé,* Brussels-Paris, Bruylant-LGDJ, 2001, (113) 145; S. Stijns, *Leerboek Verbintenissenrecht,* vol. 1, Bruges, die Keure, 2005, 170; S. Stijns, D. Van Gerven and P. Wéry, "Chronique de jurisprudence. Les obligations: les sources (1985–1995)", *JT* 1996, (689) 719. See also for French law: B. Gimonprez, *v° Mise en demeure, Rép. civ. Dalloz*, 2009, No. 11.

53 H. Geens, "Ingebrekestellingsbedingen" in S. Stijns and K. Vanderschot (eds.), *Contractuele clausules rond de (niet-)uitvoering en beëindiging van contracten,* Antwerp, Intersentia, 2006, (157) 173; W. Van Gerven and S. Covemaeker, *Verbintenissenrecht*, Leuven, Acco, 2006, 598; P. Van Ommeslaghe, *Traité de droit civil belge – Tome II: les obligations*, III, Brussels, Bruylant, 2013, No. 1504.

54 P. Wéry, *Droit des obligations*, I, Brussels, Larcier, 2011, No. 452.

55 In civil cases this is not, according to Van Ransbeeck, enough: R. Van Ransbeeck, "Sancties bij niet nakoming. Ingebrekestelling" in L. De Keyser, E. Dirix, C. Sluyts and A. Van Gelder (eds.), *Bijzondere overeenkomsten: commentaar met overzicht van rechtspraak en rechtsleer,* Antwerp, Kluwer, 2010, losbl., (1) 4.

56 Cass. 20 November 2008, *Rev. not. b.* 2009, 196 and *TBO* 2009, 26.

57 See, for example, Article 45 of the law on mortgage loans; Article VII.111 WER ("*Wetboek Economisch Recht*" or Code on Economic Law, with regard to consumer loans); and Article 70 of the new law on insurance contracts of 4 April 2014.

58 Cass. 16 September 1983, *Arr.Cass.* 1983–84, 45, *Pas.* 1984, 48 and *RW* 1984–85, 464; confirmed in Cass. 25 November 1991, *Arr.Cass.* 1991–92, 272, *Pas.* 1992, I, 231, note, *RW* 1991–92, 1364, *JT* 1992, 221 and *Soc. Kron.* 1992, 102. See also for France: B. Gimonprez, *v° Mise en demeure, Rép. civ. Dalloz*, 2009, No. 15. See also for the French case law: Cass. Fr. com. 12 October 1964, *Bull. civ.* 1964, III, No. 420; Cass. Fr. civ. 19 March 1997, No. 95–17070, *Bull. civ.* 1997, III, No. 63.

59 S. Stijns, *Leerboek Verbintenissenrecht,* vol. 1, Bruges, die Keure, 2005, 170; P. Van Ommeslaghe, *Traité de droit civil belge – Tome II: les obligations*, III, Brussels, Bruylant, 2013, No. 1504; P. Wéry, *Droit des obligations*, I, Brussels, Larcier, 2011, No. 456.

60 S. Stijns, *Leerboek Verbintenissenrecht,* vol. 1, Bruges, die Keure, 2005, 170.

61 E.g. Article 70 of the new law on insurance contracts of 4 April 2014 (the insurer must order the debtor to pay the premium within a certain period. This period may not be shorter than 15 days. The default

The question arises whether it is necessary to notify the debtor *about the intention to apply a specific sanction* in the default notice. This question is closely connected with part 3, where we will examine the 'notification to invoke remedies'. Note that in most cases,[62] it is not necessary to notify the debtor about the intention to apply a specific sanction or general legal sanctions.[63] A part of legal doctrine and jurisprudence holds the view that good faith requires that a sanction that is to be applied in the future has to be specified, when it concerns unilateral and extrajudicial sanctions (extrajudicial termination or extrajudicial replacement).[64] Although some authors seem to have rejected this point of view,[65] it is, in practice, prudent to stipulate any extrajudicial sanction in the default notice (see also *infra*, part 3).

The second question that arises is the necessity of giving the debtor *an additional period to perform* his obligations. Although the answer has a lot of practical relevance, confusion reigns. Modern legal doctrine emphasises that – when useful execution by the debtor is still possible – it is logical to give the debtor a 'reasonable additional period' to perform his obligations,[66] but does not always take a clear stance in the debate. Jurisprudence and

notice must stipulate the renewal date and the consequences of non-payment) and Article 6 of the law of 20 December 2002 on the amicable recovery of consumer debts, modified by the law of 27 March 2009.

62 Exceptions can be found in Article 1154 CC, a provision on interests on interests; see, also, on special laws: Article VII.105 WER ("*Wetboek Economisch Recht*" or Code on Economic Law, with regard to consumer loans); Article 45 and on mortgage loans; and Article 70 of the new law on insurance contracts of 4 April 2014.

63 Cass. 16 September 1983, *Arr.Cass.* 1983–1984, 45, *Pas.* 1984, 48 and *RW* 1984–85, 464 (penalty clauses); Cass. 25 November 1991, *Arr.Cass.* 1991–92, 272, *Pas.* 1992, I, 231, note, *RW* 1991–92, 1364, *JT* 1992, 221 and *Soc. Kron.* 1992, 102 (moratory interests); Cass. 18 December 1986, *Arr.Cass.* 1986–87, 525, *Pas.* 1987, 484, *RW* 1987–88, 55 and *JT* 1987, 162 (judicial termination).

64 B. De Coninck, "La mise en demeure. Rapport Belge" in M. Fontaine and G. Viney (eds.), *Les sanctions de l'inexécution des obligations contractuelles. Etudes de droit comparé*, Brussels-Paris, Bruylant-LGDJ, 2001, (113) 149–150; S. Stijns, D. Van Gerven and P. Wéry, "Chronique de jurisprudence. Les obligations: les sources (1985–1995)", *JT* 1996, (689) 719; P. Wéry, *Droit des obligations*, I, Brussels, Larcier, 2011, No. 599.

65 P. Van Ommeslaghe, *Traité de droit civil belge – Tome II: les obligations*, III, Brussels, Bruylant, 2013, No. 1504.

66 H. Geens, "Ingebrekestellingsbedingen" in S. Stijns and K. Vanderschot (eds.), *Contractuele clausules rond de (niet-)uitvoering en beëindiging van contracten*, Antwerp, Intersentia, 2006, (157) 177; P. Wéry, *Droit des obligations*, I, Brussels, Larcier, 2011, No. 460; P. Wéry, "La mise en demeure en matière d'obligations contractuelles" in P.A. Foriers (ed.), *Les obligations contractuelles*, Brussels, JBB, 2000, (285) 310–312. See also about this problem: T. Delahaye, *Résiliation et résolution unilatérales en droit commercial belge*, Brussels, Bruylant, 1984, No. 235; L. Demeyere and M. Visser, "Ingebrekestellingsclausules" in G.-L. Ballon, H. De Decker, V. Sagaert, *et al.* (eds.), *Contractuele Clausules*, II, Antwerp, Intersentia, 2013, (997) 1020–1021. See also for French law: C. Paulin, *La clause résolutoire*, Paris, LGDJ, 1996, No. 157; C. Popineau-Dehaullon, *Les remèdes de justice privée à l'inexécution du contrat*, Paris, LGDJ, 2008, No. 868 *et seq.* Compare for French law with: D. Allix, "Réflexions sur la mise en demeure", *JCP G* 1977, (2844) No. 5 ("*et la mise en demeure est le moyen donnée au créancier de fixer un terme définitif (…)*"); X. Lagarde, "Remarques sur l'actualité de la mise en demeure", *JCP G* 1996, I, (3974) No. 9 ("*l'avertissement du débiteur est réellement utile si une chance lui est donnée d'échapper aux sanctions qui le menacent*").

legal doctrine also consider an additional period imperative when the creditor uses extrajudicial sanctions, such as an extrajudicial termination or a replacement.[67] Nevertheless, urgent circumstances can make such an additional period to perform impractical or useless.[68] Furthermore, it is, of course, always possible to specify an additional period in the contract. Special laws have solved this problem in some areas by imposing a certain additional period for the debtor.[69] Finally, it is important to bear in mind that a party may never abuse his contractual rights, as may be considered to be the case in a situation where a creditor gives his debtor no additional period to perform his obligations.[70]

2.1.1.4. Effects of the default notice

The default notice has other consequences in addition to enabling the creditor to enforce his contractual rights from the moment he has put the debtor in delay.[71]

Firstly, a default notice has the effect that the moratory interest (Article 1146 CC) are due by the non-performing debtor from the moment the debtor has been put in delay. When the obligation consists in a sum of money, this default notice will set the moment from which moratory interest will run (Article 1153 CC).[72] This 'moratory interest' consists generally in the 'legal interest',[73] but if the debtor deliberately did not perform ('on

67 De Coninck thinks that an additional period is only necessary when taking extrajudicial unilateral sanctions: B. De Coninck, "La mise en demeure. Rapport Belge" in M. Fontaine and G. Viney (eds.), *Les sanctions de l'inexécution des obligations contractuelles. Etudes de droit comparé,* Brussels-Paris, Bruylant-LGDJ, 2001, (113) 150; P. Wéry, *Droit des obligations*, I, Brussels, Larcier, 2011, No. 460, P. Wéry, "La mise en demeure en matière d'obligations contractuelles" in P.A. Foriers (ed.), *Les obligations contractuelles,* Brussels, JBB, 2000, (285) 313. See also for France: C. Popineau-Dehaullon, *Les remèdes de justice privée à l'inexécution du contrat*, Paris, LGDJ, 2008, No. 865.

68 T. Delahaye, *Résiliation et résolution unilatérales en droit commercial belge*, Brussels, Bruylant, 1984 No. 235. Seems partially *contra*: C. Popineau-Dehaullon, *Les remèdes de justice privée à l'inexécution du contrat*, Paris, LGDJ, 2008, No. 875 (also in case of serious breach, an additional period of time must be given to perform the contract; nevertheless specifies in No. 878 that an additional period of time can be superfluous when such a period is useless, e.g. in case of repeated breach).

69 See Article 70 of the new law on insurance contracts of 4 April 2014; Article VII.111 WER ("*Wetboek Economisch Recht*" or Code on Economic Law with regard to consumer loans).

70 P. Wéry, *Droit des obligations*, I, Brussels, Larcier, 2011, No. 460; P. Wéry, "La mise en demeure en matière d'obligations contractuelles" in P.A. Foriers (ed.), *Les obligations contractuelles,* Brussels, JBB, 2000, (285) 313.

71 See for these consequences in French law: D. Allix, "Réflexions sur la mise en demeure", *JCP G* 1977, (2844) No. 2; B. Gimonprez, *v° Mise en demeure, Rép. civ. Dalloz*, 2009, No. 33–54; R. Libchaber, "Demeure et mise en demeure en droit français" in M. Fontaine and G. Viney (eds.), *Les sanctions de l'inexécution des obligations contractuelles*, Brussels, Bruylant, 2001, (113) No. 9–13.

72 See, for example, Cass. 28 November 2002, *Arr.Cass.* 2002, 2595, *Pas.* 2002, 11, 2277, *RGAR* 2004, 13.820, *RW* 2004–05, 1457, *T.Verz.* 2003, 587 and *Verkeersrecht* 2003, afl. 6, 198; Cass. 27 February 1989, *Arr.Cass.* 1988–89, 727, *Pas.* 1989, I, 655 and *RW* 1988–89, 1366, note. See e.g. for France: G. Guerlin, case note under Cass. Fr. civ. 14 October 2010, No. 09-12921, *EDCO* 2010, (6) 6.

73 Every January, the Ministry of Finance communicates the legal interest in the Belgian Official Gazette: in 2014, the legal interest was 2.75%.

purpose'), or if another contractual interest was negotiated, the 'moratory interest' can be higher.[74] The moratory interest is due by the debtor, even without the creditor having to prove that he has suffered damages.[75]

Secondly, a default notice has the effect that the risk of loss is transferred between the contracting parties. It concerns mainly the obligations *to give a specific good*.[76] When the debtor has been put in delay, he cannot invoke *force majeure*, and will be responsible for the shortcoming. Articles 1138 and 1302 CC deal with the transfer of risk. When the debtor – who delivers a good – has been put in delay by the creditor-owner, the risk of loss of a sold, but not yet delivered, good will transfer from the creditor-owner to the debtor (Article 1138 CC). The risk of loss will, nonetheless, stay with the creditor when the debtor can establish that the good could also have perished if it was delivered in due time (Article 1302 CC).

Recently, a law of 23 May 2013[77] introduced a new effect of a default notice *issued by a lawyer* of the creditor, a bailiff appointed by the creditor or other persons being able to represent the creditor according to Article 728, §3 of the Code of Civil Procedure (Article 2244, §2 CC). This default notice, which has to fulfil certain requirements with regard to form and content, interrupts the initial period of limitation. At the same time a new limitation period of one year[78] starts to run. However, the claim cannot be barred by prescription before the expiration of the initial period of limitation. The interruptive effect of the default notice can only be applied once.

2.1.1.5. Consequences of a lack of default notice

As already mentioned, the lack of a default notice will have the consequence that there is no transfer of risk and that the interest will not start to run. In addition, the creditor will not be able to invoke a sanction for breach of contract towards the debtor.[79] This means

74 Article 1153, 4 CC.

75 Article 1153, 2 CC.

76 S. Stijns, D. Van Gerven and P. Wéry, "Chronique de jurisprudence. Les obligations: les sources (1985–1995)", *JT* 1996, (689) 720; P. Wéry, *Droit des obligations*, I, Brussels, Larcier, 2011, No. 475.

77 Article 2 Law of 23 May 2013, *Belgian Official Gazette* 1 July 2013. See about this new rule: O. Vandenberghe and K. Balcaen, "Wet van 23 mei 2013 tot wijziging van artikel 2244 van het Burgerlijk Wetboek teneide aan de ingebrekestellingsbrief van de advocaat, van de gerechtsdeurwaarder of van de persoon die krachtens artikel 728, §3 van het Gerechtelijk Wetboek in rechte mag verschijnen, een verjaringstuitende werking te verlenen", *TBH* 2013, (672) 672–673.

78 Unless if the period of limitation is shorter than one year. In that case the extension equals the initial period of limitation.

79 See nuanced: L. Demeyere and M. Visser, "Ingebrekestellingsclausules" in G.-L. Ballon, H. De Decker, V. Sagaert, *et al.* (eds.), *Contractuele Clausules*, II, Antwerp, Intersentia, 2013, (997) 1030. See also about this consequence of a lack of a default notice: C. Popineau-Dehaullon, *Les remèdes de justice privée à l'inexécution du contrat*, Paris, LGDJ, 2008, No. 902 *et seq.* (about a lack of default notice), No. 906 *et seq.* (about an insufficient extra period of time to perform), No. 911 *et seq.* (about the breach of the formalities related to the default notice).

that in the event a default notice is needed and the creditor forgets to fulfil this obligation, he will be facing the harsh consequence of being excluded to invoke sanctions such as termination, damages, penalty clauses ...

As mentioned in the introduction, the question arises whether the duty to put ones debtor in delay can be qualified as an *Obliegenheit*. A breach of such an *Obliegenheit* cannot lead to a performance in kind.[80] Unfortunately, the scope of our contribution does not allow us to go more deeply into this last matter.

2.1.2. Other notification duties under Belgian contract law

One would think that the duty to put the debtor in delay would suffice as a 'notification-mechanism'. Nevertheless, several 'special contracts' require specific examination- and notification duties. In what follows, I will examine this specific examination- and notification duties for sales and tenancy contracts.

2.1.2.1. Examination and acceptance in sales contracts

The 'duty to put the debtor in delay' has to be read together with the buyer's examination and acceptance duties in sales contracts.[81] The rules concerning acceptance imply that the buyer has to examine the received goods.[82] If the buyer does not inform the seller of a non-conformity on the moment of receiving the goods ("*terbeschikkingstelling*", generally this will take place on the moment of delivery), the buyer is deemed to have accepted the goods ("*aanvaarding*", "*agréation*" or "*reception*").[83]

80 M. Fontaine, "Obliegenheit, incombance?" in X (ed.), *Liber Amicorum Hubert Claassens*, 1998, (151) 151–163.

81 See about acceptance: H. De Page and A. Meinertzhagen-Limpens, *Traité*, IV, Brussels, Bruylant, 1997, No. 114, 2°; D. Devos, "Chronique de jurisprudence (1980–1987), Les contrats, La vente", *JT* 1991, (161) No. 20; P.A. Foriers, "Conformité et garantie dans la vente" in B. Tilleman and P.A. Foriers (eds.), *De Koop*, Bruges, die Keure, 2002, (17) No. 8 *et seq.*; F. Glansdorff, "Panorama des actions ouvertes à l'acheteur insatisfait" in F. Glansdorff (ed.), *Actualités de quelques contrats spéciaux*, Brussels, Bruylant, 2005, (1) 3; J. Limpens, *La vente en droit belge*, Brussels, Bruylant, 1960, No. 438 *et seq.*; B. Tilleman, *Beginselen van Belgisch privaatrecht, overeenkomsten, bijzondere overeenkomsten, verkoop, gevolgen van de koop*, X, Mechelen, Kluwer, 2012, No. 271 *et seq.* See also for France: M. Alter, *L'obligation de délivrance dans la vente de meubles corporels*, Paris, LGDJ, 1972, No. 93 *et seq.*; A. Bénabent, *Droit civil. Les contrats spéciaux civils et commerciaux*, Paris, Montchrestien, 2011, No. 315; P. Malaurie and L. Aynes, *Les contrats spéciaux*, Paris, Defrénois, 2012, No. 321.

82 J. Limpens, *La vente en droit belge*, Brussels, Bruylant, 1960, No. 438. See for France: M. Alter, *L'obligation de délivrance dans la vente de meubles corporels*, Paris, LGDJ, 1972, No. 93–94; A. Bénabent, *Droit civil. Les contrats spéciaux civils et commerciaux*, Paris, Montchrestien, 2011, No. 315.

83 H. De Page and A. Meinertzhagen-Limpens, *Traité*, IV, Brussels, Bruylant, 1997, No. 114, 2°. See also: F. Glansdorff, "Panorama des actions ouvertes à l'acheteur insatisfait" in F. Glansdorff (ed.), *Actualités de quelques contrats spéciaux*, Brussels, Bruylant, 2005, (1) 3.

The acceptance signifies the recognition of the buyer that the goods have been delivered in conformity, without visible defects.[84] To put it in other words: the buyer *will renounce from his right* to call upon non-conformity or visible defects.[85, 86] This means that if the buyer has accepted the goods, he cannot invoke any sanctions, because he has renounced from his right to invoke a non-conformity or any other visible defect. Of course, the acceptance and the renunciation from rights imply that the buyer is aware of it and could or should know the non-conformity or the visible defects at the moment of delivery.[87] Consequently, acceptance will not bear on hidden defects. Acceptance can happen explicitly or impliedly.[88]

84 H. De Page and A. Meinertzhagen-Limpens, *Traité*, IV, Brussels, Bruylant, 1997, No. 114, 2°; D. Devos, "Chronique de jurisprudence (1980–1987), Les contrats, La vente", *JT* 1991, (161) No. 21; J. Herbots, S. Stijns, E. Degroote, *et al.*, "Overzicht van rechtspraak. Bijzondere Overeenkomsten 1995–1998", *TPR* 2002, (57) No. 75–76; B. Tilleman, *Beginselen van Belgisch privaatrecht, overeenkomsten, bijzondere overeenkomsten, verkoop, gevolgen van de koop*, X, Mechelen, Kluwer, 2012, No. 272; P.-F. Van den Driesche, "La Vente" in C. Jassogne (ed.), *Traité de droit commercial*, I, Waterloo, Kluwer, 2009, (453) No. 466.

85 B. Tilleman, *Beginselen van Belgisch privaatrecht, overeenkomsten, bijzondere overeenkomsten, verkoop, gevolgen van de koop*, X, Mechelen, Kluwer, 2012, No. 272, see also No. 287 *et seq*. See also: P.A. Foriers, "Conformité et garantie dans la vente" in B. Tilleman and P.A. Foriers (eds.), *De Koop*, Bruges, die Keure, 2002, (17) No. 5 (uses the term "*renonciation*"); J. Van Ryn and J. Heenen, *Principes de droit commercial*, III, Brussels, Bruylant, 1981, No. 678 (uses the term: "*une reconnaissance ou une rénonciation*"). See for France: M. Alter, *L'obligation de délivrance dans la vente de meubles corporels*, Paris, LGDJ, 1972, No. 109; P. Malaurie and L. Aynes, *Les contrats spéciaux*, Paris, Defrénois, 2012, No. 321.

86 The renunciation of rights is according to Belgian law a unilateral juridical act: S. Jansen, "Afstand van recht: een eenzijdige rechtshandeling" (case note under Cass. 24 december 2009), *TBBR* 2011, (333) 333–343.

87 P.A. Foriers, "Conformité et garantie dans la vente" in B. Tilleman and P.A. Foriers (eds.), *De Koop*, Bruges, die Keure, 2002, (17) No. 16; B. Tilleman, *Beginselen van Belgisch privaatrecht, overeenkomsten, bijzondere overeenkomsten, verkoop, gevolgen van de koop*, X, Mechelen, Kluwer, 2012, No. 272.

88 H. De Page and A. Meinertzhagen-Limpens, *Traité*, IV, Brussels, Bruylant, 1997, No. 114, 2° (an implied acceptance can be deduced from presumptions such as the fact that the buyer does not protest a non-conformity or uses the good). See similarly: D. Devos, "Chronique de jurisprudence (1980–1987), Les contrats, La vente", *JT* 1991, (161) No. 20; F. Glansdorff, "Panorama des actions ouvertes à l'acheteur insatisfait" in F. Glansdorff (ed.), *Actualités de quelques contrats spéciaux*, Brussels, Bruylant, 2005, (1) 3; J. Herbots, S. Stijns, E. Degroote, *et al.*, "Overzicht van rechtspraak. Bijzondere Overeenkomsten 1995–1998", *TPR* 2002, (57) No. 75; P.-F. Van den Driesche, "La Vente" in C. Jassogne (ed.), *Traité de droit commercial*, I, Waterloo, Kluwer, 2009, (453) No. 466. See also about express and implied acceptance: P.A. Foriers, "Conformité et garantie dans la vente" in B. Tilleman and P.A. Foriers (eds.), *De Koop*, Bruges, die Keure, 2002, (17) No. 6; L. Fredericq, m.m.v. S. Fredericq, *Handboek van Belgisch Handelsrecht*, III, Brussels, Bruylant, 1980, No. 1442; J. Limpens, *La vente en droit belge*, Brussels, Bruylant, 1960, No. 439 *et seq.*; B. Tilleman, *Beginselen van Belgisch privaatrecht, overeenkomsten, bijzondere overeenkomsten, verkoop, gevolgen van de koop*, X, Mechelen, Kluwer, 2012, No. 278–284; J. Van Ryn and J. Heenen, *Principes de droit commercial*, III, Brussels, Bruylant, 1981, No. 681. See also for France: M. Alter, *L'obligation de délivrance dans la vente de meubles corporels*, Paris, LGDJ, 1972, No. 104 ("*La protestation doit donc être diligente, sous peine de se voir opposer une agréation tacite*").

Acceptance must not necessarily take place *on the moment* of delivery or on the moment of receiving the goods. Some (complex) goods require tests or removal of packaging before acceptance can take place.[89] Although the limitation period to bring an action (for a remedy) for a non-conform delivery amounts to ten years (Article 2262*bis* CC), the buyer has to protest or to refuse to accept the goods within *a short period of time.*[90]

The consequence of a lack of a (timely) notification of non-acceptance amounts to a *deemed acceptance* of the goods in conformity with the contract. Consequently, a buyer will lose his sanctions for non-conform delivery and visible defects.

According to me, the refusal to accept the goods (by means of a notification of non-acceptance) can be *combined* with a default notice, as described before (see *supra*, 1.1.1), in the same *instrumentum*. On the one had the buyer must make clear that goods are not in conformity with the contract (*i.e.* the notification of non-acceptance) and on the other hand he makes clear that he wishes the correct performance of his contract (*i.e.* the default notice).

2.1.2.2. Notification in tenancy contracts

In general terms, the law and legal doctrine require a notification to the landlord by the tenant in the event of a reduced enjoyment, except in situations in which the landlord knows or ought to know the reduction or loss of enjoyment. This notification can also be combined with a 'default notice' in the same *instrumentum* (see *supra,* 1.1.2.1).

Article 1726 CC states e.g. that the tenant has to 'notify' the landlord of any *legal action from third parties* disturbing quite enjoyment.[91] This notification enables the landlord to

89 P.A. Foriers, "Conformité et garantie dans la vente" in B. Tilleman and P.A. Foriers (eds.), *De Koop*, Bruges, die Keure, 2002, (17) No. 7 and 16; J. Limpens, *La vente en droit belge*, Brussels, Bruylant, 1960, No. 448; B. Tilleman, *Beginselen van Belgisch privaatrecht, overeenkomsten, bijzondere overeenkomsten, verkoop, gevolgen van de koop*, X, Mechelen, Kluwer, 2012, No. 273; P.-F. Van den Driesche, "La Vente" in C. Jassogne (ed.), *Traité de droit commercial*, I, Waterloo, Kluwer, 2009, (453) No. 466; J. Van Ryn and J. Heenen, *Principes de droit commercial*, III, Brussels, Bruylant, 1981, No. 679. See also for France: P. Malaurie and L. Aynes, *Les contrats spéciaux*, Paris, Defrénois, 2012, No. 321.

90 P.A. Foriers, "Conformité et garantie dans la vente" in B. Tilleman and P.A. Foriers (eds.), *De Koop*, Bruges, die Keure, 2002, (17) No. 6; J. Limpens, *La vente en droit belge*, Brussels, Bruylant, 1960, No. 448 ("*L'acheteur ne pourra se voir opposer l'agréation tacite s'il proteste, auprès du vendeur, avant l'expiration du délai qui lui est strictement nécessaire pour examiner la chose dont il a pris livraison*"); B. Tilleman, *Beginselen van Belgisch privaatrecht, overeenkomsten, bijzondere overeenkomsten, verkoop, gevolgen van de koop*, X, Mechelen, Kluwer, 2012, No. 274. See also for France: M. Alter, *L'obligation de délivrance dans la vente de meubles corporels*, Paris, LGDJ, 1972, No. 103–104.

91 M. Dambre, "Rechten en verbintenissen van de huurder" in M. Dambre, B. Hubeau and S. Stijns (eds.), *Handboek algemeen huurrecht*, Bruges, die Keure, 2006, (399) No. 1051. See also: C.-E. de Fresart, T. Papart and D. Janssens, "Droits et obligations du bailleur" in G. Benoit, I. Durant, P.A. Foriers, *et al.* (eds.), *Le droit commun du bail*, Brussels, die Keure, 2006, (107) No. 134; M. La Haye, J. Vankerckhove, P. Coeckelberghs, *et al.*, *Les Novelles, Le louage de choses, Les baux en général*, Brussels, Larcier, 2000,

perform his obligations in kind. No specific period is prescribed within which the tenant has to notify the landlord.[92] If the tenant does *not* notify the landlord, he risks to lose the guarantee by the landlord against non-disturbance according to Article 1726 CC, which consists in the first place of performance in kind (and in the second place in a price reduction or the termination of the contract).[93] LAURENT is of the opinion that a lack of notification will not always imply that the tenant will lose his rights according to Article 1726 CC. This will only be the case if the lack of notification damages the landlord.[94]

Most authors also mention a duty to notify when *repair* by the landlord has become necessary within the framework of his liability to keep the rented good in (good) repair.[95] The tenant would lose his right to claim damages if he does not comply with this duty.[96] Moreover, he can be held liable towards the landlord.[97]

No. 652; Y. Merchiers, *Les Baux. Le bail en général*, Brussels, Larcier, 1997, No. 206. See for France: J. Ghestin, J. Huet, G. Decocq, *et al.*, *Les principaux contrats spéciaux*, Paris, LGDJ, 2012, No. 21164; M. Planiol, G. Ripert, J. Hamel, *et al.*, *Traité pratique de droit civil français*, X, Paris, LGDJ, 1956, No. 523; B. Vial-Pedroletti, *v° Article 1708–1762, Fasc. 263, Jur.-Cl. Civ.*, 2011, No. 56.

92 F. Laurent, *Principes de droit civil*, XXV, Brussels, Bruylant, 1877, No. 165.

93 M. La Haye, J. Vankerckhove, P. Coeckelberghs, *et al.*, *Les Novelles, Le louage de choses, Les baux en général*, Brussels, Larcier, 2000, No. 652 (the tenant can be held liable towards the landlord); B. Louveaux, *Le droit du bail, régime général*, Brussels, De Boeck, 1993, No. 293.

94 F. Laurent, *Principes de droit civil*, XXV, Brussels, Bruylant, 1877, No. 165.

95 M. Dambre, "Rechten en verbintenissen van de huurder" in M. Dambre, B. Hubeau and S. Stijns (eds.), *Handboek algemeen huurrecht*, Bruges, die Keure, 2006, (399) No. 1050; S. Beyaert, "Rechten en verbintenissen van de verhuurder" in M. Dambre, B. Hubeau and S. Stijns (eds.), *Handboek algemeen huurrecht*, Bruges, die Keure, 2006, (349) No. 831–832; H. De Page, *Traité*, IV, Brussels, Bruylant, 1972, No. 594a; M. La Haye, J. Vankerckhove, P. Coeckelberghs, *et al.*, *Les Novelles, Le louage de choses, Les baux en général*, Brussels, Larcier, 2000, No. 611; B. Louveaux, *Le droit du bail, régime général*, Brussels, De Boeck, 1993, No. 315; Y. Merchiers, *Les Baux. Le bail en général*, Brussels, Larcier, 1997, No. 172. See for France: C. Aubry, C. Rau and P. Esmein, *Cours de droit civil français*, V, Paris, Ed. Techniques, 1952, 211 (the tenant must only be notified of situations where repair is necessary in places where the landlord has no access); J. Ghestin, J. Huet, G. Decocq, *et al.*, *Les principaux contrats spéciaux*, Paris, LGDJ, 2012, No. 21166 (in text these authors use the term 'notification' and later in the text and in footnote 119 they mention 'the duty to put the debtor in delay'); X. Lagarde, "Remarques sur l'actualité de la mise en demeure", *JCP G* 1996, I, (3974) No. 11–12 (mentions the requirement of putting the debtor in delay but also describes the evolution that relaxes this requirement to merely a notification); M. Planiol, G. Ripert, J. Hamel, *et al.*, *Traité pratique de droit civil français*, X, Paris, LGDJ, 1956, No. 510; B. Vial-Pedroletti, *v° Art. 1708–1762, Fasc. 270, Jur.-Cl. Civ.*, 2012, No. 23 (mentions the word 'default notice').

96 S. Beyaert, "Rechten en verbintenissen van de verhuurder" in M. Dambre, B. Hubeau and S. Stijns (eds.), *Handboek algemeen huurrecht*, Bruges, die Keure, 2006, (349) No. 831; H. De Page, *Traité*, IV, Brussels, Bruylant, 1972, No. 594a; Y. Merchiers, *Les Baux. Le bail en général*, Brussels, Larcier, 1997, No. 172. Compare: B. Louveaux, *Le droit du bail, régime général*, Brussels, De Boeck, 1993, No. 315 (this would mean that the tenant renounces to any repair of the rented good).

97 S. Beyaert, "Rechten en verbintenissen van de verhuurder" in M. Dambre, B. Hubeau and S. Stijns (eds.), *Handboek algemeen huurrecht*, Bruges, die Keure, 2006, (349) No. 831; H. De Page, *Traité*, IV, Brussels, Bruylant, 1972, No. 594a; B. Louveaux, *Le droit du bail, régime général*, Brussels, De Boeck, 1993, No. 315; Y. Merchiers, *Les Baux. Le bail en général*, Brussels, Larcier, 1997, No. 172.

Also a *defect* of the rented good brings about a duty to notify.[98] The tenant would lose his rights according to Article 1721 CC if he does not comply with this duty.[99] He can also be held responsible towards the landlord in this regard.[100]

As already mentioned, an *exception* to the duty to notify exist in situations in which the landlord *knows or ought to know* the reduction or loss of enjoyment. It is for instance logical that Article 1724 (reduced enjoyment due to urgent renovations) does not require a duty to notify by the tenant. The disturbance of the tenant due to the performance of urgent renovations is likely to be known by the landlord. Moreover, a notification is *not* required as for the *non-conform delivery* and the *disturbance of enjoyment* of the tenant *through the actions of the landlord*. Indeed, in these circumstances the landlord knows or ought to know the disturbance of the tenant. Therefore, a duty to notify is not necessary.

We can conclude that a notification of a disturbance in enjoyment of a rented good is generally required, except in circumstances where the landlord knows or ought to know any shortcomings.

As already mentioned, 'the duty to put a debtor in delay' by means of a default notice also exists in tenancy law. However, it can overlap with the duty to notify and can be done in the same *instrumentum*. Nevertheless, often a default notice will not be necessary because of an exception (see for the exceptions also *supra*, 2.1.1.1, ii). For instance, there will be no need to put the debtor in delay if the rented good is not delivered in time,[101] as

98 S. Beyaert, "Rechten en verbintenissen van de verhuurder" in M. Dambre, B. Hubeau and S. Stijns (eds.), *Handboek algemeen huurrecht*, Bruges, die Keure, 2006, (349) No. 871; C.-E. de Fresart, T. Papart and D. Janssens, "Droits et obligations du bailleur" in G. Benoit, I. Durant, P.A. Foriers, *et al.* (eds.), *Le droit commun du bail*, Brussels, die Keure, 2006, (107) No. 159; H. De Page, *Traité*, IV, Brussels, Bruylant, 1972, No. 628a; J. Dewez, "Le régime des vices cachés dans les contrats de vente, de bail et d'entreprise" (case note under Bergen 24 March 2005), *TBBR* 2008, (47) No. 41; M. La Haye, J. Vankerckhove, P. Coeckelberghs, *et al.*, *Les Novelles, Le louage de choses, Les baux en général*, Brussels, Larcier, 2000, No. 668–669 (nuanced); B. Louveaux, *Le droit du bail, régime général*, Brussels, De Boeck, 1993, No. 308; Y. Merchiers, *Les Baux. Le bail en général*, Brussels, Larcier, 1997, No. 214. See for France: D. Allix, "Réflexions sur la mise en demeure", *JCP G* 1977, (2844) No. 41 (mentions a 'default notice'); J. Ghestin, J. Huet, G. Decocq, *et al.*, *Les principaux contrats spéciaux*, Paris, LGDJ, 2012, No. 21170; B. Vial-Pedroletti, *v° Art. 1708–1762, Fasc. 266, Jur.-Cl. Civ.*, 2011, No. 17 (also mentions a default notice).

99 S. Beyaert, "Rechten en verbintenissen van de verhuurder" in M. Dambre, B. Hubeau and S. Stijns (eds.), *Handboek algemeen huurrecht*, Bruges, die Keure, 2006, (349) No. 871; C.-E. de Fresart, T. Papart and D. Janssens, "Droits et obligations du bailleur" in G. Benoit, I. Durant, P.A. Foriers, *et al.* (eds.), *Le droit commun du bail*, Brussels, die Keure, 2006, (107) No. 159; H. De Page, *Traité*, IV, Brussels, Bruylant, 1972, No. 628a; B. Louveaux, *Le droit du bail, régime général*, Brussels, De Boeck, 1993, No. 308.

100 S. Beyaert, "Rechten en verbintenissen van de verhuurder" in M. Dambre, B. Hubeau and S. Stijns (eds.), *Handboek algemeen huurrecht*, Bruges, die Keure, 2006, (349) No. 871; J. Dewez, "Le régime des vices cachés dans les contrats de vente, de bail et d'entreprise" (case note under Bergen 24 March 2005), *TBBR* 2008, (47) No. 41 B. Louveaux, *Le droit du bail, régime général*, Brussels, De Boeck, 1993, No. 308. See also: Rb. Ghent 26 February 2003, *Huur* 2004, 81.

101 See already: F. Laurent, *Principes de droit civil*, XXV, Brussels, Bruylant, 1877, No. 106 ("*Si le bailleur est simplement en retard de faire la délivrance, le preneur peut réclamer des dommages-intérêts, sans être tenu de constituer le bailleur en demeure*"). See also: C.-E. de Fresart, T. Papart and D. Janssens, "Droits et

Article 1146 CC states that a default notice is not necessary if the debtor does not comply his obligation within the agreed period. A default notice is also unnecessary if performance in kind becomes impossible. This is often the case in tenancy contracts, with continuing obligations. It is for instance unlikely that a landlord can remedy an already suffered disturbance of quite enjoyment by means of a performance in kind. As a result, a default notice will, in principle, not be required for a disturbance in the past.[102] Nevertheless, a duty to notify the shortcoming is still necessary to inform the landlord to take action with regard to the future.

This illustrates the difference between a *default notice* and a *notification of a shortcoming*. A (timely) notification is always required except in the event the landlord knows or ought to know about the shortcoming. The forbearance of such a notification can trigger the accountability of the tenant and the loss of sanctions or remedies. A default notice is necessary for the passing of risk, the interests and the possibility to invoke sanctions, except if the above mentioned exceptions apply (see *supra*, 2.1.1.1, ii).

2.1.3. Duty to notify under European contract law

2.1.3.1. General

There are two important differences between Belgian contract law and European contract law with regard to the duty to notify a shortcoming. On the one hand, European instruments often differentiate between creditors that are *consumer* and creditors that are *traders*, a differentiation which is not made under Belgian contract law. European instruments, on the other hand, do *not* make the sharp distinction between situations of *excused* and *unexcused* shortcomings, as is the case under Belgian law.

First of all, the PECL does *not* contain an explicit obligation for the creditor to notify the debtor of any shortcoming (excused or not) of the contract.[103] Of course, Article 1:201(1) PECL states that each party must 'act in accordance with *good faith* and *fair dealing*', which might imply that a creditor must notify a debtor of a non-conformity in some particular situations.

obligations du bailleur" in G. Benoit, I. Durant, P.A. Foriers, *et al.* (eds.), *Le droit commun du bail*, Brussels, die Keure, 2006, (107) No. 8, M. La Haye, J. Vankerckhove, P. Coeckelberghs, *et al.*, *Les Novelles, Le louage de choses, Les baux en général*, Brussels, Larcier, 2000, No. 585; Y. Merchiers, *Les Baux. Le bail en général*, Brussels, Larcier, 1997, No. 164; S. Napora, "Effets de l'inexécution fautive et non fautive" in G. Benoit, I. Durant, P.A. Foriers, *et al.* (eds.), *Le droit commun du bail*, Brussels, die Keure, 2006, (341) No. 4. See for France: L. Guillouard, *Traité du contrat de louage*, I, Paris, Pédone-Lauriel, 1891, No. 101; M. Planiol, G. Ripert, J. Hamel, *et al.*, *Traité pratique de droit civil français*, X, Paris, LGDJ, 1956, No. 503 en 510 (no default notice would be needed for all shortcomings in delivery to receive damages). *Contra* for France: G. Baudry-Lacantinerie and A. Wahl, *Traité théorique et pratique de droit civil, Du contrat de louage*, I, Paris, Larose et Tenin, 1906, No. 312 and 317 (also in case of a breach of the duty to deliver the rented good, the landlord has to be put in delay to have a right for damages).

102 See e.g.: H. De Page, *Traité*, IV, Brussels, Bruylant, 1972, No. 597.

103 See also: B. Gimonprez, *v° Mise en demeure, Rép. civ. Dalloz*, 2009, No. 7.

As mentioned before, the DCFR and the CESL differentiate according to whether the creditor is a *consumer* or *not* with regard to the duty to notify shortcomings. It has to be noted, that these systems do not differentiate between *unexcused* and *excused* shortcomings with regard to the duty to notify. This is the reason why I will not come back to these notification duties under 2.2 ('Notifying an excused shortcoming').

The DCFR prescribes a duty to notify within a *reasonable time* when the creditor is *not* a consumer.[104] This reasonable time runs 'from the time when the goods or other assets are supplied or the service is completed; or from the time, if it is later, when the creditor discovered or could reasonably be expected to have discovered the non-conformity'.[105]

The CESL prescribes similarly that the buyer or customer (when he is *not* a consumer) must examine the goods or the service and notify within a *reasonable period of time*.[106] The buyer or customer must first '*examine* the goods within a reasonable time or cause them to be examined, not exceeding 14 days from the date of delivery of the goods, supply of digital content or provision of related services'. Further, the buyer or customer must *notify* the debtor, specifying the nature of the lack of conformity, within a reasonable period, which starts to run from the moment when the goods are supplied or when the buyer discovers or could be expected to discover the lack of conformity, whichever is later, with a maximum period of two years.

In its 19th consideration the Consumer Sales Directive mentions a possibility for Member States to set a period within which the consumer must inform the seller of any lack of conformity, which may not be shorter than two months. It also allows the Member States to ensure a higher level of protection for the consumer by not introducing such an obligation. The Belgian law maker has decided that parties may agree to set a period within which the consumer must inform the seller of any lack of conformity, without being shorter than two months as from the day the consumer has discovered the defect.[107]

2.1.3.2. Consequences of a lack of notification

If the creditor (not being a consumer) has not respected the duty to notify the debtor *within a reasonable time* (specifying the nature of the lack of conformity), the DCFR[108] prescribes that he loses the right to rely on the lack of conformity. Consequently, he loses his right to invoke a remedy (such as e.g. termination, damages, price reduction or performance).

The same was true for Article 122(1) CESL with regard to a failure to give the required notice within *a reasonable time* without taking into account the amendments of the EU

104 Article III.-3:106 DCFR.

105 Article III-3:107 DCFR. This is also the case for sale contracts: Article IV.A.-4:301 DCFR.

106 Articles 121–122 and 155.5–156 CESL.

107 Article 1649*quater*, §2 CC.

108 Article III.-1:307(1) DCFR.

parliament of 26 February 2014.[109] The first version of the Article stated that the buyer may not rely on the lack of conformity if he did not give notice to the seller within a reasonable time, specifying the lack of conformity (in a contract between traders).[110] However, Parliament proposed to amend this Article and added that the buyer *may still reduce the price or claim damages*, except for loss of profit, if he has a reasonable excuse for his failure to give the required notice. This means that some remedies can still be invoked if the buyer has a reasonable excuse for omitting his obligation to notify. The buyer loses his right to invoke the lack of conformity (and all his remedies) anyway if he fails to give notice within a *period of two years* from the time at which the goods were handed over to the buyer according to the contract.[111]

The Belgian implementation of the Consumer Sales Directive does not mention any sanction if (the agreed period for) the duty to notify has not been respected.[112]

2.2. *Notifying an excused shortcoming*

Whereas the European instruments (PECL, DCFR and CESL) do not differentiate between an *excused* and an *unexcused* shortcoming with regard to the duty to notify, important differences between both regimes exist in Belgian law.

2.2.1. No requisition of putting the debtor in delay

There exists *no 'duty to put the debtor in delay'* in the event of an excused shortcoming, which we qualify in Belgian law as *force majeure* (see about the duty of putting the debtor in delay, 2.1.1).[113] This exception to the duty to put the debtor in delay can be explained as follows. *Force majeure* requires under Belgian law that the performance is *impossible*. Indeed, the Court of Cassation decided that *force majeure* requires an insurmountable impediment to the performance of an obligation, which is not due to the debtor.[114] This means that the debtor may not be responsible for the event and that performance of the

109 See for the amendments: European Parliament legislative resolution of 26 February 2014 on the proposal for a regulation of the European Parliament and of the Council on a Common European Sales Law (COM(2011)0635 – C7-0329/2011 – 2011/0284(COD)) (Ordinary legislative procedure: first reading): www.europarl.europa.eu/sides/getDoc.do?pubRef=-//EP//TEXT+TA+P7-TA-2014-0159+0+DOC+XML+V0//EN.

110 Article 122(1) en 156(1) CESL.

111 Article 122(2) CESL.

112 Some Belgian authors claim that the consumer will be contractually liable towards the seller: C. Delforge, Y. Ninane and M.-P. Noël, "De quelques délais emblématiques du contrat de vente" in X (ed.), *Contrats spéciaux*, Limal, Anthemis, 2013, (77) No. 71.

113 See for the same solution under French law: C. Popineau-Dehaullon, *Les remèdes de justice privée à l'inexécution du contrat*, Paris, LGDJ, 2008, No. 887.

114 See e.g.: Cass. 15 February 1951, *Arr.Cass.* 1951, 327, *Pas.* 1951, I, 388 and *RW* 1950–51, 1403; Cass. 23 February 1967, *Arr.Cass.* 1967, 797 and *Pas.* 1967, I, 782; Cass. 9 December 1976, *Arr.Cass.* 1977, 404, *Pas.* 1977, 408 and *RW* 1977–78, 695; Cass. 18 November 1996, *Arr.Cass.* 1996, 1051, *Pas.* 1996, 1121, *JT* 1997, 173 and *RW* 1997–98, 604. See also in slightly different wordings e.g.: Cass. 16 March 1998, *Arr.*

obligation is *impossible*.[115] The requirement that 'performance of the obligation is impossible' is incompatible with the duty to put a debtor in delay. Indeed, we have seen before that a default notice is not required when performance has become *impossible* (in line with Articles 1145 and 1146 CC) (see *supra*, 2.1.1.1, ii). Consequently, a default notice is not necessary in the event of *force majeure* under this exception.

There is a second reason why it is not necessary to put the debtor in delay in case of an excused shortcoming: a default notice is only needed for invoking *sanctions* (remedies) of *unexcused* shortcomings such as termination, performance in kind, performance by equivalent (damages). Such a *sanctions* do not come into play in case of excused shortcomings (*force majeure*). The main consequence of *force majeure* is the liberation of the creditor of his obligations.[116] In reciprocal contracts (which do not imply the transfer of property and ownership of *species*-goods) it also means that the other party is liberated from its correlative obligations (the *res perit debitori*-rule).[117] This means that the contract ends (dissolution of the contract). Contrary to the PECL, the DCFR and the CESL, Belgian law does not consider this the same remedy as 'termination' (under Article 1184

Cass. 1998, 320, *JTT* 1999, 45 and *RW* 1998–99, 1398; Cass. 7 March 2008, *Pas.* 2008, 627 and *RW* 2011–12, 583.

115 See e.g. Brussels 17 November 1992, *Pas.* 1992, II, 123; Brussels 30 April 2010, *JT* 2011, 145. See also: A. De Boeck, "De schorsing bij overmacht in het gemene verbintenissen- en contractenrecht" in A. De Boeck, S. Stijns and R. Van Ransbeeck (eds.), *Schorsing van verbintenissen en overeenkomsten*, Bruges, die Keure, 2010, (57) 63–69; H. De Page, *Traité*, II, Brussels, Bruylant, 1964, No. 599; P.A. Foriers and C. de Leval, "Force majeure et contrat" in P. Wéry (ed.), *Le droit des obligations contractuelles et le bicentenaire du Code civil*, Brussels, die Keure, 2004, (241) No. 8; R. Kruithof, "Schuld, risico, imprevisie en overmacht bij de niet-nakoming van contractuele verbintenissen. Een rechtsvergelijkende benadering" in X (ed.), *Hulde aan René Dekkers*, Brussels, Bruylant, 1982, (281) No. 8–11; R. Kruithof, H. Bocken, F. De Ly, *et al.*, "Overzicht van rechtspraak (1981–1992), Verbintenissen", *TPR* 1994, (171) No. 221, 516; S. Stijns, *Leerboek verbintenissenrecht*, Boek 1, Bruges, die Keure, 2005, No. 211; A. Van Oevelen, "Overmacht en imprevisie in het Belgische contractenrecht", *TPR* 2008, (603) No. 4; P. Wéry, *Droit des obligations*, I, Brussels, Larcier, 2011, No. 564.

116 H. De Page, *Traité*, II, Brussels, Bruylant, 1964, No. 606*bis*, 841, 811; P.A. Foriers and C. de Leval, "Force majeure et contrat" in P. Wéry (ed.), *Le droit des obligations contractuelles et le bicentenaire du Code civil*, Brussels, die Keure, 2004, (241) No. 36; S. Stijns, *Leerboek verbintenissenrecht*, Boek 1, Bruges, die Keure, 2005, No. 214; P. Van Ommeslaghe, *Traité de droit civil belge – Tome II: les obligations*, II, Brussels, Bruylant, 2013, No. 982; P. Wéry, *Droit des obligations*, I, Brussels, Larcier, 2011, No. 572.

117 See implicitly about a labour-contract: Cass. 10 January 1994, *Arr.Cass.* 1994, 17, *JTT* 1994, 141, note, *Pas.* 1994, I, 12 and *RW* 1994–95, 51. See: P.A. Foriers and C. de Leval, "Force majeure et contrat" in P. Wéry (ed.), *Le droit des obligations contractuelles et le bicentenaire du Code civil*, Brussels, die Keure, 2004, (241) No. 32 and 38; J.-F. Germain and Y. Ninane, "Force majeure et imprévision en matière contractuelle" in X (ed.), *Droit des obligations*, Louvain-la-Neuve, Anthemis, 2011, (81) No. 54; S. Stijns, *Leerboek verbintenissenrecht*, Boek 1, Bruges, die Keure, 2005, No. 215; A. Van Oevelen, "Overmacht en imprevisie in het Belgische contractenrecht", *TPR* 2008, (603) No. 10; P. Van Ommeslaghe, *Traité de droit civil belge – Tome II: les obligations*, I, Brussels, Bruylant, 2013, No. 565; P. Wéry, *Droit des obligations*, I, Brussels, Larcier, 2011, No. 575–576. See for France: P.-H. Antonmattei, *Contribution à l'étude de la force majeure*, Paris, LGDJ, 1992, No. 227; O. Deshayes, *v° Théorie des risques, Rép. civ. Dalloz*, 2009, No. 9; C. Larroumet, *Droit civil*, III, 2e partie, Paris, Economica, 2007, No. 735; H. Mazeaud, J. Mazeaud and F. Chabas, *Leçons de droit civil*, II, vol. 1, Paris, Montchrestien, 1998, No. 1108; F. Terré, P. Simler and Y. Lequette, *Les obligations*, Paris, Dalloz, 2009, No. 667.

CC) which is reserved for (sufficiently severe) unexcused shortcomings. In principle, this dissolution has an *ex nunc* effect.[118]

However, in case of a partial impossibility due to *force majeure*, it is possible that parties of a reciprocal contract are partly liberated from their obligations. Article 1722 CC provides for tenancy contracts that in case of a partial impossibility the creditor can choose between a complete dissolution of the contract or a 'price reduction' (partial liberation of the contracting parties). This Article has to be applied by analogy to other reciprocal contracts (not implying the acquisition of a right of ownership of a *species*-good).[119] This means that the creditor has a choice between two remedies (dissolution or price reduction). The fact that the creditor has an option between two remedies will have implications on the duty to notify *a remedy*, treated in part 3.1.2.1 of this contribution.

2.2.2. Other notification duties?

The question arises whether there is a duty for the creditor to notify the debtor about a shortcoming due to *force majeure*, or the other way around, whether there is a duty for the debtor to inform the creditor about the circumstances leading to *force majeure*. Admittedly, there is almost no literature or jurisprudence about this subject matter.

Nevertheless, under Belgian law, contracts have to be performed in *good faith*. Under the *complementary function* of good faith certain information duties can arise in the capacity of the contracting parties.[120] This means that, dependent on the particular circumstances,

118 Parties are liberated *ex nunc* of their mutual obligations, without damages: H. De Page, *Traité*, II, Brussels, Bruylant, 1964, No. 848; S. Stijns, *De gerechtelijke en de buitengerechtelijke ontbinding van overeenkomsten*, Antwerp, Maklu, 1994, No. 22; P. Van Ommeslaghe, *Traité de droit civil belge - Tome II: les obligations*, I, Brussels, Bruylant, 2013, No. 568–2°. See also for contracts with continuing performances: R. Kruithof, H. Bocken, F. De Ly, *et al.*, "Overzicht van rechtspraak (1981–1992), Verbintenissen", *TPR* 1994, (171) No. 294. See for France: R. Demogue, *Traité des obligations en général*, VI, Paris, Rousseau, 1933, No. 615.

119 P.A. Foriers and C. de Leval, "Force majeure et contrat" in P. Wéry (ed.), *Le droit des obligations contractuelles et le bicentenaire du Code civil*, Brussels, die Keure, 2004, (241) No. 47; J.-F. Germain and Y. Ninane, "Force majeure et imprévision en matière contractuelle" in X (ed.), *Droit des obligations*, Louvain-la-Neuve, Anthemis, 2011, (81) No. 58; P. Wéry, "Les adages "Res perit debitori", "Res perit creditori" et "Res perit domino"" in A. Ruelle and M. Berlingin (eds.), *Le droit romain d'hier à aujourd'hui*, Brussels, FUSL, 2009, (287) No. 9 (implicitly); P. Wéry, *Droit des obligations*, I, Brussels, Larcier, 2011, No. 576. See for France: H. Capitant, *De la cause des obligations*, Paris, Dalloz, 1927, No. 144; J. Carbonnier, *Droit civil*, IV, Paris, PUF, 2000, No. 194, 349; (implicitly) R. Demogue, *Traité des obligations en général*, VI, Paris, Rousseau, 1933, No. 627; G. Ripert and J. Boulanger, *Traité de droit civil d'après le traité de Planiol*, II, Paris, LGDJ, 1957, No. 507; B. Starck, H. Roland and L. Boyer, *Obligations, 2. Contrat*, Paris, Litec, 1995, No. 1737 ("*Normalement, il y a lieu à réajustement de l'obligation qui se trouve réduite proportionnellement, ainsi que le montre la disposition de l'article 1722 du Code civil*"). Seems *contra* for France ("*Cette disposition* [Article 1722 CC] *s'explique par le caractère successif du bail*"): H. Mazeaud, J. Mazeaud and F. Chabas, *Leçons de droit civil*, II, vol. 1, Paris, Montchrestien, 1998, No. 1110.

120 S. Stijns, *Leerboek verbintenissenrecht*, Boek 1, Bruges, die Keure, 2005, No. 82–84; P. Van Ommeslaghe, *Traité de droit civil belge - Tome II: les obligations*, I, Brussels, Bruylant, 2013, No. 99.

the creditor should inform the debtor of the circumstances that amount to *force majeure* and *vice versa*. Other authors[121] remark pertinently that in this regard the complementary function of good faith also includes the duty to mitigate[122] damages. This duty will also induce a party to inform the other party of the circumstances that amount to *force majeure*. If a rented building burns down because of unforeseen circumstances, a tenant should inform the landlord about the event (when the landlord does not or ought not to know about it). The other way around, a building company should warn a client if it cannot finish the promised work in time, because of unforeseen circumstances. A duty to notify is also useful if the circumstances leading to a situation of *force majeure* are disputed and if findings about the situation are necessary. If a creditor claims that he is liberated due to *force majeure*, it is in his interest that he explains why he is liberated and notifies the *force majeure*-situation. This is even more true if the debtor does not know or ought not to know about the *force majeure*-situation. Due to the uncertainty about the duty to notify the other party about the circumstances that amount to *force majeure* it is recommended to expressly stipulate such an obligation in a contractual clause.[123]

2.3. *Conclusion of part 2*

We can conclude that a duty to *notify the shortcoming* often exists. A tendency to require this notification to be done within a *reasonable period* emerges. This requirement corresponds with the goal of such a notification, which is to enable the debtor to remedy his shortcomings (in kind). The sanction of not-observing the duty to notify within a reasonable period will often result into the creditor not being able to invoke the shortcoming and into the loss of remedies.[124] These far-reaching consequences may appear harsh for a creditor. This is especially the case for a creditor merely not notifying 'within a reasonable'

121 A. Draulans and J. Rasquin, "Overmachts-, imprevisie- en hardship-clausules" in G.-L. Ballon, H. De Decker, V. Sagaert, *et al.* (eds.), *Gemeenrechtelijke clausules*, Antwerp, Intersentia, 2013, (1191) 1217.

122 See the important ruling of the Court of Cassation in terms of *extra-contractual* liability: there is only a reasonable duty to mitigate damages: Cass. 14 May 1992, *Arr.Cass.* 1991, 855, *JLMB* 1994, 48, note D. Philippe, *Pas.* 1992, I, 798, *R.Cass.* 1992, 163, note M.E. Storme, *RGAR* 1994, 13.312, *RW* 1993–94, 1395, note A. Van Oevelen and *Verkeersrecht* 1992, 250. See similarly (but in terms of *contractual* liability): Cass. 17 May 2001, *Arr.Cass.* 2001, 923, concl. AG De Riemaecker, *JT* 2002, 467 and *Pas.* 2001, 889, concl. AG De Riemaecker; Rb. Bruges 16 May 2012, *Huur* 2012, 194, note S. Caeyers. See also: S. Stijns, *Leerboek verbintenissenrecht*, Boek 1, Bruges, die Keure, 2005, No. 82–84; P. Wéry, *Droit des obligations*, I, Brussels, Larcier, 2011, No. 394.

123 See about these contractual clauses: A. Draulans and J. Rasquin, "Overmachts-, imprevisie- en hardship-clausules" in G.-L. Ballon, H. De Decker, V. Sagaert, *et al.* (eds.), *Gemeenrechtelijke clausules*, Antwerp, Intersentia, 2013, (1191) 1217–1219; M. Fontaine, "Portée et limites du principe de la convention-loi" in X (ed.), *Les obligations contractuelles*, Brussels, JBB, 1984, (163) 187 ("*Autre caractéristique intéressante révélée par ces analyses, la force majeure est même créatrice d'obligations nouvelles. Il s'agit en premier lieu du devoir de notifier immédiatement au créancier, parfois sous certaines formes et avec certaines preuves, la survenance d'un tel événement*").

124 This duty to notify a shortcoming can – according to me – be qualified as an *Obliegenheit*. A breach of such an *Obliegenheit* cannot lead to a performance in kind (M. Fontaine, "Obliegenheit, incombance?" in X (ed.), *Liber Amicorum Hubert Claassens*, 1998, (151) 151–163). Unfortunately, the scope of our contribution does not allow us to go more deeply into this last matter.

period of time. Moreover, we must bear in mind the goal of this notification duty: to inform the debtor about the shortcoming and to offer him a second chance to remedy his shortcoming (in kind). Therefore, in future law-making, it seems advisable to differ between several situations. The legislator could take into account whether the creditor is a consumer or not (see also extensively the contribution of S. Tamboer), whether the contract is performed immediately or over a longer period, whether performance in kind is still possible, and the concrete knowledge of one of the parties of the shortcoming.

In addition to specific notification duties (e.g. in sales and tenancy law), the Belgian law of obligations requires the creditor *to put the debtor formally in delay* by means of a so-called 'default notice' to be able to invoke a *sanction* in case of an *un*excused shortcoming. It is not explicitly required that a default notice must be given within a 'reasonable period'. Nevertheless, the complementary function of good faith (see *supra* about this function, 2.2.2) can require the debtor to perform his duty of putting the debtor in delay in a timely manner.

These 'specific notification duties' and the 'duty to put one's debtor in delay' are not often linked with each other. Although I argued that both can be done in the same *instrumentum*, both seem to have different goals. It is not surprising that their scopes of application have overlapping areas, as well as genuinely independent areas.

On the one hand, a *notification* of a shortcoming (such as the duty to notify in case of sale or tenancy contracts, as mentioned before) is particularly aimed at *informing* the debtor about the shortcoming in the performance of a contract. Additionally, the duty to notify seems to enable the debtor to *remedy the contract* by means of performance in kind. For example, a landlord can repair defects for the future if he is notified about these defects of the rented good.

On the other hand, a *default notice* enables the creditor to invoke a sanction to remedy an unexcused shortcoming of the contract. This implies that a default notice aims to warn the debtor.[125] As from the moment the debtor has been put in delay the creditor can call upon any sanction. Whereas a *notification* informs the debtor merely about the shortcoming in performance, a *default notice* also will make clear that the creditor is able (and perhaps also willing) to invoke a sanction.[126] As Largarde puts it rightly with

125 L. Demeyere and M. Visser, "Ingebrekestellingsclausules" in G.-L. Ballon, H. De Decker, V. Sagaert, *et al.* (eds.), *Contractuele Clausules*, II, Antwerp, Intersentia, 2013, (997) 1005. See for France: A. Brès, *La résolution du contrat par dénonciation unilatérale*, Paris, Litec, 2009, No. 779; R. Libchaber, "Demeure et mise en demeure en droit français" in M. Fontaine and G. Viney (eds.), *Les sanctions de l'inexécution des obligations contractuelles*, Brussels, Bruylant, 2001, (113) No. 15.

126 See: T. Delahaye, *Résiliation et résolution unilatérales en droit commercial belge*, Brussels, Bruylant, 1984, No. 235 ("*Elle peut se comparer à un ultime avertissement 'avant les poursuites'*"). See also for France: X. Lagarde, "Remarques sur l'actualité de la mise en demeure", *JCP G* 1996, I, (3974) No. 2 *et seq.*; C. Popineau-Dehaullon, *Les remèdes de justice privée à l'inexécution du contrat*, Paris, LGDJ, 2008, No. 841 and 868.

regard to a notification, as opposed to a default notice: "*Il s'agit en effet d'aviser le débiteur et non de l'avertir*".[127] We can conclude that, indeed, both mechanisms overlap with each other, but have a separate right to exist.

While examining the Belgian duty to put a debtor in delay, we have already touched upon the question whether it is necessary to include in the default notice *the specific remedy* which the creditor intends to invoke (see *supra*, 2.1.1.3). Before discussing the intertwinement between the notification of shortcomings and the notification of remedies, we will examine whether a duty to notify a remedy exists.

III. Notification of the intention to invoke remedies

In this part we will examine whether a duty to notify a *remedy*, which a creditor intends to invoke, exists. This notification differs from the 'duty to notify a shortcoming' or the 'duty to put the debtor in delay', discussed in part 2. As for the duty to notify a remedy, we will observe that there is a fundamental difference between *judicial* and *extrajudicial* remedies. Finally, in part 4, this study will address the *interplay* between the notification duties with regard to shortcomings and the notification duties concerning remedies.

3.1. General rule: the difference between judicial and extrajudicial remedies

First of all, a fundamental difference between judicial remedies (which are applied after a prior intervention of a judge) and extrajudicial remedies (which are applied without any prior intervention of a judge, and can be controlled *a posteriori*) seems to exist.

3.1.1. Notifying judicial remedies

In case of a judicial remedy, the creditor will (after any required default notice or notification of a shortcoming) bring a judicial action to enforce the remedy. The creditor will specify the chosen remedy in his writ of summons or in his conclusion. Consequently, there is *no need* to give notice of the intention to invoke a remedy in a supplementary declaration. In this contribution I defend the point of view that a notification of the intention to invoke a remedy is only needed for extra-judicial remedies.

3.1.2. Notifying extrajudicial remedies

> "*Ennemie jurée de l'arbitraire, la forme est la soeur jumelle de la liberté*"[128]

Contrary to judicial remedies, the application of extra-judicial remedies require a notification. The reason why the application of extrajudicial remedies must be notified to

[127] X. Lagarde, "Remarques sur l'actualité de la mise en demeure", *JCP G* 1996, I, (3974) No. 12.

[128] R. Von Jhering and O. Meulenaere, *L'esprit du droit romain dans les diverses phases de son développement*, III, Paris, Marescq, 1880, 2e, 158.

the debtor is mainly based on *legal certainty*[129] and *clarity*. It informs the debtor about the chosen remedy.[130] For instance, if the creditor unilaterally decides not to pay the price, it can be unclear to the debtor whether the creditor wishes to terminate the contract definitively or only wishes to suspend the contract temporarily. Another important reason to notify the intention to invoke extrajudicial remedies is to enable a judge to examine *a posteriori* the unilaterally invoked remedy.[131] A unilateral remedy does not cancel out an *a posteriori* intervention of a judge. Consequently, a notification is required so that a judge can check whether the conditions of application and other requirements to apply the unilateral remedy are fulfilled. Moreover, a judge can punish a party when not respecting the requirement to notify a unilateral remedy. This implies that a procedural guarantee (the duty to notify the application of a unilateral remedy) counterbalances the far-reaching effects of a unilateral remedy.[132] As a result, the interests of the debtor are preserved when applying a unilateral remedy.[133] The formality to notify ones debtor is the price to pay for the freedom to invoke a remedy unilaterally, or as Von Jhering says: "*Ennemie jurée de l'arbitraire, la forme est la soeur jumelle de la liberté*".[134] Indeed, the fact that the application of an extrajudicial remedy can be qualified as a unilateral juridical act, requires an enhanced protection of the other party. This protection can be reached by procedural requirements.[135] As Lokiec puts it: "*Elle* [la décision unilatérale] *est ainsi soumise à un certain nombre d'exigences procédurales visant à pallier l'absence de consentement de l'assujetti*".[136]

129 See also the French authors: A. Brès, *La résolution du contrat par dénonciation unilatérale*, Paris, Litec, 2009, No. 394; P. Lemay, *Le principe de la force obligatoire du contrat à l'épreuve du développement de l'unilatéralisme*, unpublished, Université Lille Nord de France 2, 2012, No. 287.

130 P. Lemay, *Le principe de la force obligatoire du contrat à l'épreuve du développement de l'unilatéralisme*, unpublished, Université Lille Nord de France 2, 2012, No. 296.

131 P. Lemay, *Le principe de la force obligatoire du contrat à l'épreuve du développement de l'unilatéralisme*, unpublished, Université Lille Nord de France 2, 2012, No. 284, 287 and 296. *Cf.* also: R. Encinas de Munagorri, *L'acte unilatéral dans les rapports contractuels*, Paris, LGDJ, 1996, No. 268 (specifies that a notification enables to examine the existence of the will of the person that notifies). Comp. with: A. Brès, *La résolution du contrat par dénonciation unilatérale*, Paris, Litec, 2009, No. 785.

132 P. Lemay, *Le principe de la force obligatoire du contrat à l'épreuve du développement de l'unilatéralisme*, unpublished, Université Lille Nord de France 2, 2012, No. 284 and 286. See also: C. Popineau-Dehaullon, *Les remèdes de justice privée à l'inexécution du contrat*, Paris, LGDJ, 2008, No. 916 ("*Cette procédure (...) est indispensable, selon nous, à la mise en œuvre des remèdes de justice privée (...) pour protéger le débiteur contre des décisions intempestives*"). *Contra*: A. Brès, *La résolution du contrat par dénonciation unilatérale*, Paris, Litec, 2009, No. 785–786 ("*la fixation de conditions de forme ne viendrait pas neutraliser l'assouplissement des conditions de fond de la résolution par dénonciation unilatérale*").

133 P. Lemay, *Le principe de la force obligatoire du contrat à l'épreuve du développement de l'unilatéralisme*, unpublished, Université Lille Nord de France 2, 2012, No. 286 and 296.

134 R. Von Jhering and O. Meulenaere, *L'esprit du droit romain dans les diverses phases de son développement*, III, Paris, Marescq, 1880, 2e, 158. See also: P. Lemay, *Le principe de la force obligatoire du contrat à l'épreuve du développement de l'unilatéralisme*, unpublished, Université Lille Nord de France 2, 2012, No. 286.

135 See about the French legal philosophy with regard to the 'regularisation' ("*procéduralisation*") of the law of contracts): M. Fabre-Magnan, *Droit des obligations, Contrat et engagement unilatéral*, I, Paris, PUF, 2012, 89–90. See also: M. Mekki, *L'intérêt général et le contrat*, Paris, LGDJ, 2004, No. 612, 1206 *et seq.* and esp. No. 1254–1267.

136 P. Lokiec, *Contrat et pouvoir*, Paris, LGDJ, 2004, No. 342.

Also for the creditor the notification to apply an extrajudicial remedy is of importance. Indeed, the notification of the intention to invoke a unilateral act (see *infra*), such as an extrajudicial remedy, proves that the act has been addressed to the debtor.[137] Some authors even claim that the 'existence' of the unilateral act depends on its form, the notification.[138] It is certain that the effects of the invoked remedy start as from the notification to invoke the unilateral remedy.[139]

3.1.2.1. Belgian law

i. Extra-judicial remedies are the exception

Unilateral or extrajudicial *sanctions* in case of an *unexcused shortcoming* are the exception in Belgian law.[140] Some important exceptions seem to confirm this rule: such as the 'extrajudicial termination in urgent circumstances' and the 'extrajudicial replacement in extra-ordinary circumstances'. The application of these two extrajudicial sanctions does not rule out an *a posteriori* examination by the judge. The application of those two exceptions imply a notification to invoke these remedy.

In case of an *extrajudicial termination*, Stijns has convincingly demonstrated in her thesis that the application of this sanction implies its notification.[141] Also the French *Projet d'Ordonnance* of 2015 of the law of obligation requires a notification to apply an extrajudicial

137 R. Encinas de Munagorri, *L'acte unilatéral dans les rapports contractuels*, Paris, LGDJ, 1996, No. 265 and 268.

138 R. Encinas de Munagorri, *L'acte unilatéral dans les rapports contractuels*, Paris, LGDJ, 1996, No. 265–266.

139 C. Popineau-Dehaullon, *Les remèdes de justice privée à l'inexécution du contrat*, Paris, LGDJ, 2008, No. 916.

140 S. Jansen, "De rol van de rechter bij prijsvermindering in de koop: variations énigmatiques?" in S. Stijns and P. Wéry (eds.), *De rol van de rechter in het contract*, Bruges, die Keure, 2014, (471) No. 23.

141 See: S. Stijns, *De gerechtelijke en de buitengerechtelijke ontbinding van overeenkomsten*, Antwerp, Maklu, 1994, No. 350 (about express resolutory clauses) *juncto* No. 479 *et seq.* (esp. No. 482 *et seq.* about extrajudicial termination in urgent circumstances); S. Stijns, "La dissolution du contrat par un acte unilatéral en cas de faute dans l'inexécution ou de vice de formation" in X (ed.), *La volonté unilatérale dans le contrat*, Brussels, JBB, 2008, (325) No. 43 and 50; S. Stijns, C. Goethals and S. Jansen, "De ontbinding en de exceptie van niet-uitvoering bij meerpartijenovereenkomsten" in I. Samoy and P. Wéry (eds.), *Meerpartijenovereenkomsten*, Bruges, die Keure, 2013, (113) No. 53. See also: M.E. Storme, *De invloed van de goede trouw op de kontraktuele schuldvorderingen*, Brussels, Story-Scientia, 1990, No. 362–363; T. Delahaye, *Résiliation et résolution unilatérales en droit commercial belge*, Brussels, Bruylant, 1984, No. 234–235 (this authors considers a notification of a 'breach of contract' to be incompatible with a default notice). See also for Dutch law: C. Asser, A.S. Hartkamp and C.H. Sieburgh, *v° Algemeen overeenkomstenrecht, Asser-serie*, 6-III, 2014, 687 (an extrajudicial termination requires a written (or an electronically transferred) declaration. See also for French law: A. Brès, *La résolution du contrat par dénonciation unilatérale*, Paris, Litec, 2009, No. 391 *et seq.*; C. Paulin, *La clause résolutoire*, Paris, LGDJ, 1996, No. 216 *et seq.* (about express resolutory clauses). *Compare* for French law: E. Bazin, "La résolution unilatérale du contrat", *RRJ* 2000, (1381) No. 30 (according to this author the Court of Cassation seems not to require a notification in all circumstances); C. Pelletier, "Rôle de la mise en demeure dans le mécanisme de la résolution unilatérale aux risques et périls du créancier" (case note under Cass. Fr. civ. 24 September 2009, No. 08–14524), *RDCO* 2010, (690) No. 4.

termination (Article 1226).[142] This notification is necessary because the creditor has to make clear which sanction he chooses, since he can choose between several remedies according to Belgian law (the so-called 'right to choose' between termination and performance of the contract).[143] The application of an extrajudicial termination can be qualified as a *unilateral juridical act* ("*eenzijdige rechtshandeling*"/"*acte juridique unilatéral (réceptice)*") and can only resort its effects as from the moment the debtor is notified.[144] Stijns recognises in this unilateral termination a so-called 'party-decision' ("*partijbeslissing*"/"*decision de partie*"), similarly as to the extrajudicial replacement.[145] With regard to the *form* and the *content* of the notification of the extrajudicial termination I can be brief. As to the form, no formal requisitions apply,[146] however, it is advisable to send a letter by registered mail ("*aangetekend schrijven*"/"*envoi recommandé*").[147] As far as the content is concerned it is recommended that the notification makes clear that the creditor wishes to terminate the contract unilaterally, without any prior intervention of the judge: there may be no doubt about the sanction the creditor wants to invoke.[148] Furthermore, the creditor has to *motivate* why he invokes the

142 Article 132: "*La résolution résulte soit de l'application d'une clause résolutoire, soit, en cas d'inexécution suffisamment grave, d'une notification du créancier au débiteur ou d'une décision de justice*".

143 S. Stijns, *De gerechtelijke en de buitengerechtelijke ontbinding van overeenkomsten*, Antwerp, Maklu, 1994, No. 483; S. Stijns, *Leerboek verbintenissenrecht*, Boek 1, Bruges, die Keure, 2005, 286. See for the same opinion with regard to express resolutive clauses (that organises an extrajudicial termination of a contract): T. Tanghe, "Ontbindingsclausules" in G.-L. Ballon, H. De Decker, V. Sagaert, *et al.* (eds.), *Gemeenrechtelijke clausules*, II, Antwerp, Intersentia, 2013, (1557) 1568–1569.

144 S. Stijns, *De gerechtelijke en de buitengerechtelijke ontbinding van overeenkomsten*, Antwerp, Maklu, 1994, No. 484. See also for the same reasoning with regard to the 'cancellation' ("*opzegging*" or "*résiliation*") of contracts (which cannot be qualified as a remedy): F. Vermander, *De opzegging van overeenkomsten*, Antwerp, Intersentia, 2014, No. 377 and 647 *et seq.* See for the same opinion in France with regard to express resolutory clauses: C. Paulin, *La clause résolutoire*, Paris, LGDJ, 1996, No. 216 *et seq.* See also for France with regard to an extrajudicial termination: A. Brès, *La résolution du contrat par dénonciation unilatérale*, Paris, Litec, 2009, No. 393 and 411–417. See also about unilateral juridical acts for France: J. Martin de la Moutte, *L'acte juridique unilatéral*, Paris, Sirey, 1951, 343 p.

145 S. Stijns, *De gerechtelijke en de buitengerechtelijke ontbinding van overeenkomsten*, Antwerp, Maklu, 1994, No. 485.

146 M. Willemart and S. Willemart, *Les Concessions de Vente en Belgique*, Waterloo, Kluwer, 2007, 147. See also for France: C. Paulin, *La clause résolutoire*, Paris, LGDJ, 1996, No. 218.

147 S. Stijns, *De gerechtelijke en de buitengerechtelijke ontbinding van overeenkomsten*, Antwerp, Maklu, 1994, No. 487.

148 S. Stijns, *De gerechtelijke en de buitengerechtelijke ontbinding van overeenkomsten*, Antwerp, Maklu, 1994, No. 487 and 488; S. Stijns, "De buitengerechtelijke ontbinding wegens wanprestatie in wederkerige overeenkomsten: door het Hof van Cassatie erkend, doch tegelijk miskend", *TBBR* 2003, (258) No. 33–34 (criticises the imprecise terminology used by the Belgian Court of Cassation (Cass. 2 May 2002, AR C.01.0185.N, *Arr.Cass.* 2002, 1177, *Juristenkrant* 2002, afl. 53, 5, *Pas.* 2002, 1051, *RCJB* 2004, 293, note P. Wéry and *TBBR* 2003, 339; Cass. 2 May 2002, AR C.99.0277.N, *Arr.Cass.* 2002, 1167, *Juristenkrant* 2002, 5, *www.cass.be* note A. Van Oevelen, *NJW* 2002, 24, note, *Pas.* 2002, 1046, *RCJB* 2004, 291, *RW* 2002–03, 501, note A. Van Oevelen and *TBBR* 2003, 337: "*en kennis geeft aan de wederpartij dat zij de overeenkomst als beëindigd beschouwt*": 'the creditor has to notify the other party that he considers the contract to be ended'; see for the same expression: Cass. 16 February 2009, *Arr.Cass.* 2009, 537, *JT* 2010, 352, note M. Dupont, *Pas.* 2009, 485, *RW* 2011–2012, 1843, note J. Baeck, *TBH* 2009, 722 and *TBO* 2009, 245, note). See also critical about the decisions of the Court of Cassation of 2 May 2002: S. Stijns, "Actualia inzake beëindiging van overeenkomsten: de buitengerechtelijke ontbinding erkend door het hof van cassatie?" in S. Stijns (ed.), *Verbintenissenrecht*, Bruges, die Keure, 2004, (5) No. 24–28. See also: M. Willemart

termination because termination is 'fault'-based.[149] This motivation will enable the judge in a later stage, in case of an *a posteriori* examination, to check whether the unilateral termination was invoked in a regular manner (*"regelmatig"/"régulier"*) (are the conditions of application fulfilled?) and in a lawful manner (*"rechtmatig"/"légitime"*) (has the general principle that prohibits the of abuse of rights been respected?). One author also specifies that the notification of the extrajudicial termination must be done within a reasonable period of time.[150]

An *extrajudicial replacement* can also be qualified as a so-called 'party-decision' (*"partijbeslissing"* / *"decision de partie"*).[151] Some authors do not explicitly mention a duty to notify the application of an extrajudicial replacement but specify that a 'default notice' (see *supra*, 1.1.1) must make clear that in the absence of performance he will proceed to replacement (see also 1.1.1.3).[152] Indeed, without any notification it is often unclear to find out the exact intentions of a creditor if he contracts with a third party.[153] Nevertheless, case law does not

and S. Willemart, *Les Concessions de Vente en Belgique*, Waterloo, Kluwer, 2007, 147–148. See also for France: A. Brès, *La résolution du contrat par dénonciation unilatérale*, Paris, Litec, 2009, No. 401–410.

149 S. Stijns, *De gerechtelijke en de buitengerechtelijke ontbinding van overeenkomsten*, Antwerp, Maklu, 1994, No. 487. See similarly: T. Delahaye, *Résiliation et résolution unilatérales en droit commercial belge*, Brussels, Bruylant, 1984, No. 236; M.E. Storme, *De invloed van de goede trouw op de kontraktuele schuldvorderingen*, Brussels, Story-Scientia, 1990, No. 362 (the shortcoming has to be specified); M. Willemart and S. Willemart, *Les Concessions de Vente en Belgique*, Waterloo, Kluwer, 2007, 148. See also for French law: L. Aynes and A. Mazeaud, "Rupture unilatrale du contrat", *RDCO* 2004, (273) partie Mazeaud; C. Sévely-Fourné, *Essai sur l'acte juridique extinctif en droit privé français*, unpublished, Université des sciences sociales de Toulouse, 21 November 2008, No. 408. See *contra* for French law: E. Bazin, "La résolution unilatérale du contrat", *RRJ* 2000, (1381) No. 18 and 31 (although the creditor must not motivate his decision, he must be able to justify his decision: Tocqueville case Cass. Fr. civ. 13 October 1998, No. 96–21485, *Bull. Civ.* 1998, I, No. 300, nevertheless the author admits that a duty to motivate could slowly emerge). The French *Projet d'Ordonnance* of 2015 of the law of obligation requires in Article 1226 that the notification mentions the reasons to apply the extrajudicial termination).

150 T. Delahaye, *Résiliation et résolution unilatérales en droit commercial belge*, Brussels, Bruylant, 1984, No. 235.

151 See e.g.: M.E. Storme, "De bepaling van het voorwerp van een verbintenis bij partijbeslissing", *TPR* 1988, (1259) No. 1 (footnote 3: an indirect performance (Articles 1143–1144 CC, such as a new tender for a contract, a substitution-sale contract) which does not require a prior intervention of a judge can be qualified as a 'party decision'); M.E. Storme, *De invloed van de goede trouw op de kontraktuele schuldvorderingen*, Brussels, Story-Scientia, 1990, No. 364.

152 W. Geldhof and M. Somers, "Vervanging en indeplaatsstelling van de in gebreke blijvende schuldenaar. Artikelen 1143–1144 B.W. en artikel 20 §6 AAV als uitdrukking van een gemeen recht van contractenrechtelijke eigenrichting?", *TBO* 2008, (138) No. 32. In another article of the same year, a notification of the replacement is described as merely 'possible': W. Geldhof and M. Somers, "De buitengerechtelijke vervanging van de schuldenaar vanuit rechtsvergelijkend perspectief. Handelskoop en aanneming zetten de toon", *TPR* 2008, (511) 515.

153 The following authors confirm that the intention of the creditor is often unclear: W. Geldhof and M. Somers, "Vervanging en indeplaatsstelling van de in gebreke blijvende schuldenaar. Artikelen 1143–1144 B.W. en artikel 20 §6 AAV als uitdrukking van een gemeen recht van contractenrechtelijke eigenrichting?", *TBO* 2008, (138), No. 33. See also about the duty to notify and extrajudicial replacement: T. Delahaye, *Résiliation et résolution unilatérales en droit commercial belge*, Brussels, Bruylant, 1984, No. 234–235.

often require a notification of an extrajudicial replacement, apart from a default notice.[154] However, some recent decisions explicitly mention a (separate) duty to notify an extrajudicial replacement.[155]

Although a *'price reduction'* is not recognised as a general remedy under Belgian contract law, some applications in special contracts exist.[156] The question arises whether the aforementioned remedy can be applied without a prior intervention of a judge and whether a notification of its extrajudicial application is required. Article 50 of the Vienna Sales Convention, which is part of Belgian law, provides for a price reduction which can be invoked without prior intervention by a judge.[157] I argued in other contributions that also the price reduction in consumer sales contracts can be applied extra-judicially.[158] The price reduction by way of an *actio quanti minoris* (Article 1644 CC) and by way of a *réfaction* in commercial sales contracts[159] are often considered subject to a *prior* intervention by a judge.[160] Nevertheless, our previous research showed that an extrajudicial price reduction is also feasible in case of an *action quanti minoris*

154 See for case law that requires a 'default notice' but not a notification of the extrajudicial replacement: Liège 24 June 1991, *JT* 1991, 698; Liège 1 October 1991, *T.Aann.* 1993, 302, note P. Flamme; Liège 16 February 2001, *JLMB* 2001, 535; Ghent 6 May 2003, *NjW* 2003, 1005, note FB; Kh. Hasselt 14 November 1995, *RW* 1999–00, 132; Kh. Charleroi 9 June 1999, *Cah. Dr. Immo.* 1997, vol. 5, 15; Kh. Ieper 15 January, *RW* 2002–03, 349; Vred. Ghent 29 June 1992, *T.Vred.* 1993, 119.

155 See for case law that requires a 'default notice' *and* a notification of the extra judicial replacement: Bergen 16 September 2003, *TBBR* 2006, 174; Kh. Ghent 30 January 2003, *TGR* 2003, 199; Kh. Bergen 30 March 2010, *TBBR* 2011, 91. See for case law in which a 'default notice' and the notification of an extra-judicial replacement are combined in one *instrumentum*: Liège 9 January 2012, *TBBR* 2014, 348 (*"et la mettait en demeure de remédier aux défauts constatés sous peine de mise en oeuvre de la faculté de remplacement unilatéral"*).

156 E.g.: Articles 1617 and 1619 CC, Article 1644 CC, Article 1649*quiniquies* CC, Article 1722 CC, Article 1724 CC, Article 1726 CC, Article 50 CISG. See also: S. Jansen, *Prijsvermindering. Remedie tot bijsturing van contracten*, Antwerpen, Intersentia, 2015, *fortcoming.*

157 See extensively: S. Jansen, "Price Reduction under the CISG", *Journal of Law and Commerce* 2014, (325) 353–354; S. Jansen, "Prijsvermindering in de handelskoop: de *réfaction* vergeleken met artikel 50 Weens Koopverdrag" in B. Tilleman and V. Sagaert (eds.), *Contractenrecht, Themis*, Bruges, die Keure, 2014, (103) No. 40; S. Jansen, "De rol van de rechter bij prijsvermindering in de koop: variations énigmatiques?" in S. Stijns and P. Wéry (eds.), *De rol van de rechter in het contract*, Bruges, die Keure, 2014, (471) No. 36.

158 S. Jansen, "Price reduction as a remedy in European contract law and the consumer acquis" in A. Keirse and M. Loos (eds.), *Alternative Ways to Ius Commune. The Europeanisation of Private Law*, Antwerp, Intersentia, 2012, (169) 178; S. Jansen, "De rol van de rechter bij prijsvermindering in de koop: variations énigmatiques?" in S. Stijns and P. Wéry (eds.), *De rol van de rechter in het contract*, Bruges, die Keure, 2014, (471) No. 38.

159 See extensively about this remedy: S. Jansen, "De "*réfaction*" in de handelskoop", *TBH* 2014, (127) 127–151.

160 See for the *actio quanti minoris*: S. Jansen, "De rol van de rechter bij prijsvermindering in de koop: variations énigmatiques?" in S. Stijns and P. Wéry (eds.), *De rol van de rechter in het contract*, Bruges, die Keure, 2014, (471) No. 4. See for the *réfaction*: S. Jansen, "Prijsvermindering in de handelskoop: de *réfaction* vergeleken met artikel 50 Weens Koopverdrag" in B. Tilleman and V. Sagaert (eds.), *Contractenrecht, Themis*, Bruges, die Keure, 2014, (103) No. 38; S. Jansen, "De "*réfaction*" in de handelskoop", *TBH* 2014, (127) No. 34; S. Jansen, "De rol van de rechter bij prijsvermindering in de koop: variations énigmatiques?" in S. Stijns and P. Wéry (eds.), *De rol van de rechter in het contract*, Bruges, die Keure, 2014, (471) No. 12.

and of a *réfaction*.[161] Article 50 of the Vienna Sales Convention must be invoked by a unilateral declaration, which means that the application of an extrajudicial price reduction requires a notification.[162] Accordingly, the other applications of an extrajudicial price reduction require such a notification too.[163] When omitting a notification to apply an extrajudicial price reduction it would be unclear to the debtor whether the aggrieved party invokes a temporary measure such as a partial *enac* or a definitive remedy such as a price reduction. The French *Project d'Ordonnance* of 2015 of the law of obligations foresees a unilateral price reduction remedy which has to be notified to the debtor if the creditor has not yet paid his debtor (Article 1223).

With regard to the consequences of *force majeure* (excused shortcoming) an extrajudicial 'dissolution' of the contract can be observed with regard to reciprocal contracts (which do not imply a transfer of property of a *species*-good), because of the *res peril debitori*-rule. In the event of a total and permanent impossibility to perform due to *force majeure*, the majority of the authors holds that an *a priori* intervention of the judge is unnecessary.[164] Since both parties are liberated 'by right' ("*van rechtswege*"/"*de plein droit*")', no constitutive judgment is required. If the parties disagree, the judge will intervene and can merely determine whether the conditions of application are fulfilled.[165] If they are fulfilled, the judge can only confirm the liberation of the parties without any margin of

161 See for the *actio quanti minoris*: S. Jansen, "De rol van de rechter bij prijsvermindering in de koop: variations énigmatiques?" in S. Stijns and P. Wéry (eds.), *De rol van de rechter in het contract*, Bruges, die Keure, 2014, (471) No. 33–34. See for the *réfaction*: S. Jansen, "De rol van de rechter bij prijsvermindering in de koop: variations énigmatiques?" in S. Stijns and P. Wéry (eds.), *De rol van de rechter in het contract*, Bruges, die Keure, 2014, (471) No. 24–31; S. Jansen, "De "*réfaction*" in de handelskoop", *TBH* 2014, (127) No. 36–39; S. Jansen, "Prijsvermindering in de handelskoop: de *réfaction* vergeleken met artikel 50 Weens Koopverdrag" in B. Tilleman and V. Sagaert (eds.), *Contractenrecht, Themis*, Bruges, die Keure, 2014, (103) No. 42–45.

162 See extensively: S. Jansen, "Price Reduction under the CISG", *Journal of Law and Commerce* 2014, (325) 346–349. See also: S. Jansen, "Price reduction as a remedy in European contract law and the consumer acquis" in A. Keirse and M. Loos (eds.), *Alternative Ways to Ius Commune. The Europeanisation of Private Law*, Antwerp, Intersentia, 2012, (169) 203–204; S. Jansen, "Prijsvermindering in de handelskoop: de *réfaction* vergeleken met artikel 50 Weens Koopverdrag" in B. Tilleman and V. Sagaert (eds.), *Contractenrecht, Themis*, Bruges, die Keure, 2014, (103) No. 40; S. Jansen, "De prijsvermindering als proportionele remedie in het Weens Koopverdrag: enkele knelpunten" (noot onder Antwerpen 1 oktober 2012), *TBBR* 2015, 91–100.

163 See e.g. for the *réfaction*: S. Jansen, "Prijsvermindering in de handelskoop: de *réfaction* vergeleken met artikel 50 Weens Koopverdrag" in B. Tilleman and V. Sagaert (eds.), *Contractenrecht, Themis*, Bruges, die Keure, 2014, (103) No. 45 (without any notification of the *réfaction*, confusion is possible between a temporary (partial) suspension and a definitive *réfaction*); S. Jansen, "De "*réfaction*" in de handelskoop", *TBH* 2014, (127) No. 39 (idem).

164 See for Belgium: H. De Page, *Traité*, II, Brussels, Bruylant, 1964, No. 845 (the judge only has to decide when both parties disagree); S. Stijns, *De gerechtelijke en de buitengerechtelijke ontbinding van overeenkomsten*, Antwerp, Maklu, 1994, No. 22; P. Van Ommeslaghe, *Traité de droit civil belge - Tome II: les obligations*, I, Brussels, Bruylant, 2013, No. 568-A (the interference of the judge is unnecessary if both parties agree, but this will not often be the case). *Contra*: L. Herve, "Durée du bail – Extinction du bail" in X (ed.), *Les baux: commentaire pratique*, Diegem, Kluwer, 2005, (z.p.) No. 50. See for France: A. Colin and H. Capitant, *Cours élémentaire de droit civil français*, II, Paris, Dalloz, 1935, No. 93.

165 S. Beyaert, "BW Art. 1722" in E. Dirix and A. Van Oevelen (eds.), *Bijzondere overeenkomsten. Artikelsgewijze commentaar*, Mechelen, Kluwer, 2002, (z.p.) No. 12 (an interference of a judge is not

appreciation about the desirability of the rule. The judge will only be able to 'declare' the dissolution of the contract.[166]

> Because of the fact that in such circumstances both parties are liberated 'by right' (automatically), no notification of the extrajudicial dissolution of the contract is required. Indeed, neither legal doctrine nor case law requires a notification of the application of an extrajudicial dissolution due to *force majeure*.

However, in case of a partial impossibility due to *force majeure*, it is possible that parties of a reciprocal contract are only *partly* liberated from their obligations (*supra*, 2.2). Article 1722 CC provides for tenancy contracts that in case of a partial impossibility to perform due to *force majeure* the creditor can choose between a complete dissolution of the contract or a 'price reduction' (partial liberation of the contracting parties). This Article has to be applied by analogy to other reciprocal contracts (not implying an acquisition of a right of ownership of a *species*-goods).[167] This means that the creditor has a choice between two remedies (dissolution or price reduction). This implies that the creditor has to make a choice and that those remedies do not apply automatically ('by right') such as in the event of a total impossibility to perform due to *force majeure*. Belgian legal doctrine generally derives from this that the remedies in case of partial impossibility due to *force majeure* cannot be applied without prior intervention by the judge.[168] This means that there is no discussion about how to invoke these remedies extra-judicially by means of a notification.

excluded if parties disagree about the total liberation of the parties in case of a total destruction of a rented good); P. Wéry, *Droit des obligations*, I, Brussels, Larcier, 2011, No. 576.

166 *Cf.* also: S. Denoo, "Geen ontbinding van rechtswege van een huurovereenkomst bij gedeeltelijk tenietgaan van het verhuurde goed" (case note under Cass. 5 December 1996), *RW* 1998–99, (746) 746: ("*Zijn uitspraak is declaratief en werkt terug tot op het ogenblik van het zich voordoen van de overmacht. (...) Hoewel de ontbinding bij het geheel tenietgaan van het verhuurde goed een ontbinding van rechtswege is, moet ze toch nog door de rechter worden uitgesproken*": His judgement is declarative and retroacts until the moment of the circumstances of force majeure [...] Even though the parties are liberated 'by right' in case of the total destruction of the rented good, the judge still has to pronounce the dissolution).

167 P.A. Foriers and C. de Leval, "Force majeure et contrat" in P. Wéry (ed.), *Le droit des obligations contractuelles et le bicentenaire du Code civil*, Brussels, die Keure, 2004, (241) No. 47; J.-F. Germain and Y. Ninane, "Force majeure et imprévision en matière contractuelle" in X (ed.), *Droit des obligations*, Louvain-la-Neuve, Anthemis, 2011, (81) No. 58; P. Wéry, "Les adages "Res perit debitori", "Res perit creditori" et "Res perit domino"" in A. Ruelle and M. Berlingin (eds.), *Le droit romain d'hier à aujourd'hui*, Brussels, FUSL, 2009, (287) No. 9 (implicitly); P. Wéry, *Droit des obligations*, I, Brussels, Larcier, 2011, No. 576. See for France: H. Capitant, *De la cause des obligations*, Paris, Dalloz, 1927, No. 144; J. Carbonnier, *Droit civil*, IV, Paris, PUF, 2000, No. 194, 349; (implicitly) R. Demogue, *Traité des obligations en général*, VI, Paris, Rousseau, 1933, No. 627; G. Ripert and J. Boulanger, *Traité de droit civil d'après le traité de Planiol*, II, Paris, LGDJ, 1957, No. 507 (see for accessory obligations); B. Starck, H. Roland and L. Boyer, *Obligations, 2. Contrat*, Paris, Litec, 1995, No. 1737 ("*Normalement, il y a lieu à réajustement de l'obligation qui se trouve réduite proportionnellement, ainsi que le montre la disposition de l'article 1722 du Code civil*"). Seems *contra* for France ("*Cette disposition* [Article 1722 CC] *s'explique par le caractère successif du bail*"): H. Mazeaud, J. Mazeaud and F. Chabas, *Leçons de droit civil*, II, vol. 1, Paris, Montchrestien, 1998, No. 1110.

168 See similarly: S. Denoo, "Geen ontbinding van rechtswege van een huurovereenkomst bij gedeeltelijk tenietgaan van het verhuurde goed" (case note under Cass. 5 December 1996), *RW* 1998–99, (746) 746–747. See also for France: A. Colin and H. Capitant, *Cours élémentaire de droit civil français*, II, Paris, Dalloz, 1935, No. 93.

ii. The notification of extra-judicial remedies

When discussing the decision to apply an extrajudicial *termination*, we noticed that this decision can be qualified as a *unilateral juridical act* ("*eenzijdige rechtshandeling*" / "*acte juridique unilatéral*") (see *supra*).[169] A *unilateral juridical act* is a decision of a person that aims to create legal effects. This means that the decision to apply extrajudicial remedies (in general) must be qualified as a unilateral juridical act.[170] Indeed, the decision to apply an extrajudicial remedy implies the expression of the will of one person.[171] Consequently, it is not required that another party 'accepts' the unilateral juridical act.[172] Furthermore, this will of one person is aimed at generating legal effects.[173]

Doctrine specifies that this *uniltateral juridical act* has to be externalised[174] towards the person whose rights are affected. Indeed, the decision to apply an extrajudicial remedy affects the rights of the debtor. Consequently, it requires an externalisation in the form of a *notification* so that it can have its legal effects (the so-called "*acte juridique unilateral réceptice*").[175] Martin DE LA MOUTTE puts it rightly: "*Il y aura acte réceptice toutes les fois*

169 See e.g. S. Stijns, *De gerechtelijke en de buitengerechtelijke ontbinding van overeenkomsten*, Antwerp, Maklu, 1994, No. 484.

170 See e.g.: P. Lemay, *Le principe de la force obligatoire du contrat à l'épreuve du développement de l'unilatéralisme*, unpublished, Université Lille Nord de France 2, 2012, No. 293 *et seq.*

171 S. Stijns, *Leerboek verbintenissenrecht*, Boek 1, Bruges, die Keure, 2005, 5. See also for France: A. Sonet, *Le préavis en droit privé*, Aix-en-Provence, PUAM, 2003, No. 263 *et seq.*

172 J. Martin de la Moutte, *L'acte juridique unilatéral*, Paris, Sirey, 1951, No. 28 *et seq.* See e.g.: P. Lemay, *Le principe de la force obligatoire du contrat à l'épreuve du développement de l'unilatéralisme*, unpublished, Université Lille Nord de France 2, 2012, No. 294; C. Popineau-Dehaullon, *Les remèdes de justice privée à l'inexécution du contrat*, Paris, LGDJ, 2008, No. 930; C. Sévely-Fourné, *Essai sur l'acte juridique extinctif en droit privé français*, unpublished, Université des sciences sociales de Toulouse, 21 November 2008, No. 420; A. Sonet, *Le préavis en droit privé*, Aix-en-Provence, PUAM, 2003, No. 294 *et seq.*

173 See e.g.: P. Lemay, *Le principe de la force obligatoire du contrat à l'épreuve du développement de l'unilatéralisme*, unpublished, Université Lille Nord de France 2, 2012, No. 294. See also: M. Durma, *La notification de la volonté*, Paris, Sirey, 1930, No. 14 ("*L'acte juridique est une institution juridique que le droit positif met à la disposition des individus pour la production d'effets juridiques voulus*").

174 See: R. Encinas de Munagorri, *L'acte unilatéral dans les rapports contractuels*, Paris, LGDJ, 1996, No. 261–263. See also about this externalisation: M. Durma, *La notification de la volonté*, Paris, Sirey, 1930, No. 14 *et seq.* (externalisation of juridical acts in general); A. Sonet, *Le préavis en droit privé*, Aix-en-Provence, PUAM, 2003, No. 263.

175 See about the concept "*acte juridique unilateral réceptice*": J. Martin de la Moutte, *L'acte juridique unilatéral*, Paris, Sirey, 1951, No. 178–187. See also: P. Lemay, *Le principe de la force obligatoire du contrat à l'épreuve du développement de l'unilatéralisme*, unpublished, Université Lille Nord de France 2, 2012, No. 294; S. Stijns, *De gerechtelijke en de buitengerechtelijke ontbinding van overeenkomsten*, Antwerp, Maklu, 1994, No. 484; C. Popineau-Dehaullon, *Les remèdes de justice privée à l'inexécution du contrat*, Paris, LGDJ, 2008, No. 930. *Cf.* also: M. Durma, *La notification de la volonté*, Paris, Sirey, 1930, No. 78 ("*La notification est, dans ce cas* [not specified], *necessaire, constitutive, essentielle*"); R. Encinas de Munagorri, *L'acte unilatéral dans les rapports contractuels*, Paris, LGDJ, 1996, No. 267 (although considering that an extrajudicial termination is not generally recognised; this author is of the opinion that any unilateral 'breach' of contract is to be considered an *acte juridique unilatéral réceptrice*, which implies that a notification of the act is a requirement

que l'acte aura pour fonction directe soit une information ou un ordre juridique, soit une atteinte aux droits d'autrui".[176]

As to the *form* of this notification, we have seen that no formal requisitions apply in case of the notification of an extrajudicial termination, however, it is advisable to send a letter by registered mail ("*aangetekend schrijven*"/"*envoi recommandé*").[177] We can conclude that a notification of an extrajudicial remedy does not require any formality, except for reasons of proof.

As to the *content* I refer back to the notification of the application of an extrajudicial termination (see *supra*). The notification should *make clear* that the creditor wishes to apply *unilaterally* the invoked remedy, without any prior intervention of the judge: there may be no doubt about the remedy he unilaterally wants to invoke. Furthermore, the creditor has to *motivate* why he invokes the chosen remedy.[178] This motivation must give information about the shortcoming leading to the invoked remedy.[179] Some authors correctly point out the importance of (the complementary function of) good faith (Article 1134, 3th para and

with regard to its validity); C. Sévely-Fourné, *Essai sur l'acte juridique extinctif en droit privé français*, unpublished, Université des sciences sociales de Toulouse, 21 november 2008, No. 417 *et seq*.

176 J. Martin de la Moutte, *L'acte juridique unilatéral*, Paris, Sirey, 1951, No. 178–187.

177 See for the notification of an extrajudicial termination (*supra*): T. Delahaye, *Résiliation et résolution unilatérales en droit commercial belge*, Brussels, Bruylant, 1984, No. 235; S. Stijns, *De gerechtelijke en de buitengerechtelijke ontbinding van overeenkomsten*, Antwerp, Maklu, 1994, No. 487; M. Willemart and S. Willemart, *Les Concessions de Vente en Belgique*, Waterloo, Kluwer, 2007, 147. See also for termination in France: C. Paulin, *La clause résolutoire*, Paris, LGDJ, 1996, No. 218. See e.g. for the cancellation ("*opzegging*") of a contract: T. Delahaye, *Résiliation et résolution unilatérales en droit commercial belge*, Brussels, Bruylant, 1984, No. 107; F. Vermander, *De opzegging van overeenkomsten*, Antwerp, Intersentia, 2014, No. 67 *et seq*.

178 Argue strongly in favour of a duty to motivate: P. Lemay, *Le principe de la force obligatoire du contrat à l'épreuve du développement de l'unilatéralisme*, unpublished, Université Lille Nord de France 2, 2012, No. 308 *et seq.* (see especially No. 318, in which the author specifies that the (precise) motivation will be contained in the notification); C. Popineau-Dehaullon, *Les remèdes de justice privée à l'inexécution du contrat*, Paris, LGDJ, 2008, No. 831–837 (esp. 834). See also: L. Aynès, "Motivation et justification", *RDCO* 2004, (555) 555 (the duty to motivate extends to the unilateral juridical acts depriving the recipient of a right); M. Fabre-Magnan, "L'obligation de motivation en droit des contrats" in X (ed.), *Etudes offertes à Jacques Ghestin*, Paris, LGDJ, 2001, (301) No. 6 and 23 ("*On a pu également constater que les exemples d'obligations de motivation apparaissent à chaque fois qu'une partie peut exercer un droit unilatéralement*"); X. Lagarde, "La motivation des actes juridiques" in X (ed.), *La motivation, Travaux de l'Association Henri Capitant*, III, Paris, LGDJ, 2000, (71) 77–78 ("*Ainsi peut-on esquisser une définition plus générale des actes juridiques qui devraient être motivés: il s'agit des actes juridiques unilatéraux (...) dont partie ou totalité des effets se font directement ressentir dans la personne ou le patrimoine d'un tiers*"); C. Sévely-Fourné, *Essai sur l'acte juridique extinctif en droit privé français*, unpublished, Université des sciences sociales de Toulouse, 21 November 2008, No. 408 ("*Une obligation de motivation pourrait donc être utilement imposée à toute partie à un contrat désireuse de le rompre unilatéralement et à ses risques et périls en cas de faute grave du cocontractant*").

179 P. Lemay, *Le principe de la force obligatoire du contrat à l'épreuve du développement de l'unilatéralisme*, unpublished, Université Lille Nord de France 2, 2012, No. 318 (the causal link between the 'fault' and the 'sanction' must be established).

1135 CC) to explain the duty to motivate.[180] In addition, the duty to motivate will enable the judge to examine *a posteriori* whether the unilateral remedy is invoked in a correct and a just way.[181] Some authors specify that the notification should specify an additional period to perform (if performance is still possible) for the debtor.[182] Nevertheless, exceptions to the allocation of additional time exist if the performance of the contract loses all its interest or in urgent situations.[183] We have already discussed this obligation in the framework of the 'default notice' (*supra*, 2.1.1.3). The notification of an extrajudicial remedy and a 'default notice' can, however, be combined (*infra*, IV).

When does the notification take effect? Does the notification take effect at the moment of actual knowledge by the debtor or at the moment of transmission? Under the Vienna Sales Convention, for example, an (extrajudicial) price reduction declaration has effect as from the moment the buyer has sent it to the seller and alters, according to the majority of doctrine, immediately the contract.[184] The *transmission* of the unilateral declaration is at the risk of the seller: even if the declaration does not arrive, this does not deprive the buyer of the right to rely on the declaration.[185] Under Belgian law the opposite solution

180 Compare: P. Lemay, *Le principe de la force obligatoire du contrat à l'épreuve du développement de l'unilatéralisme*, unpublished, Université Lille Nord de France 2, 2012, No. 320 *et seq.* (points to '*l'exigence de loyauté*" being in direct relation with good faith, distinguishes, however, between "*la loyauté contractuelle et la loyauté des contractants*", the latter being applicable to the obligation of motivation).

181 X. Lagarde, "La motivation des actes juridiques" in X (ed.), *La motivation, Travaux de l'Association Henri Capitant*, III, Paris, LGDJ, 2000, (71) 73–84 (the duty to motivate is important in the context of a dispute in enabling the judge to examine the unilateral decision (p. 78). However, it has also a preventive role for the parties as to reflect upon a unilateral decision (pp. 81–84)); P. Lemay, *Le principe de la force obligatoire du contrat à l'épreuve du développement de l'unilatéralisme*, unpublished, Université Lille Nord de France 2, 2012, No. 323 and 328 (this authors points also correctly to a reversal of the burden of proof, see No. 329); M. Mekki, *L'intérêt général et le contrat*, Paris, LGDJ, 2004, No. 1260; C. Popineau-Dehaullon, *Les remèdes de justice privée à l'inexécution du contrat*, Paris, LGDJ, 2008, No. 835–836 (this duty to motivate implies a reversal of the burden of proof). Compare: S. Le Gac-Pech, "Rompre son contrat", *RTD Civ.* 2005, (223) No. 23.

182 P. Lemay, *Le principe de la force obligatoire du contrat à l'épreuve du développement de l'unilatéralisme*, unpublished, Université Lille Nord de France 2, 2012, No. 297–305. *Cf.* also: M. Mekki, *L'intérêt général et le contrat*, Paris, LGDJ, 2004, No. 1261. Compare with: A. Sonet, *Le préavis en droit privé*, Aix-en-Provence, PUAM, 2003, No. 312 *et seq.* (seems to require an additional period of time because of the unilateral character and the legal effects of a "*préavis*" and links this to the requirement to perform a contract in good faith (No. 450 *et seq.*)). *Contra*: C. Sévely-Fourné, *Essai sur l'acte juridique extinctif en droit privé français*, unpublished, Université des sciences sociales de Toulouse, 21 November 2008, No. 416 (in case of sanctions, an additional period of time must only be granted in the default notice, another additional time to perform is not required).

183 P. Lemay, *Le principe de la force obligatoire du contrat à l'épreuve du développement de l'unilatéralisme*, unpublished, Université Lille Nord de France 2, 2012, No. 306. See within the framework of an extrajudicial termination: E. Bazin, "La résolution unilatérale du contrat", *RRJ* 2000, (1381) No. 30.

184 M.R. Will, "Art. 50" in M.C. Bianca and M.J. Bonell (eds.), *Bianca-Bonell Commentary on the International Sales Law*, Milan, Giuffrè, 1987, (368) 372, No. 2.1.3. *Accord* I. Bach, "Art. 50" in S. Kröll, L. Mistelis and P.P. Viscasillas (eds.), *CISG*, Munich, Beck, 2011, (748) 757; P. Huber and A. Mullis, *The CISG*, Munich, Sellier, 2007, 250. *Contra*: C. Benicke, "Art. 50 CISG" in K. Schmidt (ed.), *Municher Kommentar Handelsgesetzbuch*, VI, Munich, Beck, 2004, (573) No. 14.

185 Article 27 CISG. *Accord* M.R. Will, "Art. 50" in M.C. Bianca and M.J. Bonell (eds.), *Bianca-Bonell Commentary on the International Sales Law*, Milan, Giuffrè, 1987, (368) 372, No. 2.1.3. *See also*: I. Bach,

is defended with regard to extrajudicial termination. The notification of the extrajudicial termination can only resort its effects as from the moment the debtor is actually notified and has knowledge of the notification.[186]

If a procedural requirement, such as the duty to notify the application of extrajudicial remedies, is violated this *lack of notification* can be *sanctioned*.[187, 188] The opinions about the appropriate sanction of a lack of notification (or other procedural requirements such as a default notice) are divided. Some authors suggest a moderation or a refusal of the claim in damages (in addition to the invoked extrajudicial remedy),[189] while other authors defend a more radical solution. The latter are of the opinion that the unilateral decision loses its effect.[190] This means, in the case of an extrajudicial termination, that the entire contract is maintained. Some authors elaborate on this and state that a lack of notification amounts to a shortcoming of a contract.[191] This means that the relevant remedies apply, such as damages or the performance of the contract (the last remedy is, however, the exception).[192, 193]

"Art. 50" in S. Kröll, L. Mistelis and P.P. Viscasillas (eds.), *CISG*, Munich, Beck, 2011, (748) 757; P. Huber and A. Mullis, *The CISG*, Munich, Sellier, 2007, 250; K.H. Neumayer and C. Ming, *Convention de Vienne sur les contrats de vente internationale de marchandises*, Paris, Litec, 1993, 355; U. Magnus, "Art. 50 CISG" in M. Martinek (ed.), *von Staudingers Kommentar zum BGB, Wiener UN-Kaufrecht*, III, Berlin, Sellier – de Gruyter, 2004, (530) No. 15; A.K. Schnyder and R.M. Straub, "Art. 50" in H. Honsell (ed.), *Kommentar zum UN-Kaufrecht*, Berlin, Springer, 1997, (581) No. 29.

186 S. Stijns, *De gerechtelijke en de buitengerechtelijke ontbinding van overeenkomsten*, Antwerp, Maklu, 1994, No. 484. See also: T. Delahaye, *Résiliation et résolution unilatérales en droit commercial belge*, Brussels, Bruylant, 1984, No. 243 ("*Elle prend date au moment de sa notification*"). See for France: J. Martin de la Moutte, *L'acte juridique unilatéral*, Paris, Sirey, 1951, No. 197–204. See for the same reasoning in case of cancellation ("*opzegging*"): F. Vermander, *De opzegging van overeenkomsten*, Antwerp, Intersentia, 2014, No. 661 *et seq.*

187 Some authors call the violations of procedural requirements (such as the duty to notify) the '*irregularity*' of the extrajudicial remedy (France: P. Lemay, *Le principe de la force obligatoire du contrat à l'épreuve du développement de l'unilatéralisme*, unpublished, Université Lille Nord de France 2, 2012, No. 289), while others reserve this term for the violation of the substantial conditions of application (the term 'unlawfulness' is reserved for the violation of the good faith requirement) (S. Stijns, *De gerechtelijke en de buitengerechtelijke ontbinding van overeenkomsten*, Antwerp, Maklu, 1994, No. 509–510 (about the extra-judicial termination) *juncto* S. Stijns and S. Jansen, "Actuele ontwikkelingen inzake de basisbeginselen van het contractenrecht" in S. Stijns, V. Sagaert, I. Samoy, *et al.* (eds.), *Verbintenissenrecht, Themis*, Bruges, die Keure, 2012, (1), No. 55 (about express resolutory clauses)).

188 See also about the possible sanctions in the event the extrajudicial remedy (termination) is not (sufficiently) motivated: A. Brès, *La résolution du contrat par dénonciation unilatérale*, Paris, Litec, 2009, No. 781–785.

189 See e.g.: S. Stijns, *De gerechtelijke en de buitengerechtelijke ontbinding van overeenkomsten*, Antwerp, Maklu, 1994, No. 509 and 510.

190 P. Lemay, *Le principe de la force obligatoire du contrat à l'épreuve du développement de l'unilatéralisme*, unpublished, Université Lille Nord de France 2, 2012, No. 289 *Comp.*: E. Bazin, "La résolution unilatérale du contrat", *RRJ* 2000, (1381) No. 29 (not specifically about formal requirements such as a notification).

191 P. Lemay, *Le principe de la force obligatoire du contrat à l'épreuve du développement de l'unilatéralisme*, unpublished, Université Lille Nord de France 2, 2012, No. 289.

192 P. Lemay, *Le principe de la force obligatoire du contrat à l'épreuve du développement de l'unilatéralisme*, unpublished, Université Lille Nord de France 2, 2012, No. 352.

193 P. Lemay, *Le principe de la force obligatoire du contrat à l'épreuve du développement de l'unilatéralisme*, unpublished, Université Lille Nord de France 2, 2012, No. 289 and 252–258.

3.1.2.2. European contract law

A duty to notify the application of a remedy is relatively scarce in European contract law. The PECL only lays down a duty to notify the debtor of a chosen remedy in case of termination. If the creditor wishes to terminate the contract he has to notify the debtor within a reasonable period of time ('notice of termination', Article 9:303 PECL).[194] The creditor will lose his right to terminate if he does not give notice of termination within a reasonable time after he has or ought to have become aware of the shortcoming. The PECL does not require this notification in case of e.g. a price reduction (Article 9:401 PECL),[195] the right to withhold performance (Article 9:201 PECL) or to perform (Articles 9:101 *et seq.* PECL). Also the DCFR does not generally require a notification of the chosen remedy.[196, 197] The same exception with regard to termination applies: if the creditor wants to terminate the contract, he must notify the debtor of his intention to do so within a reasonable time (Articles III.-3:507 and III.-3:508 DCFR). The DCFR does not require this notification in case of e.g. a price reduction (Article III.-3:601 DCFR), or the right to withhold performance (Article III.-3:401 DCFR). It is true – as SAMOY and DANG VU have stated – that a lack of duty to inform the debtor when invoking a remedy, results in an enhanced flexibility to apply remedies, but at the same time, the protection of creditor and debtor will be significantly affected.[198]

> We might wonder if a duty to notify the debtor *to invoke the remedy* is necessary if there is a duty to notify *a non-conformity*. First of all, there is not always a duty under the DCFR to notify *a non-conformity*: this is not the case if the creditor is a consumer (see *supra*, 1.1.3.1). Consequently, it is in our view, advisable that the creditor informs the debtor about a *non-conformity* with the contract within a reasonable period, for reasons of proof concerning the passing of risk (has the non-conformity of the good appeared before or after the passing of risk?). Furthermore, it is in our opinion advisable that the creditor informs the debtor somehow about his intention to invoke an extrajudicial remedy. This might also be necessary

194 See Article 9:303 PECL and the exceptions of this principle. O. Lando and H. Beale (eds.), *Principles of European Contract Law, Parts I and II,* The Hague, Kluwer Law International, 2000, 413–416. See also: J.M. Smits, "Non-Performance and Remedies in General" in D. Busch and E. Hondius (eds.), *The Principles of European Contract Law and Dutch Law,* The Hague, Kluwer Law International, 2002, (325) 326 (nevertheless, we do not agree with Smits' point of view that only a termination for a non-fundamental delay in performance requires a notification of termination; Article 9:303 PECL states generally that a notification is required to call upon termination).

195 S. Jansen, "Price reduction as a remedy in European contract law and the consumer acquis" in A. Keirse and M. Loos (eds.), *Alternative Ways to Ius Commune. The Europeanisation of Private Law,* Antwerp, Intersentia, 2012, (169) 202.

196 See also: I. Samoy and T. Dang Vu, "Performance and non-performance in the DCFR" in V. Sagaert, M. Storme and E. Terryn (eds.), *The draft common frame of reference: a national and comparative perspective,* Antwerp, Intersentia, 2012, (53) 81.

197 With regard to the duty to notify termination or price reduction, the *Acquis principles* state that there is an insufficient base to formulate such a rule (see the commentaries of Article 8:302 ACQP).

198 I. Samoy and T. Dang Vu, "Performance and non-performance in the DCFR" in V. Sagaert, M. Storme and E. Terryn (eds.), *The draft common frame of reference: a national and comparative perspective,* Antwerp, Intersentia, 2012, (53) 81.

for reasons of proof about the question of which remedy the creditor has chosen[199] (in case the judge exercises an *a posteriori* control after the extrajudicial or unilateral use of a remedy). Indeed, the judge must be able to examine the choice of the creditor with regard to the conditions of application of the remedy. A notification of the application of an extrajudicial remedy will facilitate this task of the judge.

Under the CESL, there is no general principle to notify the debtor in order to invoke a remedy.[200] Articles 118 and 138 of the CESL actually establish a duty to notify the debtor should the creditor wish to invoke the right to terminate the contract, as under the PECL and the DCFR.[201] This obligation is not provided for in the case of other remedies and we might raise the same concerns in relation to the practical applicability of those remedies (see *supra*).

The Consumer Sales Directive does not comment on the duty to notify the application of the chosen remedies.[202] In Belgium, legal doctrine is convinced that the choice of the consumer to invoke a remedy must be *notified* to the seller; the consumer must make clear which remedy he has chosen.[203] Article 1649*quinquies*, §2 and §3 CC states

199 Confusion is possible between partial termination or price reduction, suspension or price reduction, damages or price reduction, … Müller-Chen correctly points out the ambiguity if the creditor pays a reduced price with a notice of defect, since this only makes clear that there is a temporary retention of part of the price, but not a final selection of a remedy: M. Müller-Chen, 'Art. 50' in P. Schlechtriem and I. Schwenzer (eds.), *Commentary on the UN Convention on the international sale of goods (CISG)*, Oxford, OUP, 2005, 598, No. 4.

200 F. Faust, "Das Kaufrecht im Vorschlag für ein Gemeinsames Europäisches Kaufrecht" in H. Schulte-Nölke, F. Zoll, N. Jansen, *et al.* (eds.), *Der Entwurf für ein optionales europäisches Kaufrecht*, Munich, Sellier, 2012, (251) 264 (it is therefor not clear whether it is a "*Gestaltungsrecht*", because neither a duty to notify nor a prescription period has been set out for the price reduction); S. Jansen, "Price reduction as a remedy in European contract law and the consumer acquis" in A. Keirse and M. Loos (eds.), *Alternative Ways to Ius Commune. The Europeanisation of Private Law*, Antwerp, Intersentia, 2012, (169) 204; A. Schopper, "Verpflichtungen und Abhilfen der Parteien eines Kaufvertrages oder eines Vertrages über die Bereit-stellung digitaler Inhalte (Teil IV CESL-Entwurf)" in C. Wendehorst and B. Zöchling-Jud (eds.), *Am Vorabend eines Gemeinsamen Europäischen Kaufrechts*, Wien, Manzsche Verlags- und Universitätsbuchhandlung, 2012, (107) 139 (because of this problem, German scholars debate whether the right to reduce a price is still a "*Gestaltungsrecht*"). *Contra*: M. Schmidt-Kessel, "Artikel 120 GEK-E" in M. Schmid-Kessel (ed.), *Der Entwurf für ein Gemeinsames Europäisches Kaufrecht*, Munich, Sellier, 2014, (600) No. 16 (a price reduction 'declaration' is required in conformity with Article 10 CESL; but the author admits that there is no clear solution to this question); F. Zoll, "Article 120" in R. Schulze (ed.), *Common European Sales Law (CESL)*, Munich, Beck, 2012, (526) 527 (price reduction has to be exercised by means of a notification to the seller).

201 See also Article 10 of the CESL, which elaborates on the notification. If the creditor does not notify the debtor within a reasonable time, he loses his right to terminate. See also Articles 115 and 135 CESL: termination for delay in delivery after a notice fixing an additional time for performance.

202 S. Jansen, "Price reduction as a remedy in European contract law and the consumer acquis" in A. Keirse and M. Loos (eds.), *Alternative Ways to Ius Commune. The Europeanisation of Private Law*, Antwerp, Intersentia, 2012, (169) 183–184.

203 S. Stijns, 'De remedies van de koper bij niet-conformiteit' in S. Stijns and J. Stuyck (eds.), *Het nieuwe kooprecht. De wet van 1 september 2004 betreffende de bescherming van de consumenten bij verkoop van consumptiegoederen*, Antwerp, Intersentia, 2005, (53) 68; P. Wéry, 'Les droits légaux du consommateur

that the consumer has the right to 'claim' ("*eisen*" or "*verlangen*"/"*exiger*") a remedy.[204] These terms are not by any means clarified. WÉRY holds the opinion that repair or replacement (§2) has to be 'claimed' orally or in written, without going to court. This implies, if the judge does not intervenes *a priori*, the *choice* for one of the four remedies and its *notification* to the debtor.[205] This notification must be clear and the consumer may leave no doubt about his choice.[206] In many cases the consumer will not have a *real* choice, taking into account the hierarchy of the remedies, prescribed by the Consumer Sales Directive. If the seller does not act upon the notification, the consumer has to put the seller in delay (see *supra*, 2.1.1), if he has not already done this.[207] The same reasoning applies to an extrajudicial price reduction[208] or a termination in §3 (the latter can only be invoked extra-judicially in extra-ordinary circumstances). The consumer must inform the seller about the (extrajudicial) remedy chosen.

3.1.3. Notification to invoke extrajudicial defences

I defended that the *enac* does not require a formal 'default notice' because it must be considered a *temporary* defence (*supra*, 2.1.1.1, iii). Nevertheless, the question arises

en cas de défaut de conformité' in C. Biquet-Mathieu and P. Wéry (eds.), *La nouvelle garantie des biens de consommation et son environnement légal*, Brussels, die Keure, 2005, (127) 143–144.

204 See extensively: P. Wéry, "Les droits légaux du consommateur en cas de défaut de conformité" in C. Biquet-Mathieu and P. Wéry (eds.), *La nouvelle garantie des biens de consommation et son environnement légal*, Brussels, die Keure, 2005, (127) 136–137.

205 P. Wéry, "Les droits légaux du consommateur en cas de défaut de conformité" in C. Biquet-Mathieu and P. Wéry (eds.), *La nouvelle garantie des biens de consommation et son environnement légal*, Brussels, die Keure, 2005, (127) No. 13 and 20. See also: S. Jansen, "Price reduction as a remedy in European contract law and the consumer acquis" in A. Keirse and M. Loos (eds.), *Alternative Ways to Ius Commune. The Europeanisation of Private Law*, Antwerp, Intersentia, 2012, (169) 183–184; R. Steennot and S. Dejonghe, *Consumentenbescherming en Handelspraktijken*, Antwerp, Intersentia, 2007, No. 1080; S. Stijns, "De remedies van de koper bij niet-conformiteit" in S. Stijns and J. Stuyck (eds.), *Het nieuwe kooprecht, De wet van 1 september 2004 betreffende de bescherming van de consumenten bij verkoop van consumptiegoederen*, Antwerp, Intersentia, 2005, (53) No. 38. See similarly: M.C. Bianca, "Article 3. Droits et remèdes du consommateur" in M.C. Bianca (ed.), *La directive communautaire sur la vente, Commentaire*, Brussels-Paris, Bruylant-LGDJ, 2004, (179) No. 65 (about the choice between repair and replacement).

206 S. Stijns, "De remedies van de koper bij niet-conformiteit" in S. Stijns and J. Stuyck (eds.), *Het nieuwe kooprecht, De wet van 1 september 2004 betreffende de bescherming van de consumenten bij verkoop van consumptiegoederen*, Antwerp, Intersentia, 2005, (53) No. 38; S. Stijns, "De consumentenkoop: actuele knelpunten" in B. Tilleman and A. Verbeke (eds.), *Knelpunten verkoop roerende goederen*, Antwerp, Intersentia, 2009, (21) No. 58; P. Wéry, "Les droits légaux du consommateur en cas de défaut de conformité" in C. Biquet-Mathieu and P. Wéry (eds.), *La nouvelle garantie des biens de consommation et son environnement légal*, Brussels, die Keure, 2005, (127) No. 13.

207 P. Wéry, "Les droits légaux du consommateur en cas de défaut de conformité" in C. Biquet-Mathieu and P. Wéry (eds.), *La nouvelle garantie des biens de consommation et son environnement légal*, Brussels, die Keure, 2005, (127) No. 20.

208 See about extrajudicial price reduction in consumer sales: S. Jansen, "Price reduction as a remedy in European contract law and the consumer acquis" in A. Keirse and M. Loos (eds.), *Alternative Ways to Ius Commune. The Europeanisation of Private Law*, Antwerp, Intersentia, 2012, (169) 177–178.

whether a duty to notify the application of the *enac* exists.[209] Can the obligation to perform contracts in good faith (Article 1134, third para CC) result in a duty of the *excipiens* to notify the debtor of his intention to invoke the *enac* and to suspend his performance?[210]

When discussing the requisition of putting the debtor in delay, it became clear that, in principle, the aggrieved party does not have to indicate which sanction he will invoke (*supra*, 2.1.1.3).[211] He must merely make it clear for the debtor that he is ordered to perform his obligation. Most authors only require that the sanction must be specified in the default notice if the creditor wishes to exercise an extrajudicial sanction (such as an extrajudicial termination) (*supra*, 2.1.1.3).[212] If we transpose these rules to a possible duty to notify in good faith in case of the *enac*, it has to be taken into account that the *enac* can be invoked *without prior intervention* by a judge (extrajudicial *enac*). On the other side the *enac* is not considered an irreversible definitive *sanction*, but a reversible temporary *defence*. Because of this *temporary and reversible character* of the *enac*-defence, the *excipiens* is *not* always required to notify the debtor about his intention to apply it.

Nevertheless, an important condition of application of the *enac* is the requirement for the *excipiens* to act in good faith. As a consequence, under some circumstances, *good faith* will require the aggrieved party to notify the debtor about his intention to invoke the *enac*. This is the case if there is any doubt about who has to perform first or about the invoked shortcoming.[213] Another example is the situation in which the possibility to perform can become impossible due to the application of the *enac* (if the *enac* is not considered to be a definitive sanction under these circumstances, *supra* 2.1.1.1, iii).[214] Under those circumstances it seems indispensable to notify the intention to invoke the

209 Compare for France: Cass. Fr. civ. 26 May 1992, No. 90–15.883, *Bull civ.* 1992, III, No. 176 (*enac* and the duty to notify or to inform).

210 In favour a duty to notify the *enac* in good faith: H. Van Gompel, "Vereist de toepassing van de exceptie van niet-uitvoering een voorafgaande ingebrekestelling?" (case note under Antwerp 9 December 2009), *Limb. Rechtsl.* 2010, (116) No. 6 ("*Een te goeder trouw toepassing van de exceptie van niet-uitvoering vereist wel dat de excipiens de wederpartij op het ogenblik van de toepassing van de exceptie hiervan op gemotiveerde wijze in kennis stelt*").

211 Cass. 16 September 1983, *Arr.Cass.* 1983–1984, 45, *Pas.* 1984, 48 and *RW* 1984–85, 464 (penalty clause); Cass. 18 December 1986, *Arr.Cass.* 1986–87, 525, *Pas.* 1987, 484, *RW* 1987–88, 55 and *JT* 1987, 162 (judicial termination); Cass. 25 November 1991, *Arr.Cass.* 1991–92, 272, *Pas.* 1992, I, 231, note, *RW* 1991–92, 1364, *JT* 1992, 221 and *Soc. Kron.* 1992, 102 (moratory interests).

212 B. De Coninck, "La mise en demeure. Rapport Belge" in M. Fontaine and G. Viney (eds.), *Les sanctions de l'inexécution des obligations contractuelles. Etudes de droit comparé*, Brussels-Paris, Bruylant-LGDJ, 2001, (113) 149–150; S. Stijns, *Leerboek Verbintenissenrecht*, Vol. 1, Bruges, die Keure, No. 240; P. Wéry, *Le droit des obligations*, I, Brussels, Larcier, 2011, No. 459. *Contra*: P. Van Ommeslaghe, *Traité de droit civil belge – Tome II: les obligations*, III, Brussels, Bruylant, 2013, No. 1504 (implicitly).

213 S. Stijns, *Leerboek verbintenissenrecht*, Vol. 1, Bruges, die Keure, 2005, No. 293. See also: S. Stijns, S. Jansen and F. Peeraer, "Schorsing en beëindiging van de huurovereenkomst naar gemeen recht" in M. Dambre, B. Hubeau and S. Stijns (eds.), *Handboek algemeen huurrecht*, Bruges, die Keure, 2015, (685), nr. 20; H. Van Gompel, "Vereist de toepassing van de exceptie van niet-uitvoering een voorafgaande ingebrekestelling?" (case note under Antwerp 9 December 2009), *Limb. Rechtsl.* 2010, (116) No. 6.

214 See e.g.: Antwerp 30 September 2013, *Limb. Rechtsl.* 2014, 131, note I. Samoy and S. Jansen.

enac to the other party. It will not suffice that the *excipiens* sends a 'default notice' to the debtor. A default notice merely makes clear that the *excipiens* wants to undertake a (not specified) *action* to obtain performance by the debtor. It does not specify the intention of the *excipiens* to invoke the *enac*-defence upon an attack of the debtor himself.

3.2. *Conclusion of part 3*

The analysis of *Belgian law* confirms the fundamental difference between judicial remedies (which are applied after a prior intervention of a judge) and extrajudicial remedies (which are applied without any prior intervention of a judge, and can be controlled *a posteriori*).

In case of a *judicial sanction* (such as judicial termination, judicial price reduction or judicial performance), the creditor will (after any required default notice or notification of a shortcoming) bring a judicial action to enforce the remedy under Belgian law. The creditor will specify the chosen remedy in his writ of summons or in his conclusion. Consequently, there is no need for any extra notification of the remedy. In case of an extrajudicial sanction (such as an extrajudicial termination, an extrajudicial replacement or an extrajudicial price reduction) a notification of the unilateral application of this remedy is required.

As for the consequences of *force majeure* in reciprocal contracts (not implying a transfer of property of *species*-goods), dissolution of the contract automatically takes place in case of a total impossibility to perform. Consequently, a notification to 'invoke' the consequences is not necessary. A partial impossibility to perform due to force majeure will imply a prior intervention by a judge with regard to its consequences. Consequently a notification (to invoke an extrajudicial remedy) is ruled out.

The *new instruments in European contract law* (PECL, DCFR and CESL) only prescribe a duty to notify the debtor about the intention to invoke termination. Other extrajudicial remedies do not require such a notice. Nevertheless, a notification to invoke an extrajudicial remedy might benefit the creditor as well as the debtor (see *supra*, 3.1.2, introduction). First of all, this notification might be necessary for reasons of proof with regard to the question of which remedy the creditor has chosen (because the judge can exercise an *a posteriori* control after the extrajudicial or unilateral use of a remedy). Such a notification enables the judge to examine the conditions of application of the chosen remedy (e.g. by looking at the motivation in the notification). A notification also implies that the creditor reflects upon the application of an extrajudicial remedy and that the debtor is well informed about the creditor's intentions.

As for the *enac* we must conclude that the temporary and reversible character of this (extrajudicial) defence often makes the requirement to notify the intention to invoke the 'enac' superfluous. Nevertheless, the obligation to perform contracts in good faith (in its complementary function, Articles 1134, para 3 and 1135 CC) may require the *excipiens* to inform the other party about his intention to apply the *enac*.

IV. The interplay between the notification of shortcomings and of remedies

In the two previous parts we discussed the different notification duties under Belgian (and European) contract law and the circumstances in which they can be required. We differentiated between 1) the formal requisition to put a debtor in delay ('a default notice'), 2) a notification of a shortcoming and 3) the duty to notify the application of an extrajudicial remedy. The question arises whether these different notification duties can be contained in the same '*instrumentum*' or act.

As for the formal requisition of putting a debtor in delay ('default notice') and the other notification duties of a shortcoming in sale and tenancy contracts, I am of the opinion that both can be done in the same *instrumentum*. A default notice only requires that it is clear to the debtor that he is ordered to perform his obligation. A notification of shortcoming will, moreover, require that the precise shortcomings will be specified.

As for the formal requisition of putting a debtor in delay ('default notice') and the notification to invoke an extrajudicial termination in case of extraordinary circumstances or when applying an express resolutory clause, legal doctrine expressly accepts that both can be combined in the same act.[215] Nevertheless, it must be clear that the creditor wishes also, in addition to putting the debtor in delay, to exercise the extrajudicial termination of the contract.[216] As seen before, a default notice must specify an additional time in which the debtor can perform if the creditor wishes to exercise an extrajudicial remedy (see *supra*, 2.1.1.3). This implies that the creditor must make clear in a combined 'default notice' and 'notification of the application of an extrajudicial termination' that after this additional period of time the extrajudicial termination will have its effects.[217] The same reasoning can be applied for the other

215 See e.g.: S. Stijns, *De gerechtelijke en de buitengerechtelijke ontbinding van overeenkomsten*, Antwerp, Maklu, 1994, No. 350 (implicitly: extrajudicial termination due to an express resolutive clause) and No. 481 (extrajudicial termination in case of extraordinary circumstances). See also: T. Delahaye, *Résiliation et résolution unilatérales en droit commercial belge*, Brussels, Bruylant, 1984, No. 235 (implicitly: "*Cette manifestation de volonté se prouve par la notification et/ou la mise en demeure*"). See for French law: A. Brès, *La résolution du contrat par dénonciation unilatérale*, Paris, Litec, 2009, No. 393 (implicitly); C. Paulin, *La clause résolutoire*, Paris, LGDJ, 1996, No. 218 (implicitly and nuanced); C. Popineau-Dehaullon, *Les remèdes de justice privée à l'inexécution du contrat*, Paris, LGDJ, 2008, No. 931. The same is true under Dutch law: C. Asser, A.S. Hartkamp and C.H. Sieburgh, *v° Verbintenis in het algemeen, eerste gedeelte, Asser-serie*, 6-I, 2011, No. 388 (the 'default notice' ("*ingebrekestelling*") can be combined with a declaration for an extrajudicial-termination). See for a similar technique under Article 70 of the new Law of 4 April 2014 concerning Insurances (*Belgian Official Gazette* 30 April 2014) (about the cancellation ("*opzegging*") instead of the termination ("*ontbinding*") of the contract).

216 See: S. Stijns, *De gerechtelijke en de buitengerechtelijke ontbinding van overeenkomsten*, Antwerp, Maklu, 1994, No. 481.

217 See: S. Stijns, *De gerechtelijke en de buitengerechtelijke ontbinding van overeenkomsten*, Antwerp, Maklu, 1994, No. 481.

remedies which can be invoked extra-judicially, such as price reduction and replacement.[218]

The fact that a default notice can be combined with other notifications of shortcomings and that it can be combined with the notification of the application of an extrajudicial remedy implies that the three notification duties can be combined in one and the same instrument or act. However, one must always be cautious to make sure that the three elements are clearly present in the act, and that all the requirements with regard to form and content are met.

V. Conclusion

This contribution endeavoured to examine the clash between different notification duties in Belgian contract law in comparison with European contract law.

At first sight the 'specific notification duties' (e.g. in sale and tenancy contracts) and the 'duty to put one's debtor in delay' are not linked with each other *under Belgian law*. Nevertheless, we found that both can be combined in the same *instrumentum*. Furthermore, we concluded that their scopes of application have overlapping as well as genuinely independent areas. Whereas a *notification* merely informs the debtor about the shortcoming in performance, a *default notice* also will make clear that the creditor is able (and perhaps also willing) to invoke a sanction. If a comparison is made with the European instruments with regard to the notification of a shortcoming, we must conclude that those instruments often differentiate between creditors that are *consumers* and creditors that are *traders* (e.g. DCFR and CESL). Only creditor that are traders must notify a shortcoming to a debtor, consumers are not obliged to do so.

With regard to the duty to notify the application of a *remedy*, the analysis of *Belgian law* confirms the fundamental difference between *judicial* remedies (which are applied after a prior intervention of a judge) and *extrajudicial* remedies (which are applied without any prior intervention of a judge, and can be controlled *a posteriori*). In case of a judicial remedy (such as judicial termination, judicial price reduction or judicial performance ...), the creditor will (after any required default notice or notification of the shortcoming) bring a judicial action to enforce the remedy under Belgian law. This means that the creditor will specify the chosen remedy in his writ of summons or in his conclusion. Consequently, there is no need for any extra notification for the remedy. In case of an extrajudicial remedy (such as an extrajudicial termination, an extrajudicial replacement or an extrajudicial price reduction) a notification of the decision to invoke this sanction is required. An exception applies to the consequences of the total impossibility to perform due to *force majeure* in reciprocal contracts (not implying the transfer of property of *species*-goods). Indeed, the dissolution of the contracts will take place

218 See similarly: P. Lemay, *Le principe de la force obligatoire du contrat à l'épreuve du développement de l'unilatéralisme*, unpublished, Université Lille Nord de France 2, 2012, No. 292.

automatically ('by right'), ruling out a notification of the remedy. The *new European contract law instruments* (PECL, DCFR and CESL) only prescribe a duty to notify the debtor about the intention to invoke termination. Other remedies do not require such a notice.

Finally, the three duties to notify interact with each other and can be combined in the same *instrumentum*. Indeed, the fact that a default notice can be combined with other notifications of shortcomings and that it can be combined with the notification of the application of an extrajudicial remedy implies that the three notification duties can be combined in one and the same instrument or act. However, one must always be cautious to make sure that the three elements are clearly present in the act, and that all the requirements with regard to form and content are met.

Johanna Waelkens*

ARTICLE 5 UNFAIR TERMS DIRECTIVE 93/13/EEC: TRANSPARENCY AND INTERPRETATION IN CONSUMER CONTRACTS

I. Introduction

Prior to 1993, in many European Member States, laws existed relating to unfair terms in consumer contracts. However, the laws showed marked divergences, with the result that the national markets for the sale of goods and services to consumers differed from each other. Consequently, distortions of competition could arise amongst the sellers and the suppliers. The Council of the European Communities introduced Directive 93/13/EEC on Unfair Terms in Consumer Contracts in order to tackle these disparities, with the aim, according to the sixth recital in its preamble, "*to safeguard the citizen in his role as consumer when acquiring goods and services under contracts.*" One of the ways in which the citizen in his role as consumer was safeguarded, was by means of introducing a transparency and interpretation rule in all consumer contracts. The need for such a provision arose from the fact that parties do not always act on the same footing when concluding a contract. In numerous kinds of contracts, one of the parties holds an inferior or a weak position, because he suffers from a shortage of information or from a lack of knowledge about the exact content of the agreement. Weakness can also arise when one party has no influence upon the substance of the contract, because of the absence of previous negotiations in which each party can make himself felt. In order to counter this asymmetry, rules have been developed to protect weak contracting parties.

In contracts concluded between a business and a consumer, Article 5 Unfair Terms Directive 93/13/EEC functions as such a counterforce, protecting the consumer, by means of introducing a transparency and interpretation rule in all consumer contracts. A consumer is presumed to be weaker than a professional contracting party in the sense that he often lacks a strong negotiating position. Moreover, a consumer in many cases has no option but to contract with a certain counterparty or has no option but to adhere to a standard agreement. Article 5 Unfair Terms Directive 93/13/EEC runs as follows: "*In the case of contracts where all or certain terms offered to the consumer are in writing, these*

* PhD Candidate Centre for Methodology of Law, KU Leuven.

terms must always be drafted in plain, intelligible language. Where there is doubt about the meaning of a term, the interpretation most favourable to the consumer shall prevail. This rule on interpretation shall not apply in the context of the procedures laid down in Article 7 (2)." When a seller or a supplier does not make sure that the contracts he concludes with consumers are perfectly clear, he provokes an interpretation at his disadvantage.[1] He formulates the contract and should not have the opportunity to profit from any inaccuracy.

Article 5 Directive 93/13/EEC is only applicable in consumer contracts, where an agreement is concluded between a consumer and a professional seller or supplier.[2] Article 2 of the Directive defines the parties as follows: "*For the purposes of this Directive: [...] (b) 'consumer' means any natural person who, in contracts covered by this Directive, is acting for purposes which are outside his trade, business or profession; (c) 'seller or supplier' means any natural or legal person who, in contracts covered by this Directive, is acting for purposes relating to his trade, business or profession, whether publicly owned or privately owned.*" Besides, the Directive only applies to terms which have not been individually negotiated.[3]

In this contribution, we investigate the transparency and interpretation rule from a European perspective. Since a Directive needs to be implemented in the Member States in order to function concretely, a bottom-up approach is needed. Therefore, apart from investigating European sources, like European legislation and the case law of the European Court of Justice, an analysis of legal doctrine and jurisprudence of different Member States is essential. We examine case law and scholarly debate in Belgium, France, the Netherlands and England, because of the different systems of contract interpretation existing in those countries. In Belgian and French law, a subjective interpretation of contracts prevails: the common intention is the vital criterion that governs the explanation of agreements. Situated on the other end of the scale, is the objective English system, where the meaning which the document would convey to a

1 M. Lamoureux, "L'interprétation des contrats de consommation", *D.* 2006, (2848) No. 5; S. Lebeau, "L'application de la LPMPC à la location immobilière", *Jurim Pratique* 2012, 216; G. Paisant, "Les clauses abusives et la présentation des contrats dans la loi No. 95-96 du 1er février 1995", *D.* 1995, (99) No. 41; T. Ravel d'Esclapon, "Protection du consommateur: interprétation d'un contrat d'assurance" (note under Cass. fr. (2e civ.) 1 June 2011), *D.* 2011, 1612; R.P.J.L. Tjittes, *Uitleg van schriftelijke contracten*, Nijmegen, Ars Aequi Libri, 2009, 41.

2 A. Cruquenaire, "L'interprétation du contrat de vente", *TBBR* 2008, 313, 317; A. Cruquenaire, "L'incidence du droit commun des obligations sur les règles d'interprétation préférentielle: réflexions à partir de l'exemple des contrats relatifs au droit d'auteur", *TBBR* 2008, 602; C. Paris, "L'interprétation des clauses d'une police d'assurance and cas de doute" (note under Bergen 6 May 2003), *JLMB* 2003, 1825; R. Steennot, "Interpretatie in het voordeel van de consument" (note under JoP Zelzate 30 June 2009), *T.JoP* 2012, 359.

3 Directive 2005/29/EC concerning unfair business-to-consumer commercial practices in the internal market, recital 12 ("*Whereas, in particular, only contractual terms which have not been individually negotiated are covered by this Directive.*"); OFT v Abbey National Plc [2009] UKSC 6; [2010] 1 A.C. 696; [2009] 3 W.L.R. 1215; [2010] 1 All E.R. 667; [2010] 2 All E.R. (Comm) 945; [2010] 1 Lloyd's Rep. 281; [2010] 1 C.M.L.R. 44; [2010] Eu. L.R. 309; (2009) 159 N.L.J. 1702 ("*The Directive and the 1999 Regulations apply only to terms which have not been individually negotiated.*").

reasonable person predominates. An intermediary system is found in the Netherlands. Decisive is the sense the contracting parties (subjective) could mutually reasonably (objective) attach to the stipulations in the present circumstances and that which they could reasonably (objective) expect from each other to that matter.

II. Implementation of Article 5 Unfair Terms Directive 93/13/EEC

Under Article 10(1) of the Unfair Terms Directive 93/13/EEC, European Member States were required to bring into force the laws, regulations and administrative provisions necessary to comply with the Directive no later than 31 December 1994.

Two different systems of implementation of the Directive can be discerned. In England, the entire Directive was laid down almost literally in a separate law, namely the Unfair Terms in Consumer Contracts Regulations 1994,[4] which were in 1999 replaced by the Unfair Terms in Consumer Contracts Regulations 1999.[5] The transparency and interpretation rule was laid down in Article 7 UTCCR: "*(1) A seller or supplier shall ensure that any written term of a contract is expressed in plain, intelligible language. (2) If there is doubt about the meaning of a written term, the interpretation which is most favourable to the consumer shall prevail but this rule shall not apply in proceedings brought under regulation 12.*" This way of implementing the Directive raised some critical voices, since the regime concerning unfair contract terms existing before 1993, namely the Unfair Contract Terms Act 1977, continued to be in place.[6] The existence of two different sets of rules regarding unfair contract terms, which partly overlap, operating alongside each other, might give rise to uncertainties. However, in practice, no problems should arise, since, when a conflict arises between the Unfair Contract Terms Act 1977 and the UTCCR, the latter law prevails.[7]

4 Unfair Terms in Consumer Contracts Regulations 1994, *SI* 1994/3159.

5 Unfair Terms in Consumer Contracts Regulations 1999, *SI* 1999/2083, hereafter UTCCR.

6 N. Andrews, *Contract Law*, Cambridge, Cambridge University press, 2011, 438; P. Britton, "The architect, the banker, his wife and the adjudicator: construction and the changing law of unfair contract terms", *Const. L.J.* 2006, 40; M. Ebers, "Unfair Contract Terms Directive (93/13)" in H. Schulte-Nölke, C. Twigg-Flesner and M. Ebers (eds.), *EC Consumer Law Compendium: The Consumer Acquis and its transposition in the Member States*, München, Sellier, 2008, 220; J. Poole, *Textbook on Contract Law*, Oxford, Oxford University Press, 2012, 260–261; K. Reid, "Unfair Terms in Consumer Contract Regulations 1994", *Comp. Law.* 1995, 280; G.G. Howells and R. Brownsword, "The implementation of the EC Directive on unfair terms in consumer contracts – some unresolved questions", *J.B.L.* 1995, 243–244; J.K. MacLeod, *Consumer sales law*, London, Cavendish Publishing, 2002, 382; J. O'Sullivan and J. Hilliard, *The Law of Contract*, Oxford, Oxford Univeristy Press, 2010, 209; F. M. B. Reynolds, "Unfair Contract Terms", *L.Q.R.* 1994, 110; R. Sudbury and D. Marchese, "The UK Unfair Terms in Consumer Contracts Regulations 1994", *ICCLR* 1995, 388.

7 P. Britton, "The architect, the banker, his wife and the adjudicator: construction and the changing law of unfair contract terms", *Const. L.J.* 2006, 25–26. Contra: AJ Building and Plastering Ltd v Turner [2013] EWHC 484 (QB); [2013] WL 617792, §47, 53–54: "*If the normal principles of construction led to a firm conclusion as to the meaning of a document, there would be no room for reg.7(2) to apply. However, if the process of construction did not lead to a firm conclusion and the court was left with two or more interpretations that it could not reject on other grounds, reg.7(2), which is not materially different from the contra proferentem rule, would operate as a tie-breaker.*"

In other countries, for instance Belgium, France and the Netherlands, the Directive was integrated in existing laws. This did not happen without a struggle. In Belgium, the authorities were of the opinion that it was not necessary to transpose Article 5 Unfair Terms Directive 93/13/EEC, since the content of the article was merely a repetition of the existing Article 1162 CC. However, the European Commission did not agree, arguing that Article 1162 CC was only a partial transposition of Article 5 Unfair Terms Directive, because Article 1162 CC is a subsidiary provision, that only comes into place when the content of the contract cannot be discovered using the primary interpretation rules.[8] Article 5 Unfair Terms Directive, on the other hand, has to be applied as from the moment a stipulation in a consumer contract is unclear, irrespective of the other interpretation rules. Besides, the first part of Article 5 Unfair Terms Directive, describing a transparency rule, was not included in Article 1162 CC. The Belgian lawmaker reacted to the criticism and inserted Article 5 Unfair Terms Directive's transparency and interpretation requirement in the *Wet van 14 juli 1991 betreffende de handelspraktijken en de voorlichting en bescherming van de consument (WHPC)*, namely in Article 31 §4 WHPC. The transparency and the interpretation rule were included in Article 31 WHPC, a provision that described unfair contract terms. This positioning was a bit ill-chosen, seeing that an unclear or an ambiguous stipulation is not always unfair.[9] When drafting the WMPC,[10] the successor of the WHPC, it was therefore decided to give the transparency and the interpretation rule an autonomous position. That way the general scope of the rule was emphasised: the rule is applicable to all stipulations in consumer contracts, not only to unfair contract terms. Nowadays, the WMPC is replaced by book VI of the Belgian Wetboek van economisch recht, which has come into force on 31 May 2014. The transparency and interpretation rule is copied from the WMPC. Article VI. 37 WER states: "*§1. Indien alle of bepaalde bedingen van een overeenkomst tussen een onderneming en een consument schriftelijk zijn, moeten ze op duidelijke en begrijpelijke wijze zijn opgesteld. §2. In geval van twijfel over de betekenis van een beding, prevaleert de voor de consument gunstigste interpretatie. Deze interpretatieregel is niet van toepassing in het kader van de vordering tot staking bedoeld in boek XVII. [...]*".

A similar process took place in France, where Article 5 Unfair Terms Directive was first regarded as being incorporated in Article 1162 CC and where the European Commission opposed to this view.[11] This resulted in 1995 in the adoption of Article L133-2 Code de

8 Wetsontwerp tot wijziging van de wet van 14 juli 1991 betreffende de handelspraktijken and de voorlichting and bescherming van de consument, *Parl. St.* Kamer 1997–1998, No. 49–1565/1, 6; Verslag namens de commissie over wetsontwerp tot wijziging van de wet van 14 July 1991 betreffende de handelspraktijken and de voorlichting and bescherming van de consument, *Parl. St.* Kamer 1997–1998, No. 49–1565/3, 27.

9 E. Van den Haute, "Le règlement général des opérations de banque et les clauses abusives: vers la consécration du concept du 'consommateur responsable'?" (note under Liège 26 January 2007), *Bank Fin. R.* 2007, 355.

10 Wet van 6 april 2010 betreffende de marktpraktijken en consumentenbescherming.

11 V. Avena-Robardet, "Le doute profite toujours au consommateur" (note under Cass. fr. (1e civ.) 21 January 2003), *D.* 2003, 693; C. Bourrier, *La faiblesse d'une partie au contrat*, Louvain-la-Neuve,

la Consommation: "*Les clauses des contrats proposés par les professionnels aux consommateurs ou aux non-professionnels doivent être présentées et rédigées de façon claire et compréhensible. Elles s'interprètent en cas de doute dans le sens le plus favorable au consommateur ou au non-professionnel. Le présent alinéa n'est toutefois pas applicable aux procédures engagées sur le fondement de l'article L. 421-6.*"

In the Netherlands, at first, no steps were taken to transpose Article 5 Unfair Terms Directive in national law. The Dutch government considered such an action unnecessary, on the ground that the existing Dutch legislation already was in conformity with the Directive, since it secured the aims pursued by the Directive.[12] On some topics, the Dutch Civil Code was at variance with the Directive, but an interpretation of the legislation in conformity with the Directive would provide a sufficient consumer protection.[13] However, the European Commission did nog agree with the Dutch lawmaker, as it was of the opinion that the Directive had not been fully transposed into Dutch law within the prescribed period.[14] The Commission initiated the infringement procedure and delivered a reasoned opinion on 6 April 1998, calling upon the Netherlands to take the measures necessary to comply with the Directive within two months of receipt of the opinion. However, the Kingdom of the Netherlands failed to comply, so the European Commission called upon the Court of Justice to determine whether the obligation incumbent upon the Kingdom of the Netherlands to transpose into national law Council Directive 93/13/EEC of 5 April 1993 might be deemed to have been discharged by virtue of the fact that the Dutch Civil Code already contained provisions allegedly in conformity with the Directive, in particular regarding Articles 4(2) and 5 of the Directive.[15] This resulted in a judgment on 10 May 2001 (C-144/99), in which the Court of Justice decided that the Kingdom of the

Academia-Bruylant, 2004, 392; M. Luby, "Contrats et clauses abusives: transposition de la directive No. 93/13 du 5 avr. 1993 (note under CoJ 9 September 2004), *RTD Com.* 2005, 183.

12 M.L. Hendrikse, "De contra proferentem-regel en het notariaat", *WPNR* 2000, 521; E. Hondius, "Non-implementation of the Directive on Unfair Contract Terms: the Dutch case", *ERPL* 1997, 193; C.M.D.S. Pavillon, "De wisselende betekenis van de Richtlijn oneerlijke bedingen in de Nederlandse rechtspraak: een drieluik", *VrA* 2006, 29.

13 E. Hondius, "Non-implementation of the Directive on Unfair Contract Terms: the Dutch case", *ERPL* 1997, 193–194; C.M.D.S. Pavillon, "De wisselende betekenis van de Richtlijn oneerlijke bedingen in de Nederlandse rechtspraak: een drieluik", *VrA* 2006, 30.

14 CoJ 10 May 2001, C-144/99, Commission of the European Communities v Kingdom of the Netherlands, http://curia.europa.eu; HR 19 September 1997, *NJ* 1998, 6 ("*Daarbij verdient aandacht dat de Nederlandse regels betreffende algemene voorwaarden, waarvan de wetgever heeft geoordeeld dat zij de richtlijn incorporeren, aldus moeten worden uitgelegd dat zij aan – kort gezegd – consumenten tenminste dezelfde bescherming bieden als de richtlijn, terwijl de richtlijn aan een verder gaande bescherming in het Nederlandse recht niet in de weg staat.*"); M.B.M. Loos, "Veroordeling Nederland wegens niet-omzetting Richtlijn oneerlijke bedingen", *NTER* 2001, 242–244; C.M.D.S. Pavillon, "De wisselende betekenis van de Richtlijn oneerlijke bedingen in de Nederlandse rechtspraak: een drieluik", *VrA* 2006, 32.

15 CoJ 10 May 2001, C-144/99, Commission of the European Communities v Kingdom of the Netherlands, http://curia.europa.eu.

Netherlands had failed to fulfil its obligations under the Directive.[16] The Court passed judgment as following: "*As regards the argument advanced by the Netherlands Government that, if the Netherlands legislation were interpreted in such a way as to ensure conformity with the Directive – a principle endorsed by the Hoge Raad der Nederlanden (Netherlands) – it would be possible in any event to remedy any disparity between the provisions of Netherlands legislation and those of the Directive, suffice it to note that, [...] even where the settled case-law of a Member State interprets the provisions of national law in a manner deemed to satisfy the requirements of a directive, that cannot achieve the clarity and precision needed to meet the requirement of legal certainty. That, moreover, is particularly true in the field of consumer protection.*" The Dutch government decided to comply with its duty to transpose the Directive, which resulted in Article 6:238, 2 Dutch CC: "*Bij een overeenkomst als bedoeld in de artikelen 236 en 237 moeten de bedingen duidelijk en begrijpelijk zijn opgesteld. Bij twijfel over de betekenis van een beding, prevaleert de voor de wederpartij gunstigste uitleg.*"

III. Content of Article 5 Unfair Terms Directive 93/13/EEC

3.1. *Functioning of the rule*

Article 5 Unfair Terms Directive 93/13/EEC consists of two parts: an information or transparency requirement on the one hand and an interpretation rule on the other hand. Both rules are intertwined, since the second sentence functions as a sanction for non-compliance with the first sentence.[17] Any lack of transparency suffices to ensure that the

16 CoJ 10 May 2001, C-144/99, Commission of the European Communities v Kingdom of the Netherlands, http://curia.europa.eu.

17 V. Avena-Robardet, "Le doute profite toujours au consommateur" (note under Cass. fr. (1e civ.) 21 January 2003), *D.* 2003, 693; S. Ben Hadj Yahia, "L'assurance de groupe aux confins du droit des obligations et du droit de la consommation" (note under Cass. fr. (1e civ.) 22 May 2008), *Gaz. Pal.* 2009, (20) No. 29; P. Cambie, *Onrechtmatige bedingen*, Brussels, Larcier, 2009, 137; M. Bruschi, "Information des consommateurs et formation des contrats" (note under Cass. fr. civ. 1e 21 January 2003), *RDC* 2003, 91; H. Claret, "Contrats de consommation. Interprétation d'une clause ambiguë d'un contrat d'assurance" (note under Cass. fr. 2e civ. 1 June 2011), *Petites Affiches* 2011, 15; G. Courtieu, "Le doute doit toujours profiter à l'assuré", *Resp. civ. et assur.* 2003, chron. 13; A. Cruquenaire, *L'interprétation des contrats and droit d'auteur*, Brussels, Larcier, 2007, 230; A. Cruquenaire, "L'incidence du droit commun des obligations sur les règles d'interprétation préférentielle: réflexions à partir de l'exemple des contrats relatifs au droit d'auteur", *TBBR* 2008, 602; P. Erneux, "Promotions immobilières et protection du consommateur. Pratique contractuelle des ventes d'immeubles et loi sur les pratiques du commerce", *Jurim Pratique* 2008, 186; E. Ferrante, "Contractual Disclosure and Remedies under the Unfair Contract Terms Directive" in G. Howells, A. Janssen and R. Schulze (eds.), *Information Rights and Obligations: A Challenge for Party Autonomy and Transactional Fairness*, Ashgate, Aldershot, 2004, 121; J. Ghestin and I. Marchessaux-Van Melle, "L'application en France de la directive visant à éliminer les clauses abusives après l'adoption de la loi nos 95–96 du 1er février 1995", *JCP* 1995, 278; C. Grimaldi, "Paradoxes autour de l'interprétation des contrats", *RDC* 2008, (207) No. 25; L. Grynbaum, "De l'art de la mesure dans la protection du consentement", *RDC* 2007, 973; M. Lamoureux, "L'interprétation des contrats de consommation", *D.* 2006, (2848) No. 5, 8; S. Lebeau,

interpretation rule comes into effect. The rules are considered to be two sides of the same coin: the first one is preventive, the second one is punitive.[18]

When faced with a dispute regarding the interpretation of a consumer contract, Article 5 Unfair Terms Directive 93/13/EEC provokes an approach in two steps.[19] In a first phase, the question needs to be answered whether a contract, a clause or a term is (1) clear and

"L'application de la LPMPC à la location immobilière", *Jurim Pratique* 2012, 216; J.K. MacLeod, *Consumer sales law*, London, Cavendish Publishing, 2002, 385; J. Mestre and B. Fages, "Le doute profite au consommateur" (note under Cass. fr. (1e civ.) 21 January 2003), *RTD Civ.* 2003, 292; A. Pélissier, "Contrat d'assurance. Interprétation" (note under Cass. fr. (2e civ.) 1 June 2011), *RGDA* 2012, 33; J. Poole, *Textbook on Contract Law*, Oxford, Oxford University Press, 2012, 273; T. Ravel d'Esclapon, "Protection du consommateur: interprétation d'un contrat d'assurance" (note under Cass. fr. (2e civ.) 1 June 2011), *D.* 2011, 1612; K. Reid, "Unfair Terms in Consumer Contract Regulations 1994", *Comp. Law.* 1995, 280; P. Richards, *Law of contract*, Harlow, Pearson Education Limited, 2007, 207; N. Sauphanor-Brouillaud, "Droit des contrats et droit de la consommation" (note under Cass. fr. (3e civ.) 9 February 2011 and Cass. fr. (1e civ.) 3 March 2011), *RDC* 2011, (877) No. 3; N. Sauphanor-Brouillaud, "Une clause ambiguë d'un contrat d'assurance doit s'interpréter dans le sens le plus favorable à l'assuré " (note under Cass. fr. (2e civ.) 1 June 2011), *EDC* 2011, 3; E.J.H. Schrage, "Contra proferentem", *VrA* 2005, 58; A. Sériaux, "Lien contractuel direct entre l'adhérent et l'assureur du fait de l'adhésion à un contrat d'assurance de groupe et interprétation d'une clause abusive" (note under Cass. fr. (1e civ.) 22 May 2008), *JCP G* 2008, II, 10138; E. Swaenepoel, S. Stijns and P. Wéry, "Onrechtmatige bedingen", *DCCR* 2009, 157; E. Swaenepoel, *Toetsing van het contractuele evenwicht*, Antwerp, Intersentia, 2011, 520; M. Tenreiro and J. Karsten, "Unfair terms in consumer contracts: uncertainties, contradictions and novelties of a directive" in H. Schulte-Nölke and R. Schulze (eds.), *Europaïsche Rechtsangleichung und nationale Privatrechte*, Baden-Baden, Nomos, 1999, 243; The Law Commission, *Consultation Paper No 166*, The Scottish Law Commission, *Discussion Paper No 119*, htttp://lawcommission.justice.gov.uk/docs/cp166_Unfair_Terms_In_Contracts_Consultation.pdf, 49; E. Van den Haute, "Le règlement général des opérations de banque et les clauses abusives: vers la consécration du concept du 'consommateur responsable'?" (note under Liège 26 January 2007), *Bank Fin. R.* 2007, 355; P. Wéry, "Les clauses abusives relatives à l'inexécution des obligations contractuelles dans les lois de protection des consommateurs du 14 juillet 1991 et du 12 août 2002", *JT* 2003, 802; S. Whittaker, "The Language or Languages of Consumer Contracts", *Cambridge Y.B. Eur. Legal Stud.* 2005–2006, 247; C. Willett, "The Directive on Unfair Terms in Consumer Contracts and its implementation in the United Kingdom", *ERPL* 1997, 231; C. Willett, "Good Faith in Consumer Contracts: Rule, Policy and Principle" in A.D.M. Forte (ed.), *Good Faith in Contract and Property Law*, Oxford, Hart Publishing, 1999, 196.

18 A. Sériaux, "Lien contractuel direct entre l'adhérent et l'assureur du fait de l'adhésion à un contrat d'assurance de groupe et interprétation d'une clause abusive" (note under Cass. fr. (1e civ.) 22 May 2008), *JCP G* 2008, II, 10138.

19 M. Ebers, "Unfair Contract Terms Directive (93/13)" in H. Schulte-Nölke, C. Twigg-Flesner and M. Ebers (eds.), *EC Consumer Law Compendium: The Consumer Acquis and its transposition in the Member States*, München, Sellier, 2008, 248; E. Ferrante, "Contractual Disclosure and Remedies under the Unfair Contract Terms Directive" in G. Howells, A. Janssen and R. Schulze (eds.), *Information Rights and Obligations: A Challenge for Party Autonomy and Transactional Fairness*, Ashgate, Aldershot, 2004, 122–123; M.L. Hendrikse, "Uitleg van verzekeringsvoorwaarden", *NTHR* 2008, 137–146; M.L. Hendrikse, "Verzekeringsrecht en algemene voorwaarden" in M.L. Hendrikse, P.H.J.G. van Huizen and J.G.J. Rinkes, *Verzekeringsrecht praktisch belicht*, Deventer, Kluwer, 2008, 28; M.L. Hendrikse, "De reikwijdte van het contra-proferentembeginsel in het verzekeringsrecht", *NTHR* 2010, 95–103; M.B.M. Loos, *Algemene voorwaarden*, Den Haag, Boom Juridische Uitgevers, 2013, 176; G. McMeel, *The Construction of Contracts*, Oxford, Oxford University Press, 2007, 456; B. Wessels and

intelligible, (2) unclear or (3) unintelligible. In order to do that, it is necessary to interpret the text provisionally, because it is not possible to examine whether more than one reading of a text can exist without turning to interpretation.[20] In a second phase, consequences need to be attached to the results of the first phase. Three different outcomes can arise. First, the reader might conclude that the clause is completely clear and intelligible. Only one meaning is possible, so no interpretation is needed. A second situation arises when the clause can have more than one meaning: it is unclear. Than it needs to be interpreted *in favorem consumentis*. This interpretation in favour of the consumer can lead to two different outcomes. On the one hand, the judge can merely draw a conclusion concerning the meaning of the contract that is advantageous for the consumer. On the other hand, the judge might interpret the contract in such a way that an unclear clause must be characterised as unfair and therefore needs to be declared null or void. Not every unclear of ambiguous clause is unfair.[21] Still, an unclear stipulation can in many cases be deemed unfair, for instance when a certain interpretation of the stipulation makes it unfair. A third scenario happens when no meaning can be attached to a clause. It is not intelligible, so it cannot be interpreted. Such an incomprehensible clause is unfair, so incomprehensibility results in nullity of the clause.[22]

3.2. *Transparency rule: clarity and intelligibility*

3.2.1. Reference person

Who determines whether a consumer contract is plain and intelligible? In a first stage, the consumer does. He only takes legal action when he decides that he does not understand the agreement. From the moment the action is brought before a judge, that judge has to ascertain whether or not a clause is plain and intelligible.[23] In this operation,

R.H.C. Jongeneel, "Uitgangspunten bij het opstellen van algemene voorwaarden" in B. Wessels (ed.), *Contracten maken*, Deventer, Kluwer, 2004, 33.

20 M.H.. Wissink, "Europese uitleg van onduidelijke algemene voorwaarden" in *BW-Krant Jaarboek 1995*, Arnhem, Gouda Quint, 1995, 167.

21 M.B.M. Loos, *Algemene voorwaarden*, Den Haag, Boom Juridische Uitgevers, 2013, 179; E. Van den Haute, "Le règlement général des opérations de banque et les clauses abusives: vers la consécration du concept du 'consommateur responsable'?" (note under Liège 26 January 2007), *Bank Fin. R.* 2007, 355.

22 P. Cserne, "Policy considerations in contract interpretation: the contra proferentem rule from a comparative law and economics perspective" in G. Radhika, *Contract Theory – Corporate Law*, Hyderabad, ICFAI University Press, 2009, 92; M.L. Hendrikse, "Uitleg van verzekeringsvoorwaarden", *NTHR* 2008, 146; M.L. Hendrikse, "Verzekeringsrecht en algemene voorwaarden" in M.L. Hendrikse, P.H.J.G. van Huizen en J.G.J. Rinkes, *Verzekeringsrecht praktisch belicht*, Deventer, Kluwer, 2008, 28; M.L. Hendrikse, "De reikwijdte van het contra-proferentembeginsel in het verzekeringsrecht", *NTHR* 2010, 95–103; J. Hijma, *Algemene voorwaarden*, Deventer, Kluwer, 2003, 34; M.B.M. Loos, *Algemene voorwaarden*, Den Haag, Boom Juridische Uitgevers, 2013, 173–174; E. Swaenepoel, *Toetsing van het contractuele evenwicht*, Antwerpen, Intersentia, 2011, 520–521.

23 F. Bogaert and B. Van Baeveghem, "Contractuele aspecten van de wet marktpraktijken" in *Economisch recht: ondernemingen, concurrenten and consumenten*, Malines, Kluwer, 2011, 29.

the judge should not check if he thinks that the stipulation under investigation lacks clarity, but he is obliged to imagine himself in the situation in which the consumer finds himself.[24]

On the 18th of April 2000 Mr and Mrs X. concluded a contract with a real estate agent, Immo 5 Cantons. The agent was to sell their apartment. In the agreement, the parties included a clause stating that the owners of the apartment were not allowed to sell it without the agency of the real estate agent for a certain period. If they would sell, they would have to pay a fine. The contract stated as follows: "*Le présent mandat est consenti et accepté avec exclusivité pour une période irrévocable de trois mois à compter de ce jour. Sauf dénonciation, à l'expiration de cette période initiale, il sera prorogé pour une durée maximale d'une année au terme de laquelle il prendra automatiquement fin. Chacune des parties pourra, moyennant un préavis de quinze jours, par lettre recommandée avec avis de réception, y mettre fin au terme de la période initiale ou à tout moment pendant sa prorogation.*" Mr and Mrs X sold their property on the 12th of September 2000, without any intervention of the real estate agent. They had ended the contract by registered mail, which had arrived at Immo 5 Cantons on the 11th of September. The real estate agent argued that a fine needed to be paid, since the letter had not immediately ended the contract, but had merely started a period of notice of 15 days. Mr and Mrs X referred to Article L133-2 Code de la Consommation and said that the time clause was not clear. The judge decided: "*Il ne s'agit donc pas de savoir si la clause est en soi claire ou si son interprétation est nécessaire, mais si pour le consommateur ou le non professionnel, la lecture de la clause laissait place à une interprétation qui rend son erreur éventuelle de compréhension excusable et non fautive. [...] Comme l'a relevé exactement le premier Juge, la clause contractuelle peut être lue dans le sens où le préavis de quinze jours n'est exigé que pour mettre un terme au contrat à l'issue de la période initiale. Au contraire, pendant la période de prorogation d'un an, la résiliation peut intervenir à tout moment. Cette ambigité manifeste ne peut que profiter aux époux X. en application de l'article L133-2 du Code de la Consommation [...]*".[25]

The reference person, in relation to which the judge has to ascertain the clearness of a consumer contract, is the consumer. But which consumer? Is it the consumer who is a party in the concrete action brought before the judge (consumer *in concreto*)? Or should the judge have recourse to an abstract reference person? One might think a control *in concreto* is to be preferred, so that the individual character of the consumer is to be taken into account.[26] However, such an approach can be problematic when interpreting a clause in a consumer contract. In practice it might not be possible to work out whether a

24 Pau 9 February 2004, No. 02/001705; M. Lamoureux, "L'interprétation des contrats de consommation", *D.* 2006, (2848) No. 11; R. Sudbury and D. Marchese, "The UK Unfair Terms in Consumer Contracts Regulations 1994", *ICCLR* 1995, 390.

25 Pau 9 February 2004, No. 02/001705.

26 Pres. Comm. C. Brussels 16 June 2003, *DCCR* 2004, 104, note L. Kerzmann; *Jaarboek Handelspraktijken and Mededinging* 2003, 334; *TBH* 2003, 893, note L. Kerzmann ("*Le §3 suppose dès lors un contrôle concret et non abstrait des rapports individuels entre un consommateur et un vendeur.*"); H. Claret, "Interprétation des contrats d'assurance et droit de la consommation" (note under Cass. fr. (1e civ.) 21 January 2003), *D.* 2003, (2600) n°6.

specific consumer has actually understood the stipulation he claims is unclear. In order to force a favourable interpretation, he can pose as someone less intelligent than he actually is. That way every consumer bringing an action about the lack of transparency in a consumer contract would be put in the right. This is, of course, untenable. Therefore, the investigation of the transparency requirement has to be an abstract inquiry, using the consumer *in abstracto* as a benchmark. However, having to assess the consumer *in abstracto*, not taking into account his individual character, does not mean excluding all elements particular to the case at hand: the judge must have regard to the particular circumstances of the case.[27]

The obvious abstract reference person is the "*average consumer*".[28] The average consumer test is commonly used in EU-law in the context of consumer protection, namely in the

27 CoJ 21 March 2013, C-92/11, RWE Vertrieb v. Verbraucherzentrale Nordrhein-Westfalen, http://curia.europa.eu, opinion V. Trstenjak ("*Articles 3 and 5 of Directive 93/13 [...] must be interpreted as meaning that, [...] It is for the national court to carry out that assessment with regard to all the circumstances of the particular case.*"); CoJ 30 April 2014, C-26/13, Kásler, http://curia.europa.eu ("*In that context, it is for the national court to determine, taking account of the criteria laid down in Articles 3(1) and 5 of Directive 93/13, whether, having regard to the particular circumstances of the case, such a term meets the requirements of good faith, balance and transparency laid down by that directive.*"); M. Asser, P. Clausing and J.H. Wansink, *Bijzondere Overeenkomsten. De Verzekeringsovereenkomst*, Deventer, Kluwer, 2007, 276–277; M.L. Hendrikse, "De reikwijdte van het contra-proferentembeginsel in het verzekeringsrecht", *NTHR* 2010, 97–98; M.B.M. Loos, *Consumentenkoop*, Deventer, Kluwer, 2004, 35; M.B.M. Loos, *Algemene voorwaarden*, Den Haag, Boom Juridische Uitgevers, 2013, 177; J.M. van Dunné, *Verbintenissenrecht. Deel 1. Contractenrecht*, Deventer, Kluwer, 2001, 209, 226.

28 CoJ 30 April 2014, C-26/13, Kásler, http://curia.europa.eu ("*It is for the referring court to determine whether, having regard to all the relevant information, including the promotional material and information provided by the lender in the negotiation of the loan agreement, the average consumer, who is reasonably well informed and reasonably observant and circumspect, would not only be aware of the existence of the difference [...].*"); OFT v Abbey National plc and Others [2008] EWHC 875 ("*Some would regard the United Kingdom system as being, in some sense at least, obviously unfair, though Mr. Sumption QC (for the banks) vigorously disputed Lord Mance's suggestion that his clients were engaged in a sort of 'reverse Robin Hood exercise'. That is an imponderable question which depends partly on whether one's perception of the* average customer *who incurs unauthorised overdraft charges is that he is spendthrift and improvident, or that she is disadvantaged and finding it hard to make ends meet. But it is not the question for the Court*"); OFT v Ashbourne Management Services Ltd and Others [2011] EWHC 1237 (Ch) ("*The concept of a* typical or average consumer *is a familiar one in European consumer law extending also into the law of registered trade marks. Such a person is generally assumed to be reasonably well informed and reasonably observant and circumspect, and to read the relevant documents and to seek to understand what is being read. The standard is a variable one and must, I believe, take colour from the context. For example, consumers who are financially sophisticated may be expected to bring to bear a greater understanding of the meaning and implications of the terms of a contract than consumers who are vulnerable as a result of their naivety or credulity. As will be seen, this typical consumer is relevant not only to the assessment of fairness but also the consideration of whether a particular term is expressed in clear intelligible language*".); Den Bosch 29 May 2012, HD 200.080.411 and HD 200.089.618, *TvC* 2012, 292, note V. Mak (HD 200.080.411: "*Aangezien deze begrippen vergelijkbaar zijn met het in het geding zijnde begrip vaste opslag, is het hof evenals de rechtbank van oordeel dat mag worden aangenomen dat de gemiddelde consument bij lezing van de offerte zal denken dat met vaste opslag wordt bedoeld een (rente)opslag van een bepaald percentage (in de offerte is de hoogte van de opslag niet afzonderlijk vermeld), welk percentage gedurende de looptijd van de*

case of unfair business-to-consumer commercial practices.[29] In the European Unfair Commercial Practices Directive, the average consumer is described as a "*notional, typical consumer*."[30] The Directive "*takes as a benchmark the average consumer, who is reasonably well-informed and reasonably observant and circumspect, taking into account social,*

overeenkomst niet verandert. [...] Ook de stelling van Obvion dat gezien de werking van het in- and uitlenen van financiële middelen, zoals geschetst in de memorie van grieven, een onveranderlijke opslag onlogisch zou zijn, leidt niet tot een ander oordeel. De gemiddelde consument *zal doorgaans immers niet op de hoogte zijn van de werking van de financiële markten and hoeft dat ook niet te zijn*"; HD 200.089.618: "*Aangezien deze begrippen vergelijkbaar zijn met het in het geding zijnde begrip vaste opslag, is het hof van oordeel dat mag worden aangenomen dat de* gemiddelde consument *bij lezing van de offerte zal denken dat met vaste opslag wordt bedoeld een (rente)opslag van een bepaald percentage (in de offerte is de hoogte van de opslag niet afzonderlijk vermeld), welk percentage gedurende de looptijd van de overeenkomst niet verandert.*"); C. Amsterdam 18 May 2011, *IER* 2011, 463, note W. Leppink ("*Voor de* gemiddelde consument *had het – zeker vanaf het najaar van 2008 tegen de achtergrond van de mondiale kredietcrisis – duidelijk moeten zijn dat de aangeboden spaarrente van 4% niet tot in lengte van dagen ongewijzigd zou blijven, maar dat de hoogte daarvan ook afhankelijk zou kunnen zijn van zich wijzigende marktomstandigheden. De gemiddelde consument heeft op basis van de toegezonden Handleiding and de Voorwaarden Toprekening over voldoende informatie over de aard and omvang van de te vergoeden rente kunnen beschikken om een geïnformeerd besluit te nemen al dan niet op de Toprekening te gaan sparen. Daarbij is van belang dat van de gemiddelde consument mag worden verwacht dat hij kennis neemt van de aan hem verstrekte informatie.*"); C. Armbrüster, "Standard Contract Terms and Information Rules" in H. Collins (ed.), *Standard Contract Terms in Europe*, Alphen aan den Rijn, Kluwer, 2008, 169; A. Arora, "Unfair contract terms and unauthorised bank charges: a banking lawyer's perspective", *JBL* 2012, 61–62; P. Butt, *Modern Legal Drafting: A Guide to Using Clearer Language*, Cambridge, Cambridge University Press, 2013, 121; A.G. Castermans, "Misleidende omissie bij het aangaan van overeenkomsten. Reflexwerking van de regeling oneerlijke handelspraktijken", *MvV* 2011, 202–207; M. Chen-Wishart, "Transparency and fairness in bank charges", *LQR* 2010, 161; H. Claret, "Contrats de consommation. Interprétation d'une clause ambiguë d'un contrat d'assurance" (note under Cass. fr. (2e civ.) 1 June 2011), *Petites Affiches* 2011, 15; M.B.M. Loos, *Algemene voorwaarden*, Den Haag, Boom Juridische Uitgevers, 2013, 174; V. Mak, Note under Den Bosch 29 May 2012, HD 200.080.411 and HD 200.089.618, *TvC* 2012, 294, "Europese uitleg van onduidelijke algemene voorwaarden" in *BW-Krant Jaarboek 1995*, Arnhem, Gouda Quint, 1995, 166; E. McKendrick, *Contract Law: Text, Cases, and Materials*, Oxford, Oxford University Press, 2012, 468; OFT, *Unfair contract terms guidance. Guidance for the Unfair Terms in Consumer Contracts Regulations 1999*, 2008, www.oft.gov.uk/shared_oft/reports/unfair_contract_terms/oft311.pdf, 85; J. O'Sullivan and J. Hilliard, *The Law of Contract*, Oxford, Oxford Univeristy Press, 2010, 213; M. Schillig, "Directive 93/13 and the 'price term exemption': a comparative analysis in the light of the 'market for lemons' rationale", *ICLQ* 2011, 959–960; C. Willett, "Good Faith in Consumer Contracts: Rule, Policy and Principle" in A.D.M. Forte (ed.), *Good Faith in Contract and Property Law*, Oxford, Hart. Publishing, 1999, 195–196; C. Willett, "The functions of transparency in regulating contract terms: UK and Australian approaches", *ICLQ* 2011, 379–380.

29 Article 6 Directive 2005/29/EC concerning unfair business-to-consumer commercial practices in the internal market; V. Mak, Note under Den Bosch 29 May 2012, HD 200.080.411 and HD 200.089.618, *TvC* 2012, 295; J.G.J. Rinkes, "Europees Consumentenrecht" in E.H. Hondius and G.J. Rijken (eds.), *Handboek Consumentenrecht*, Zutphen, Paris, 2011, 47–52; J.K. Winn and M. Webber, "The Impact of EU Unfair Contract Terms Law on US Business-to-Consumer Internet Merchants", *Bus. Law* 2006–07, 216.

30 Directive 2005/29/EC concerning unfair business-to-consumer commercial practices in the internal market, recital 18.

cultural and linguistic factors."[31] However, it is commonly agreed that, in assessing the transparency requirement of Article 5 Unfair Terms Directive 93/13/EEC, the notion of average consumer is somewhat more flexible: the judge does not have to take into account the level of circumspection and attentiveness.[32] The slightest reasonable doubt suffices to conclude that the transparency requirement is breached.

X bought a house and took out a mortgage loan when he was 54 years old. He also contracted an insurance to cover the balance outstanding in case of death, permanent total invalidity and full temporary disability. Four years later, X took out another mortgage loan, and contracted another insurance to cover the balance outstanding. Half a year after signing the second contract, X suffered from a temporary disability. One year later, he was declared 100% invalid. He asked the insurance company to pay out the balance outstanding. However, the insurer did not agree that payment was in order. The special conditions of the insurance contract included a stipulation stating that full temporary disability would only be covered until the 60th birthday of the policyholder. However, X claimed that he was entitled to he money, since the individual proposal form only referred to "*une quotité assurée de 100% pour une durée de cent quarante quatre mois*". He thought both provisions constituted a contradiction, so that the contract violated Article L133-2 Code de la Consommation. The French Cour de Cassation was of the opinion that both provisions were actually not conflicting, but acknowledged that, from the viewpoint of an inexperienced consumer, the words could be seen as lacking transparency: "*Mais attendu que l'arrêt retient que s'il ressort clairement des indications portées aux conditions particulières que la couverture en matière d'incapacité temporaire totale s'arrête au soixantième anniversaire de l'adhérent, ces mentions sont toutefois en apparente contradiction avec celles figurant sur la demande d'adhésion, aux termes desquelles il est fait état dans un même encadré d'un financement de 300 000 francs, d'une quotité assurée de 100%, pour une durée de cent quarante quatre mois, soit jusqu'au 1er septembre 2006, alors que lesdites mentions n'étaient que partiellement valables, à savoir seulement pour la couverture des risques décès et invalidité permanente et absolue, et non pour la couverture du risque Incapacité temporaire totale; qu'il a pu en résulter une confusion pour M. X., qui doit être résolue en sa faveur, [...]*".[33]

As the benchmark of the average consumer is by and large interpreted differently in the framework of the Unfair Terms Directive 93/13/EEC than in the framework of the European Unfair Commercial Practices Directive, it might be appropriate to look for another term than "*average consumer*", in order to describe the reference person. Within

31 Directive 2005/29/EC concerning unfair business-to-consumer commercial practices in the internal market, recital 18.

32 Cass. fr. (2e civ.) 24 May 2006, No. 04-14.024; H. Claret, "Contrats de consommation. Interprétation d'une clause ambiguë d'un contrat d'assurance" (note under Cass. fr. (2e civ.) 1 June 2011), *Petites Affiches* 2011, 15; J. Elvin, "The Application Of The Unfair Terms In Consumer Contracts Regulations 1999", *KCLJ* 2003, 39, 49; M. Lamoureux, "L'interprétation des contrats de consommation", *D.* 2006, (2848) No. 11; H. Lécuyer and J.-B. Seube, "L'interprétation du contrat dans un sens favorable au consommateur" (note under Cass. fr. (2e civ.) 1 June 2011), *Defrénois* 2011, (1485) No. 40154; R.P.J.L. Tjittes, *Uitleg van schriftelijke contracten*, Nijmegen, Ars Aequi Libri, 2009, 41.

33 Cass. fr. (2e civ.) 24 May 2006, No. 04-14.024.

the framework of Directive 93/13/EG, the reference person regarding the transparency rule should rather be referred to as the *"naïve and inexperienced consumer"*,[34] the *"everyday layman"*,[35] or the *"non-jurist"*.[36]

> This benchmark was used in a Belgian case. Consumers' organisation *TestAankoop* brought an action against insurance company ING, because ING was accustomed to include clauses in its standard insurance contracts which TestAankoop regarded as unfair or unclear. Among other things, TestAankoop heaped criticism on the following stipulation: "*la déchéance lorsque le sinistre garanti est provoqué par les cas, énumérés ci-après, de faute grave de la part de l'assuré, du preneur d'assurance ou du bénéficiaire ou par toute autre personne ayant un intérêt à toucher les allocations. Sont considérées comme fautes graves: [...] les actes clairement téméraires dont on est censé savoir qu'ils constituent une menace à l'intégrité physique; sauf dans les cas de tentative de sauvetage de personnes ou de biens.*" The consumers' organisation was of the opinion that it was not clear which acts had to be deemed clearly impetuous in the sense of this clause. The court reflected on the normal meaning of the words and stated: "*Le fait que, selon les circonstances, un acte puisse être considéré ou non comme clairement téméraire n'implique pas que la clause ne soit pas claire pour le consommateur nonjuriste.*" For instance, the same act of descending on skis a black piste could be, depending upon the skills of the skier, impetuous or not. The everyday layman should himself be capable of evaluating the level of recklessness of such an act.[37]

Using as a benchmark the everyday layman raises the question what should happen when a consumer, who concludes a contract with a professional, is assisted by a legal adviser. In that case, he cannot be deemed an everyday layman, so it is appropriate to take this factor into account when assessing the transparency in a consumer contract.[38]

34 J. Elvin, "The Application Of The Unfair Terms In Consumer Contracts Regulations 1999", *KCLJ* 2003, 49; C. Twigg-Flesner, *The Europeanisation of Contract Law: Current Controversies in Law*, Abingdon, Routledge, 2013, 99.

35 M.A. Clarke, *The law of insurance contracts*, London, Informa, 2006, 398; M. Ebers, "Unfair Contract Terms Directive (93/13)" in H. Schulte-Nölke, C. Twigg-Flesner and M. Ebers (eds.), *EC Consumer Law Compendium: The Consumer Acquis and its transposition in the Member States*, München, Sellier, 2008, 247.

36 Cass. fr. (2e civ.) 21 October 2004, No. 03-16.328 ("*Qu'il n'apparaît pas que le calcul du taux d'invalidité tel qu'il est présenté puisse apparaître comme ambigu et nécessitant une interprétation même pour un* non-juriste, *au point que M. X... ait pu se méprendre sur la proposition d'assurance qui lui était faite.*"); Pres. Comm. C. Brussels 16 June 2003, *DCCR* 2004, 104, note L. Kerzmann; *Jaarboek Handelspraktijken & Mededinging* 2003, 334; *TBH* 2003, 893, note L. Kerzmann ("*Le fait que, selon les circonstances, un acte puisse être considéré ou non comme clairement téméraire n'implique pas que la clause qui prévoit que 'sont considérées comme fautes graves [...] les actes clairement téméraires dont ont est censé savoir qu'ils constituent une menace à l'intégrité physique', ne soit pas claire pour* le consommateur nonjuriste."); J. Elvin, "The Application Of The Unfair Terms In Consumer Contracts Regulations 1999", *KCLJ* 2003, 48-49.

37 Pres. Comm. C. Brussels 16 June 2003, *DCCR* 2004, 104, note L. Kerzmann; *Jaarboek Handelspraktijken & Mededinging* 2003, 334; *TBH* 2003, 893, note L. Kerzmann.

38 M. Asser, P. Clausing and J.H. Wansink, *Bijzondere Overeenkomsten. De Verzekeringsovereenkomst*, Deventer, Kluwer, 2007, 276-277; P. Erneux, "Promotions immobilières et protection du consommateur.

However, the assistance of a learned intermediary does not always lead to a better understanding by a consumer. Therefore, it is important that the judge takes into consideration the concrete circumstances of every case when investigating the transparency of a consumer contract.[39] For instance, when a seller or a supplier can prove that a legal adviser has informed a consumer about the meaning of a certain clause before he concluded a contract, the consumer cannot claim that the clause at hand is unclear.[40]

Van Zaanen concluded a travel insurance contract with Postbank. A term of the policy stated: "*Postbank Verzekeringen vergoedt schade wegens diefstal van in of op het motorrijtuig of de caravan achtergelaten bagage uitsluitend als [...] de bagage was opgeborgen in een afgesloten bagageruimte en er verder geen bagage van buitenaf zichtbaar was.*" During the trip, the closed trunk of the car was ransacked. Van Zaanen had left some clothes on the back seat of the car. Postbank refused to pay for the damage, because of the fact that some items were left on the back seat. A conflict arose about the meaning of "luggage": were the clothes on the back seat luggage or not? The court referred to the transparency requirement and stated: "*Daarbij is van belang dat schriftelijke, door de verzekeraar vastgestelde en gehanteerde algemene voorwaarden ten opzichte van de niet-professionele verzekerde, zoals in het onderhavige geval Van Zaanen c.s., steeds duidelijk en begrijpelijk moeten zijn geformuleerd. In geval van twijfel over de betekenis van een voorwaarde prevaleert de voor de verzekerde gunstigste interpretatie. Bij een zonder bijstand van een onafhankelijke tussenpersoon gesloten reisverzekering als de onderhavige kan de betekenis die een bepaald begrip in het algemeen spraakgebruik heeft, een belangrijke rol by de uitleg spelen.*"[41] A contract concluded without assistance of a well-versed intermediary, was deemed to be unclear. It can be argued *a contrario* that, if Van Zaanen had had judicial advice before he concluded the contract, he could not have claimed that the stipulation in het contract lacked transparency.[42]

Pratique contractuelle des ventes d'immeubles et loi sur les pratiques du commerce", *Jurim Pratique* 2008, 185; M.L. Hendrikse, "Uitleg van verzekeringsvoorwaarden", *NTHR* 2008, 138; M.L. Hendrikse, "Verzekeringsrecht en algemene voorwaarden" in M.L. Hendrikse, P.H.J.G. van Huizen and J.G.J. Rinkes, *Verzekeringsrecht praktisch belicht*, Deventer, Kluwer, 2008, 23–24; M.B.M. Loos, *Consumentenkoop*, Deventer, Kluwer, 2004, 35; J.M. van Dunné, *Verbintenissenrecht. Deel 1. Contractenrecht*, Deventer, Kluwer, 2001, 209.

39 CoJ 21 March 2013, C-92/11, RWE Vertrieb v. Verbraucherzentrale Nordrhein-Westfalen, http://curia.europa.eu, opinion V. Trstenjak ("*Articles 3 and 5 of Directive 93/13 [...] must be interpreted as meaning that, [...] It is for the national court to carry out that assessment with regard to all the circumstances of the particular case.*"); CoJ 30 April 2014, C-26/13, Kásler, http://curia.europa.eu ("*In that context, it is for the national court to determine, taking account of the criteria laid down in Articles 3(1) and 5 of Directive 93/13, whether, having regard to the particular circumstances of the case, such a term meets the requirements of good faith, balance and transparency laid down by that directive.*"); M. Asser, P. Clausing and J.H. Wansink, *Bijzondere Overeenkomsten. De Verzekeringsovereenkomst*, Deventer, Kluwer, 2007, 276–277; M.L. Hendrikse, "De reikwijdte van het contra-proferentembeginsel in het verzekeringsrecht", *NTHR* 2010, 97–98; M.B.M. Loos, *Consumentenkoop*, Deventer, Kluwer, 2004, 35; J.M. van Dunné, *Verbintenissenrecht. Deel 1. Contractenrecht*, Deventer, Kluwer, 2001, 209, 226.

40 J.M. van Dunné, *Verbintenissenrecht. Deel 1. Contractenrecht*, Deventer, Kluwer, 2001, 226.

41 Den Haag 12 September 2006, *NJF* 2006, 546.

42 M.L. Hendrikse, "Uitleg van verzekeringsvoorwaarden", *NTHR* 2008, 138.

3.2.2. Plain language

The transparency rule in Article 5 Unfair Terms Directive 93/13/EEC demands consumer contracts to be drafted in plain language. Thus the rule entails a clarity requirement. Clarity arises when no ambiguity, misunderstanding or doubt exists regarding the content and the scope of stipulations, because they are clear, transparent, obvious, accurate and concrete.[43] Clarity encompasses a formal and a substantive component.[44] Formal clarity originates when a consumer has knowledge of his rights and obligations as a result of having easy access to the stipulations. Recital 20 of the Unfair Terms Directive 93/13/EEC mentions this requirement: "*Whereas contracts should be drafted in plain, intelligible language, the consumer should actually be given an opportunity to examine all the terms.*" Hence, a consumer must always be provided with the opportunity to have a look at the stipulations of a consumer contract, which must be readily available. The consumer should have the opportunity to examine the contract extensively before the conclusion of the agreement.[45] Another aspect of formal clearness is the requirement for the contract to be easy to read. The contract has to be structured in a transparent way, it must be clearly presented and it must be drafted in a font that is legible.[46] The character size, the colour of the lettering, the colour of the background and the paper quality are

[43] I. Demuynck, "Bedingen tot bepaling van de dekkingsomvang in verzekeringsovereenkomsten: toetsbaar (onrechtmatig) beding of ontoetsbaar kernbeding?", *TBBR* 2002, 421; M. Ebers, "Unfair Contract Terms Directive (93/13)" in H. Schulte-Nölke, C. Twigg-Flesner and M. Ebers (eds.), *EC Consumer Law Compendium: The Consumer Acquis and its transposition in the Member States*, München, Sellier, 2008, 246; S. Stijns and E. Swaenepoel, "De evolutie van de basisbeginselen in het contractenrecht, geïllustreerd aan de hand van het contractueel evenwicht" in I. Samoy (ed.), *Evolutie van de basisbeginselen van het contractenrecht*, Antwerp, Intersentia, 2010, 50; E. Swaenepoel, S. Stijns and P. Wéry, "Onrechtmatige bedingen", *DCCR* 2009, 157; E. Swaenepoel, *Toetsing van het contractuele evenwicht*, Antwerp, Intersentia, 2011, 519.

[44] M. Ebers, "Unfair Contract Terms Directive (93/13)" in H. Schulte-Nölke, C. Twigg-Flesner and M. Ebers (eds.), *EC Consumer Law Compendium: The Consumer Acquis and its transposition in the Member States*, München, Sellier, 2008, 246; J. Mestre and B. Fages, "Le doute profite au consommateur" (note under Cass. fr. (1e civ.) 21 January 2003), *RTD Civ.* 2003, 292; H.-W. Micklitz, "Unfair terms in consumer contracts" in H.-W. Micklitz, N. Reich and P. Rott (eds.), *Understanding EU Consumer Law*, Antwerp, Intersentia, 2009, 135; E. Swaenepoel, S. Stijns and P. Wéry, "Onrechtmatige bedingen", *DCCR* 2009, 157; E. Swaenepoel, *Toetsing van het contractuele evenwicht*, Antwerp, Intersentia, 2011, 519.

[45] CoJ 21 March 2013, C-92/11, RWE Vertrieb v. Verbraucherzentrale Nordrhein-Westfalen, http://curia.europa.eu, opinion V. Trstenjak ("*Information, before concluding a contract, on the terms of the contract and the consequences of concluding it is of fundamental importance for a consumer.*"); CoJ 30 April 2014, C-26/13, Kásler, http://curia.europa.eu ("*As regards Article 5, the Court has already held that information, before concluding a contract, on the terms of the contract and the consequences of concluding it is of fundamental importance for a consumer.*"); S. Whittaker, "The Language or Languages of Consumer Contracts", *Cambridge Y.B. Eur. Legal Stud.* 2005–2006, 246–247.

[46] V. Christianos and F. Picod, "Consommateurs" in *Répertoire de droit Communautaire*, Paris, Editions Dalloz, losbl., No. 284; J. Ghestin and I. Marchesseaux-Van Melle, "Les contrats d'adhésion et les clauses abusives and droit français et and droits européens" in J. Ghestin and M. Fontaine (eds.), *La protection de la partie faible dans les rapports contractuels: comparaisons franco-belges*, Paris, LGDJ, 1996, 23–24; J. Mestre and B. Fages, "Le doute profite au consommateur" (note under Cass. fr. (1e civ.) 21 January 2003), *RTD Civ.* 2003, 292; E. Swaenepoel, S. Stijns and P. Wéry, "Onrechtmatige bedingen", *DCCR* 2009, 157; E. Swaenepoel, *Toetsing van het contractuele evenwicht*, Antwerp, Intersentia, 2011, 519.

also relevant.[47] Substantive clarity comes into being when the content of a clause bears no secrets for the everyday layman, because the professional party presents the content of the clauses in a plain way, not resorting to long and obscure sentences or legal jargon.[48] Also, for a contract to be substantively clear, the drafter must ensure that it contains no clauses that are mutually contradictory.

> The Governor of the Peabody Trust was a social landlord and charity providing low cost residential accommodation. Clause 5 of the "General Terms" of the standard form of tenancy agreement used by the Governors of the Peabody Trust read: *"Altering the Agreement. (a) With the exception of any changes in Rent this Agreement may only be altered by the agreement in writing of both the Tenant and the Trust. (b) The terms of this Agreement may be varied by the Trust by a notice of variation served on the Tenant and the provisions of section 103 of the Housing Act 1985 shall apply to this Agreement as if this tenancy were a secure tenancy provided that in no case shall the variations be such as to be properly regarded as creating a new tenancy"*. The landlord unilaterally varied the terms of the Tenancy Agreement. Mr. Reeve, one of the tenants, was of the opinion that the Trust was not allowed to unilaterally change the agreement. He claimed that the two parts of clause 5 appeared to be contradictory. The court followed his argument and decided: *"Accordingly, given that there is 'doubt' as to the meaning of clause 5 as a whole, and, in the light of the contradictory terms of the sub-clauses, as to the meaning of the sub-clauses themselves, I am obliged in terms of Regulation 7(2) to adopt the interpretation most favourable to the consumer, in other words the tenant in this case. That interpretation must in my judgment be that there can be no variation of the Tenancy Agreement without the agreement in writing of both parties."*[49]

3.2.3. Intelligible language

The transparency rule in Article 5 Unfair Terms Directive 93/13/EEC also demands consumer contracts to be drafted in intelligible language. The intelligibility and comprehensibility requirement prescribes that an everyday layman should be able to understand the meaning and the sense of the stipulations.[50] This does not mean that every word considered on its own should be understandable, but rather that the general

47 OFT, *Unfair contract terms guidance. Guidance for the Unfair Terms in Consumer Contracts Regulations 1999*, 2008, www.oft.gov.uk/shared_oft/reports/unfair_contract_terms/oft311.pdf, 86.

48 M. Ebers, "Unfair Contract Terms Directive (93/13)" in H. Schulte-Nölke, C. Twigg-Flesner and M. Ebers (eds.), *EC Consumer Law Compendium: The Consumer Acquis and its transposition in the Member States*, München, Sellier, 2008, 246; M.B.M. Loos, *Algemene voorwaarden*, Den Haag, Boom Juridische Uitgevers, 2013, 177; E. Swaenepoel, S. Stijns and P. Wéry, "Onrechtmatige bedingen", *DCCR* 2009, 157; E. Swaenepoel, *Toetsing van het contractuele evenwicht*, Antwerp, Intersentia, 2011, 519.

49 The Governors of the Peabody Trust v Mr Michael Reeve [2008] EWHC 1432; [2008] WL 2148300.

50 I. Demuynck, "Bedingen tot bepaling van de dekkingsomvang in verzekeringsovereenkomsten: toetsbaar (onrechtmatig) beding of ontoetsbaar kernbeding?", *TBBR* 2002, 421; H. Schulte-Nölke, C. Twigg-Flesner and M. Ebers, *EC Consumer Law Compendium*, München, Sellier, 2008, 246; S. Stijns and E. Swaenepoel, "De evolutie van de basisbeginselen in het contractenrecht, geïllustreerd aan de hand van het contractueel evenwicht" in I. Samoy (ed.), *Evolutie van de basisbeginselen van het contractenrecht*, Antwerp, Intersentia, 2010, 50; E. Swaenepoel, S. Stijns and P. Wéry, "Onrechtmatige

sense of the contract and of each individual clause is to be intelligible: the consumer must be able to gather from the contract the content and the range of his rights and obligations.[51] For every clause in a consumer contract, at least one plausible construction must exist.[52] Intelligibility is very close to clearness, for only clear language is understandable. Accordingly, some of the criteria of both pillars of transparency are the same. For instance, the need for comprehensibility entails the obligation to avoid legal or technical jargon.[53] Consumers should be able to understand a consumer contract all by themselves, without having to resort to legal advice.[54] When drafting a consumer contract, a supplier or a seller has to make use of common terminology and use the words according to their normal meaning.[55] If technical or legal terms are inserted, the inclusion of a definition is necessary.[56] The use of short sentences and subtitles also contributes to intelligibility.[57]

The former Office of Fair Trading, a public body with the mission to make markets work well for consumers, brought an action against some banks. The OFT was of the opinion that the system of bank charges levied on personal current account customers in respect of unauthorised overdrafts (including unpaid item charges and other related charges) was excessive in relation to the services supplied to the customers and therefore unfair. The Office

bedingen", *DCCR* 2009, 157; E. Swaenepoel, *Toetsing van het contractuele evenwicht*, Antwerp, Intersentia, 2011, 519.

51 OFT v Abbey National plc and Others [2008] EWHC 875; A. Arora, "Unfair contract terms and unauthorised bank charges: a banking lawyer's perspective", *JBL* 2012, 61; E. McKendrick, *Contract Law: Text, Cases, and Materials*, Oxford, Oxford University Press, 2012, 468; OFT, *Unfair contract terms guidance. Guidance for the Unfair Terms in Consumer Contracts Regulations 1999*, 2008, www.oft.gov.uk/shared_oft/reports/unfair_contract_terms/oft311.pdf, 85.

52 M.L. Hendrikse, "Uitleg van verzekeringsvoorwaarden", *NTHR* 2008, 137; M.L. Hendrikse, "De reikwijdte van het contra-proferentembeginsel in het verzekeringsrecht", *NTHR* 2010, 95.

53 M. Ebers, "Unfair Contract Terms Directive (93/13)" in H. Schulte-Nölke, C. Twigg-Flesner and M. Ebers (eds.), *EC Consumer Law Compendium: The Consumer Acquis and its transposition in the Member States*, München, Sellier, 2008, 246; M.B.M. Loos, *Algemene voorwaarden*, Den Haag, Boom Juridische Uitgevers, 2013, 177; E. Swaenepoel, S. Stijns and P. Wéry, "Onrechtmatige bedingen", *DCCR* 2009, 157; E. Swaenepoel, *Toetsing van het contractuele evenwicht*, Antwerp, Intersentia, 2011, 519.

54 J.K. MacLeod, *Consumer sales law*, London, Cavendish Publishing, 2002, 384; OFT, *Unfair contract terms guidance. Guidance for the Unfair Terms in Consumer Contracts Regulations 1999*, 2008, www.oft.gov.uk/shared_oft/reports/unfair_contract_terms/oft311.pdf, 86; J.K. Winn and M. Webber, "The Impact of EU Unfair Contract Terms Law on US Business-to-Consumer Internet Merchants", *Bus. Law* 2006–07, 218.

55 A. Cruquenaire, "L'interprétation la plus favorable au consommateur, principe efficace ou gadget inutile?" (note under Liège 27 March 2012), *For.ass.* 2013, 139; OFT, *Unfair contract terms guidance. Guidance for the Unfair Terms in Consumer Contracts Regulations 1999*, 2008, www.oft.gov.uk/shared_oft/reports/unfair_contract_terms/oft311.pdf, 86; P. Wéry, *Droit des obligations, vol. I, Théorie générale du contrat*, Brussels, Larcier, 2011, 408; J.K. Winn and M. Webber, "The Impact of EU Unfair Contract Terms Law on US Business-to-Consumer Internet Merchants", *Bus. Law* 2006–07, 218.

56 J.K. MacLeod, *Consumer sales law*, London, Cavendish Publishing, 2002, 384.

57 OFT, *Unfair contract terms guidance. Guidance for the Unfair Terms in Consumer Contracts Regulations 1999*, 2008, www.oft.gov.uk/shared_oft/reports/unfair_contract_terms/oft311.pdf, 86; J.K. Winn and M. Webber, "The Impact of EU Unfair Contract Terms Law on US Business-to-Consumer Internet Merchants", *Bus. Law* 2006–07, 218.

stated that the charges were in fact default payments, imposed not as a hefty element in the price that the Banks hope that customers will pay for their services, but by way of sanctions to discourage them from overdrawing on their current accounts. SMITH J., judge of the High Court, dwelled upon the intelligibility requirement. He stated: "*Regulation 6(2),*[58] *as the OFT submits and as I accept, requires not only that the actual wording of individual clauses or conditions be comprehensible to consumers, but that the typical consumer can understand how the term affects the rights and obligations that he and the seller or supplier have under the contract*".[59] This interpretation of intelligibility was not only applicable to Regulation 6, but also to Regulation 7: "*This was said about the plain and intelligible language provision in regulation 6(2), but OFT considers it applies equally to the requirement in regulation 7*".[60]

3.3. *Interpretation of unclear clauses*

3.3.1. Precedence of the rule

The sanction for non-compliance with the transparency-duty consists of an interpretation in favour of the consumer. This rule provides the consumer with the possibility to anticipate the outcome of an interpretation dispute, since it prevails over all other interpretation rules.[61] The precedence of the rule *in favorem consumentis* is to be

[58] Regulation 6 UTCCR states: "*Assessment of unfair terms. (1) Without prejudice to regulation 12, the unfairness of a contractual term shall be assessed, taking into account the nature of the goods or services for which the contract was concluded and by referring, at the time of conclusion of the contract, to all the circumstances attending the conclusion of the contract and to all the other terms of the contract or of another contract on which it is dependent. (2) In so far as it is in plain intelligible language, the assessment of fairness of a term shall not relate (a) to the definition of the main subject matter of the contract, or (b) to the adequacy of the price or remuneration, as against the goods or services supplied in exchange.*"

[59] OFT v Abbey National plc and Others [2008] EWHC 875; A. Arora, "Unfair contract terms and unauthorised bank charges: a banking lawyer's perspective", *JBL* 2012, 44–70; M. Schillig, "Directive 93/13 and the 'price term exemption': a comparative analysis in the light of the 'market for lemons' rationale", *ICLQ* 2011, 933–963.

[60] OFT, *Unfair contract terms guidance. Guidance for the Unfair Terms in Consumer Contracts Regulations 1999*, 2008, www.oft.gov.uk/shared_oft/reports/unfair_contract_terms/oft311.pdf, 85, note 46.

[61] W.D.H. Asser, "Uitleg van verzekeringsovereenkomsten in cassatie. Opmerkingen naar aanleiding van HR 31 March 2000, *NJ* 2000, 357" in T. Hartlief and M. M. Mendel (eds.), *Verzekering and maatschappij*, Deventer, Kluwer, 2000, 24; M. Asser, P. Clausing and J.H. Wansink, *Bijzondere Overeenkomsten. De Verzekeringsovereenkomst*, Deventer, Kluwer, 2007, 265; P. Britton, "The architect, the banker, his wife and the adjudicator: construction and the changing law of unfair contract terms", *Const. L.J.* 2006, 25–26; A. Cruquenaire, "L'interprétation du contrat de vente", *TBBR* 2008, 316; A. Cruquenaire, "L'incidence du droit commun des obligations sur les règles d'interprétation préférentielle: réflexions à partir de l'exemple des contrats relatifs au droit d'auteur", *TBBR* 2008, 603; A. Cruquenaire, "L'interprétation la plus favorable au consommateur, principe efficace ou gadget inutile?" (note under Liège 27 March 2012), *For.ass.* 2013, 139; P. Erneux, "Promotions immobilières et protection du consommateur. Pratique contractuelle des ventes d'immeubles et loi sur les pratiques du commerce", *Jurim Pratique* 2008, 186; J. Hijma, *Algemene voorwaarden*, Deventer, Kluwer, 2010, 33–34; M. Lamoureux, "L'interprétation des contrats de consommation", *D.* 2006, (2848) No. 2; S. Lebeau, "L'application de la LPMPC à la location immobilière", *Jurim Pratique* 2012, 216; M.B.M. Loos, *Consumentenkoop*, Deventer, Kluwer, 2004, 35; F.H.J. Mijnssen, *Verzekering*, Deventer, Kluwer, 2012,

grounded on its aim to fully protect the consumer.[62] This precedence assures an uncomplicated functioning of the rule: from the moment when a non-individually negotiated clause in a consumer contract is untransparent onwards, interpretation must be carried out in favour of the consumer.[63]

3.3.2. Interpretation *in favorem consumentis*

Article 5 Unfair Terms Directive 93/13/EEC includes the interpretation rule *in favorem consumentis*, stating that interpretation of unclear consumer contracts needs to be carried out in a way most favourable to the consumer. The interpretation most favourable to the consumer is the construction that burdens the consumer the least, the interpretation that makes his rights as extensive as possible and his obligations as limited as possible.[64] Interesting in this regard is the question who should determine which construction is most advantageous: the consumer or the judge. It might seem logical to confer this task on the consumer.[65] The aim of the rule is consumer protection, and how can he be better protected than by complying with his demands?

> X. concluded an insurance contract with insurer Ethias. The contract among others covered the costs for legal assistance. Article 21 restricted the intervention of the insurer as follows: "*L'intervention de la société mutuelle est limitée à 100% du montant du litige et, dans tous les cas, à 500.000 BEF par sinistre*". A dispute arose concerning the words "*montant du litige*".

24; C.M.D.S. Pavillon, "De wisselende betekenis van de Richtlijn oneerlijke bedingen in de Nederlandse rechtspraak: een drieluik", *VrA* 2006, 40; R. Steennot, "Interpretatie in het voordeel van de consument" (note under JoP Zelzate 30 June 2009), *T.JoP* 2012, 358; R.P.J.L. Tjittes, *Uitleg van schriftelijke contracten*, Nijmegen, Ars Aequi Libri, 2009, 40; J.M. van Dunné, *Verbintenissenrecht. Deel 1. Contractenrecht*, Deventer, Kluwer, 2001, 227; M.M. van Rossum, "Uitleg van algemene voorwaarden" in B. Wessels, R.H.C. Jongeneel and M.L. Hendrikse, *Algemene Voorwaarden*, Deventer, Kluwer, 2006, 60; P. Wéry, "L'interprétation contra profèrentem" (note under Bergen 13 January 2005), *JLMB* 2005, 1050.

62 Cass. 26 May 2005, *Arr.Cass.* 2005, 1119; *JT* 2005, 679; *Pas.* 2005, 1115; *Res Jur.Imm.* 2006, 26; *RW* 2007–08 (samenvatting), 609; *TBBR* 2007, 52; Brussels 10 April 2009, *Res Jur.Imm.* 2009, 200; JoP Brussels 26 July 1995; *RW* 1996–97, 264, note F. Mortier ("*artikel 31 WHPC is van dwingend recht*"); S. Ben Hadj Yahia, "L'assurance de groupe aux confins du droit des obligations et du droit de la consommation" (note under Cass. fr. (1e civ.) 22 May 2008), *Gaz. Pal.* 2009, (20) No. 29; A. Cruquenaire, "L'interprétation du contrat de vente", *TBBR* 2008, 316; M. Lamoureux, "L'interprétation des contrats de consommation", *D.* 2006, (2848) No. 13.

63 Cass. fr. (1e civ.) 21 January. 2003, *Bull. civ.* 2003, I, 13; *D.* 2003, 693, note V. Avena-Robardet, 2600, note H. Claret; *RDC* 2003/1, 93, note M. Bruschi; *RTD civ.* 2003, 292, note J. Mestre and B. Fages; S. Ben Hadj Yahia, "L'assurance de groupe aux confins du droit des obligations et du droit de la consommation" (note under Cass. fr. (1e civ.) 22 May 2008), *Gaz. Pal.* 2009, (20) No. 29; M. Lamoureux, "L'interprétation des contrats de consommation", *D.* 2006, (2848) No. 13.

64 M.L. Hendrikse, "Uitleg van verzekeringsvoorwaarden", *NTHR* 2008, 141–142; M.L. Hendrikse, "Verzekeringsrecht en algemene voorwaarden" in M.L. Hendrikse, P.H.J.G. van Huizen and J.G.J. Rinkes, *Verzekeringsrecht praktisch belicht*, Deventer, Kluwer, 2008, 29.

65 H. Claret, "Contrats de consommation. Interprétation d'une clause ambiguë d'un contrat d'assurance" (note under Cass. fr. (2e civ.) 1 June 2011), *Petites Affiches* 2011, 16; A. Cruquenaire, "L'interprétation du contrat de vente", *TBBR* 2008, 315; A. Cruquenaire, "L'interprétation la plus favorable au consommateur, principe efficace ou gadget inutile?" (note under Liège 27 March 2012), *For.ass.* 2013, 139.

Ethias said these terms were not ambiguous. They clearly meant "*l'enjeu raisonnable du litige*", the reasonable estimation of what was at stake in the dispute. The assessment of what was reasonably at stake had to be carried out by Ethias: Ethias had to verify whether the sum asked by the insurer was reasonable or not. The insurer, however, stated that this terms were undoubtedly unclear. The Commission mixte de Protection juridique, the arbitrator in this case judged: "*à défaut de définition de la notion de 'montant du litige' la commission estime que cette notion doit être interprétée dans le sens le plus favorable à l'assuré, à savoir la réclamation formulée par l'assuré lors de l'introduction de la procédure*".[66]

However, in general, consumers are laymen who are often not able to evaluate how to best promote their own interests.[67] Judges are more acquainted with evaluating contracts than consumers. Therefore, it is appropriate to let the judge decide which construction has, in the case at hand, the most favourable outcome for the consumer.[68]

Mrs. Cahalene was the leasehold owner of a flat under a lease for 125 years granted to her by the London Borough of Wandsworth (LBW), in December 1997. In October 2004, LBW started a major works programme to the Estate, which consisted of six blocks of flats, of which Mrs. Cahalene's flat was one. As part of the works programme, the timber windows of some apartments were replaced with PVC units. LBW did not replace the windows of Mrs. Cahalene's flat. LBW levied service charges amounting to £7,251 in respect of the works. However, Mrs. Cahalene contended that, under the terms of her lease, she was not obliged to pay for works to the windows of other flats. The issue was one of construction of the lease contract. The Fourth Schedule to the contract imposed some obligations on the landlord, namely: "(2) *to repair cleanse uphold support and maintain the exterior of the Block and the communal television aerials door entry systems fences walls and the entrance ways paths lifts staircases main walls party walls roof foundations and all structural parts thereof [...]*" and "(3) *To repair and maintain the exterior of the window frames window sashes and balcony or patio doors and of the frames thereof (if any) of the Flat and as often as may be necessary to replace the whole or part of the window frames window sashes window furniture and balcony or patio doors and frames and furniture thereof (if any).*" Every leasehold owner had to bear 3.617% of the costs and expenses made by the landlord. Mrs. Cahalene argued that on a proper construction of the lease she only had to pay for the repair and maintenance of the exterior of the window frames of the Flat, as provided for by paragraph 3 of the Fourth Schedule. Paragraph 2 did

66 Commission Mixte De Protection Juridique 15 September 2006, *RGAR* 2008, No. 14.419.

67 H. Claret, "Contrats de consommation. Interprétation d'une clause ambiguë d'un contrat d'assurance" (note under Cass. fr. (2e civ.) 1 June 2011), *Petites Affiches* 2011, 16; A. Cruquenaire, "L'interprétation du contrat de vente", *TBBR* 2008, 315; A. Cruquenaire, "L'interprétation la plus favorable au consommateur, principe efficace ou gadget inutile?" (note under Liège 27 March 2012), *For.ass.* 2013, 139.

68 The Governors of the Peabody Trust v Mr Michael Reeve [2008] EWHC 1432; [2008] WL 2148300 ("*I am obliged in terms of Regulation 7(2) to adopt the interpretation most favourable to the consumer, in other words the tenant in this case.* That interpretation must in my judgment be *that there can be no variation of the Tenancy Agreement without the agreement in writing of both parties.*"); A. Cruquenaire, "L'interprétation du contrat de vente", *TBBR* 2008, 315; J.-F. Leclercq and C. Jassogne, "Notions essentielles du droit des obligations contractuelles" in *Traité pratique de droit commercial*, Brussels, Kluwer, 2009, 342.

mention the exterior of the Block, i.e. the other Flats, but not the windows of the Block. The judge decided that the contract was not unclear: "*There is, in my judgment, no doubt that the words in paragraph 2 providing for the repair and maintenance of 'the exterior of the Block' and 'all structural parts thereof' are apt to cover repair and maintenance of the exterior windows*". He continued: "*Even if there were doubt as to the scope of paragraph 2 I am by no means sure that case law and the Unfair Contracts Regulations would require the doubt to be resolved in favour of the lessee in the present case. Paragraph 2 imposes obligations on the landlord, and in other circumstances the lessee might be disposed to contend that the obligations extended to the repair and maintenance of the windows of other flats in the block. The value of her flat and her enjoyment of it could be adversely affected if lack of repair of these adversely affected the appearance of the block. It is only the service charge consequences in a situation where the council have replaced some windows in the block but not hers that causes her to argue for a limited meaning to be given to the obligations of the council under paragraph 2. It does not seem to me that to construe the provision* contra proferentem *would require that the obligation should be construed narrowly or that such narrow interpretation would necessarily be the one 'most favourable to' the lessee'.*"[69]

The interpretative task of the judge consists of different steps.[70] First, he has to work out which different meanings can be bestowed upon the unclear clause. The next step is considering which of these meanings is the most favourable for the consumer. This is an evaluation *in concreto*: which outcome is the most beneficial for this specific consumer, at this moment, given these circumstances?[71] His margin of appreciation has a limited scope. He cannot interpret in *a* way that is interesting for the consumer, but has to balance the different possible outcomes in order to find out the interpretation that is *most* favourable.[72] However, an important remark comes up: only reasonable constructions of a clause can be considered.[73]

69 Ms G.C. Cahalane v London Borough of Wandsworth [2008] WL 4698844.

70 A. Cruquenaire, "L'interprétation du contrat de vente", *TBBR* 2008, 315; A. Cruquenaire, "L'interprétation la plus favorable au consommateur, principe efficace ou gadget inutile?" (note under Liège 27 March 2012), *For.ass.* 2013, 139; P. Wéry, *Droit des obligations. 1: Théorie générale du contrat*, Brussels, Larcier, 2010, 516.

71 H. Claret, "Contrats de consommation. Interprétation d'une clause ambiguë d'un contrat d'assurance" (note under Cass. fr. (2e civ.) 1 June 2011), *Petites Affiches* 2011, 16.

72 Cass. fr. (1e civ.) 11 March 2010, *EDC* 2010, note N. Sauphanor-Brouillaud; Ms G C Cahalane v London Borough of Wandsworth [2008] WL 4698844; C. Brussels 8 May 2006, *TBBR* 2006, 436; A. Cruquenaire, "L'interprétation du contrat de vente", *TBBR* 2008, 315; I. Demuynck, "Interpretatie van verzekeringsovereenkomsten" (note under JoP Sint-Kwintens-Lennik 13 November 2000), *DCCR* 2002, 78; P. Erneux, "Promotions immobilières et protection du consommateur. Pratique contractuelle des ventes d'immeubles et loi sur les pratiques du commerce", *Jurim Pratique* 2008, 188; S. Stijns and E. Swaenepoel, "De evolutie van de basisbeginselen in het contractenrecht, geïllustreerd aan de hand van het contractueel evenwicht" in I. Samoy (ed.), *Evolutie van de basisbeginselen van het contractenrecht*, Antwerp, Intersentia, 2010, 50; P. Wéry, "Les clauses abusives relatives à l'inexécution des obligations contractuelles dans les lois de protection des consommateurs du 14 juillet 1991 et du 12 août 2002", *JT* 2003, 803; P. Wéry, "L'interprétation contra proferentem" (note under Bergen 13 January 2005), *JLMB* 2005, 1053.

73 M.L. Hendrikse, "De contra proferentem-regel en het notariaat", *WPNR* 2000, 521.

X concluded a pension insurance contract with Axa France. The contract stated: "*UAP-VIE majorera votre compte de la façon suivante: de la onzième année et jusqu'à la quinzième année incluse. UAP-VIE investit sur votre compte 110% de votre prime périodique annuelle*". X was under the impression that, from the moment he got into retirement onwards, he would draw an annual pension pay constituted of an amount of 110% of the sum he previously had paid annually. Axa however interpreted the clause as if it said: "*de la 11e à la 15e année, UAP investira sur votre compte votre prime périodique annuelle majorée de 10%.*" X did not agree and asked Axa to pay the sum Axa, according to X's interpretation, owed him, which was 1325 euro. The French judge decided there was "*une confusion dans l'interprétation des clauses du contrat qui a sa source dans l'ambiguïté rédactionnelle*". He sentenced Axa to pay 500 euro. However, the Cour de Cassation stated that the lower judge had not applied Article L133-2 Code de la Consommation properly. The clause was ambiguous, hence the interpretation had to be chosen which was most favourable for X. Receiving 500 euro in compensation was not the most beneficial outcome, since the sum Axa owed X, if the clause was constructed in the way X interpreted it, was 1325 euro.[74]

Contradictory as it may sound, in some cases, the most beneficial interpretation for the consumer is the least advantageous one.[75] This happens when the judge is of the opinion that, even according to its most favourable construction, a stipulation still has adverse effects for the consumer. If it comes to that, it might be most advantageous for the consumer to interpret an unclear clause in a way that is not most favourable, but in a way that has the effect that the clause is to be characterised as unfair. Then the stipulation needs to be declared null and void, which means it cannot contain any bad consequence for the consumer. An interpretation that leads to nullity can in some cases indeed be more favourable for a consumer than an interpretation that leaves the clause unchanged, since a clause, even when it is interpreted in the consumer's favour, can still be unappealing to him.

74 Cass. fr. (1e civ.) 11 March 2010, *EDC* 2010, note N. Sauphanor-Brouillaud.

75 P. Cserne, "Policy considerations in contract interpretation: the contra proferentem rule from a comparative law and economics perspective" in G. Radhika, *Contract Theory – Corporate Law*, Hyderabad, ICFAI University Press, 2009, 96; E. Ferrante, "Contractual Disclosure and Remedies under the Unfair Contract Terms Directive" in G. Howells, A. Janssen and R. Schulze (eds.), *Information Rights and Obligations: A Challenge for Party Autonomy and Transactional Fairness*, Ashgate, Aldershot, 2004, 123; J. Hijma, *Algemene voorwaarden*, Deventer, Kluwer, 2010, 34; M.B.M. Loos, *Algemene voorwaarden*, Den Haag, Boom Juridische Uitgevers, 2013, 176; H. Macdonald, "But which Interpretation favours the Consumer", *C and CC* 1997, 9; The Scottish Law Commission, *Discussion Paper No 119*, htttp://lawcommission.justice.gov.uk/docs/cp166_Unfair_Terms_In_Contracts_Consultation.pdf, 49; C. Willett, "The Directive on Unfair Terms in Consumer Contracts and its implementation in the United Kingdom", *ERPL* 1997, 231; C. Willett, *Fairness in consumer contracts: the case of unfair terms*, Aldershot, Ashgate Publishing Ltd., 2007, 260–262; C. Willett, "The functions of transparency in regulating contract terms: UK and Australian approaches", *ICLQ* 2011, 379–380; M.H.. Wissink, "Europese uitleg van onduidelijke algemene voorwaarden" in *BW-Krant Jaarboek 1995*, Arnhem, Gouda Quint, 1995, 166. Contra A. Cruquenaire, "L'interprétation la plus favorable au consommateur, principe efficace ou gadget inutile?" (note under Liège 27 March 2012), *For.ass.* 2013, 139.

3.3.3. Exception

Article 5 Unfair Terms Directive 93/13/EEC contains an exception to the general interpretation rule *in favorem consumentis*: "*This rule on interpretation shall not apply in the context of the procedures laid down in Article 7 (2).*" The actions referred to in paragraph 7(2) of the Directive are collective actions for cessation, procedures "*whereby persons or organizations, having a legitimate interest under national law in protecting consumers, may take action according to the national law concerned before the courts or before competent administrative bodies for a decision as to whether contractual terms drawn up for general use are unfair, so that they can apply appropriate and effective means to prevent the continued use of such terms.*" The interpretation rule is, according to this exception, not applicable in collective actions for cessation brought by persons or organisations representative of the collective interest of consumers. After all, in such cases, the common interpretation rules can result in wider consumer protection.[76] The interpretation rule *in favorem consumentis* obliges the judge to look in every case for the *in concreto* most favourable construction of a provision, which benefits one specific consumer immediately.[77] Consumer organisations however focus on consumer protection in general, trying to achieve the best possible result for all consumers as a whole. The common interpretation rules are more suitable to achieve that general aim than the concrete rule *in favorem consumentis*. In collective actions for cessation, judges therefore should make an assessment *in abstracto* of the construction, and of the unfair character, of terms which may be incorporated into contracts which are not yet concluded.

The importance of this exception is clearly shown in the case *Commission v Spain*.[78] The Commission criticised the Kingdom of Spain for the fact that the last sentence of Article 5 Unfair Terms Directive 93/13/EEC was not transposed in its national legislation. That

76 CoJ 9 September 2004, C-70/03, *Commission v Spain*, http://curia.europa.eu, opinion L. Geelhoed; F. Bogaert and B. Van Baeveghem, "Contractuele aspecten van de wet marktpraktijken" in *Economisch recht: ondernemingen, concurrenten and consumenten*, Malines, Kluwer, 2011, 26; H. Claret, "Contrats de consommation. Interprétation d'une clause ambiguë d'un contrat d'assurance" (note under Cass. fr. (2e civ.) 1 June 2011), *Petites Affiches* 2011, 16; W.C.H. Ervine, "The Unfair Contract Terms Regulations Mark II", *SLT* 1999, 255; J. Ghestin and I. Marchesseaux-Van Melle, "Les contrats d'adhésion et les clauses abusives and droit français et and droits européens" in J. Ghestin and M. Fontaine (eds.), *La protection de la partie faible dans les rapports contractuels: comparaisons franco-belges*, Paris, LGDJ, 1996, 43; R. Steennot, "Algemene bepalingen betreffende de verkopen van producten and diensten aan consumenten", *TPR* 2009, 272; R. Steennot, F. Bogaert, D. Bruloot and D. Goens, *Wet Marktpraktijken*, Antwerp, Intersentia, 2010, 198; C. Willett, *Fairness in consumer contracts: the case of unfair terms*, Aldershot, Ashgate Publishing Ltd., 2007, 98.

77 CoJ 9 September 2004, C-70/03, *Commission v Spain*, http://curia.europa.eu, opinion L. Geelhoed; B. Gelot, *Finalités et méthodes objectives d'interprétation des actes juridiques*, Paris, LGDJ, 2003, 272; J. Ghestin and I. Marchesseaux-Van Melle, "Les contrats d'adhésion et les clauses abusives and droit français et and droits européens" in J. Ghestin and M. Fontaine (eds.), *La protection de la partie faible dans les rapports contractuels: comparaisons franco-belges*, Paris, LGDJ, 1996, 43.

78 CoJ 9 September 2004, C-70/03, *Commission v Spain*, http://curia.europa.eu, opinion L. Geelhoed. See also M. Audit, "Condamnation de l'Espagne pour transposition incorrecte de la directive du 5 avril 1993 concernant les clauses abusives dans les contrats conclus avec les consommateurs" (note under

omission could compromise the effectiveness of collective actions for cessation, as a seller or supplier was able to prevent an intransparent term, liable to be interpreted as unfair, from being prohibited, by referring to the interpretation rule *in favorem consumentis*. The Court of Justice scrutinised this exception and stated: "*The distinction made in Article 5 of the Directive concerning the applicable rule of interpretation, as between actions involving an individual consumer and actions for cessation which involve persons or organisations representative of the collective interest of consumers may be accounted for by the different aims pursued by those actions. In the former case, the courts or competent bodies are required to make an assessment in concreto of the unfair character of a term contained in a contract which has already been concluded, while in the latter case it is their task to assess in abstracto the unfair character of a term which may be incorporated into contracts which have not yet been concluded. In the former case, an interpretation favourable to the individual consumer concerned benefits him or her immediately. By contrast, in the latter case, in order to obtain, by way of prevention, the most favourable result for consumers as a whole, it is not necessary, where there is doubt, to interpret the term in a manner favourable to them. Accordingly, an objective interpretation makes it possible to prohibit more frequently the use of an unintelligible or ambiguous term, which results in wider consumer protection.*"

The fact that the general interpretation rules should be applied in collective actions generates an additional sanction for unclear clauses in consumer contracts.[79] Instead of maintaining the existence of a clause and constructing it in favour of the consumer, another sanction takes effect, namely the elimination of unclear clauses in adhering contracts.[80] The general interpretation rules indeed often lead to a conclusion that an unclear clause is unfair, having the effect that such a construction frequently allows to prohibit the use of an unintelligible or ambiguous term in general.[81]

The Belgian consumer organisation TestAankoop brought an action against banker Dexia. Quite a few standard clauses Dexia used in its general conditions were unfair, according to TestAankoop, since they caused a significant imbalance in the parties' rights and obligations arising under the contract, to the detriment of the consumer. The judge concluded that some of the clauses were ambiguous, making different interpretations possible. However, the rule *in favorem consumentis* could not be applied in this case, since it was brought by a consumer organisation. The judges ordered the cessation of the use of two clauses by reason of their inclarity, which resulted in them being unfair. Regarding Article 94, the judge stated: "*Par*

CoJ 9 September 2004), *RCDIP* 2005, 451 and M. Luby, "Contrats et clauses abusives: transposition de la directive No. 93/13 du 5 avr. 1993 (note under CoJ 9 September 2004), *RTD Com.* 2005, 183.

79 E. Van den Haute, "Le règlement général des opérations de banque et les clauses abusives: vers la consécration du concept du 'consommateur responsable'?" (note under Liège 26 January 2007), *Bank Fin. R.* 2007, 355.

80 M. Flamee and K. Troch, "De invloed van de E.G.-Richtlijnen van 5 April 1993 betreffende oneerlijke bedingen in consumentenovereenkomsten op het heersend Belgisch recht", *TBH* 1996, 51; E. Van den Haute, "Le règlement général des opérations de banque et les clauses abusives: vers la consécration du concept du 'consommateur responsable'?" (note under Liège 26 January 2007), *Bank Fin. R.* 2007, 355.

81 CoJ 9 September 2004, C-70/03, *Commission v Spain*, http://curia.europa.eu, opinion L. Geelhoed.

contre, la généralité des termes de l'article 94 – les frais qui ont été "causés" par le client, ladite cause pouvant éventuellement avoir une origine fautive – nécessite, en application de l'article 31 LPCC tel qu'il doit être interprété au vu de l'arrêt de la Cour de justice du 9 septembre 2004 (C.J.C.E. Commission contre Espagne, C-70/03, spécial. Considérant 16), que la cessation de son utilisation, tel que formulé, soit ordonnée." Article 252 was considered unfair as well: *"Le caractère abusif de cette clause, telle que rédigée, réside non pas dans ce droit de modification détenu par Dexia, mais plutôt dans le fait qu'il n'est pas précisé sous quelle(s) condition(s) une telle modification peut intervenir. [...] Il y a lieu d'ordonner la cessation de l'utilisation de cette clause, telle que formulée."*[82]

The constraint on the applicability of Article 5 Unfair Terms Directive 93/13/EEC only extends to the interpretation rule, having no influence upon the transparency requirement. Hence, consumer organisations are allowed to bring actions in order to challenge the transparency of consumer contracts.[83] After all, the evaluation of the clearness and intelligibility as prescribed by Article 5 Unfair Terms Directive 93/13/EEC is an abstract assessment, using the average layman as its benchmark. Unlike the interpretation rule *in favorem consumentis*, it is perfectly usable within the framework of protecting the collective interest of consumers in general.

3.4. *Nullity of unintelligible clauses*

To some clauses, no meaning can be attached at all: they are unintelligible. Than the transparency requirement is not complied with. However, the sanction of interpretation *in favorem consumentis* can not be applied in such cases, since there are no different conceivable constructions of the clause to choose from. Such an incomprehensible clause is unfair, which means that the clause has to be declared null and void.[84] This can be derived from Article 4(2) Unfair Terms Directive 93/13/EEC, which gives: *"Assessment of the unfair nature of the terms shall relate neither to the definition of the main subject matter of the contract nor to the adequacy of the price and remuneration, on the one hand,*

82 Liège 26 January 2007, *Bank Fin. R.* 2007, 344, note E. Van den Haute; R. Steennot, "Algemene bepalingen betreffende de verkopen van producten and diensten aan consumenten", *TPR* 2009, 276–278; E. Van den Haute, "Le règlement général des opérations de banque et les clauses abusives: vers la consécration du concept du 'consommateur responsable'?" (note under Liège 26 January 2007), *Bank Fin. R.* 2007, 351–355.

83 Eg. Pres. Comm. C. Brussels 16 June 2003, *DCCR* 2004, 104, note L. Kerzmann; *Jaarboek Handelspraktijken and Mededinging* 2003, 334; *TBH* 2003, 893, note L. Kerzmann.

84 P. Cserne, "Policy considerations in contract interpretation: the contra proferentem rule from a comparative law and economics perspective" in G. Radhika, *Contract Theory – Corporate Law*, Hyderabad, ICFAI University Press, 2009, 92; M.L. Hendrikse, "Uitleg van verzekeringsvoorwaarden", *NTHR* 2008, 146; M.L. Hendrikse, "Verzekeringsrecht en algemene voorwaarden" in M.L. Hendrikse, P.H.J.G. van Huizen en J.G.J. Rinkes, *Verzekeringsrecht praktisch belicht*, Deventer, Kluwer, 2008, 28; M.L. Hendrikse, "De reikwijdte van het contra-proferentembeginsel in het verzekeringsrecht", *NTHR* 2010, 95–103; J. Hijma, *Algemene voorwaarden*, Deventer, Kluwer, 2003, 34; M.B.M. Loos, *Algemene voorwaarden*, Den Haag, Boom Juridische Uitgevers, 2013, 173–174; E. Swaenepoel, *Toetsing van het contractuele evenwicht*, Antwerpen, Intersentia, 2011, 520–521.

as against the services or goods supplies in exchange, on the other, in so far as these terms are in plain intelligible language." This Article was commented upon in the above-mentioned case Commission of the European Communities v Kingdom of the Netherlands.[85] Advocate-General Tizzano stated: "*First, it should be recalled that Article 4(2) of the Directive expressly provides that, if terms are obscure or ambiguous, even those relating to the definition of the main subject matter of the contract or to the adequacy of the price and remuneration, on the one hand, as against the services or goods supplied in exchange, on the other, may be regarded as unfair. This means, clearly and unambiguously, that the consumer may rely on such terms for the purposes of securing the protection guaranteed him under Article 6(1) of the Directive, that is to say, for a ruling that he is not bound by those terms*".[86] So, if a clause is unclear, a choice has to be made between interpretation *in favorem consumentis* or nullity. If a clause is unintelligible, only one sanction can be applied, namely the nullity of the clause.

IV. Conclusion

Article 5 Directive 93/13/EEC encompasses an information or transparency requirement and an interpretation rule aimed at protecting the consumer against the power of professional sellers and suppliers. Both rules are inextricably bound up: a construction *in favorem consumentis* functions as a sanction for unclearness and intelligibility. Since the interpretation rule prevails over all other rules of construction, this sanction is to be applied automatically as from the moment a clause is untransparent. However, if an investigation of a clause shows that no meaning can be attached to it at all, the sanction of interpretation *in favorem consumentis* cannot be applied. Another sanction comes into place, namely the nullity of the unintelligible – and therefore unfair – clause.

The transparency and interpretation requirement are important rules, resulting in a wide consumer protection. It is therefore regrettable that lawyers and courts often are oblivious to the interpretation rule *in favorem consumentis*, applying rules like *contra proferentem*, *contra venditorem* or *contra stipulatorem* instead. The interpretation rule in favour of the consumer prevails over all other interpretation rules and therefore deserves a significant place in jurisprudence – a place more significant than it has nowadays.

[85] E. Swaenepoel, *Toetsing van het contractuele evenwicht*, Antwerp, Intersentia, 2011, 521.

[86] CoJ 10 May 2001, C-144/99, Commission of the European Communities v Kingdom of the Netherlands, http://curia.europa.eu.

Johan Vannerom*

THE CONSUMER'S RIGHT TO INFORMATION

A 'Reality Check', on the Boundaries of a Duty to Inform and a Proposed Regulatory Reform

> *"Education is an admirable thing. But it is well to remember from time to time that nothing that is worth knowing can be taught"*
>
> O. Wilde, *A Few Maxims For The Instruction Of The Over-Educated*, 1894

I. Introduction

(Shortcomings of the) Information Paradigm – When overlooking European Consumer (Credit) legislation, one notices the information paradigm takes a leading role as the optimal consumer protection mechanism.[1] According to the information paradigm, the stronger contracting party has to provide mandatory information to its weaker counterparty, *in casu* the consumer. After having read, studied and analysed the information the weaker contracting party is able to make a carefully thought-out decision. The consumer can thus give its informed consent. The outcome is an agreement, which is supposed to be in the best interest of both.

The information paradigm is seriously criticised. Studies in (behavioural) economics illustrate that the information paradigm is not flawless.[2] The consumer is overloaded with documents and brochures and it is not always clear whether he understands or even reads all the documents.[3] Furthermore it is questionable whether the information leaflets will protect the consumer suffering from unforeseen economic loss. For example losses suffered due to the economic crisis or to an illness.

* Attorney at Law, Janson Baugniet Brussels, Affiliated Senior Researcher KU Leuven.

1 E.g. Article 4, 5–7 and 10–12, incl. Annexes II and III Directive 2008/48/EC of 23 April 2008 on credit agreements for consumers and repealing Council Directive 87/102/EEC, *Pb.L.* 133 of 22 May 2008, 66–92.

2 A.o. I. Ramsay, "From Truth in Lending to Responsible Lending" in G. Howells, A. Janssen and R. Schulze (eds.), *Information rights and obligations. A challenge for party autonomy and transactional fairness*, Hampshire, Ashgate, 2005, 51.

3 G. Howells en T. Wilhelmsson, "EC Consumer Law: Has It Come of Age?", *E.L.Rev.* 2003, 380–381; C. Sunstein (ed.), *Behavioral law and economics*, Cambridge, Cambridge University Press, 2000, 59–187.

Lack off Interest for Alternative Policy Choices – Although the positive effect of (pre-) contractual information on the level of consumer protection is criticised, no profound (European) research has so far been conducted on contractual protection mechanisms vis-à-vis consumer credit agreements. Examples of such mechanisms are interest rate caps, the right of early repayment and the termination of a credit agreement in case of default.

Limited Balance of Interests – Another problem that occurs is highlighted by law and economics' studies. They indicate that rules on consumer protection can only be effective if the legal framework achieves a high standard of consumer protection at a minimal cost to creditors.[4] It is questionable whether European and national legislators take these Law and Economics' findings into account, since they disregard studies which show the disproportional costs of the information paradigm for creditors.

Paper overview – The paper starts with the main reason for choosing the information paradigm in current EU consumer credit regulation, i.e. the information asymmetry. Though also a creditor is confronted with a certain lack of information vis-à-vis the consumer (e.g. when conducting the consumer's creditworthiness assessment), we will only focus on the information asymmetry on the consumer side. The information paradigm is currently the readiest response of European and national legislators to tackle the problems arising from the information asymmetry. This paper will list the shortcomings of the information paradigm in the field of consumer credit. Secondly, we will address the consumer image. We will see that the consumer image is not unproblematic. In fact, even the Court of Justice uses two different consumer images. In an attempt to enhance consumer protection, we propose to set up a new multi-layered consumer image in a final paragraph. To make it more viable, we shall apply our multi-layered consumer image to consumer credit law.

II. Information paradigm

Information asymmetry on consumer side – When signing a(n) (credit) agreement the consumer should pay attention to the specific characteristics of the product or service. Moreover, he must know the normal use of that product or service. There will not be a truly informed decision ("*informed consent*") if he does not have a correct understanding of these two elements.[5] If not, an information asymmetry exists. There are two ways to solve this information asymmetry.[6] Either one merely has confidence in the functioning of the free market or one accepts that information requirements have to be legally imposed.

4 IP/A/IMCO/ST/2006-20, *Broad economic analysis of the impact of the proposed directive on consumer credit*, www.europarl.europa.eu/comparl/imco/studies/0704_consumercredit_en.pdf, 42.

5 O. Bar-Gill, "The Behavioral Economics of Consumer Contracts" in O. Bar-Gill and R. Epstein, *Consumer Contracts: Behavioral Economics vs. Neoclassical Economics. An exchange between Oren Bar-Gill and Richard A. Epstein*, http://ssrn.com/abstract=982527, New York University School of Law, 2007, 38.

6 There exists also an information asymmetry on creditor side. After all, he must assess the creditworthiness of the consumer. He does not have perfect information here. The consultation of data bases or direct information gathering of the consumer does not give him a complete and/or accurate picture of the financial situation of the consumer. In this paper we do not look closer at this problem. After all, we focus on a critical evaluation of the information paradigm as a method of consumer protection.

Criticism on the information paradigm – In this paragraph we discuss both solutions, although the legislator often (instantly) chooses for mandatory information disclosure. However (behavioural) law and economics studies show certain market failures undermine the usefulness of the information paradigm as an optimal method of consumer protection in the field of consumer credit. Examples of such market failures are higher transaction costs, the free-rider problem, behavioural abnormalities which cause consumers to not always act rationally, a lack of real choice for the consumer, etc. We look at this in more detail below.

2.1. *Solutions via the free market*

The market mechanism – In principle, the free market itself should provide for a correct and competitive price(-setting). Ideally, the consumer is looking for and collecting information on the terms and conditions of the credit agreement. Creditors, who charge too much, thus price themselves outside the competitive market. This mechanism operates in a market with (*quasi*-)perfect information for all parties involved. Ideally, the creditor even provides willingly prospective consumers all the information needed in order to attract as many clients as possible. The prospective consumer studies the terms and conditions and finally takes a rational decision, based upon the information obtained and acquired. Some observations to this ideal image of the free market have to be made.

Transaction costs of seeking consumer – Firstly, the image of the seeking consumer is an utopian image.[7] Not every consumer is looking long enough or even looking for the correct information. Sometimes this behaviour can be explained by the irrational choices certain consumers make. Nonetheless, also rational consumers shall stop at a certain stage their quest for information. More precisely, when the research costs outweigh the advantage that one hopes to achieve from the credit agreement.[8]

Free-rider problem – Secondly, a creditor does not always benefit if he willingly and fully discloses information to the consumer. The free-rider problem tempers his desire to give complete and accurate information. The hope of a competitive advantage is after all rather quickly superseded by the fear that the transaction costs made, will also serve for the benefit of competing creditors. After all, they have little additional transaction costs. Indeed the creditor, who fully informed the consumer, has already provided lots of general information that should not be repeated by other creditors.[9]

7 R. Hynes and R. Posner, "The Law and Economics of Consumer Finance", *AM.L. and Econ. Rev.* 2002, 172–173.

8 A.I. Ogus, *Regulation: Legal Form and Economic Theory*, Oxford, Clarendon Press, 1994, 128. Cf. also Posner: "*(...) incompletely informed decisions are rational when the costs of acquiring more information exceed the likely benefits in being able to make a better decision*". Cf. R. Posner, *Economic analysis of law*, New York, Aspen Law and Business, 2003, 18.

9 O. Bar-Gill and E. Warren, "Making Credit Safer", *U. Pa. L. Rev.* 2008, 117–120; C. Camerer, S. Issacharoff, G. Loewenstein, T. O'Donoghue and M. Rabin, "Regulation for Conservatives: Behavioral Economics and the Case for 'Asymmetric Paternalism'", *U. Pa. L. Rev.* 2003, 1252; R. Hynes and R. Posner, "The Law and Economics of Consumer Finance", *AM.L. and Econ. Rev.* 2002, 173.

Behavioural deviations – Thirdly, certain behavioural abnormalities lead to market failures in the market for (consumer) credit. The main behavioural abnormalities are:

- *"information overload"*;
- procrastination of the consumer;
- *"mental accounting"*; and
- the *"status quo bias"*.[10]

Behavioural deviation (I): information overload – Consumers are inundated with advertisements, prospectuses, pre-contractual information brochures, etc.[11] This information overload leads to three possible market failures, i.e.:

- the consumer does not read the information;
- he incorrectly processes the obtained information; and
- the deception of the consumer.

Firstly, many consumers lose their mind when overlooking the vast amount of information leaflets. They then choose to avoid all of it or almost everything.[12] This does not necessarily include irrational behaviour. The high information processing costs do not outweigh the eventual benefits, such as obtaining a cheaper credit agreement.[13]

Secondly, the unclear information overload also emphasis the negative consequences of cognitive defects each man have. A consumer possibly incorrectly processes the information. He may also overestimate his own financial knowledge.[14] This 'knowledge'-

10 CBFA, *Verslag over het bevorderen van de financiële kennis in België*, www.cbfa.be/nl/consultations/lop/pdf/2008-10_promotion.pdf, 2008, 23–25; D. de Meza, B. Irlenbusch and D. Reyniers, *Financial Capability: A Behavioural Economics Perspective*, www.fsa.gov.uk/pubs/consumer-research/crpr69.pdf, 2008, 22–52.

11 E.g. the General Regulations of April 1, 2010 of ING Belgium NV is 77 pages long. (www.ing.be/xpedio/groups/transaction/@transaction/@ibe/@homebank/documents/portalcontent/060776_nl.pdf).
Bayot, Monnier and Roland analysed on behalf of the POD Maatschappelijke integratie the socially responsible nature of advertisements for credit facilities in the Belgian market. Cf. B. Bayot, T. Monnier and L. Roland, *Zijn reclame en verkooppraktijken voor kredietopeningen verantwoord?*, Réseau Financement Alternatif, 2010, 18–45.
Cf. also a study of OIVO showing that consumers become more critical in the processing of advertising messages. OIVO, *Het verzet van de consument*, www.oivo-crioc.org/files/nl/6208nl.pdf, 2011, 37 p.; X, "Belgische consument wantrouwt reclame", *De Standaard* October 19, 2011.

12 G. Howells and T. Wilhelmsson, "EC Consumer Law: Has It Come of Age?", *E.L.Rev.* 2003, 380–381; Th. Wilson, N. Howell and G. Sheehan, "Protecting the Most Vulnerable in Consumer Credit Transactions", *JconsP* 2009, 124.

13 V.P. Goldberg, "Institutional Change and the Quasi-Invisible Hand", *Journal of Law and Economics* 1974, 485; D.M. Grether, A. Schwartz and L.L. Wilde, "The Irrelevance of Information Overload: an Analysis of Search and Disclosure", *S. Cal. L. Rev.* 1985–86, 279–280; C. Willett, *Fairness in consumer contracts: the case of unfair terms*, Aldershot, Ashgate, 2007, 42–43.

14 D. de Meza, B. Irlenbusch and D. Reyniers, *Financial Capability: A Behavioural Economics Perspective*, www.fsa.gov.uk/pubs/consumer-research/crpr69.pdf, 2008, 50; I. Ramsay, "From Truth in Lending to

optimism is common to both low- as high-skilled individuals.[15] Finally, the average consumer often does not understand the language and content of the information brochures. Thus, De Muynck states that *"a common critique is that European information requirements tend to prefer the side of the seller's/provider's professional wording instead that of the consumer"*.[16] It is therefore important that the creditor provides the information in an understandable manner to the consumer.[17]

Thirdly, the information overload increases the risks on misleading consumers. It leads consumers in fact away from the core (terms and conditions) of the credit agreement. The more information you give or how more certain elements of the information are emphasised, the more likely it is that people are being misled.[18] This criticism is often tackled by adopting formal requirements.[19]

Responsible Lending" in G. Howells, A. Janssen and R. Schulze (eds.), *Information rights and requirements. A challenge for party autonomy and transactional fairness*, Hampshire, Ashgate, 2005, 52.

15 G. Howells and T. Wilhelmsson, "EC Consumer Law: Has It Come of Age?", *E.L.Rev.* 2003, 381; C. Sunstein (ed.), *Behavioral Law and Economics*, Cambridge, Cambridge University Press, 2000, 59–187.

16 M. De Muynck, "Credit Cards, Overdraft Facilities and European Consumer Protection. A Blank Cheque for Unfairness?", *ERPL* 2010, 1222.

17 Cf. also Article 5 Directive 93/13/EC which states that *"in the case of contracts where all or certain terms offered to the consumer are in writing, these terms must always be drafted in plain, intelligible language. Where there is doubt about the meaning of a term, the interpretation most favorable to the consumer shall prevail"*; BIS, "A Better Deal for Consumers. Economic Narrative", www.bis.gov.uk/files/ file52074.pdf, 2009, 22; R. Incardona and C. Poncibò, "The average consumer, the unfair commercial practices directive, and the cognitive revolution", *JconsP* 2007, 34; J. Köndgen, "Policy Responses to Credit Crises: Does the Law of Contract Provide an Answer?" in S. Grundmann and Y.M. Atamer (eds.), *Financial Services, Financial Crisis and General European Contract Law. Failure and Challenges of Contracting*, Kluwer Law International, Alphen aan den Rijn, 2011, 46; R. Steennot, "Sanctionering van inbreuken op het consumentenrecht: de zoektocht naar een rechtvaardige oplossing" in F. Evers and P. Lefranc (eds.), *Kiezen tussen recht en rechtvaardigheid*, Bruges, die Keure, 2009, 146; A. Tiffe in cooperation with M. Feigl, "Best Practice beim verantwortlichen Kreditgeschäft – Corporate Social Responsibility in der Bankenpraxis", www.verantwortliche-kreditvergabe.net, 2008, 82–83.

18 D. de Meza, B. Irlenbusch and D. Reyniers, *Financial Capability: A Behavioural Economics Perspective*, www.fsa.gov.uk/pubs/consumer-research/crpr69.pdf, 2008, 49–50; H. Jacquemin, "Focus sur certains mécanismes de protection du consommateur de produits et services financiers en matière contractuelle" in H. Daems, I. De Meuleneere, R. Feltkamp, C. Houssa and R. Steennot (eds.), *Bescherming van de consument in het financieel recht. La protection du consommateur en droit financier*, Limal/Antwerp, Anthemis/Intersentia, 2012, 134; J. Lacko and J. Pappalardo, *The effect of mortgage broker compensation disclosures on consumers and competition: A controlled experiment*, www.ftc.gov/os/2004/01/030123mortgagefullrpt.pdf, 2004, 7–8; R. Steennot, "Sanctionering van inbreuken op het consumentenrecht: de zoektocht naar een rechtvaardige oplossing" in F. Evers and P. Lefranc (eds.), *Kiezen tussen recht en rechtvaardigheid*, Bruges, die Keure, 2009, 146–147.

19 C. Camerer, S. Issacharoff, G. Loewenstein, T. O'Donoghue and M. Rabin, "Regulation for Conservatives: Behavioral Economics and the Case for 'Asymmetric Paternalism'", *U. Pa. L. Rev.* 2003, 1230; R. Incardona and C. Poncibò, "The average consumer, the unfair commercial practices directive, and the cognitive revolution", *JconsP* 2007, 32; R. Steennot, "Informatieverplichtingen als beschermingstechniek bij de verwerving van beleggingsdiensten door consumenten" in H. De Wulf, R. Steennot, M. Tison and C. Van der Elst (eds.), *Van alle markten. Liber Amicorum Eddy Wymeersch*, Antwerp, Intersentia, 2008, 795; A.S. Vandenberghe, "Over de nieuwe zwakheden van de consument en wat eraan te doen", *Ars Aequi* 2009, 393; T. Van Dyck, *De geharmoniseerde prospectusplicht. Kritische*

Behaviour deviation (II): procrastination – Research showed that every man wants to consume in short term, but to pass the costs of consuming on to the future.[20] This behaviour is not entirely irrational. Money has after all a time value, i.e. by taking into account the future value of X EUR today.[21] Information, in particular advertising, however, can play a negative role. Emphasising the need to possess a particular good in conjunction with advertisements for obtaining easy credit may encourage consumers to consume rather than to save money and/or to pay off other debts. The rules on misleading and aggressive commercial practises are adopted in order to prevent excesses. One can also warn borrowers about the consequences of their procrastinating behaviour.[22] De Muynck pleads for a text message that should alert consumers when using credit cards:

> *"Dear Sir/Madam. The funds on your current account are insufficient to cover the cost of this transaction. If you wish to pursue your buying, be aware that besides a charge of x EUR, an interest rate of x percent will be due. Please press 1) CANCEL if you wish to refrain from the transaction of 2) OK if you wish to continue".*[23]

Behaviour deviation (III): mental accounting – People divide their assets in different 'mental' accounts. One account is reserved for the education and training of children, another for retirement savings, yet another for the purchase of food and medicine. However, money is money. Thaler found that consumers sometimes choose to buy a TV, a car, etc. on instalments, while they still have sufficient money standing on their saving account. In the consumer's head these savings are, however, reserved for another purpose. This is no rational behaviour.[24]

analyse van de geharmoniseerde prospectusplicht in de Prospectusrichtlijn 2003/71/EG en haar omzettingswetten in België, Nederland, Frankrijk, het Verenigd Koninkrijk en Duitsland, Bruges, die Keure, 2010, 98.

20 R.H. Strotz, "Myopia and inconsistency in dynamic utility maximization", *Review of Economic Studies* 1956, 180. This idea is also found in behavioural economic studies under the term *"Hyperbolic Discounting Utility"*, cf. a.o. D. de Meza, B. Irlenbusch and D. Reyniers, *Financial Capability: A Behavioural Economics Perspective*, www.fsa.gov.uk/pubs/consumer-research/crpr69.pdf, 2008, 23; E. Phelps and R. Pollak, "On Second-Best National Saving and Game-Equilibrium Growth", *Review of Economic Studies* 1968, 185–199.

21 A. Van de Velde, *Inleiding tot het financiewezen. Financiële markten, producten en instellingen analyse, werking en risico's*, Bruges, die Keure Business and Economics, 2011, 43; C. Van Hulle with the cooperation of M. Dutordoir, K. Smedts, K. De Cock, H. Drijkoningen, T. Lievens and A. Vanderlinden, *Bank- en financiewezen*, I, Leuven, Acco, 2010, 12.

22 D. de Meza, B. Irlenbusch and D. Reyniers, *Financial Capability: A Behavioural Economics Perspective*, www.fsa.gov.uk/pubs/consumer-research/crpr69.pdf, 2008, 30.
Cf. also Article 5, §2 WCK, that oblige lenders to include in certain advertising messages following sentence: *"caution, borrowing money has also to be paid"*.

23 M. De Muynck, "Credit Cards, Overdraft Facilities and European Consumer Protection. A Blank Cheque for Unfairness?", *ERPL* 2010, 1228.
Cf. also the warning that the lender, pursuant to Article 11 WCK, should include in the Standard European Consumer Credit Information form on *"Missing payments could have severe consequences for you (e.g. forced sale) and make obtaining credit more difficult."* Cf. Annex I to the WCK.

24 R. Thaler, "Mental Accounting and Consumer Choice", *Marketing Science* 1985, 199–200.

Behaviour deviation (IV): 'status quo'-bias – Men like to stay with their initial choice. They fear that a change of mind/direction will deteriorate their position or their assets. A loss arising from an action outweighs any loss caused by an omission to take action.[25] This behavioural deviation plays a role when reviewing credit agreements and/or choosing for an early repayment.[26] One must admit, though, that sometimes the information vis-à-vis early repayment and/or the revision of credit agreements is unclear or lacking.[27]

Lack of real choice – Finally, the consumer does not always have a real choice when signing a credit agreement.[28] This defect may arise from the financial need for money to buy certain goods or services. It may also be the result of a weaker negotiating position. Indeed, it is often difficult for a consumer to negotiate in full equality the terms and conditions of the credit agreement.[29]

The creditor's reputation as a solution? – Imperfect information does not necessarily lead to inefficient results. A creditor abusing the consumer's information asymmetry to achieve higher profits may suffer reputational damage in the long run.[30] However, the competition on the credit market is sometimes biased. Credit agreement are sometimes tailor-made, i.e. it takes into account the creditworthiness of a specific consumer.[31] It is thus difficult for consumers to share their experiences with certain creditors.[32] Difficult, but not impossible though. It just takes longer to expose the bad reputation of a particular

25 W. Samuelson and R. Zeckhauser, "Status Quo Bias in Decision Making", *Journal of Risk and Uncertainty* 1988, 38.

26 H. Shui and L. Ausubel, *Time Inconsistency in the Credit Card Market*, http://ssrn.com/abstract=586622, 2004, 50p., showing that consumers of their own will not often change from lender.

27 J.P. Abraham, "La formation des taux d'intérêt en Belgique. Le point de vue économique", *T.Vred.* 1995, 1995, 63; L. Coppens, "Gevangen in je woonkrediet", *De Standaard* August 20, 2011.

28 Th. Wilson, N. Howell and G. Sheehan, "Protecting the Most Vulnerable in Consumer Credit Transactions", *JconsP* 2009, 120–125.
Cf. BIS, "A Better Deal for Consumers. Economic Narrative", www.bis.gov.uk/files/file52074.pdf, 2009, 3 and 5–8.

29 J. Drexl, *Die wirtschaftliche Selbstbestimmung des Verbrauchers*, Tübingen, Mohr Siebeck, 1998, 329; V. Roppo, "From Consumer Contracts to Asymmetric Contracts: a Trend in European Contract Law?", *ERCL* 2009, 332; Th. Wilson, N. Howell and G. Sheehan, "Protecting the Most Vulnerable in Consumer Credit Transactions", *JconsP* 2009, 120–125.

30 V.P. Goldberg, "Institutional Change and the Quasi-Invisible Hand", *Journal of Law and Economics* 1974, 486; A. Griffiths, "Brands, business and social responsibility" in M. Faure and F. Stephen (eds.), *Essays in the Law and Economics of Regulation. In Honour of Anthony Ogus*, Antwerp, Intersentia, 2008, 204; L. Kaplow and S. Shavell, "Fairness versus welfare", *Harv. L. Rev.* 2001, 1157–1162; I. Ramsay, "Regulation of consumer credit" in G. Howells, I. Ramsay, T. Wilhelmsson and D. Kraft (eds.), *Handbook of research on international consumer law*, Cheltenham, Edward Elgar, 2010, 387.
Cf. for investment products, current and savings accounts, a recent study indicates that a bank best positions itself as a trusted contract counterpart which guarantees proper and correct information. Cf. W. Sinn, D. Vater, D. Lubig and M. Kasch, *Was Bankkunden wirklich wollen*, Munich/Zürich, Bain and Company Germany/Switzerland Inc., 2012, 23.

31 O. Bar-Gill and E. Warren, "Making Credit Safer", *U. Pa. L. Rev.* 2008, 122.
Or as Coase put it: *"Nothing could be more diverse than the actual transactions which take place in our modern world"*. Cf. R.H. Coase, "The Nature of the Firm", *Economica* 1937, 396.

32 Cf. for example concerning the obscurity of rates for home loans: J.P. Abraham, "La formation des taux d'intérêt en Belgique. Le point de vue économique", *T.Vred.* 1995, 1995, 63; L. Coppens, "Woonkrediet

creditor.[33] But the risk of reputational damage alone seems inadequate and/or insufficient to protect consumers in the field of consumer credit. Nonetheless, initiatives to introduce the creditor's reputation as a method of consumer protection are always welcome. The Belgian government, for example, wants to condemn financial institutions that repeatedly offer risky investments to their clients to higher penalties. The penalty can also be made public, so that the financial institution could suffer reputational damage.[34]

2.2. *Solutions through legislation*

Need for rules – We can conclude that the market mechanism insufficiently provides (objective) information to the consumer. Thus, the legislator should intervene. He may impose information requirements to the creditor. Examples range from merely handing over information brochures to providing personal advice. The manner in which information is transmitted also plays an important role. One can also tackle the problem preventatively by offering financial education. This formation is independent of a specific loan request. The purpose is to give every man the possibility to acquire a basic understanding of economic and legal concepts and of financial services.

2.2.1. Information requirements

Information and advice requirements – We limit ourselves below to a discussion of the information and advice requirements[35] in European consumer (credit) law *sensu stricto*[36], since the information requirements were fully harmonised by the European legislator.

wordt valstrik", *De Standaard* July 8, 2011; concerning the lack of clarity of bank tariffs: IP/10/1369 [Investments, real estate and internet access: examples of inadequate consumer markets].

33 Mouth-to-mouth advertising about a cheap and correct seller of household appliances or *vice versa* comments on a bad one will lead much faster to the build up or respectively the deterioration of a reputation.

34 N. Tanghe, "Regering voert schandpaal in voor banken", *De Standaard* February 15, 2013.

35 For the differences and similarities between an information and advice requirement: J. Vortmann, *Aufklärungs- und Beratungspflichten der Banken*, Cologne, RWS Verlag Kommunikationsforum GmbH, 2009, 1–4.

36 Cf. also the information requirements in Directive 2014/17/EU; Directive 2011/83/EU; Directive 2008/48/EC; Directive 2005/29/EC; Directive 2002/65/EC of the European Parliament and of the Council of September 23, 2002 concerning the distance marketing of consumer financial services and amending Council Directive 90/619/EEC and Directives 97/7/EC and 98/27/EC, *Pb.L.* October 9, 2002, 16–24; Directive 2000/31 of the European Parliament and of the Council of June 8, 2000 on certain legal aspects of information society services, in particular electronic commerce in the Internal Market, *Pb.L.* July 17, 2000, 1–16; Directive 98/6/EC of the European Parliament and of the Council of February 16, 1998 on consumer protection in the indication of prices or products offered to consumers, *Pb.L.* March 18, 1998, 27–31; Directive 94/47/EC of the European Parliament and of the Council of October 26, 1994 on the protection of purchasers in respect of certain aspects of contracts relating to the purchase of the right to use immovable properties on a timeshare basis, *Pb.L.* October 29, 1994, 83–87; Directive 87/102/EEC etc. Also the proposals of the European Commission for new Directives start from information paradigm.

Below three types of information requirements are mentioned. More specifically, the rules on (i) advertising, (ii) pre- and (iii) contractual information.

Advertising – Commercials are a first introduction to a credit agreement. The creditor wants to praise its credit agreement and its indispensability as good as possible. Correct advertising is thus important. Directive 2005/29/EC protects consumers in general terms against misleading and unfair commercial practices, including advertising.[37, 38] Article 4 Directive 2008/48/EC contains some standard clauses that a creditor must include in its advertising. The information must state *"in a clear, concise and prominent way by means of a representative example"* the basic contractual terms of the credit agreement. This includes a.o. information on the borrowing rate, the total amount of credit, the annual percentage rate, the duration of the credit agreement, the default interest rate, etc.[39] Creditors have to take into account both provisions.[40] In case of a conflict of law the principle *"lex specialis derogat legi generali"* applies. Unfortunately, the European legislator did not adopt a general framework on advertisements for credit agreements. The information requirements only apply if the advertisements mention the cost of credit.[41] The national legislator can oblige creditors to include standard information in any advertising for a consumer credit agreement *sensu stricto*.[42]

Pre-contractual information – The creditor shall also inform the consumer during the contract negotiations that lead to the signing of the credit agreement.[43] The creditor shall provide the information on the basis of an European Standard Form, which is included in Annex II to Directive 2008/48/EC.[44] If the creditor has given this form to the

37 This prohibition of the diffusion of misleading information is a negative information requirement. There exist also positive disclosure requirements. A positive information requirement requires producers and suppliers of services to provide to the consumer the objective information needed so that he can close the agreement with knowledge. Cf. E. Terryn, *Bedenktijden in het consumentenrecht. Het herroepingsrecht als instrument van consumentenbescherming*, Antwerp, Intersentia, 2008, 34–35; T. Van Dyck and V. Colaert, "Reclameregulering als vorm van consumentenbescherming" in C. Bruyneel, J.P. Buyle, M. Delierneux, J.F. Romain and E. Van den Haute (eds.), *Liber Amicorum A. Bruyneel*, Brussels, Larcier, 2008, 35–36.

38 Moreover Article 3 (9) Directive 2005/29/EC allows Member States to introduce more stringent provisions for *"financial services as indicated in* Directive *2002/65/EC and immovable goods"*.

39 Article 4 (2) Directive 2008/48/EC.

40 Article 4 (4) Directive 2008/48/EC.

41 In an earlier phase, it was possible to deduct a comprehensive framework for advertising from the wording of COM (2004) 747 final. [Amended proposal for a Directive of the European Parliament and the Council on the harmonisation of laws, regulations and administrative provisions of the Member States concerning consumer credit, repealing Directive 87/102/EEC and amending Directive 93/13/EEC], 5–6, Eq. Recital 18 *in fine* Directive 2008/48/EC, see also V. Colaert and E. Terryn, "Kredietpromotie" in E. Terryn (ed.), *Handboek Consumentenkrediet*, Bruges, die Keure, 2007, 66–70.

42 Consideration 9, 10 and 18 and *in fine* Article 22 (1) Directive 2008/48/EC; E. Terryn and J. Vannerom, "De nieuwe richtlijn consumentenkrediet en de implicaties voor de Belgische wetgeving" in VRG-Alumni (ed.), *Recht in beweging – 16de VRG Alumnidag*, Antwerp, Maklu, 2009, 30–31.

43 Also, the credit intermediary is subject to these pre-contractual information requirements (Article 5(1) Directive 2008/48/EC. Pursuant to Article 7 Directive 2008/48/EC are *"suppliers of goods or providers of services which ancillary act as credit intermediaries"* exempted from these pre-contractual information requirements.

44 There apply additional or specific information requirements for credit agreements in the form of an authorised overdraft on an account and for certain specific credit agreements (Article 6 Directive

consumer, he is presumed to have met his information obligation.[45] It is a rebuttable presumption.[46] Furthermore, the creditor shall provide the consumer with the standard form and a free copy of the credit agreement in due course before the credit agreement.[47]

The consumer should also have sufficient time to reflect and overlook his options.[48] The consumer shall receive the necessary information in good time before signing the credit agreement in order to reflect quietly whether or not the credit agreement offered to him best suits his needs and capabilities.[49] Directive 2008/48/EC does not define the term 'in good time'. The creditor and, in case of dispute, the court will interpret the concept of 'good time' *in concreto*.[50] Such an open standard has advantages and disadvantages. On one hand it provides flexibility for the contracting parties. On the other hand it leads to legal uncertainty. Ideally, the preparatory work had given an indication and/or criteria.

Appropriate explanation – The creditor must in some cases give the consumer an appropriate explanation about the credit agreement.[51] This appropriate explanation is not an abstract concept, but should always be assessed *in concreto*.[52] It must allow the consumer to give his informed consent.[53] Thus the consumer must be informed about (i) the content and characteristics of the credit agreement and (ii) the utility and the purpose

2008/48/EC). The information requirements are more limited in case of communication via speech recognition (Article 5 (2) Directive 2008/48/EC).

45 Article 5(1) *in fine* Directive 2008/48/EC.

46 Cf. also the prejudicial question of the Tribunal d'instance d'Orléans of May 30, 2013 in the case ECJ C-298/13, *Facet SA and BNP Paribas Personal Finance SA v. Saïda Bouchelaghem a.o.*

47 If the lender has decided at the time of the request not to grant a credit to the consumer, then he may refuse to issue a draft credit agreement free of charge (Article 5(4) *in fine* Directive 2008/4).

48 At this stage we do not yet discuss about a cooling off period *sensu stricto*. Terryn defines the cooling off period *sensu stricto* as *"de 'afkoelmogelijkheid' na de totstandkoming van een zekere wilsovereenstemming, ongeacht of de overeenkomst nu als 'voorlopig' of 'definitief' gesloten moet worden beschouwd"*. Cf. E. Terryn, *Bedenktijden in het consumentenrecht. Het herroepingsrecht als instrument van consumentenbescherming*, Antwerp, Intersentia, 2008, 22.

49 Article 5(1) Directive 2008/48/EC.

50 Cf. to make general conditions (*"Allgemeine Geschäftsbedingungen"*) opposable under German law, §305(2) BGB requires that *"wenn der Verwender bei Vertragsschluss [...] 2. der anderen Vertragspartei die Möglichkeit verschafft, in zumutbarer Weise, die auch eine für den Verwender erkennbare körperliche Behindering der anderen Vertragspartei angemessen berücksichtigt, von ihrem Inhalt Kenntnis zu nehmen"*. Cf. also T. Wilhelmsson and C. Willet, "Unfair terms and standard form contracts" in G. Howells, I. Ramsay, T. Wilhelmsson and D. Kraft (eds.), *Handbook of research on international consumer law*, Cheltenham, Edward Elgar, 2010, 170.

51 J. Vortmann, *Aufklärungs- und Beratungspflichten der Banken*, Keulen, RWS Verlag Kommunikationsforum GmbH, 2009, 2.

52 E. Terryn and J. Vannerom, "De nieuwe richtlijn consumentenkrediet en de implicaties voor de Belgische wetgeving" in VRG-Alumni (ed.), *Recht in beweging – 16de VRG Alumnidag*, Antwerp, Maklu, 2009, 33–34.

53 Article 5(6) Directive 2008/48/EC states that *"that creditors [...]provide adequate explanations to the consumer, <u>in order to place</u> the consumer in a position enabling him to assess whether the proposed credit agreement adapted to his needs and to his financial situation"* (own emphasis added). Cf. also consideration 27 Directive 2008/48/EC.

for which such type of credit agreement is normally used.[54] The creditor's explanation shall take into account (i) the repayment ability of the consumer, (ii) the risk, (iii) whether or not there is a fixed timetable, (iv) the ways of drawdown, and (v) the purpose of the requested credit.[55] The proposal of the European Commission in 2002 went even further. Creditors were required to request collateral and to grant an appropriate credit.[56] However, at the end of the legislative process the European legislator laid the final decision making power with the consumer.

Contractual information – The third and final part of the information requirements concern the information that the lender must provide in the credit agreement itself.[57] The credit agreement must list the basic terms and conditions.

The creditor must also communicate any change in the borrowing rate to the consumer during the execution of the contract. The notification should be made before the new borrowing rate is applied.[58] The creditor may also provide this information to the consumer periodically. This possibility should be stipulated in the credit agreement. Moreover, the new borrowing rate should be the result of a change in a reference rate, of which consumers can take note appropriately and which can be consulted in the offices of the creditor.[59]

2.2.2. Financial education

Some recent initiatives – A final way to inform the consumer is by giving financial education. The OECD and the World Bank published hereabout some recommendations.[60] Number of initiatives are launched within the EU.[61] In Belgium schools already offered

54 O. Bar-Gill, "The Behavioral Economics of Consumer Contracts" in O. Bar-Gill and R. Epstein, *Consumer Contracts: Behavioral Economics vs. Neoclassical Economics. An exchange between Oren Bar-Gill and Richard A. Epstein*, http://ssrn.com/abstract=982527, New York University School of Law, 2007, 38.

55 COM(2002) 443 final, 14; cf. also Article 6 (2) COM(2002) 443 final, 38.

56 Article 10(2) Directive 2008/48/EG; C. Herresthal, "Die Verpflichtung zur Bewertung der Kreditwürdigkeit und zur angemessenen Erläuterung nach der neuen Verbraucherkreditrichtlinie 2008/48/EG", *WM* 2009, 1177–1179.

57 Article 10(5) and 12 Directive 2008/48/EC contain specific regulations for credit agreements in the form of authorised overdrafts on an account.

58 Article 11(1) Directive 2008/48/EC.

59 Article 11(2) Directive 2008/48/EC.

60 OECD, "Recommendation of the Council on Good Practices on Financial Education and Awareness Relating to Credit", 2009, http://acts.oecd.org/Instruments/ShowInstrumentView.aspx?InstrumentID=78 andLang=en andBook=False; OECD, "Recommendation on Principles and Good Practices for Financial Education and Awareness", 2005, www.oecd.org/finance/financial-education/35108560.pdf, 7 p.; World bank, "Good Practices for Financial Consumer Protection", 2012, http://responsiblefinance.worldbank.org, 102 p.

61 Concerning European initiatives: European Insurance and Occupational Pensions Authority, "Report on Financial Literacy and Education. Initiatives by Competent Authorities", 2011, https://eiopa.europa.eu/fileadmin/tx_dam/files/publications/reports/Report_on_Financial_Literacy_and_Education__EIOPA-CCPFI-11-018_.pdf, 38p.
An information site for consumers exists in France and in the United Kingdom: www.lafinancepourtous.com and https://www.moneyadviceservice.org.uk.

lessons on economics, money management...[62] As from 2014 economics became a mandatory course in schools for secondary education.[63]

Furthermore, the European Commission aims to boost the quality of financial education. While this is, according to the Commission, is essentially the responsibility of the Member States, the Commission proposes some possible action plans to install a better financial basic knowledge of consumers. This may include:

- financing existing projects. The European Commission has already contributed in the past to support some projects[64];
- developing guidelines;
- identifying and promoting best practices;
- drafting innovative proposals.[65]

The purpose of education is fuelling financial capability – Financial education should lead to financially capable consumers, which can process the information obtained and actually implement it in their everyday lives.[66] The term 'financial capability includes more than the term 'financial knowledge'. It means that the consumer:

In Germany the Bankenverband (a German association representing the interests of private banks) Has started with some projects on financial education. For example Schul/Bank, an information platform for schools and teachers with information and teaching materials on economics and finance: www.schulbank.de.
Cf. concerning this matter S. De Brouwer, "Financial Literacy in Europe" *Bank Fin.* 2011, 263–265; L. Van Cauter, "De bescherming van de financiële consument – Een overzicht van het regelgevend kader" in H. Daems, I. De Meuleneere, R. Feltkamp, C. Houssa and R. Steennot (eds.), *Bescherming van de consument in het financieel recht. La protection du consommateur en droit financier*, Limal/Antwerp, Anthemis/Intersentia, 2012, 31–32.

62 For a brief overview of existing Belgian information programs: CBFA, *Verslag over het bevorderen van de financiële kennis in België*, www.cbfa.be/nl/consultations/lop/pdf/2008-10_promotion.pdf, 2008, 18–22.

63 C. De Herdt, "Economie wordt verplicht schoolvak", *De Standaard* October 11, 2011.
Cf. also the call of the Vlaamse Juristenvereniging for a debate on juridical literacy (B. De Groote, "Geen juridische geletterdheid zonder toegang tot juridische basisinformatie", *RW* 2010–11, 302).

64 For example: the online information platform Dolceta (www.dolceta.eu/).

65 COM(2007) 226 def. [Green paper on Retail Financial Services for Consumers in the Single Market], 18–19; cf. also S. De Brouwer, "Financial Literacy in Europe", *Bank Fin.* 2011, 261–263.

66 Y.M. Atamer, "Duty of Responsible Lending: Should the European Union Take Action?" in S. Grundmann and Y.M. Atamer (eds.), *Financial Services, Financial Crisis and General European Contract Law. Failure and Challenges of Contracting*, Kluwer Law International, Alphen a/d Rijn, 2011, 188–189; L. Van Cauter, "De bescherming van de financiële consument – Een overzicht van het regelgevend kader" in H. Daems, I. De Meuleneere, R. Feltkamp, C. Houssa and R. Steennot (eds.), *Bescherming van de consument in het financieel recht. La protection du consommateur en droit financier*, Limal/Antwerp, Anthemis/Intersentia, 2012, 31; T. Van Dyck, *De geharmoniseerde prospectusplicht. Kritische analyse van de geharmoniseerde prospectusplicht in de Prospectusrichtlijn 2003/71/EG en haar omzettingswetten in België, Nederland, Frankrijk, het Verenigd Koninkrijk en Duitsland*, Bruges, die Keure, 2010, 85.

- has the necessary financial knowledge;
- adopts an attitude reflecting his financial knowledge; and
- also acts/behaves in a manner that is consistent with the financial knowledge he claims to possess.[67]

Mandatory financial information alone is not sufficient. Financial education should ensure that consumers ultimately act consistently.[68]

Target group of financial education – According to the European Commission, it is best to start as soon as possible with financial education.[69] A Dutch study shows that a large majority of young people feel that schools have a role to play alongside the parents.[70, 71]

III. Multi-layered consumer image

Information is good, but not always sufficient – Legislators are *de lege lata* in favour of the information paradigm. We have shown that the information paradigm alone falls short as a method of consumer protection.[72] Firstly, more information means in principle more responsibility for the consumer on the choices made by him.[73] If one does not accept this, one has to deal with (a hidden form) of paternalism. Secondly, the functioning of the market alone will not lead to sufficient and correct information. Thus the legislator had to intervene to safeguard the (substantive) freedom of contract. Here, however, one took too little account of the various market distortions.

This paper does not plead to throw everything overboard. No, mandatory information disclosure can be useful, but perhaps combined with other methods of consumer protection.

Overview of difficulties – Looking for other methods of consumer protection, some questions and comments arise. Firstly, we note that the current definition of the consumer

67 A. Atkinson, S. McKay, E. Kempson and S. Collard, *Levels of financial capability in the UK: results of a baseline survey*, www.fsa.gov.uk/pubs/consumer-research/crpr47.pdf, 2006, 10–11; D. Loerwald, "How can we measure financial literacy", abstract written following an oral presentation during the Workshop "Are we Financially Illiterate? – Evaluation of knowledge and capabilities?" on the Internationale Konferenz zu Finanzdienstleistungen, *Finanzdienstleister und Verbraucherschutz – zwei Welten?*, Konferenz Reader, 2010, 38.

68 D. de Meza, B. Irlenbusch and D. Reyniers, *Financial Capability: A Behavioural Economics Perspective*, www.fsa.gov.uk/pubs/consumer-research/crpr69.pdf, 2008, 2–4.

69 COM(2007) 808 [Communication of the Commission – Financial education], 7–9.

70 Nibud in cooperation with CentiQ, "Financiële opvoeding 2010", NIBUD, 2010, 8 p.

71 The Specific Teacher Training of Commercial Sciences at Hogeschool Gent started in 2010 with a project on "financial literacy". The purpose of the project is the elaborating of lessons for secondary education. The European Economic and Social Committee also argues for the inclusion of financial education in the curricula of the schools. Cf. CES/11/82 of July 14, 2011, www.eesc.europa.eu; ECO/297, "Opinion of July 14, 2011 of the European Economic and Social Committee on Financial education and responsible consumption of financial products (own-initiative opinion), www.eesc.europa.eu/?i=portal.en.eco-opinions.15375, 2 en 4–6.

72 ???

73 ???

notion is still under discussion. Some legislative texts define the consumer as a natural person who acquires or uses products/services principally for non-professional purposes. Other legislation applies a more restrictive view of the non-professional nature. The consumer is a natural person acting exclusively for non-commercial purposes. The legal doctrine and justice is divided on this point.[74]

Secondly, limiting the scope of application *ratione personae* of consumer law using the current consumer notion is not unproblematic. The majority assumes that the aim of consumer law is to protect the consumer against a stronger negotiating party. Recently, however, the question is whether one should not abandon a person-oriented view of the consumer and focus more on the interrelationship of the contracting parties. Consumer law should not protect only consumers but each party who is in a weaker bargaining position in a specific contractual relationship. One may wonder whether the definition of consumer credit should not be extended to small and medium sized enterprises (SMEs). In principle one abolishes in this way consumer law *sensu stricto*. Only the consumer law *sensu lato* which aims to protect the weaker party against market failures subsists.

Finally, we note that the consumer image is two-fold and that it has its shortcomings. The reference point is the average-informed and reasonably observant and circumspect consumer, who is able to take a rational decision provided he obtained sufficient and correct information. This forms the basis for the assessment of the legislative and judicial action in a situation-specific consumer law. Legal rules are not written tailor-made to each specific, individual consumer, but are drafted in accordance to the image of an abstract, average consumer. After the legislator and/or the judge have/has investigated the circumstances under which the average consumer suffers from market failures – and thus encounters disadvantages of his weaker bargaining position – they seek to restore the market failure as optimal as possible.[75] This is a correct, but insufficient working hypothesis.

3.1. Consumer image and the Court of Justice

Double consumer image – In the jurisprudence of the Court of Justice a double consumer image emerges. As we shall see below, the Court of Justice takes the image of the average informed consumer as the starting point in its jurisprudence on primary European Union law or on unfair commercial practices. In its jurisprudence on unfair terms the Court of Justice emphasises the weaker bargaining position of consumers. As such the Court of Justice authorises a more far-reaching interference by the legislator and the national judges in the contractual relationship between the consumer and the trader.

74 For an overview: see a.o. J. Vannerom, "Consumer Notion: Natural or Legal Persons and Mixed Contracts" in E. Terryn, G. Straetmans and V. Colaert (eds.), *Landmark Cases of EU Consumer Law. In Honour of Jules Stuyck*, Antwerp, Intersentia, 2013, 53–72.

75 For England: Crowther Committee, *Consumer Credit. Report of the Committee*, I, *Report*, London, HM Stationery Office, Cmnd 4596, 1971, 151–153.

3.1.1. The consumer in the internal market and the law on commercial practices

Development of the consumer image in the internal market – The primary European Union law regulates the functioning of the European Union and its internal market. It guarantees freedom of goods, persons, services and capital.[76] Member States may not impose quantitative import and export restrictions impeding intra-EU-trade.[77] Such national restrictions can be challenged before the Court of Justice. We speak about negative harmonisation. Indeed, here the European legislator does not actively regulate a particular product, service or sales method. The Court of Justice provides for an integrated internal market by eliminating national protectionist rules.[78] Consumer protection is often cited as a justification for such national restrictions. However, the Court of Justice inveighed against purely protectionist provisions enacted under the guise of consumer protection, but merely aimed to protect the national market. The judgment in *Rewe-Zentral* about the French liqueur Cassis de Dijon is probably the best known.[79] There were also a number of Belgian cases.[80] In reviewing national restrictions, the Court of Justice had to define who the consumer is or better what degree of protection he needs. The European consumer image is so largely developed by the jurisprudence of the Court of Justice on the freedom of goods and services.

Jurisprudential evolution – The jurisprudential development started with a judgment of the Court of Justice of February 20, 1979.[81] In a case concerning the free movement of goods Rewe-Zentral AG asked to the *'Bundesmonopolverwaltung für Branntwein'* an authorisation for the import of the spirit *'Cassis de Dijon'* on the German market. A permit was not necessary according to the Bundesmonopolverwaltung. However it was not to be imported, as suppliers might only introduce on the market drinks with an alcohol content of at least 32%. The ban of import intended a.o. to protect the consumer against false assumptions about the consumed beverage. Rewe-Zentral appealed the

76 Resp. Article 28, 45 and 49, 56, 63 VWEU.

77 Article 34–35 VWEU.

78 J. Goddaer, E. Terryn and J. Vannerom, "Invloed van het Europese recht op het consumenten(contracten) recht" in I. Samoy, V. Sagaert and E. Terryn (eds.), *Invloed van het Europese recht op het Belgische privaatrecht*, Antwerp-Cambridge, Intersentia, 2012, 473–478; I. Ramsay, *Consumer Law and Policy: Text and Materials on Regulating Consumer Markets. Third Edition*, Oxford, Hart, 2012, 30–33.

79 ECJ 120/78, *Rewe-Zentral AG v. Bundesmonopolverwaltung für Branntwein*.

80 Cf. a.o. ECJ C-205/07, *Criminal proceedings v. Lodewijk Gysbrechts and Santurel Inter BVBA*; ECJ C-20/03, *Criminal proceedings v. Marcel Burmanjer, René Alexander Van Der Linden and Anthony De Jong*; ECJ C-239/02, *Douwe Egberts NV v. Westrom Pharma NV and Christophe Souranis and Douwe Egberts NV v. FICS-World BVBA*; ECJ C-50/85, *Berhard Schloh v. PVBA Auto contrôle technique*; ECJ C-261/81, *Walter Rau Lebensmittelwerke v. De Smedt PVBA*.
For a detailed discussion: J. Goddaer, E. Terryn and J. Vannerom, "Invloed van het Europese recht op het consumenten(contracten)recht" in I. Samoy, V. Sagaert and E. Terryn (eds.), *Invloed van het Europese recht op het Belgische privaatrecht*, Antwerp-Cambridge, Intersentia, 2012, 474–478.

81 S. Grundmann and Y.M. Atamer, "European Contract Law and Banking Contracts after the Financial Crisis: Challenges for Contracting and Market Transactions" in S. Grundmann and Y.M. Atamer (eds.), *Financial Services, Financial Crisis and General European Contract Law. Failure and Challenges of Contracting*, Kluwer Law International, Alphen a/d Rijn, 2011, 16.

decision. Ultimately the case came before the Court of Justice. The Court of Justice ruled that the information about the origin of the drink and the alcohol content[82] was a less far-reaching restriction on cross-border trade than the imposition of a minimum alcohol content. The information paradigm as a means of consumer protection was born.

Also in the case, *the European Commission against Germany*, the Court of Justice confirmed that the mandatory information disclosure to consumers is preferred above a ban on imports of products from other Member States. The German '*Reinheitsgebot*' states that only beverages made from malted barley, hops, yeast and water may be traded as beer in Germany. The beer imported from another Member State did not comply with this requirement. The Court of Justice preferred again mandatory information requirements over a ban. It is sufficient for a trader to notify the consumer that the beer, which he is to purchase does not meet the German '*Reinheitsgebot*', for example. The consumer can then with full knowledge make his choice.[83]

The Court of Justice confirmed this view on the quest of the consumer to the '*characteristics*' of a product in the *Pall v. Dahlhausen* judgment and continues to repeat it in subsequent judgments on the free movement of goods and services.[84] Some two years before the *Pall v. Dahlhausen* judgment the Court of Justice even ruled that each consumer has a right on information in the *GB Inno* case.[85]

Basic knowledge of the average consumer – In the jurisprudence on the internal market and on misleading and unfair commercial practices the Court of Justice takes the average consumer as the standard for information disclosure.[86] In the *Van Bennekom* case the Court of Justice indicated for the first time what basic level of knowledge one can expect from the consumer. The consumer who evaluates medicinal products has an average discernment.[87] The Court of Justice refined this consumer image and speaks about the "*average consumer who is reasonably well informed and reasonably observant*

82 Consideration 14 ECJ 120/78, *Rewe-Zentral AG v. Bundesmonopolverwaltung für Branntwein*; cf. also consideration 25 Concl. N. Fennely ECJ C-220/98, *Estée Lauder Cosmetics GmbH and Co. OHG v. Lancaster Group GmbH.*

83 Consideration 35 and 36 ECJ 178/84, *Commission v. Germany (Reinheitsgebot).*

84 Consideration 19 ECJ C-238/89, *Pall Corp. v. P.J. Dahlhausen and Co.*; cf. also consideration 24 ECJ C-470/93, *Verein gegen Unwesen in Handel und Gewerbe Köln eV. v. Mars GmbH*; ECJ C-315/92, *Verband Sozialer Wettbewerb eV v. Clinique Laboratoires SNC and Estée Lauder Cosmetics GmbH*; consideration 17 ECJ C-126/91, *Schutzverband gegen Unwesen in der Wirtschaft eV. v. Yves Rocher GmbH*; consideration 15–17 ECJ C-373/90, *Nissan.*

85 ECJ 362/88, *GB Inno SA v. Confédération du Commerce luxembourgeois ASBL*; L. Gormley, "The Consumer Acquis and the Internal Market", *EBLR* 2009, 417; J. Stuyck and G. Straetmans, *Financiële diensten en de consument. Bankdiensten – Consumentenkrediet – Hypothecair krediet – Verzekeringen – Handelspraktijken volgens het Belgisch en Europees recht*, Antwerp, Kluwer, 1994, 31–32; T. Wilhelmsson, G. Howells and H.-W. Micklitz, "European Consumer Law" in M. Bussani and F. Werro (eds.), *European Private Law: a Handbook*, Bern, Stämpfli, 2009, 270–271.

86 R. Incardona and C. Poncibò, "The average consumer, the unfair commercial practices directive, and the cognitive revolution", *JconsP* 2007, 24.

87 Consideration 18 ECJ 227/82, *Criminal proceeding v. Leendert Van Bennekom.*

and circumspect".[88] The national courts may in their review of misleading and unfair commercial practices assume that a consumer is able to estimate the value of standard information. Advocate General Geelhoed even believes that a consumer, before he (first) purchases a product or service, will always take knowledge of the information on the label.[89] In the *Darbo* case also the Court of Justice held that the average informed and reasonable observant and circumspect consumer first looks at the list of ingredients. For example, if in this list the ingredient 'pectin' is mentioned, consumers can value the indication *"purely natural"* on the label. According to the Court of Justice, the labelling was not misleading.[90]

The image of the 'searching informed consumer' – The Court of Justice adopts in its jurisprudence on the internal market and on misleading and unfair commercial practices the image of the average informed and reasonable observant and circumspect consumer.[91] The consumer is actively seeking information. Once he has sufficient and correct information, he can make a free and conscious decision.[92]

3.1.2. The consumer in case of positive harmonisation

Ex officio review of unfair terms – In the jurisprudence of the Court of Justice on unfair terms, however, a different consumer image emerges. The Court of Justice has repeatedly ruled that Directive 93/13/EEC misses its goal, if the consumer himself has to raise the unfairness of a contract term. The consumer is in fact in a weak bargaining position, partly because he has less information than the company.[93] According to the Court of

88 Consideration 27 ECJ C-220/98, *Estée Lauder Cosmetics GmbH and Co. OHG v. Lancaster Group GmbH*; consideration 36 ECJ C-303/97, *Verbraucherschutzverein eV v. Sektkellerei G.C. Kessler GmbH und Co*; consideration 31 ECJ C-210/96, *Gut Springenheide GmbH en Rudolf Tusky v. Oberkreisdirektor des Kreises Steinfurt*; G. Straetmans, "Het Europese consumentenacquis: genese en toekomstblik" in J. Meeusen, G. Straetmans and A.-M. Van den Bossche (eds.), *Het EG-consumentenacquis: nu en straks*, Antwerp, Intersentia, 2009, 7–8.

89 Consideration 54 conc L.L.A. Geelhoed by ECJ C-239/02, *Douwe Egberts NV v. Westrom Pharma NV and Christophe Souranis and Douwe Egberts NV v. FICS-World BVBA*.
This was already been mentioned. Cf. consideration 25 Concl. N. Fennely by ECJ C-220/98, *Estée Lauder Cosmetics GmbH and Co. OHG v. Lancaster Group GmbH.*
Cf. also R. Incardona and C. Poncibò, "The average consumer, the unfair commercial practices directive, and the cognitive revolution", *JconsP* 2007, 30.

90 Consideration 20 ECJ C-465/98, *Verein gegen Unwesen in Handel und Gewerbe Köln eV v. Adorf Darbo AG.* Cf. also consideration 12 ECJ 27/80, *Criminal proceeding v. Anton Adriaan Fietje* in which the Court stated that in some cases indications and signs are sufficient.

91 Consideration 27 ECJ C-220/98, *Estée Lauder Cosmetics GmbH and Co. OHG v. Lancaster Group GmbH*; consideration 36 ECJ C-303/97, *Verbraucherschutzverein eV v. Sektkellerei G.C. Kessler GmbH und Co*; consideration 31 ECJ C-210/96, *Gut Springenheide GmbH and Rudolf Tusky v. Oberkreisdirektor des Kreises Steinfurt.*

92 J. Stuyck and G. Straetmans, *Financiële diensten en de consument. Bankdiensten – Consumentenkrediet – Hypothecair krediet – Verzekeringen – Handelspraktijken volgens het Belgisch en Europees recht*, Antwerp, Kluwer, 1994, 31–32.

93 Consideration 25–26 ECJ C-240/98-C-244/98, *Oceano Grupo Editorial SA v. Rocio Murciano Quintero.* Cf. also consideration 41 ECJ C-618/10, *Banco Espanol de Credito SA v. Joaquin Calderon Camino*; consideration 48–49 ECJ C-137/08, *VB Pénzügyi Lízing Zrt. v. Ferenc Schneider*; consideration 31 ECJ

Justice article 6 of Directive 93/13/EEC aims to *"replace the formal balance which the latter establishes between the rights and obligations of the parties with an effective balance which re-establishes equality between them"*.[94] Therefore, the court must assess *ex officio* unfair terms. The *ex officio* assessment offers the consumer also a preventative protection against unfair terms. Traders will abstain from including unfair terms in the agreement. Indeed, the court has to declare the unfair contract term as not binding.[95] When assessing out of its own motion unfair terms, the national court may not violate the right of defence, though. The Court of Justice extended this *ex officio* assessment of unfair terms to all types of consumer contracts. It is only required that the agreement falls *ratione materiae* and *personae* within the scope of Directive 93/13/EEC. Thus, the national court should also assess of its own motion interest clauses and clauses for non-performance in a consumer credit agreement.[96] The Court of Justice also emphasised

C-40/08, *Asturcom Telecomunicaciones SL v. Cristina Rodríguez Nogueira*; consideration 26 and 38 ECJ C-168/05, *Elias Maria Mostaza Claro v. Centro Movil Milenium*; consideration 33 ECJ C-473/00, *Cofidis SA v. Jean-Louis Fredout*; I. Demuynck, *De inhoudelijke controle van onrechtmatige bedingen: onderzoek van de Wet van 14 juli 1991 op de handelspraktijken en de voorlichting van de consument*, doctoraatsthesis UGent, 2000, 711; R. Steennot, "Sanctionering van inbreuken op het consumentenrecht: de zoektocht naar een rechtvaardige oplossing" in F. Evers and P. Lefranc (eds.), *Kiezen tussen recht en rechtvaardigheid*, Bruges, die Keure, 2009, 147; A. Van Oevelen, "Enkele actuele knelpunten in het verbintenissenrecht", *RW* 2011–12, 56; C. Willett, *Fairness in consumer contracts: the case of unfair terms*, Aldershot, Ashgate, 2007, 99–101.

94 Consideration 36 ECJ C-168/05, *Elias Maria Mostaza Claro v. Centro Movil Milenium.*
Cf. also consideration 45 ECJ C-415/11, *Mohamed Aziz v. Caixa d'Estalvis de Catalunya, Tarragona i Manresa (Catalunyacaixa)*; consideration 20 ECJ C-472/11, *Banif Plus Bank Zrt v. Csaba Csipai and Viktoria Csipai*; consideration 40 ECJ C-618/10, *Banco Espanol de Credito SA v. Joaquin Calderon Camino.*

95 Consideration 28 ECJ C-240/98-C-244/98, *Oceano Grupo Editorial SA v. Rocio Murciano Quintero.*
Cf. also consideration 41 ECJ C-76/10, *Pohotovost' s.r.o. v. Iveta Korckovska*; consideration 27 ECJ C-168/05, *Elias Maria Mostaza Claro v. Centro Movil Milenium*; consideration 32 ECJ C-473/00, *Cofidis SA v. Jean-Louis Fredout*; J. Goddaer, E. Terryn and J. Vannerom, "Invloed van het Europese recht op het consumenten(contracten)recht" in I. Samoy, V. Sagaert and E. Terryn (eds.), *Invloed van het Europese recht op het Belgische privaatrecht*, Antwerp-Cambridge, Intersentia, 2012, 537.
Cf. consideration 32 ECJ C-243/08, *Pannon GSM Zrt. v. Erzsébet Sustikné Györfi*; consideration 23 ECJ C-472/11, *Banif Plus Bank Zrt v. Csaba Csipai and Viktoria Csipai*; consideration 43 ECJ C-618/10, *Banco Espanol de Credito SA v. Joaquin Calderon Camino.*

96 Consideration 61–63 ECJ C-429/05, *Max Rampion and Marie-Jeanne Godard v. Franfinance SA and K par K SAS*; consideration 32 ECJ C-473/00, *Cofidis SA v. Jean-Louis Fredout*; C. Biquet-Mathieu, "Les contrats du consommateur en Belgique" in X (ed.), *Travaux de l'Association Henri Capitant des amis de la culture juridique française*, LVII/2007, Brussels, Bruylant, 2010, 42.
Cf. also ECJ C-415/11, *Mohamed Aziz v. Caixa d'Estalvis de Catalunya, Tarragona i Manresa (Catalunyacaixa)*; ECJ C-227/08, *Eva Martin Martin v. EDP Editores, SL*; prejudicial question of the Tribunal d'instance d'Orléans of May 30, 2013 in the case ECJ C-298/13, *Facet SA and BNP Paribas Personal Finance SA v. Saïda Bouchelaghem e.a.*; ECJ C-280/13, *Barclays Bank S.A. v. Sara Sanchez Garcia en Alejandro Chacon Barrera*; Joined Cases ECJ C-537/12, Banco Popular Español SA v Maria Teodolinda Rivas Quichimbo and Wilmar Edgar Cun Pérez and C-116/13, *Banco de Valencia SA v. Joaquin Valldeperas Tortosa en Maria Angeles Miret Jaume*; ECJ C-482/12, Peter Macinsky and Eva Macinska v. Getfi n s.r.o. and Financreal s.r.o.

that a court must investigate *ex officio* whether a term falls within the scope of Directive 93/13/EEC.[97]

Ex officio review of remedies – Recently, the Court of Justice in the *Duarte Hueros* case said that a court should raise *ex officio* the remedies granted by Directive 1999/44/EC[98], if the consumer in his initial claim can not specify himself his remedies or is not authorised to introduce a new procedure. The Court of Justice firstly points out the principle of procedural autonomy of the Member States.[99] National procedural rules must not violate the principle of effectiveness, though. They may not make the enforcement by the consumer of his rights under Directive 1999/44/EC extremely difficult or impossible.[100]

Distance contracts – The consumer image of the weaker contracting party does not only appear in the jurisprudence on unfair terms. The Court of Justice also cites other reasons for which the consumer is in a weaker bargaining position. For example, the consumer can be in a vulnerable position because the trader is looking for him at his home. In those cases, the Court of Justice put forward more stringent requirements on the protection of consumers, a.o. through stricter information requirements.[101] In the *Buet* case representatives of SARL Educational Business Services visited consumers at their home and offered them English courses. The Court of Justice ruled that certain distance contracts put consumers in a particularly vulnerable position. "*The potential purchaser often belongs to a category of people who, for one reason or another, are behind with their education and are seeking to catch up. That makes them particularly vulnerable when faced with salesmen of educational material who attempt to persuade them that if they use that material they will have better employment prospects*".[102]

97 Consideration 56 ECJ C-137/08, *VB Pénzügyi Lízing Zrt. v. Ferenc Schneider.*
Cf. in the *Pannon* case the Court of Justice ruled for the first time the national court has to investigate the unfair character of a contract term. However, the court had to rely on the factual and legal material given by the parties of the trial. Cf. consideration 32 ECJ C-243/08, *Pannon GSM Zrt. v. Erzsébet Sustikné Györfi.*

98 Directive 1999/44/EC of the Europeans Parliament and the Council of May 25, 1999 on certain aspects of the sale of consumer goods, *Pb.L.* July 7, 1999, 12–16.

99 Consideration 31 ECJ C-32/12, *Soledad Duarte Hueros v. Autociba SA and Automoviles Citroën Espana SA.*

100 Considerations 39 and 41 ECJ C-32/12, *Soledad Duarte Hueros v. Autociba SA and Automoviles Citroën Espana SA.*

101 ECJ C-382/87, *Criminal proceeding v. R. Buet and SARL Educational Business Services*; J. Stuyck and G. Straetmans, *Financiële diensten en de consument. Bankdiensten – Consumentenkrediet – Hypothecair krediet – Verzekeringen – Handelspraktijken volgens het Belgisch en Europees recht*, Antwerp, Kluwer, 1994, 31.

102 Consideration 13 ECJ C-382/87, *Criminal proceeding v. R. Buet and SARL Educational Business Services. Contra*: consideration 20 ECJ C-239/90, *SCP Boscher, Studer and Fromentin v. SA British Motors Wright and others*; J. Stuyck and G. Straetmans, *Financiële diensten en de consument. Bankdiensten – Consumentenkrediet – Hypothecair krediet – Verzekeringen – Handelspraktijken volgens het Belgisch en Europees recht*, Antwerp, Kluwer, 1994, 32. In the arrest *Boscher* the Court of Justice stated that obstacles to the free movement of goods are not allowed because the sales in question were directed to "*buyers who particularly wary.*" They were, after all, specialised buyers. More importantly here is the observation that the judgment was about the single market, where The Court of Justice is more reticent.

The image of the 'consumer in a weaker (bargaining) position' – The Court of Justice uses a different consumer image in its jurisprudence on unfair terms and on the remedies which can be claimed under Directive 1999/44/EC. It is a consumer image which we also found in the jurisprudence on distance contracts. In these areas the Court of Justice is less reluctant to and accepts easier certain restrictions on the freedom of contract justified by the need for consumer protection. This enhanced protection is, according to the Court of Justice, justified because the consumer is in a weaker bargaining position. The consumer can not easily negotiate contractual terms.[103] Often, the trader will submit its standard agreement for signature without the consumer being able to amend or negotiate certain terms.[104] Moreover, the consumer can not always (fully) enforce his rights, because it is made extremely difficult or impossible by national procedural law.[105]

3.1.3. Double consumer image

Double consumer image: two criteria – The consumer image can not be reduced to a homogeneous image. The Court of Justice uses in certain cases, the image of the 'searching informed consumer'. In other judgments it stresses the consumer's weaker bargaining position. The consumer is someone who is not able to claim the rights he possesses out of his own motion. In the current legal doctrine one finds possible explanations for the double consumer image.

Specific circumstances as criterion – Stuyck and Straetmans deduce from the jurisprudence of the Court of Justice a double consumer image.[106] The Court of Justice starts, in principle, from a rational consumer who is looking for useful information and

[103] ECJ C-240/98-C-244/98, *Oceano Grupo Editorial SA v. Rocio Murciano Quintero*, where the Court of Justice is suggesting that *"system of protection elaborated by the Directive is based on the idea that the consumer is against the seller in a weak bargaining position and has less information than the latter"* (consideration 25).
Cf. also consideration 46 ECJ C-137/08, *VB Pénzügyi Lízing Zrt. v. Ferandc Schneider*; consideration 29 ECJ C-40/08, *Asturcom Telecomunicaciones SL v. Cristina Rodríguez Nogueira*; consideration 25 ECJ C-168/05, *Elias Maria Mostaza Claro v. Centro Movil Milenium*; J. Stuyck, "Consumentenbescherming in tijden van economische crisis", *Jura Falc.* 2009–2010, 328.

[104] Consideration 46 ECJ C-137/08, *VB Pénzügyi Lízing Zrt. v. Ferenc Schneider*; consideration 29 ECJ C-40/08, *Asturcom Telecomunicaciones SL v. Cristina Rodríguez Nogueira*; consideration 25 ECJ C-168/05, *Elias Maria Mostaza Claro v. Centro Movil Milenium*; J. Rinkes, "De consument als zwakke partij", *Ars Aequi* 2009, 381–382; E. Swaenepoel, *Toetsing van het contractueel evenwicht*, Antwerp, Intersentia, 2011, 24–25.

[105] ECJ C-32/12, *Soledad Duarte Hueros v. Autociba SA and Automoviles Citroën Espana SA.*

[106] G. Straetmans, "Some thoughts on the future European consumer acquis", *EBLR* 2009, 429; G. Straetmans, "Het Europese consumentenacquis: genese en toekomstblik" in J. Meeusen, G. Straetmans and A.-M. Van den Bossche (eds.), *Het EG-consumentenacquis: nu en straks*, Antwerp, Intersentia, 2009, 8; J. Stuyck and G. Straetmans, *Financiële diensten en de consument. Bankdiensten – Consumentenkrediet – Hypothecair krediet – Verzekeringen – Handelspraktijken volgens het Belgisch en Europees recht*, Antwerp, Kluwer, 1994, 30 and 272–273.
Cf. also P. Rott, "'Responsible lending' – Vorsorge statt Nachsorge?" in G.M. Peer (ed.), *Die soziale Dimension des Zivilrechts – Zivilrecht zwischen Liberalismus und sozialer Verantwortung: Salzburger Tagung 10. bis 13. Sept. 2003*, Munich, Boorberg, 2004, 181–182.

who, once he has the correct information, can make a free and informed decision.[107] Opposite, stands the weak consumer or the consumer who is particularly vulnerable in certain situations.[108]

Harmonisation method as criterion – Unberath and Johnston link the rationale of the double consumer image to the chosen harmonisation method.[109] In case of negative harmonisation they see a certain reluctance of the Court of Justice to accept national restrictions on fundamental freedoms. On the contrary, when positive harmonisation is at hand, the Court of Justice gives a broader significance and interpretation to (the protection of the consumer in) the European directives. They conclude that the consumer image in negative harmonisation is more limited than in positive harmonisation.[110] Some authors stress, though, European consumer law in practice is not as black or white as this criterion might suggest this split. Indeed, the Court of Justice does not always give a broad interpretation to European directives.[111]

IV. Proposal for a multi-layered consumer image

4.1. Notion of the 'Multi-Layered Consumer'

Going further... – To get out of this impasse, there are *grosso modo* two options.[112] We can either join one (majority) group or depart from it and propose our own working hypothesis. As the title of this chapter suggests, we choose the latter option. This does not mean that we reject the current consumer notion and image. They have their merits and are still the reference point for the current legislation, doctrine and jurisprudence. We would like to build further on it. The truth lies indeed somewhere in the middle.

Consumer Notion – Firstly, we want to address shortly the consumer notion. We prefer to limit the consumer notion to any natural person acting primarily for non-

107 Examples: ECJ C-210/96, *Gut Springenheide GmbH and Rudolf Tusky v. Oberkreisdirektor des Kreises Steinfurt*; ECJ C-126/91, *Schutzverband gegen Unwesen in der Wirtschaft eV. v. Yves Rocher GmbH*; ECJ C-238/89, *Pall Corp. v. P.J. Dahlhausen and Co.*; ECJ 362/88, *GB Inno SA v. Confédération du Commerce luxembourgeois ASBL*; ECJ 178/84, *Commissie v. Bondsrepubliek Duitsland (Reinheitsgebot).*

108 Example: ECJ 382/87, *Criminal proceeding v. R. Buet and SARL Educational Business Services*; J. Stuyck and G. Straetmans, *Financiële diensten en de consument. Bankdiensten – Consumentenkrediet – Hypothecair krediet – Verzekeringen – Handelspraktijken volgens het Belgisch en Europees recht*, Antwerp, Kluwer, 1994, 39.

109 H. Unberath and A. Johnston, "The Double-Headed Approach of the ECJ concerning Consumer Protection", *CMLR* 2007, 1281.

110 H. Unberath and A. Johnston, "The Double-Headed Approach of the ECJ concerning Consumer Protection", *CMLR* 2007, 1281–1282.

111 J. Stuyck, "Setting the scene" in H.-W. Micklitz, J. Stuyck, E. Terryn and D. Droshout (eds.), *Cases, Materials and Text on Consumer Law. Ius Commune Casebooks for the Common Law of Europe*, Portland, Hart, 2010, 39 with reference to ECJ C-402/03, *Skov AEg v. Bilka Lavprisvarehus A/S and Bilka Lavprisvarehus A/S v. Jette Mikkelsen and Michael Due Nielsen.*

112 Or as T. Hobbes wrote it in 1651: *"by this it appears how necessary it is for any man that aspires to true Knowledge, to examine the Definitions of former Authors; and either to correct them, when they are negligently set down; or to make them himselfe"* (T. Hobbes, *Leviathan*, London, Andrew Crooke, 1651, 17).

business purposes. Thus we use the traditional consumer notion, but we do not follow its restrictive interpretation. In addition, we keep the policy choice open to provide in certain situations a similar protection to other weaker contracting parties, such as SMEs.

Our proposal: the 'multi-layered consumer' – Our proposed consumer image is somewhat innovative. Starting from the situation-specific nature of consumer law, it seems logical that the consumer image may change in function of specific situations in which the consumer finds himself. For some consumers it is sufficient to provide information, for others the way the information is received is equally important, while for some other consumers it is necessary for the legislator to intervene in the substantive contract equilibrium between the rights and obligations of the contracting parties resulting from the (credit) agreement. It is also of great importance to define the situations in which we will apply our model. This study does not claim that the model should be used as a working hypothesis and the basis for all legal rules on consumer (contracts). According to us, it may offer advantages in consumer credit law. We propose a three-part model and introduce the image of the 'Informed Consumer', the 'Advised Consumer' and the 'Weak Consumer'.[113]

The consumer image of the first category (the *'Informed Consumer'*) corresponds to the consumer image developed by the Court of Justice in its jurisprudence on the internal market and unfair commercial practices. Legal provisions for this category are to based upon the image of the average informed, observant and circumspect consumer who is searching information and can give an informed consent afterwards. Although he is formally free to enter into agreements, he nonetheless is in a weaker bargaining position as a consumer due to the initial information asymmetry. Providing correct and complete information is sufficient for him to take a correct and rational decision.[114] The legal provisions that are to be introduced for this category of consumers, ensure the substantive contractual freedom of the consumer. It is important that the information

[113] An impetus for diversification among consumers, we also found by M. De Muynck, "Credit Cards, Overdraft Facilities and European Consumer Protection. A Blank Cheque for Unfairness?", *ERPL* 2010, 1223–1225; I. Ramsay, "Regulation of consumer credit" in G. Howells, I. Ramsay, T. Wilhelmsson and D. Kraft (eds.), *Handbook of research on international consumer law*, Cheltenham, Edward Elgar, 2010, 387; G. Straetmans, "Het Europese consumentenacquis: genese en toekomstblik" in J. Meeusen, G. Straetmans and A.-M. Van den Bossche (eds.), *Het EG-consumentenacquis: nu en straks*, Antwerp, Intersentia, 2009, 26–28.

[114] In Germany we find a practical example. ING Diba AG offers on its website a comparison of its various products. The standard information offered consists of two parts. Firstly, the consumer obtains a schematic comparison of the key elements of the credit agreement. More specifically: the amount of credit ("*Kreditbetrag*"), the amount of the repayment and the repayment terms ("*Rate*"), the retributive interest rate ("*Sollzins*") and Annual Charge Rate ("*Effektivzins*") are published. However, the consumer can also, via a link, find out *in concreto* which credit agreement, in practice would best suit him. One speaks of a "*interaktiver Kredit-Check*". The consumer chooses, but at the end of the electronic questionnaire ING Diba indicates what type of its credit agreements *in concreto* is appropriate or not. Both options are offered to the consumer searching for a consumer credit agreement *sensu stricto* and for a mortgage loan. Cf. https://www.ing-diba.de/kredit/ (situation June 11, 2013).

provided is accurate, realistic[115] and sufficient and allows for comparison between creditors.[116]

The consumer image of the second category (the 'Advised Consumer') is based on the condition precedent that a consumer does not always (fully) read or understand the information he receives. This consumer must receive additional personal advice before entering into a credit agreement. Based on the information obtained and the personal advice provided he can freely conclude a credit agreement. For this category of consumers the rules still ensure a substantive freedom of contract. However, they impose an additional mandatory information requirement to the creditor.

The consumer image of the third and last category (the 'Weak Consumer') is partly based on the results of behavioural economic studies that show that some consumers need permanent assistance. They can not take any rational decision, because they are financially incapable of doing so. Indeed any kind of information or advice here seems inefficient from a cost-benefit analysis. This group includes also the consumer who is, due to his weak financial situation, in a vulnerable position. For this group, the legal provisions must not only guarantee the substantive contractual freedom of the consumer, they should also ensure that there exists a (substantive) contract equilibrium, for example through the introduction of legal interest rate caps, rules on compound interest, default interest rate caps, etc.[117] Here the corrective function of consumer contract law is the greatest. The legislator and the judge restrict the freedom of choice of the parties the most. Consequently one should be careful when classifying certain types of consumers into this category. Consumer contract law gets here, after all, a redistributive function.

4.2. *Applicability in consumer credit legislation*

Applicability in consumer credit legislation – After defining our three categories, we examine how the creditor can classify *in concreto* a consumer into one of the categories. The answer looks simple. The creditor, whether he grants credit to a professional borrower

115 Here we mean that the information offered, and perhaps especially vis-à-vis advertising, concerning certain services grossly corresponds with the reality. For example, one should not advertise (see Article 5, §1 WCK) for a mortgage credit for residential property which is repayable within five years. The information offered must allow the consumer to estimate the full scope and realistic and effective duration of its commitments.

116 Cf.: a study shows the wealthy customers attach great importance to the quality of the advices of their banker (the study related mainly to investments, current and savings accounts). Information on the offered product stands for them centrally. Cf. W. Sinn, D. Vater, D. Lubig and M. Kasch, *Was Bankkunden wirklich wollen*, Munich/Zürich, Bain and Company Germany/Switzerland Inc., 2012, 18–19.

117 EESC, "Opinion of the European Economic and Social Committee on the Proposal for a Directive of the European Parliament and of the Council on the harmonisation of the laws, regulations and administrative provisions of the Member States concerning credit for consumers", *Pb.C.* September 30, 2003, 4, No. 2.2.4.5.; S. Brown, "Using the law as a usury law: definitions of usury and recent developments in the regulation of unfair charges in consumer credit transactions", *J.B.L.* 2011, 102.

or to a consumer, shall examine his creditworthiness. He may use the results of this assessment to classify the prospective borrower into one of the categories. We introduce a 'know-your-borrower'-rule.[118] Thus the creditor is able to restrict his operational costs, since he is either way obliged to perform a creditworthiness assessment.[119] We only propose to add *de lege ferenda* to this credit assessment a suitability assessment. In addition to assessing the financial strength, the creditor would question the prospective borrower about the content, scope, ... and expectations about the credit agreement offered. On this basis, the creditor, could classify the (prospective) borrower into one of the three categories. The criteria used to categorise shall be made transparent and public. The borrower must be able to ascertain these criteria. Secondly, it is equally important that a court can review *a posteriori* the classification.[120] In addition, the supervisory authority for financial institutions could play a role in the approval and review of the criteria used by the creditor.

Critical evaluation of the model – New proposals must be received and evaluated critically. Although we argue below that the new model is not earth-shattering, we still try to refute some possible criticisms. Following three questions arise:

- How does the trend to extend consumer protection to other weaker contracting parties – such as SMEs – suit in the proposed model?
- Does the model not introduce an assessment *in concreto*? Do we not incur the risk of making the consumer image status dependent?
- How does this model relate to the proportionality rule[121] in consumer law?

An attentive reader will already have got some flashes of recognition. Our proposed Multi-Layered Consumer Image and its implementation sounds like to the 'know-your-client'-rule and the three categories of investor protection. The proposed model is based on intra- and interdisciplinary (legal) comparison. Intradisciplinary, because it falls back to the legal provisions on investor protection. From the MiFID legislation, we learn among others that the degree of the restrictions on freedom of contract of the financial institution do not necessarily have to be the same for every investor.[122] Financial law already knows for some time the possibility to fill in the rules of conduct, the information requirements applicable to certain institutions, etc. differently depending on the category

118 J. Köndgen, "Policy Responses to Credit Crises: Does the Law of Contract Provide an Answer?" in S. Grundmann and Y.M. Atamer (eds.), *Financial Services, Financial Crisis and General European Contract Law. Failure and Challenges of Contracting*, Kluwer Law International, Alphen a/d Rijn, 2011, 50.

119 Either because of an explicit legal provision imposes on him the requirement or because he brings his liability (*culpa in contrahendo*) compromised.

120 The judge of peace is indeed competent *ratione materiae* to deal with cases concerning consumer credit agreements.

121 J. Drexl, *Die wirtschaftliche Selbstbestimmung des Verbrauchers*, Tübingen, Mohr Siebeck, 1998, 362–363; E. Swaenepoel, *Toetsing van het contractueel evenwicht*, Antwerp-Cambridge, Intersentia, 2011, 531–532.

122 S. Grundmann and Y.M. Atamer, "European Contract Law and Banking Contracts after the Financial Crisis: Challenges for Contracting and Market Transactions" in S. Grundmann and Y.M. Atamer (eds.), *Financial Services, Financial Crisis and General European Contract Law. Failure and Challenges of Contracting*, Kluwer Law International, Alphen a/d Rijn, 2011, 15.

of persons entitled to protection.[123] In this paper we proposed to extend the creditworthiness assessment by the creditor with a suitability test. The creditor must *de lege lata* examine each prospective borrower on its financial capacity. *De lege ferenda* he should also ascertain the financial capability of the prospective borrower.

Interdisciplinary we rely on certain behavioural economic studies that show that the group of consumers is not a homogeneous one. These studies show that some consumers are more susceptible to misleading information and are more financially incompetent than others.[124] The group of consumers is too heterogeneous to enact rules based on one consumer image. A diversifying approach is more desirable.

The consumer credit law *sensu stricto* allows a certain degree of diversification of consumers. Article 5 (6) Directive 2008/48/EC obliges a creditor to provide to the consumer appropriate explanations so that the latter can make an informed decision. The appropriate explanation involves more than delivering a information leaflet with mere general information on interest rates, etc. It is an obligation to give personal explanations. Opposite to our model article 5 (6) Directive 2008/48/EC suggests an assessment *in concreto* of each individual consumer, while our model consists of three abstract categories that determine the degree of legal or judicial restrictions/interference in the freedom of contract (of the creditor). However our model is not necessarily in contradiction with article 5 (6) Directive 2008/48/EC. We do not require the creditor to give each consumer a personalised appropriate explanation. In our model the personal appropriate explanations are limited to the second (and third) category of consumers. We only use the discretionary power left by the European legislator to the Member States to fill in the appropriate explanations depending on *"the specific circumstances of the situation in which the credit agreement is offered, the person to whom it is offered and the type of credit offered"*.[125] Although we use an abstract category that introduces a seemingly *per se* obligation to give personalised advice to certain categories of consumers. It is always up to the creditor to determine *in concreto* which consumer falls under which category. It remains, albeit indirectly, an assessment *in concreto* whether a consumer needs a personalised appropriate explanation.[126] Thus, it does not go further than Directive 2008/48/EC. Although the content of the information and advice

123 Article 45, §2, paragraph 2 WFT; L. Van Cauter, "De bescherming van de financiële consument – Een overzicht van het regelgevend kader" in H. Daems, I. De Meuleneere, R. Feltkamp, C. Houssa and R. Steennot (eds.), *Bescherming van de consument in het financieel recht. La protection du consommateur en droit financier*, Limal/Antwerp, Anthemis/Intersentia, 2012, 26.

124 Cf. also T. Van Dyck, *De geharmoniseerde prospectusplicht. Kritische analyse van de geharmoniseerde prospectusplicht in de Prospectusrichtlijn 2003/71/EG en haar omzettingswetten in België, Nederland, Frankrijk, het Verenigd Koninkrijk en Duitsland*, Bruges, die Keure, 2010, 77.

125 Article 5(6) *in fine* Directive 2008/48/EG (own emphasis added).

126 de Patoul indicates *"plus le candidat emprunteur est expérimenté et familier avec l'opération qu'il s'apprête à conclure, moins l'on se montrera exigeant quant à l'étendue des informations que le prêteur devra lui communiquer"*. F. de Patoul, "Le devoir d'information et de conseil du prêteur" in C. Biquet-Mathieu and E. Terryn (eds.), *Hypothecair krediet – Crédit hypothécaire*, Bruges, die Keure, 2010, 330. Cf. also Liège 28 January 2010, *TBBR* 2010, 475; Brussels 10 September 1987, *TBH* 1989, 67; Kh. Ghent 11 April 1997, *TBH* 1998, 832; Kh. Brussels 4 October 1988, *JT* 1989, 456.

requirements are set *in abstracto*, a specific consumer is not blindly assigned to one category. Firstly, there will be a thorough *in concreto* assessment per individual consumer by the creditor. Based on the concrete result the consumer will be categorised into one of the categories. So there is no general *per se* obligation to provide advice or information to each consumer, but only for those consumers belonging to a category requiring additional protection. Also under article 5(6) Directive 2008/48/EC, these consumers shall – even without categorisation in our model – obtain appropriate explanations to make an informed decision. The model can further absorb the rapid changes in the field of credit services without having to adapt each time the legislation.[127] The basic principles of the model, i.e. only provide information, appropriate explanations and information or permanent substantive advice and support where needed, are independent of concrete products. Finally, as clarified above vis-à-vis investor protection, it is clear the multi-layered consumer image is not earth-shattering. Let us now discuss the above-mentioned three critical questions.

Firstly, it is clear that a multi-layered consumer image does not prevent the level of consumer protection provided to be extended to other weaker contracting parties such as SMEs. The legislator may subject professional borrowers to the same 'know-your-borrower' rule and offer them a similar protection.[128]

The criticism that a multi-layered consumer image could degenerate into a 'status dependent' consumer image dividing consumers into compartments according to their education, their social origin, etc., is unjustified. An abstract distinction between categories of consumers does not stigmatise the individual consumer in a concrete situation. It also does not necessarily lead to social exclusion. To make a quip, a lawyer is not necessarily an Informed Consumer. Each consumer will have to demonstrate *in concreto* during the creditworthiness/suitability assessment his level of financial capability.[129] Moreover, *de lege lata* courts take already into account the specific situation of the (contracting) parties. Through the moderating effect of good faith, the court can indeed take into account in its assessment the weaker bargaining power of a particular contracting party.

The multi-layered consumer image also takes into consideration the subsidiarity and proportionality requirement. Under these requirements, preference should be given to the least intrusive legal measure and the least intrusive judicial action.[130] For the first

127 De Muynck argues for *"intelligent, multi-layered regulation"*. M. De Muynck, "Credit Cards, Overdraft Facilities and European Consumer Protection. A Blank Cheque for Unfairness?", *ERPL* 2010, 1217.

128 Directive 2008/48/EC also does not preclude an extension of the scope *ratione personae* of the legislation of the member states of. Consideration 10 Directive 2008/48/EC allows Member States to extend their scope to other areas. This may be B2B credit agreements or, more limited, credit agreements to SMEs, start-ups, etc.

129 E.g.: when the 'Know-your-borrower'-rule suggests that the relevant consumer usually takes the correct decisions, and that he needs only some information about specific types of credit, he can still be placed in the category of 'Informed consumer' or at least in the category of the 'Advised Consumer'. The lender may be assured that the consumer concerned, after he has received the necessary generic or personalised information respectively, can take the rational credit decision.

130 J. Drexl, *Die wirtschaftliche Selbstbestimmung des Verbrauchers*, Tübingen, Mohr Siebeck, 1998, 450–452; R. Steennot, "De impact van het privaat financieel recht op de wilsautonomie, de

two categories of consumers the mandatory information requirements and cooling-off periods should, in principle, be sufficient to ensure that the substantive contractual freedom is assured. For the Weak Consumer, the legislator and the courts should possibly also provide for a substantive assessment of the contract equilibrium.

V. Conclusion

Substantive rules in consumer credit legislation – Legislators introduce more and more restrictions on the freedom of contract of the stronger contracting party. In (consumer) credit legislation this trend was already present for a longer time. The lack of information and the weaker bargaining position resulting of the financial necessity to buy goods or services on credit is indeed more robustly present in (consumer) credit law. Most restrictions safeguard not only the substantive contractual freedom of the consumer, but they want to prevent that the consumer enters into a negative debt spiral (e.g.: rules of compound interest) or that he has to pay an unreasonable and unbalanced price for obtaining credit (e.g.: prohibition of usury interest and legal interest rate caps[131]). In addition to these legal restrictions courts may also interfere in the contract equilibrium of the parties in case of unforeseen changes in circumstances. He may grant a deferred payment or other repayment facilities. These legal and judicial reviews mostly are in favour of or are introduced to protect the consumer. It is justified by the lack of information and his weaker bargaining position.

Multi-layered Consumer Image – We introduced a multi-layered consumer image. Its goal is to distribute as efficiently as possible the need for legal consumer protection. Behavioural law and economics indicated that not all consumers are in need of the same level of protection. For some mandatory information requirements is sufficient. For others advise or even substantive consumer protection, such as interest rate caps, are to be adopted. Our goal was to set up the legal framework. We strongly recommend economists to pick up this idea and enrol empirical studies to (i) analyse if the multi-layered consumer image can be a workable hypothesis in consumer credit law and (ii) provide empirical data that should enable legislators, courts, creditors… fine-tuning the legal framework in practice. Economists could empirically analyse if the multi-layered consumer image maximises the cooperative surplus of the contracting parties.[132]

contractvrijheid en het consensualisme", www.law.ugent.be/fli/wps/pdf/WP2010-15.pdf, 2010, 37; J. Stuyck, "Consumentenbescherming in tijden van economische crisis", *Jura Falc.* 2009–2010, 327.
Th. Wilson, N. Howell and G. Sheehan, "Protecting the Most Vulnerable in Consumer Credit Transactions", *JconsP* 2009, 134, referring to a proposal from 2008 by the Australian "Productivity Commission" to give layered information to consumers.

131 K. Byttebier and M. Flamée, "Het vraagstuk van ethisch financieren toegepast op de interestheffing mede vanuit een elementair rechtshistorisch perspectief. Stof voor een morele uitweg uit een wereld in (financiële) crisis" in X (ed.), *Een leven van inzet. Liber amicorum Michel Magits*, Mechelen, Kluwer, 2013, 33; H. de With and A. Nack, "Der Moderne Schuldturm", *ZRP* 1984, 3; J.M. Keynes, *A General Theory of Employment, Interest and Money*, London, Macmillan, 1936, 350.

132 C. Camerer, S. Issacharoff, G. Loewenstein, T. O'Donoghue and M. Rabin, "Regulation for Conservatives: Behavioral Economics and the Case for 'Asymmetric Paternalism'", *U. Pa. L. Rev.* 2003, 1236–1237.

C.E. (Carien)
de Jager*

'WHO ARE YOU, INVESTOR: MR. SPOCK, CAPTAIN KIRK OR SOMEWHERE IN BETWEEN?'

A Behavioural Finance Exploration and Suggestions for Better Informing Investors about Complex Investment Products Through Information Disclosure

I. Introduction

Star Trek is a well-known science fiction television show as well as a popular movie franchise. One consistent theme pervading Star Trek is embodied by two men, Mr. Spock and Captain Kirk. Both of these characters make important decisions about for instance the survival of the star ship Enterprise and its crew. In these situations, Mr. Spock is very rational and almost always emotionless, basing decisions on facts and probabilities. In contrast, Captain Kirk makes decisions based on his emotions and his 'gut feeling'.

In the financial markets, investors have to make decisions on a daily basis as well. However, a recent study concluded that around 60% of sales in complex financial products across the EU may be deemed unsuitable for consumers.[1] The 'Woekerpolis' and 'Effectenlease' scandals in the Netherlands are just two of the many examples of the mis-selling of financial products to consumers.[2] In its efforts to prevent these kinds of practices in the future and to restore trust in the financial markets, the European Union heavily relies upon information disclosure by financial institutions.[3]

* PhD researcher and Lecturer at the Department of Private Law and Notarial Law at the Faculty of Law, University of Groningen.

1 Commission Staff Working Document 'Impact Assessment Accompanying the Proposal for a Regulation of the European Parliament and of the Council on key information documents for investment products', SWD(2012) 187, p. 22; Synovate 2011.

2 These products allowed retail investors to purchase securities with borrowed money (Effectenlease) and life insurances (Woekerpolis) with an investment element. Commissie Geschillen Aandelenlease 2004; Autoriteit Financiële Markten 2008. About the miss-selling of financial products to consumers across the EU: Moloney 2012, p. 176; Ferran 2012, p. 249.

3 See about the underlying ideology of information disclosure Moloney 2010, p. 53 ff.

The retail investment market is dominated by so-called 'Packaged Retail Investment and Insurance Products' (PRIIPS). A PRIIP could be described as:

> *"...a product where the amount payable to the investor is exposed to fluctuations in the market value of assets or pay-outs from assets, through a combination or wrapping of those assets, or other mechanisms than a direct holding."*[4]

In April 2014, the European Parliament and the Council reached an agreement on a mandatory Key Information Document (KID) for those kinds of investment products.[5] Recently, the Council of the European Union has adopted a Regulation regarding an information document designed specifically for non-professional investors (so-called retail investors).[6] The two main objectives of this document are:[7]

1. Improving the *comprehensibility* of financial products;
2. Improving the *comparability* of financial products.

The focus on information disclosure through such a document as an instrument of retail investor protection suggests a belief that retail investors will make better choices if they are provided with information about financial products. As the European Commission states, such documents serve as 'the foundation' for investment decisions by retail investors.[8]

Research in the field of Behavioural Finance, a science that uses psychological and sociological concepts to describe and analyse both market 'behaviour' and behaviour of (financial) market participants, suggests that the link between information disclosure and informed and optimal decision-making is not always clear.[9] Suboptimal consumer decisions arise from a tendency in people to act irrationally. This irrational financial

4 Commission Staff Working Document 'Impact Assessment Accompanying the Proposal for a Regulation of the European Parliament and of the Council on key information documents for investment products', SWD(2012) 187, p. 32.

5 European Commission, *Proposal for a Regulation of the European Parliament and of the Council on key information documents for investment products*, Strasbourg: 2 July 2012 (COM(2012) 352 final) and European Parliament 2014.
The introduction of an information document for consumers of investment products is not a new phenomenon. Examples of such information documents at a national level are the financial information leaflet for complex financial products (*Financiële Bijsluiter)* used in the Netherlands, a Key Features Document for 'packaged products' used in the United Kingdom and a Product Information Sheet (*Produktinformationsblatt*) in Germany.

6 The European Parliament and the Council, *Regulation of the European Parliament and of the Council on key information documents for packaged retail and insurance-based investment products (PRIIPs)*, Brussels: 24 October 2014. The articles and recitals referred to in the text are part of this Regulation.

7 European Parliament and the Council 2014, recital 15,.

8 European Commission, *Proposal for a Regulation of the European Parliament and of the Council on key information documents for investment products*, Strasbourg: 2 juli 2012 (COM(2012) 352 final), p. 16. In other words on p. 15: *"Retail investors should be provided with the information necessary for them to take an informed investment decision and compare different investment products..."*

9 Shiller 1999. Behavioural Finance is a positive science (as opposed to normative science).

behaviour results from 1) personal factors, such as (the lack of) financial knowledge and cognitive limitations, 2) social factors such as culture, the complexity of the financial market and financial products and 3) mental shortcuts such as biases and heuristics.[10]

This chapter will focus on the mental shortcuts that may result in suboptimal financial decisions. Insights from Behavioural Finance are especially valuable in this regard. They allow for a greater predictability of suboptimal investors' behaviour, since this behaviour is caused by certain heuristics (mental shortcuts) and biases (errors caused by these mental shortcuts). Despite individual differences, these heuristics and biases are common among all investors.

This chapter, which is meant as a first exploration of the subject, aims to examine 1) to what extent the proposed KID is likely to be effective in achieving its objectives, 2) whether it needs to be improved and 3) if so, in what way. First, the focus is on the proposal for a Key Information Document for PRIIPS (section 2). Section 3 examines the so-called 'normative model', which describes the mechanisms behind human rational behaviour. Section 4 will focus on the 'positive model', which describes how people actually behave.[11] Finally, section 5 will explore ways in which the proposed information document could be adjusted in order to improve EU consumers' investment decisions.

II. A new information document for retail investors: a brief overview

Investing in the financial markets was once a privilege for the fortunate few. Now, it has become an essential part of EU citizens' everyday life. Financial services, such as loans, mortgages, investments and insurance facilitate citizens' full participation in the economy, enabling them to plan for the long term and protecting them from unforeseen changes in circumstances. A single retail market, which has been the overall EU objective in the last decade, is also of great significance for the EU economy.[12]

The retail investment market is dominated by PRIIPs. These products, taken together, make up 10 trillion Euros in the European financial markets.[13] PRIIPs have four characteristics. They:[14]

- combine exposures to multiple underlying assets;
- are designed to deliver capital accumulation over a medium- to long-term investment period;
- entail a degree of investment risk;
- are usually marketed directly to retail investors.

10 Capuano and Ramsay 2011, p. 77–167.
11 Given the size of this chapter, only a selection of the existing heuristics and biases can be discussed. For more details, see section 4.
12 White Paper on Financial Services 2005–2010, COM (2005) 629; Green Paper on Retail Financial Services, COM (2007) 226; Initiatives in the Area of Retail Financial Services: Accompanying Document to the Communication from the Commission to the European Parliament, the Council, the European Economic and Social Committee and the Committee of the Regions (COM, 2007) 724 final.
13 European Commission 2014, p. 1.
14 European Parliament and the Council 2014, Article 4.

These complex financial products can, broadly speaking, be categorised into four groups: investment funds, insurance-based investment products, retail structured securities and structured term deposits.[15]

The introduction of a KID aims to increase the comprehensibility and comparability of PRIIPs by the creation of a standardised and readily understandable document for retail investors containing information about the main features of an investment product, such as the costs and risks involved.[16] The KID will answer a standard set of questions, such as: 'What is this product?', 'What are the risks and what could I get in return?', 'What happens if [the name of the PRIIP manufacturer] is unable to pay out?, and 'What are the costs'.[17] The proposed information document is designed for the retail investor rather than the professional. It should help them make a more informed decision on whether a financial product is suitable for them.

PRIIPs manufacturers should draw up the information document and publish it on their website before the product can be sold to retail investors.[18] In addition, retail investors must receive the KID before a binding agreement is made.[19] To promote comparability, every document will have the same structure and should be drawn up in a standardised format.[20] It must be an accurate, fair, clear, and not-misleading document.[21] Furthermore, the KID must be a short document with a maximum of three sides of A4-sized paper.[22]

The details of the information to be included in the KID and the presentation of this information will be further harmonised by means of so-called Level 2 instruments, which are delegated acts.[23] These instruments must:

> "*...take into account existing and ongoing research on consumer behaviour, including results from testing the effectiveness of different ways of presenting information with consumers.*"[24]

However, up until now, very little research has been conducted into the way in which the provision of information to investors by means of a short information document can be made effective. Existing research mostly concerns self-reporting with the investors' perception of understanding a document as the prime consideration, instead of the question whether the information is actually understood.[25] Besides, such research hardly

15 European Commission 2014, p. 1.
16 European Parliament and the Council 2014, recital 15.
17 European Parliament and the Council 2014, Article 8.
18 European Parliament and the Council 2014, Article 5 paragraph 1.
19 European Parliament and the Council 2014, Article 13 paragraph 1.
20 European Parliament and the Council 2014, recital 17.
21 European Parliament and the Council 2014, Article 6 paragraph 1.
22 European Parliament and the Council 2014, Article 6 paragraph 4.
23 European Parliament and the Council 2014, Article 8 paragraph 5.
24 European Parliament and the Council, recital 17. It is striking that article 8, paragraph 5 merely provides that '*the capabilities of retail investors...*' need to be taken into account when developing draft regulatory technical standards. This formulation is less concrete.
25 See e.g. FSA 2003; IFF andYouGov 2009 and Millward Brown / Centrum 2004. The most relevant research in this context was done by Chater. Huck and Inderst 2010. However, this research has some limitations as well, see e.g. p. 298–299.

ever takes into account what is generally known about the ways in which investors read a text, understand it, and make decisions.[26] It also remains to be seen to what extent the results of existing research apply to the KID. Among others the wide geographic reach of this document, the fact that many different kinds of products are considered PRIIPs, and the complexity of these products could prevent this.

III. The normative model: *homo economicus*

According to Jeremy Bentham, a British philosopher, people seek the pursuit of pleasure and the avoidance of pain.[27] This idea is, to some extent, related to the basic assumption of the proposed information document. As already described, this document is primarily based on the assumption that investors act rationally and will attempt to maximise their utility by choosing the financial product with the highest monetary gains, just like Mr. Spock from Star Trek. In the ideal situation an investor takes into account all relevant information and in the end comes up with the best decision given the circumstances. In other words: such a rational investor is capable of making optimal investment decisions.

This idea is based on the normative model, which describes the assumed mechanisms behind human rational behaviour. Some characteristics of this normative model are:

a. Actively open-minded thinking: Openness to information that is not consistent with people's opinions or beliefs.
b. Probability theory: Applying mathematical and statistical rules to determine the probability of events to occur.[28]
c. Logic: A decision should be based on valid reasoning.[29]
d. Expected utility theory: Based on this theory the optimum action on a problem which involves risk[30] can be determined by calculating the utility of each possible outcome and multiply the outcomes by their probabilities.[31] Based on the results, people should choose the option with the highest expected utility.

Through the years, researchers have found that people often do not behave in accordance with the normative model. For example, Kahneman and Tversky introduced an

26 Chater, Huck and Inderst 2010 does take this into account.

27 Bentham 1789/2000, p. 14.

28 The classical definition of probability is e.g. described by Ash (2008, p. 1) as follows: "...*the probability of an event is the number of outcomes favourable to the event, divided by the total number of outcomes, where all outcomes are equally likely...*".

29 For example based on the Bayes' theorem, however, in practice people are prone to ignore the base rate, which is called 'base rate neglect', see Kahneman and Tversky 1973, p. 237–251.

30 In a risky situation, people know the possible outcomes and can assign a probability to each of these outcomes. In case of uncertainty, the possible outcomes are unknown or it is not possible to assign probabilities to known outcomes. Ackert and Deaves 2010 p. 6 en 7; Knight 1921, p. 19–20;.

31 See Bernouilli 1954; Hardman 2009, p. 66. The modern utility theory is developed by Neumann and Morgenstern: Neumann and Morgenstern 1944. The theory of expected value theory is closely connected to the expected utility theory. This theory says that a rational decision-maker should weigh the *value* of outcomes by their probability of outcomes.

alternative to expected utility theory, the so-called prospect theory.[32] Among others, according to prospect theory, people underweigh outcomes that are merely probable in comparison with outcomes that are obtained with certainty.[33] They also developed a modified version of this theory to explain decision making when uncertainty is involved, the cumulative prospect theory.[34] Furthermore, research shows that people use mental shortcuts which are not in line with the normative model. For example, the way in which information is framed influences how people make decisions. The next section focuses on these mental shortcuts.

IV. The positive model: *homo sapiens*

In 1974, Tversky and Kahneman gave a very detailed description of people's decision-making process in case of uncertainty:

> *"Many decisions are based on beliefs concerning the likelihood of uncertain events such as the outcome of an election, the guilt of a defendant, or the future value of the dollar. These beliefs are usually expressed in statements such as "I think that...," "chances are...," "it is unlikely that..." and so forth. Occasionally, beliefs concerning uncertain events are expressed in numerical form as odds or subjective probabilities. What determines such beliefs? How do people assess the probability of an uncertain event or the value of an uncertain quantity? (...) "...people rely on a limited number of heuristic principles which reduce the complex task of assessing probabilities and predicting values to simpler judgemental operations. In general, these heuristics are quite useful, but sometimes they lead to severe and systematic errors."*[35]

As follows from this passage, people use mental processes to reduce cognitive effort, especially when faced with complex problems, just like Captain Kirk from Star Trek. An increase in the complexity of a decision will increase the use of mental shortcuts, such as heuristics. These heuristics enable people to simplify matters and speed up the decision-making process. As a drawback, these mental shortcuts sometimes cause errors: biases.

In this section, various heuristics and biases will be described, more specifically the anchoring and adjustment heuristic, the recognition heuristic, the representativeness heuristic and the availability heuristic. Next, the following biases will be examined:

32 Kahneman and Tversky 1979; Tversky and Kahneman 1992. However, prospect theory is not 'the final word'. Other alternatives to expected utility have been produced over the years. Amongst others, Allais rebutted one of the assumptions of expected utility theory, Savage's sure-thing principle (Savage 1954) by the Allais paradox: a prospect choice problem which is first proposed by Allais: Allais 1953a; Allais 1953b. Furthermore, Bernouilli described a game, the so-called 'St. Petersburg paradox' which shows that the Expected Value Theory must be wrong: Bernouilli 1954. Furthermore, despite the fact that prospect theory has been the prominent behavioural theory, there is also criticism, see amongst others Hogarth and Reder 1986. Despite this criticism, most results of experiments are consistent with prospect theory.

33 Kahneman and Tversky 1979, p. 263.

34 Kahneman and Tversky 1992. Later, this theory was combined with support theory resulting in a two-stage model: Tversky and Koehler 1994; Fox and Tversky 1998. See also Fox and See 2003.

35 Tversky and Kahneman 1974, p. 1124.

choice and information overload, framing effect, overconfidence bias, confirmation bias, ambiguity aversion and the salience bias. Naturally, this is a selection of heuristics and biases. In making this selection, among others it was taken into account that the market for PRIIPs is very complex, that decision making involves uncertainty, and that most investors have little or no knowledge of and experience with financial products.[36]

4.1. *Heuristics*

When people consider buying a product, for instance a financial product, they do this with a comparison or estimate in mind. This comparison or estimate is the anchor. When receiving new information about the product, investors need to adjust their initial expectations. The anchor, however, will interfere with this adjustment. Due to this *anchoring and adjustment heuristic*, investors sometimes fail to get a proper understanding of a financial product, since the anchor continuously influences their view of it.

The anchoring and adjustment heuristic can be illustrated by a more general example.[37] In an experiment, people were instructed to take a quick look at the following numbers:

$1 \times 2 \times 3 \times 4 \times 5 \times 6 \times 7 \times 8$

Then they were asked to estimate, without explicitly calculating, the final answer of the product of these eight numbers. Most of the participants used the first few numbers of the sequence as an anchor. Therefore, they unconsciously multiplied the first numbers in the sequence. The median answer was 512, whereas the true answer is 40.320. However, when the sequence was shown to them in the following way, the outcome was slightly better:

$8 \times 7 \times 6 \times 5 \times 4 \times 3 \times 2 \times 1$

Since the first numbers, and therefore the first steps of multiplication, are higher in the first sequence than in the second one, the former expression is judged larger than the latter. As a result, the median answer people gave in the descending case was higher as well, namely 2250. It appeared that using the product of the first numbers as an anchor still led to insufficient adjustment.

The *recognition heuristic* is the mechanism that leads people to prefer a familiar object over an unfamiliar one.[38] As a result, investors may attach value to a financial product based on recognition and familiarity, which could lead to a suboptimal investment decision. It could also have the effect of making an investment product of a familiar company seem less risky in comparison with an investment product of an unfamiliar company. Furthermore, the recognition heuristic could give rise to *proximity bias*, which is a fear of the unknown leading to proximity driven investments where investments one feels close to are preferred. This bias has various subforms such as *home*

36 Nevertheless, other heuristics and biases can be relevant as well.

37 Tversky and Kahneman 1974.

38 Goldstein and Gigerenzer 2002.

bias, *local bias*, *own-company bias* and *own-industry bias*.[39] These biases cause investors to buy a financial product from a local, regional or national business. Therefore, greater gains from international diversification are lost.[40]

In the precontractual phase, an investor tries to assess for example the returns of a financial product. When judging probability, people are sometimes influenced by the *representativeness heuristic*:

> *"Representativeness is an assessment of the degree of correspondence between a sample and a population, an instance and a category, an act and an actor or, more generally, between an outcome and a model."*[41]

This heuristic could lead investors to assess the future performance of a financial product on the basis of its past performance.

Furthermore, Tversky and Kahneman have shown that judgments of frequency sometimes form the basis for estimating probabilities, the so-called *availability heuristic*:

> *"A person is said to employ the availability heuristic whenever he estimates frequency or probability by the ease with which instances or associations could be brought to mind. To assess availability it is not necessary to perform the actual operations of retrieval or construction. It suffices to assess the ease with which these operations could be performed, much as the difficulty of a puzzle or mathematical problem can be assessed without considering specific solutions."*[42]

One of the factors associated with this heuristic relevant to finance is imaginability, meaning that investors tend to perceive an investment as very risky when the risks involved are vividly presented.

4.2. *Biases*

In general, people prefer choice over no-choice, since keeping our options open could yield us with better outcomes. In this regard, the market for financial products is wonderful: a great number of strongly differing products is offered and this number and diversity keep increasing.[43]

39 French and Poterba 1991 (home bias), Huberman 2001; Seasholes and Zhu 2010 (local bias), Bernatzi et al. 2007 (own-company bias) and Døskeland and Hvide, 2011 (own-industry bias).

40 Baker and Nofsinger 2002, p. 101–102.

41 Tversky and Kahneman 1983, p. 295. Furthermore, Kahneman and Tversky wrote approximately a decade earlier: *"A person who follows this heuristic evaluates the probability of an uncertain event, or a sample, by the degree to which it is: (i) similar in essential properties to its parent population; and (ii) reflects the salient features of the process by which it is generated."* Kahneman and Tversky 1972, p. 431.

42 Tversky and Kahneman 1973, p. 208. Criticism of the availability heuristic see e.g. Betsch and Pohl 2002.

43 E.g. Commission Staff Working Document 'Impact Assessment Accompanying the Proposal for a Regulation of the European Parliament and of the Council on key information documents for investment products', SWD(2012) 187, p. 13 and 14.

However, research shows that more choice is not always better.[44] More specifically, people can face difficulties when they need to process a large amount of information. This could lead to confusion and decision avoidance induced by profusion of information or choices that is difficult to assimilate. This behaviour is known as *information overload* or *choice overload*.[45]

This bias is often studied with regard to 'menu choices'. In one study, a tasting booth with jam was set up inside a grocery store.[46] Two research assistants, dressed as store employees, invited passing customers to 'come and try our Wilkin and Sons jams'. On the table were either 6 flavours of jam (the limited-selection condition) or 24 different jams (extensive-choice condition). The displays were rotated hourly. The study demonstrated that people liked the idea of ample choice, which was confirmed by the fact that the table with 24 flavours of jam attracted larger crowds. Surprisingly, the table with 6 different jams led to the most sales. The results prove that whereas the provision of a great many choices may seem highly appealing to consumers, it can reduce their motivation to actually make a choice.[47]

Figure 1. Müller-Lyer illusion

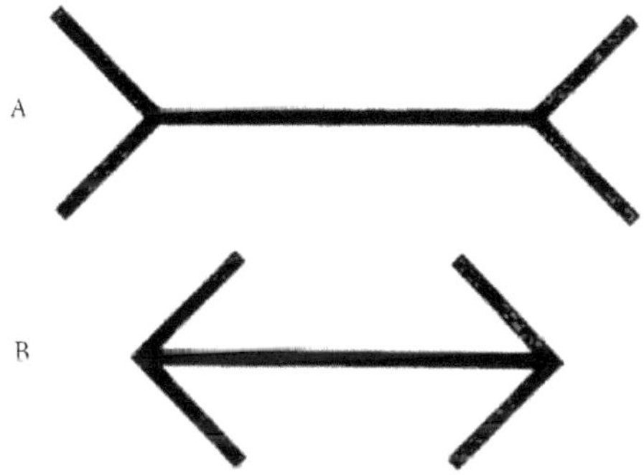

According to utility theory, only the outcomes and associated probabilities should determine which option is preferred by the decision maker. However, research shows that the way in which a question is asked to or a problem is mentally viewed by a decision maker has a strong impact on the answer given or the decision made (*framing effect*). The manner in which a decision scenario is described and presented is called *framing*. An analogy can be drawn between framing and visual perception, as shown by the *Müller-Lyer illusion* (figure 1).[48] Influenced by the context of the inward or outward arrows, most of the people agree that line A looks longer than line B. However, in fact both lines are the same length.

44 Iyengar and Lepper 2000, p. 995–1006.
45 Ackert and Deaves, p. 86 en 362.
46 Iyengar and Lepper 2000, p. 995–1006.
47 For several potential limitations to this initial field experiment see Iyengar and Lepper 2000, p. 997 en 998.
48 Müller-Lyer 1889.

Positive or negative framing of the same problem can have a substantial influence on people's decision-making process. A classical example illustrating this is the Asian Disease scenario.[49] In this study, people were asked to imagine that the U.S. was preparing for the outbreak of an unusual Asian disease, which was expected to kill 600 people. Two alternative programs for combating the disease were proposed, namely a survival frame and a mortality frame:

Survival Frame (N = 152)	Mortality Frame (N = 155)
– If Program A is adopted, 200 people will be saved. [72%] – If Program B is adopted, there is 1/3 probability that 600 people will be saved, and 2/3 probability that no people will be saved. [28%]	– If Program A is adopted 400 people will die. [22%] – If Program B is adopted there is 1/3 probability that nobody will die, and 2/3 probability that 600 people will die. [78%]

The majority of the respondents reading the survival frame preferred option A, which could be characterised as the riskless option as it guarantees that 200 people will be saved compared to the possibility of loss for option B which makes gambling less attractive. Despite the fact that the options in the mortality frame are exactly the same, except that the outcomes are framed in terms of lives that might be lost, respondents reading the mortality frame preferred the risky option.[50] This study illustrates that by changing the phrasing of information, people's preference pattern is changed. When the options are framed in terms of gains, decision makers tend to be *risk averse*, that is, they wish to hold on to what they already have and refuse to gamble. In contrast, if the frame presents the choice in terms of losses, participants tend to be *risk seeking*.

Furthermore, many people are overconfident. The so-called *overconfidence bias* takes account of this overconfidence and addresses the tendency for people to overestimate their knowledge, skills, abilities and the accuracy of their information.[51] Resulting from this, investment decisions are often based on conjecture and not on fundamental value. Research suggests that overconfidence in connection with personal-finance decision-making is widespread. For example, while 65% of the participants in a survey conducted in the United States thought they were very or highly knowledgeable about their personal finance, it turned out that many fell short on objective questions'.[52]

49 Tversky and Kahneman 1981. See also about choice in risky and riskless contexts: Kahneman and Tversky 1984.

50 Remarkably, McNeil et al. showed that not just laypeople but also experts were susceptible to framing: McNeil, Pauker, Sox and Tversky 1982. Furthermore, studies indicated that positive and negative framing is associated with different levels of cognitive processing, see among others: Dunegan 1993; Gonzales, Dana, Koshino and Just 2005; Payne, Bettman and Johnson 1993. An fMRI study of framing suggest a role for affective influences: De Martino, Kumaran, Seymour and Dolan 2006.

51 For instance, Alpert and Raiffa 1982 and Block and Harper 1991 about overconfidence in connection with the accuracy of people's estimations. However, some studies document 'underconfidence' (or the 'below average effect'), especially in complex situations, e.g. Kruger 1999. Research suggest that men are much more optimistic than women when it comes to key economic and financial performance indicators, see Jacobsen, Lee and Marquering 2008.

52 Willis 2008, p. 235–236, in which he refers to a press release on MoneyWise's website, *National MoneyWi$e Survey Shows Americans Are Not Financially Fit*, September 2005. Unfortunately, the

According to psychological literature, two factors contribute to overconfidence. First of all, the *illusion of knowledge* is related to the incorrect assumption that a large amount of information leads to a more informed decision, without taking account of the skills of the person interpreting the information.[53] Second, *illusion of control* refers to people's belief to have control over uncontrollable events. In other words, people underestimate the probability of unpleasant events. For instance, they often assume that a negative event, like losing a job, will not happen to them. Research shows that this illusion of control strengthens optimism.[54]

In addition, people have a tendency to search for information that confirms their own opinions and do not search for or ignore evidence that contradicts these beliefs, a phenomenon known as *confirmation bias*.[55] For instance, this could cause people to decide to invest in a financial product and ignore information that is not in favour of the investment.[56] Another consequence could be that investors overlook the risks a financial product entails. Furthermore, mental processing could alter key information in such a way that a specific investment decisions is favoured.

Furthermore, people tend to prefer risks that are known and predictable over unknown risks. This *ambiguity aversion* influences human behaviour in many ways.[57] This bias is demonstrated in the *Ellsberg paradox*.[58] In this classic demonstration, subjects preferred to bet that a red (or black) ball could be drawn from an urn with 50 red balls and 50 black balls to one in which they were only informed that the urn contained 100 balls but the number of black or red balls was unknown. This choice is driven by the fact that people prefer risk to uncertainty.

Finally, people's attention is more easily drawn to conspicuous objects rather than ordinary objects. This propensity is known as the *salience bias*. It has important implications for the way people should be informed about financial products. After all, by ignoring less prominent information, investors could overlook important parts of an information document like the KID. Instead, they will focus on the information that *looks* important.

V. The effectiveness of the Key Information Document and suggestions for improvement

In this section, the described heuristics and biases will be used to assess the likely effectiveness of information provision by means of the KID when it comes to the two main objectives of this information document: improving the comprehensibility and comparability of financial products. In addition, various recommendations for promoting this effectiveness are formulated. For the sake of clarity, the analysis of the effectiveness

report on which this press release is based, is not available on this website.

53 E.g. Willis 2008, p. 235.

54 Capuano and Ramsay 2011, p. 133.

55 This confirmation bias is one of the drivers of overconfidence.

56 Pompian 2006, p. 187–190.

57 See amongst others Ahn, Choi, Gale and Kariv 2013, which shows that individual differences exist as well.

58 Ellsberg 1961.

of the KID and the various recommendations will be described below on the basis of the two purposes of the KID. In this regard, it should be noted that, naturally, there will some overlap.

5.1. Comprehension of complex financial products

Various heuristics and biases appear to prevent investors from making better investment decisions through the KID. First, the fact that investors prefer products offered by a known or geographically close provider (recognition heuristic) raises the question whether the KID will actually be able to reduce this tendency and adequately inform investors. Conceivably, certain preferences of investors are hard to change by means of such a short information document.

Second, considering the representativeness heuristic, there is a risk that investors make the mistake of considering past performance of a financial product to be a good indicator for its future performance. However, this performance naturally depends on, among others, the development of the underlying assets of the financial product. It is therefore important to make clear to investors that the information in the KID is only helpful to a certain extent when it comes to predicting future returns. In this regard, it could be helpful for the Level 2 instruments to provide that the KID state that past performance offers no guarantees for future results.[59]

Furthermore, in the financial markets, investors are commonly flooded with information.[60] In combination with the large number of financial products this could lead to choice and information overload. Consequently, investors will tend to follow their gut feeling when purchasing a financial product, hardly make any use of financial knowledge and ignore information documents such as the KID. In addition, the KID will initially appear to investors to be yet another information document, and may therefore lead to a greater information overload. It is therefore important for the KID to actually contribute to a greater clarity regarding the financial product. If the KID outlines the most important information about a financial product in an intelligible way and in practice functions as an easy-to-read summary, it might reduce information overload. On the other hand, this could cause investors to perceive the financial product as easy to understand, which, among others, may have the effect of them not analysing the product sufficiently.

However, examination of existing short information documents shows that these often contain complicated language, which could lead consumers to having little incentive to actually make the effort to try to understand the document. Considering the complexity and large number of PRIIPs available this will likely to be a more prominent problem. It is therefore to be welcomed that the KID must be written in a concise manner on a maximum of three sides of A4-sized paper and composed in a language that is clear, succinct and comprehensible.[61] In this context, however, it should be noted that a similar rule also applies

[59] This is not required as yet. Such a statement is required for the Key Investor Information Document for UCITS: Article 15 paragraph 5, sub a Commission Regulation (EU) No 583/2010.

[60] See e.g. Willis 2008, p. 228–229.

[61] European Parliament and the Council 2014, Article 6 paragraph 4.

to various existing information documents.[62] Examination of these particular documents, however, shows that they also often contain complicated language and jargon. Therefore, this point also requires attention when it comes to the new information document.

The requirement that an explanatory statement emphasising this purpose be placed underneath the title is therefore to be welcomed.[63] However, research suggest that text above the title often goes unnoticed by investors, something which may be true for statements underneath the title as well.[64] Therefore, the practical usefulness of such a statement is questionable. Besides, before they come across this explanatory statement, investors already need to have taken the step to read the KID. Perhaps herein lies an important role for financial advisors.

However, despite the regulations and recommendations described above, the question remains whether the new information document will sufficiently motivate investors to try to really understand financial products and compare them. Especially, as already noted, since there is such a large number of financial products available. In the literature, Willis also argues that the availability of an overwhelming number of financial products contributes to people frequently not applying a rational decision-making strategy or financial knowledge.[65] The introduction of the KID will not cause a decrease in the number of these financial products, nor diminish their complexity. Instead, this complexity should be reduced by means of an information document. Not least in view of the information overload and choice overload it remains to be seen whether the KID will be effective in informing investors about financial products.

Fourth, the effectiveness of the KID when it comes to informing investors appears to be very much dependent on the ways in which the information is presented and phrased. This seems especially to be of importance considering the availability heuristic, framing effect and the ambiguity aversion bias. When, for instance, risks are presented vividly, investors often consider the risks to be higher than when this is not the case (availability heuristic). It is therefore important for those risks to be described in a similar manner in the various KIDs. After all, if one document describes the risks of a certain financial product much more realistically than another, this could lead to an incorrect assessment, i.e. an overestimation or underestimation of the risk. Standardisation of the ways in which for instance the risks and costs of a financial product are presented is therefore a good thing.[66] This also applies to the technical standards that will be developed regarding, among others, the methodology for the presentation of the risks and costs in the KID.[67] Standardisation could perhaps be promoted in practice by the provision of a KID

62 E.g. Article 78 paragraph 5 Directive 2009/65/EU.

63 This statement reads as follows: "*This document provides you with key information about this investment product. It is not marketing material. The information is required by law to help you understand the nature, risks, costs, potential gains and losses of this product and to help you compare it with other products.*" (European Parliament and the Council 2014, Article 8 paragraph 2).

64 Financial Services Authority 2003, p. 26.

65 Willis 2008, p. 228–229.

66 European Parliament and the Council 2014, Article 8.

67 European Parliament and the Council 2014, Article 8 paragraph 5.

generator. In the Netherlands, composers of a Financial Leaflet can use such a computer program for the creation of this document.

Besides, the framing effect also illustrates that positive or negative framing of information can have a substantial influence on people's decision making process. If, for instance, information is framed negatively, an investor will be more inclined to take risks. It is therefore vital for the information in the KID to be balanced, since, for instance an overemphasis on costs and losses can serve as a warning, but can also induce high-risk behaviour in investors. When used in practice, it will become clear if the information in the KID is balanced enough. In addition, considering the framing effect, merely prescribing which information needs to be included in the document and how the document needs to be designed will most likely not suffice. Differences in phrasing among various documents could lead to suboptimal decisions, and therefore defeat the purpose of the KID.[68] A certain standardisation of the phrasing of information is therefore recommended. The KID generator proposed above could probably also promote uniform phrasing the largest extent possible.

In addition, people tend to be ambiguity averse and choose risks they know over risks they do not know. This ambiguity aversion influences also the way in which investors take decisions. Considering this bias, it is also important for the description of risks in the various KIDs to take place in a similar manner and that the clarity level concerning risks is the same to the maximum extent possible. After all, if this is not the case, this can for instance lead to investors choosing a predictable greater risk over an unknown, but lower risk. At present, however, it is still unclear how this will be further harmonised through Level 2 instruments.

The KID is not expected to prevent investors from overestimating their own knowledge and being too optimistic about the future (overconfidence bias). Research demonstrates that overconfidence bias can be reduced by the provision of detailed information regarding the actual risks and consequences a certain decision entails.[69] It seems therefore desirable for the information in the KID to be sufficiently specific. This, however, is not likely to be achieved by means of the KID, since it is but a short document.[70] Findings of the examination of existing short information documents are consistent with this observation. Often, the information in these documents is very general with investors being referred to an advisor or other documents for further information. In the KID, it will be allowed to refer to other, more detailed documents, such as the Prospectus.[71] However, this means that consumers actually need to take the step to consult these other documents. Since many consumers overestimate their own financial knowledge as a result of overconfidence bias, it remains to be seen whether they are actually going to do this. Also relevant in this context is the fact that, when presented with choice, people tend to choose the option that needs little or no work.[72]

68 Whether such a case constitutes a misleading document in the sense of Article 6 European Parliament and Council 2014, is unknown.

69 Capuano and Ramsay 2011, p. 132–133.

70 European Parliament and the Council 2014, Article 6 paragraph 4.

71 European Parliament and the Council 2014, Article 6 paragraph 2.

72 Capuano and Ramsay 2011, p. 133.

Furthermore, the confirmation bias is expected to have an effect on the way investors perceive information provided by a short information document, as the KID. With regard to this bias, investors tend to select information which is consistent with their own wants, and ignore other information. In addition, mental processing could alter key information in such a way that a specific investment decision is favoured. Combined with the fact that this bias could also lead investors to overlook certain risks involved in a highly wanted financial product it is doubtful whether the KID will give investors a greater insight into a particular financial product. With regard to this bias as well, it seems to be desirable to promote the comparing of financial products by investors and to provide information which is sufficiently concrete in this regard. However, the latter will not expected to be possible, considering that the limited size of the KID leaves much room for interpretation on the side of the investor. As a consequence, the information could be interpreted in such a way, that it appears to be consistent with the investors' personal preferences and views, whereas this might not be the case objectively.

Considering the salience bias, important for the KID to be effective, is that it needs to *look* like an important document. In this regard, the document should be carefully designed and the content needs to be easy to understand. Among other things, this fits the requirements that the information in the KID must be accurate and clear.[73] The requirement that the KID be clearly distinguishable from marketing materials in this context is also important, as is the requirement that the KID state that it is, in fact, a legally required document.[74] However, regarding the latter requirement, it needs to be noted that, in order to notice this statement, consumers already need to have taken the step to read the KID. Therefore, it remains to be seen whether such a statement makes this document look sufficiently clear compared to other documents.[75] Furthermore, the requirement that the KID be clearly distinguishable from marketing material alone, does not suffice, since the KID also needs to look more *important* than promotional materials. This could perhaps be achieved by placing the logo of the *European Securities and Markets Authority* on it. Further research will have to show whether this will actually lead consumers to regard this document as important.[76]

Finally, considering the salience bias, the most important parts of the KID need to *look* the most important. In fact, if one part stands out more than others, such as for instance an infographic, chances are that another part is overlooked. Knowledge of this bias therefore also offers the opportunity to emphasise the most important information in the KID.

5.2. Comparing complex financial products

First, examination of the heuristics and biases demonstrates that it appears to be a good thing that the purpose of the KID is to enable investors to compare financial products.

73 European Parliament and the Council 2014, Article 6 paragraph 1.

74 European Parliament and the Council 2014, Article 6 paragraph 2 and Article 8 paragraph 2 respectively.

75 See footnote 64.

76 European investors may not be familiar with this authority.

Research shows that increased effort and motivation to compare financial products can reduce the influence of the anchoring and adjustment heuristic:

> *"...adjustment is effortful, and so anything that increases a person's willingness or ability to seek more accurate estimates tends to reduce the magnitude of adjustment-based anchoring biases."*[77]

The fact that the KID endeavours to make it easier for investors to compare financial products is, considering this heuristic, desirable. This increased comparability reduces for instance the influence of the anchor thus expectedly limiting the role of the anchoring and adjustment heuristic.

However, given the recognition heuristic, it remains to be seen to which extent the KID will actually lead consumers to actually consider foreign products and providers when comparing financial products. After all, financial products from a familiar or geographically close provider are by definition deemed better. It appears unlikely for the KID to change this.

In any event, it is important for consumers to experience as few barriers as possible when it comes to the comparison of financial products. After all, if the comparison of products requires a lot of effort and motivation, investors will be more inclined to use mental shortcuts, such as the described heuristics. In this context, the fact that the content and design of the KID must be standardised seem to be a step in the right direction.[78] In addition, the requirement that the document must be short, concise, and easy to understand, will likely lead to it requiring less effort and motivation of consumers when it comes to comparing financial products.[79] Besides, it is therefore only to be welcomed that the Regulation offer room for the development of calculation tools, allowing investors to easily calculate costs of various products.[80]

The comparability of documents is likely to increase if they can be accessed on a central website.[81] In addition, consideration could be given to the introduction of a product comparison website for complex financial products. At present, comparison websites already exist for many different kinds of products such as car insurance and electronics, and are being visited by many people.[82] Such a website may be helpful to investors as well.

It is furthermore vital for investors themselves to be aware of the importance of comparing financial products. By means of Level 2 instruments could perhaps be stipulated that the document needs to explicitly state that it is of great importance to compare various products in order to be able to gain insight into the risks and possibilities they entail. Additionally, financial advisors could make investors aware of this.

77 Epley and Gilovich 2006, p. 316.

78 European Parliament and the Council 2014, recital 17.

79 European Parliament and the Council 2014, Article 6 paragraph 4.

80 European Parliament and the Council 2014, recital 36.

81 And thus not only on the website of the PRIIPs manufacturer, European Parliament and the Council 2014, Article 5 paragraph 1.

82 A well-known website in the Netherlands is www.independer.nl.

VI. Final remarks

Finally, research suggest, that the described heuristics and biases cannot be prevented by informing investors about them, and that these errors are also likely to occur when people are trying their best to be careful.[83] An important cause of this appears to be the fact that they are unconscious cognitive processes that are hard to influence. In addition, increasing financial knowledge is not expected to prevent the errors described, since even experts make these errors.[84] It is therefore extra important for policymakers to take these heuristics and biases into account when drafting regulations such as for instance the new information document.

Considering the described heuristics and biases, it seems doubtful whether the new information document will be effective when it comes to informing investors and stimulating them to compare financial products. However, the analysis of the likely effectiveness of the KID and the formulated recommendations are not meant as a final step, but rather as a first exploration of the subject. After all, experimental research offers ways to study more concretely whether, and if so how, the content and design of the KID can actually contribute to consumers being adequately informed and able to compare financial products. Insights from Behavioural Finance, a selection of which were discussed in this chapter, allow for a greater predictability of investors' behaviour and therefore hopefully constitute an initial step into the right direction.

It must be noted that this chapter does not elaborate on the question to which extent an information document for complex financial products is desirable, since the European legislature has already made the decision to introduce such a document.[85] However, it is questionable whether the recommendations formulated in this chapter will actually lead consumers to better understand financial products and compare them with each other. First, these recommendations and the goals of the KID may clash. For example, the documents being short could help improve the comparability of information documents, while, on the other hand, more information could possibly enhance their comprehensibility. Second, a part of the research described is based on laboratory studies and does therefore not necessarily apply to information provision by means of a short information document like the KID. Besides, it should be noted that many heuristics and biases could prevent a proper provision of information through an information document.[86] Only a small number of heuristics and biases were described in this chapter. Partly in view of the aforementioned, experimental research could be helpful in exploring whether an

83 Daniel Kahneman, Nobel laureate, admits in his book (Kahneman 2011, p. 417): "*...my intuitive thinking is just as prone to overconfidence, extreme predictions, and the planning fallacy as it was before I made a study of these issues.*" See also Arkes 1991; Financial Services Authority 2008, p. 54; Hertwig and Ortmann 2003.

84 See amongst others Hilton 2003; Kahneman 2013.

85 About the effectiveness of mandated disclosure e.g. Ben-Shahar and Schneider 2014.

86 For example, Ben-Shahar and Schneider 2014, p. 115: "*In short, since biases and heuristics are so many and since people respond so variously, nobody could write mandates that can account for that chaos of thought and passion, all confused*". See also Van Boom, Giesen and Verheij 2013, p. 1179–1189 which clearly shows that empirical research and the ensuing results are not always directly applicable when it comes to the drafting of laws and regulations.

information document could actually lead to consumers being adequately informed about a financial product and stimulate them to compare financial products with each other. Probably other alternatives, such as choice architecture, will be more helpful to consumers.[87]

Now, back to the question posed in the title of this chapter: 'Who are you, investor: Mr. Spock, Captain Kirk, or somewhere in between?' As it turns out, investors are not as rational as Mr. Spock, but have more in common with Captain Kirk. However, when thinking about an answer to this question, the decisions made by Mr. Spock and Captain Kirk do not really matter that much. After all, even though Captain Kirk and Mr. Spock have been known to make many important decisions, they did so within the realm of science *fiction*. The consequences of purchasing an unsuitable financial product are *real* and include for instance becoming homeless or spending one's old age worrying about money and suffering the ensuing emotional and social consequences. As was established earlier in this chapter, insights from Behavioural Finance can help discover who these investors are and how they make decisions. Therefore, despite the apparently dubious link between information disclosure and investor decision making, fine-tuning of the proposed regulation regarding a Key Information Document based on these insights seems at least helpful when it comes to achieving its two main objectives: improving the comprehensibility and comparability of financial products. This can only be achieved by taking into account how investors actually understand and compare financial products.

VII. References

L.F. Ackert & R. Deaves, *Behavioral Finance. Psychology, Decision-Making and Markets*, South Western: Cengage Learning 2010.

D. Ahn, S. Choi, D. Gale & S. Kariv, *Estimating Ambiguity Aversion in a Portfolio Choice Experiment*, Berkeley: 2013.

M. Allais, 'L'Extension des Theories de l'Equilibre Economique General et du Rendement Social au Cas du Risque', *Econometrica* 1953a, 21, p. 269–290.

M. Allais, 'Le Comportement de l'Homme Rationnel devant le Risque: Critique des Postulats et Axiomes de l'Ecole Americaine', *Econometrica* 1953b, 21, p. 503–546.

M. Alpert & H. Raiffa, 'A progress report on the training of probability assessors', in: D. Kahneman, P. Slovic & A. Tversky (Eds.), *Judgment under uncertainty: Heuristics and biases*, Cambridge, England: Cambridge University Press 1982.

H.R. Arkes, 'Costs and benefits of judgment errors: Implications for debiasing', *Psychological Bulletin* 1991, 110, p. 486–498.

R.B. Asch, *Basic Probability Theory*, Meneola/New York: Dover Publications 2008.

Autoriteit Financiële Markten, *Feitenonderzoek Beleggingsverzekeringen, in opdracht van het ministerie van Financiën*. Uitgevoerd door de Autoriteit Financiële Markten (AFM) in samenwerking met MoneyView, Amsterdam: 2008.

H.K. Baker & J.R. Nofsinger, 'Psychological Biases of Investors', *Financial Services Review* 2002, 11, p. 97–116.

87 E.g. Thaler and Sunstein 2008, p. 81–100.

S. Benartzi, R.H. Thaler, S.P. Utkus, C.R. Sunstein, 'The Law and Economics of Company Stock in 401(k) Plans', *Journal of Law and Economics* 2007, 50, p. 45–79.

O. Ben-Shahar & C.E. Schneider, *More than You Wanted to Know. The Failure of Mandated Disclosure*, Princeton and Oxford: Princeton University Press 2014.

J. Bentham, *An Introduction to the Principles of Morals and Legislation*, Kitchener: Botoche Books 1781/2000.

D. Bernoulli, 'Exposition of a New Theory on the Measurement of Risk', *Econometrica* 1954, 22, p. 23–36.

T. Betsch & D. Pohl, 'Tversky and Kahneman's availability approach to frequency judgment: A critical analysis', in: P. Sedlmeier & T. Betch (Eds.), *Etc.: Frequency processing and cognition*, New York: Oxford University Press 2002, p. 109–119.

R.A. Block & D.R. Harper, 'Overconfidence in Estimation: Testing the Anchoring-and-Adjustment Hypothesis', *Organizational Behaviour and Human Decision Processes* 1991, 49, p. 188–207.

W.H. van Boom, I. Giesen & A.J. Verheij, *Capita Civilologie. Handboek empirie en privaatrecht*, Den Haag: Boom Juridische uitgevers 2013.

A. Capuano & I. Ramsay, *What causes suboptimal financial behavior? An exploration of financial literacy, social influences and behavioral economics.* Research Report, Financial Literacy Project. University of Melbourne: March 2011. Accessed 29 October 2014.

N. Chater, S. Huck and R. Inderst, *Consumer Decision-Making in Retail Investment Services: A Behavioural Economics Perspective.* Report to the European Commission Directorate-General Health and Consumers (SANCO), Brussels: SANCO 2010.

Commissie Geschillen Aandelenlease, *Over lenen, leasen en verliezen. Eindrapport van de Commissie Geschillen Aandelenlease*, Den Haag: juli 2004.

T.M. Døskeland & H.K. Hvide, 'Do Individual Investors Have Asymmetric Information Based on Work Experience?', *The Journal of Finance* 2011, 66, p. 1011–1041.

K.J. Dunegan, 'Framing, cognitive models, and Image Theory: Toward an understanding of a glass half full', *Journal of Applied Psychology*, 1993, 78(3), p. 491–503.

D. Ellsberg, 'Risk, ambiguity and the Savage axioms', *Quarterly Journal of Economics*, 75, p. 643–669.

N. Epley & T. Gilovich, 'The Anchoring and Adjustment Heuristic. Why the Adjustments Are Insufficient', *Psychological Science* 2006, 17, p. 311–318.

European Commission, *Key Information Documents (KIDs) for packaged retail investment and insurance products – Frequently asked questions. Memo*, Brussel: European Commission 15 April 2014.

European Parliament and the Council, *Regulation of the European Parliament and of the Council on key information documents for packaged retail and insurance-based investment products (PRIIPs)*, Brussels: 24 October 2014.

European Parliament, *Legislative Resolution of 15 April on the proposal for a regulation of the European Parliament and the Council on key information documents for investment products (COM(2012)0352 – C7-0179/2012 – 2012/0169(COD)*, Strasbourg: 15 April 2014.

E. Ferran, 'Regulatory Lessons from the Payment Insurance Mis-selling Scandal in the UK', *European Business Organization Law Review* 2012, 13, p. 247–270.

Financial Services Authority, *Financial Capability: A Behavioural Economics Perspective.* Prepared for the Financial Services Authority by D. Meza, B. Irlenbusch, & D. Reyniers, from the London School of Economics, Consumer Research 69, FSA: London 2008.

Financial Services Authority, *The development of more effective product disclosure. Report on market research commissioned by the Financial Services Authority*, London: Financial Services Authority 2003.
C.R. Fox & K.E. See, 'Belief and Preference in Decision Under Uncertainty', in: D. Hardman & L. Macchi (eds.), *Thinking: Psychological Perspectives on Reasoning, Judgment and Decision Making*, Chichester: John Wiley & Sons 2003, p. 273–314.
C.R. Fox & A. Tversky, 'A Belief-Based Account of Decision under Uncertainty', *Management Science* 1998, 44, p. 879–895.
K.R. French & J.M. Poterba, *Investor Diversification and International Equity Markets*, NBER Working Paper Series No. 3609, Cambridge: National Bureau of Economic Research 1991.
D.G. Goldstein & G. Gigerenzer, 'Models of Ecological Rationality: The Recognition Heuristic', *Psychological Review* 2002, 109, p. 75–90.
C. Gonzalez, J. Dana, H. Koshino & M. Just, 'The Framing Effect and Risky Decisions: Examining Cognitive Functions with fMRI', *Journal of Economic Psychology* 2005, 26, p. 1–20.
D. Hardman, *Judgment and Decision Making. Psychological Perspectives*, Chichester: John Wiley & Sons 2009.
R. Hertwig & A. Ortmann, 'Economists' and psychologists' experimental practices: How they differ, why they differ, and how they could converge', in: I. Brocas & J.D. Carillo (Eds.), *The psychology of economic decisions: Rationality and well-being*, New York: Oxford University Press 2003, p. 253–272.
D.J. Hilton, 'Psychology and the financial markets: Applications to understanding and remedying irrational decision-making', in: I. Brocas & J.D. Carillo (Eds.), *The psychology of economic decisions: Rationality and well-being*, New York: Oxford University Press 2003, p. 273–297.
R.M. Hogarth & M.W. Reder, 'Editors' comments: Perspectives from economics and psychology', *Journal of Business* 1986, 59, p. 185–207.
G. Huberman, 'Familiarity Breeds Investment', *The Review of Financial Studies* 2001, 14, p. 659–680.
IFF Research & You Gov, *UCITS Disclosure Testing Research Report,* 2009.
S.S. Iyengar & M.R. Lepper, 'When Choice is Demotivating: Can One Desire Too Much of a Good Thing?', *Journal of Personality and Social Psychology* 2000, 79, p. 995–1006.
B. Jacobsen, J.B. Lee & W. Marquering, 'Are Men More Optimistic', 2008 (available at SSRN, accessed 24 December 2014).
D. Kahneman, *Thinking, fast and slow*, New York: Farrar, Straus and Giroux 2011.
D. Kahneman & A. Tversky, 'Choices, Values, and Frames', *American Psychologist* 1984, 39, p. 341–350.
D. Kahneman & A. Tversky, 'Prospect Theory: An Analysis of Decision under Risk', *Econometrica* 1979, 47, p. 263–292.
D. Kahneman & A. Tversky, 'On the psychology of prediction', *Psychological Review*, 1973, 80, p. 237–251.
D. Kahneman & A. Tversky, 'Subjective Probability: A Judgment of Representativeness', *Cognitive Psychology* 1972, 3, p. 430–454.
F.H. Knight, *Risk, Uncertainty and Profit* (thesis Cornell University 1921), Boston and New York: Houghton Mifflin Company, The Riverside Press Cambridge 1921.

J. Kruger, 'Lake Wobegon Be Gone! The 'Below-Average Effect' and the Egocentric Nature of Comparative Ability Judgements', *Journal of Personality and Social Psychology*, 1999, 77, p. 221–232.

B. de Martino, D. Kumaran, B. Seymour & R.J. Dolan, 'Frames, Biases, and Rational Decision-Making in the Human Brain', *Science* 2006, 313, p. 684–687.

B.J. McNeil, S.G. Pauker, H.C. Sox Jr. & A. Tversky, 'On the elicitation of preferences for alternative therapies', *New England Journal of Medicine*, 1982, 306(21), p. 1259–1262.

Millward Brown / Centrum, *Evaluatie van de Financiële Bijsluiter. Resultaten van onderzoek onder consumenten, intermediairs en aanbieders*, Amsterdam: Autoriteit Financiële Markten 2004.

N. Moloney, 'The Investor Model Underlying the EU's Investor Protection Regime: Consumers or Investors?', *European Business Organization Law Review* 2012, 13, p. 169–193.

N. Moloney, *How to protect Investors. Lessons from the EC and the UK*, Cambridge: Cambridge University Press 2010.

F.C. Müller-Lyer, 'Optische Urteilstäuschungen', *Archiv für Physiologie, Physiologische Abtheilung des Archives für Anatomie und Physiologie. Supplement-band* 1889, p. 263–270.

J. Neumann & O. Morgenstern, *Theory of Games and Economic Behavior*, Princeton: Princeton University Press 1944.

J.W. Payne, J.R. Bettman & E.J. Johnson, *The adaptive decision maker*, Cambridge: Cambridge University Press 1993.

M. Pompian, *Behavioral Finance and Wealth Management: How to Build Optimal Portfolios that Account for Investor Biases*, Hoboken: John Wiley & Sons 2006.

L.J. Savage, *The foundation of statistics*, New York: Wiley 1954.

M.S. Seasholes & N. Zhu, 'Individual Investors and Local Bias', *The Journal of Finance* 2010, 65, p. 1987–2010.

R.J. Shiller, 'Human Behavior and the Efficiency of the Financial System', in: J.B. Thaler & M. Woodford (eds.), *Handbook of Macroeconomics*, Amsterdam: Elsevier 1999.

Synovate, *Consumer Market Study on Advice within the Area of Retail Investment Services*. Final Report, 2011.

R.H. Thaler & C.R. Sunstein, *Nudge: Improving Decisions About Health, Wealth, and Happiness*, New Have & London: Yale University Press 2008.

A. Tversky & D. Kahneman, 'Advances in Prospect Theory: Cumulative Representation of Uncertainty', *Journal of Risk and Uncertainty* 1992, 5, p. 297–323.

A. Tversky & D. Kahneman, 'Extensional Versus Intuitive Reasoning: The Conjunction Fallacy in Probability Judgment', *Psychological Review* 1983, 90, p. 293–315.

A. Tversky & D. Kahneman, 'The Framing of Decisions and the Psychology of Choice', *Science* 1981, 211, p. 453–458.

A. Tversky & D. Kahneman, 'Judgment under Uncertainty: Heuristics and Biases. Biases in judgments reveal some heuristics of thinking under uncertainty', *Science* 1974, 185, p. 1124–1131.

A. Tversky & D. Kahneman, 'Availability: A heuristic for judging frequency and probability', *Cognitive Psychology* 1973, 4, p. 207–232.

A. Tversky & D.J. Koehler, 'Support Theory: A Nonextensional Representation of Subjective Probability', *Psychological Review* 1994, 101, p. 547–567.

L.E. Willis, 'Against Financial Literacy Education', *Iowa Law Review* 2008, 228, p. 197–285.

Joasia Luzak*

ONLINE DISCLOSURE RULES OF THE CONSUMER RIGHTS DIRECTIVE: PROTECTING PASSIVE OR ACTIVE CONSUMERS?

I. Introduction

Despite the growing academic criticism of using mandatory information duties as one of the main consumer protection measures in consumer law[1], the recently adopted Consumer Rights Directive[2] (hereafter, the "CRD") maintains this trend in Europe.[3] The long and detailed list of information duties provided for traders in Articles 5 and 6 of the CRD applies to any sale and services consumer contract that falls under the scope of application of the CRD. For traders, however, fulfilling this obligation may seem to be an exercise in futility due to little evidence that consumers read these disclosures and actually benefit from them.[4] Instead of understanding the duty to disclose as a duty to

* Dr. Joasia Luzak is Assistant Professor at the Centre for the Study of European Contract Law of the University of Amsterdam in the Netherlands and member of the Ius Commune Research School. This paper has been presented at the Ius Commune conference in Edinburgh in November 2014.

1 O. Ben-Shahar and C. E. Schneider, *More Than You Wanted to Know*, Princeton: Princeton University Press, 2014, 229 p.; O. Bar-Gill, *Seduction by Contract*, Oxford: Oxford University Press, 2012, 280 p.; K. Tonner, 'The Consumer Rights Directive and its Impact on Internet and other Distance Consumer Contracts', in: N. Reich, H.-W. Micklitz, P. Rott and K. Tonner (eds.), *European Consumer Law*, Cambridge: Intersentia, 2014, p. 402; N. Helberger, L. Guibault, M. Loos, C. Mak, L. Pessers, B. van der Sloot, *Digital Consumers and the Law*, Alphen aan den Rijn: Wolters Kluwer, 2013, p. 66–80; A. Nordhausen Scholes, 'Information Requirements', in: G. Howells, R. Schulze (eds.), *Modernising and Harmonising Consumer Contract Law*, Munich: Sellier, 2009, p. 213–216; G. Howells, T. Wilhelmsson, 'EC Consumer Law: Has it Come of Age?', *European Law Review*, vol. 4, 2003, p. 380–381.

2 Directive 2011/83/EU of the European Parliament and of the Council of 25 October 2011 on consumer rights, *OJ* 2011, L 304/64 ("CRD").

3 See: CRD, Articles 5 and 6.

4 C. Leone, 'Transparency revisited – on the role of information in the recent case-law of the CJEU', *European Review of Contract Law*, vol. 10, 2014, pp. 312–325; E. Wauters, V. Donoso, E. Lievens, 'Optimizing transparency for users in social networking sites', *Info*, vol. 16, 2014, p. 10; T. Wilhelmsson, 'Cooperation and Competition Regarding Standard Contract Terms in Consumer Contracts', *European Business Law Review*, vol. 1, 2006, p. 55; O. Ben-Shahar and C. E. Schneider (footnote 1), 229 p; Y. Bakos, F. Marotta-Wurgler, D. R. Trossen, 'Does Anyone Read the Fine Print? Consumer Attention to Standard Form Contracts', *NYU Law and Economics Research Paper Series*, working paper no. 09–40, October 2009, p. 1–35.

actually inform consumers we could see it as a duty to reach consumers with the disclosure, so that consumers possessed the information contained in it when they needed it for reference.[5] With this in mind it is important to inquire what efforts traders must undertake to ascertain that the disclosure reaches consumers and whether they could rely on an, at least partially, active behaviour of consumers in obtaining this information. This conundrum plays a special role in online transactions, where the direct contact between traders and consumers does not occur and methods of providing consumers with information differ from the offline world. The Consumer Rights Directive was adopted, among other things, to update the so-far existing rules on consumer distance selling contracts to the modern technologies, especially the Internet.[6] Its Article 8 determines formal requirements for providing information to consumers, establishing, among other things, the extent of the obligation of a trader with regard to providing consumers with mandatory online disclosures and whether any activity is required from a consumer to obtain such disclosures.

Internet users, as consumers concluding contracts at a distance, are perceived as being at a disadvantage compared to consumers shopping in stores. Due to the lack of direct contact with the trader and with the goods, consumers purchasing goods at a distance are likely to encounter more difficulties in establishing the trader's trustworthiness, as well as the goods' quality.[7] Therefore, the European legislator considers it necessary to compensate for the weaker transactional position of such consumers by granting them more information rights. However, the question remains whether the difference between consumer shopping experiences online and offline results also in different attitudes of internet users to disclosures provided to them on the Internet or in traditional stores. For example, if behavioural studies showed that it is more difficult to draw consumers' attention to disclosures online rather than offline, this could signalise that consumers would tend to be more passive in obtaining information online. Under such circumstances, the European legislator should consider demanding more activity from traders in conveying mandatory online disclosures if it aimed to improve consumer protection online. This paper analyses not only what scope of consumer protection the new formal requirements of Article 8 of the CRD regarding online disclosures introduce but also whether they reflect the findings of behavioural studies on how consumers approach online disclosures.

To date, in order to balance the interests of both contractual parties in consumer contracts, European substantive consumer law[8] has mostly protected active consumers.

5 P. Mankowski, 'Information and Formal Requirements in EC Private Law', *European Review of Private Law*, vol. 6, 2005, p. 782–783, 787.

6 See e.g. CRD, Recitals 5 and 20.

7 J. A. Luzak, 'To Withdraw Or Not To Withdraw? Evaluation of the Mandatory Right of Withdrawal in Consumer Distance Selling Contracts Taking Into Account Its Behavioural Effects on Consumers', *Journal of Consumer Policy*, vol. 37, 2014, p. 98–100; G. Borges and B. Ilrenbusch, 'Fairness Crowded Out by Law: An Experimental Study on Withdrawal Rights', *Journal of Institutional and Theoretical Economics*, vol. 163, 2007, p. 85; S. Harridge-March, 'Can the Building of Trust Overcome Consumer Perceived Risk Online?', *Marketing Intelligence and Planning*, vol. 24 (7), 2006, p. 746.

8 In this paper the notion "European substantive consumer law" is used to distinguish it from procedural rules within the area of European consumer law. It does not refer to the difference between the notions

The next paragraph briefly introduces the justifications for distinguishing between passive and active consumers and their protection in European substantive consumer law. It is important to review whether and under what circumstances European substantive consumer law currently extends its scope of protection to passive consumers, what the trend in protecting online consumers is and whether it is changing due to special characteristics of online trade. After providing general background information on the trend observed in European substantive consumer law, I turn my attention to the focus of this paper, namely, the analysis of the formal requirements for online disclosures and the consumer image (passive or active) they apply to. In paragraph three, I first discuss the interpretation of the previously binding formal requirements for online disclosures under the Distance Selling Directive[9] (hereafter, the "DSD") in the Court of Justice of the European Union's (hereafter, the "CJEU") judgment in the *Content Services* case.[10] Then, in paragraph four, I analyse the new wording of Article 8 of the CRD and compare it to the previously binding requirements. I report there also the first reactions of national legislators, on the example of the Netherlands and the UK, to the new formal requirements of the CRD. This allows me to predict the likely interpretation of these provisions in future case law, that is to say whether the courts would incline towards extending their scope to protect passive consumers. Paragraph five addresses the consumers' attitudes to online disclosures, presenting behavioural studies on whether and to what extent consumers may pay attention to online disclosures. It illustrates also the similarities and differences in attracting consumers' attention to offline and online disclosures. These behavioural insights are important to consider in examining whether the European institutions should take special needs of internet users into account when setting the formal requirements for online disclosures in the CRD. This could be the case if, e.g., consumers encountered more difficulties in noticing disclosures online rather than offline. In the conclusions readers will find an answer to the question whether there is a new European trend to protect passive consumers online in substantive European consumer law and whether the evidence from behavioural studies shows that consumers may require more protection online due to approaching disclosures with more difficulties than offline.

II. Passive vs. active consumers in substantive European consumer law

European consumer law uses more than just one notion of a "consumer". While many European consumer law measures define the consumer as a natural person acting for purposes which are not related to her trade, business, profession[11], some other refer to a

of substantive or formal requirements for disclosures, but, among other things, it encompasses within its scope information duties, corresponding to them formal requirements, the right of withdrawal.

9 Directive 97/7/EC of 20 May 1997 on the protection of consumers in respect of distance contracts, *OJ* 1997, L 144/19 ("DSD"), repealed by the new provisions of the CRD.

10 CJEU 5 July 2012, case C-49/11, ECLI:EU:C:2012:419 (*Content Services*).

11 See e.g. Directive 1999/44/EC of the European Parliament and of the Council of 25 May 1999 on certain aspects of the sale of consumer goods and associated guarantees, *OJ* 1999, L 171/12 ("Consumer Sales Directive"); Article 1 Para. 2(a); Council Directive 93/13/EEC of 5 April 1993 on unfair terms in consumer contracts, *OJ* 1993, L 95/29, Article 2(b) ("UCTD"); CRD, Article 2(1).

person concluding a given contract.[12] Authors predominantly argue that a person concluding a mixed purpose contract, that is to say, when the purchased goods would be at least partially used by this person for professional purposes, could not currently fall under the scope of the definition of a European "consumer".[13] The notion is interpreted narrowly due to consumer protection rules having been introduced as an exception from general contractual rules. The European legislator repeatedly invokes consumers' transactional weakness as a justification for granting consumers additional rights.[14] This justification seems, however, inconsistent with the above-described limitation of the scope of the notion of a "consumer". After all, just the fact that an object would not be used by its buyer for a professional purpose does not need to signify the buyer's transactional weakness.

The European legislator perceives consumers as a weaker party in the transaction. This view has been plausibly justified by vast empirical evidence that consumers suffer from information asymmetry and from many cognitive biases during their decision-making process.[15] This disqualifies them as rational agents in a market, that is to say persons who would always act reasonably, in their own best interests.[16] To the contrary, consumers have frequently proven that their decision-making is far from rational.[17] In

12 Council Directive 90/314/EEC of 13 June 1990 on package travel, package holidays and package tours, *OJ* 1990, L 158/59, Article 2 Para. 4.

13 See e.g.: D. Staudenmayer, 'The Directive on the Sale of Consumer Goods and Associated Guarantees – a Milestone in the European Consumer and Private Law', *European Review of Private Law*, vol. 4, 2000, p. 548–549; H. Schulte-Nölke, 'Scope and Role of the Horizontal Directive and its Relationship to the CFR', in: G. Howells, R. Schulze (eds.), *Modernising and Harmonising Consumer Contract Law*, Munich: Sellier, 2009, p. 37–38; M.B.M. Loos and J. A. Luzak, 'De nieuwe Richtlijn consumentenrechten', *Tijdschrift voor Consumentenrecht and Handelspraktijken*, vol. 5, 2011, p. 185–186; H.-W. Micklitz, N. Reich, 'The Commission Proposal for a "Directive on Consumer Rights"', *Common Market Law Review*, vol. 46, 2009, p. 481–484. See to the contrary e.g.: N. Reich and H.-W. Micklitz, 'Economic Law, Consumer Interests, and EU Integration', in: N. Reich, H.-W. Micklitz, P. Rott and K. Tonner (eds.), *European Consumer Law*, Cambridge: Intersentia, 2014, p. 52, 55–56.

14 See e.g.: EUROPA, 'Convention on the law applicable to contractual obligations (Rome Convention)', available at http://europa.eu/legislation_summaries/justice_freedom_security/judicial_cooperation_in_civil_matters/l33109_en.htm, last accessed online on 14 January 2015; European Parliament resolution of 8 June 2011 on policy options for progress towards a European Contract Law for consumers and businesses, 2011/2013(INI), P7_TA(2011)0262, points 11, 16; CURIA, 'The Court sets out the scope of consumer protection in cross-border sales', Press Release No 134/13, 17 October 2013, http://curia.europa.eu/jcms/upload/docs/application/pdf/2013-11/cp130134en.pdf, last accessed online on 14 January 2015.

15 T. Hansen, 'Perspectives on Consumer Decision Making: An Integrated Approach', *Journal of Consumer Behaviour*, vol. 4, 2005, pp. 420–425; H. Luth, *Behavioural Economics in Consumer Policy*, Antwerp: Intersentia, 2010, p. 48–50.

16 C. Camerer, S. Issacharoff, G. Loewenstein, T. O'Donoghue, M. Rabin, 'Regulation for conservatives: behavioral economics and the case for "assymetric paternalism"', *University of Pennsylvania Law Review*, vol. 151, 2003, p. 1238; G. Loewenstein, 'Emotions in Economic Theory and Economic Behavior', *The American Economic Review*, vol. 90, 2000, p. 428; C.R. Sunstein and R.H. Thaler, 'Libertarian paternalism is not an oxymoron', *John M. Olin Law and Economics Working Paper No. 185*, 2003, www.law.uchicago.edu/Lawecon/index.html last accessed online on 14 January 2015, p. 29.

17 J. R. Bettman, M. F. Luce, J. W. Payne, 'Constructive Consumer Choice Processes', *Journal of Consumer Research*, vol. 25, 1998, p. 187–200; G. Loewenstein, 'Emotions in Economic Theory and Economic

light of the empirical evidence to the above, the European legislator decided to adopt varied consumer protection measures that could contribute to the strengthening of the internal market by empowering consumers as market agents.

Some authors believe, however, that granting consumers additional rights, e.g., information rights or the right of withdrawal, could have a counter-effect.[18] That is to say, it could discourage consumers from spending any time or effort on trying to familiarize themselves with the transaction they are concluding, from gathering the necessary information and then trying to understand it. For example, due to the right of withdrawal consumers may have no incentive to properly inquire about the goods until after the purchase, knowing that the costs of returning the goods during the cooling-off period are low.[19] Under such circumstances consumer protection measures instead of empowering consumers could systematically weaken them. If further empirical evidence confirms this finding as to consumer behaviour, this could undermine the validity of introducing special consumer protection measures, such as mandated disclosures for distance selling consumer transactions, in Europe. After all, granting consumers additional rights in any case increases transaction costs that in the end rest on consumers, therefore, there needs to be a good reason for it.[20]

The above-described criticism of the consumer protection system in Europe could be the reason why the CJEU mostly applies substantive European consumer protection rules in favour of active consumers, as I will illustrate further in this paragraph. The distinction between active and passive consumers in the substantive European consumer law, as applied in this paper, tests whether any and what kind of activities are demanded from consumers in order for them to obtain necessary information, to make use thereof and to use their rights. On the one hand, consumers could receive all necessary information to make a transactional decision from the trader, would not need to read it and their rights could be recognised *ex officio* (passive consumers). On the other hand, consumers might be required to search for the necessary information in order to obtain it, familiarise themselves with this information and they would need to claim their rights for these to protect them (active consumers). Prior to assessing which consumer image applies to obtaining mandatory online disclosures, I will present how in substantive European consumer law the other two points differentiating between passive and active consumers are addressed. That is to say, whether consumers could remain passive and not read the information provided to them, as well as not invoke their rights and still be protected by substantive European consumer law measures.

At a first glance, it seems that European consumer law measures protect exclusively consumers who have used the information made available to them. The fact that the

Behavior', *The American Economic Review*, vol. 90, 2000, p. 430; R. A. Hillman and J. J. Rachlinski, 'Standard-form contracting in the electronic age', *New York University Law Review*, vol. 77, 2002, p. 479–483.

18 H. Eidenmüller, 'Why Withdrawal Rights?', *European Review of Contract Law*, vol. 1, 2011, p. 21.

19 R.E. Scott and G.G. Triantis, 'Embedded Options and the Case against Compensation in Contract Law', *Columbia Law Review*, vol. 104, p. 1424; J. Luzak (footnote 7), p. 106.

20 H. Eidenmüller, 'Party Autonomy, Distributive Justice and the Conclusion of Contracts in the DCFR', *European Review of Contract Law*, vol. 5, 2009, p. 119–121.

CJEU adopted a high standard of an "average" consumer in its case law, that is to say, of a consumer who is reasonably well-informed, reasonably observant and circumspect, corresponds to this idea.[21] A passive consumer who would not try to gather any information on the transaction she is about to conclude and who would not attempt to protect her own interests by trying to understand this information, would be unlikely to benefit from the protection of European consumer law. Originally, the CJEU and national courts adopted this high standard of an average consumer exclusively in case law pertaining to the assessment of misleading advertising and other unfair commercial practices cases. In assessing whether a given commercial practice is unfair, the national courts need to examine, among other things, whether a consumer who disposed of all the correct facts and was not under any undue pressure would have altered her transactional decision.[22] It is in this assessment that courts look at a well-informed consumer: whether she could have been and was swayed by the misleading information or undue pressure. Additionally, the national courts examine whether the consumer should have been able to understand the product's description and characteristics. A passive consumer, who, e.g., ignored some available information and did not try to understand it, would not be seen as a victim of an unfair commercial practice. For example, already in the *Mars*[23] case, pre-dating the introduction of the UCPD, the CJEU determined that reasonably circumspect consumers should realise that, if there is a marking on the product's packaging saying that this product is now available in a bigger quantity for the same price as previously, the marking's size on the packaging does not need to correspond to the size of the increase.[24] The court considers, therefore, the average consumer to be an active one, who would take her time to think this offer through and not merely assume that the marking on the packaging has a particular meaning. The latter consumer would not be protected under European consumer law regulating unfair commercial practices.

Recently, the CJEU adopted a similar high standard for the consumers' awareness when interpreting provisions of the Unfair Contract Terms Directive (hereafter, the "UCTD").[25] The *Kásler* case concerned a consumer who concluded a mortgage loan in a foreign currency, Swiss francs. Under the terms of the credit contract the consumer had to pay back the loan's amount at the buying rate of Swiss francs, but the monthly repayment instalments had to be calculated pursuant to the selling rate of Swiss francs. One of the questions raised in this case was how to determine the transparency of a contractual term that sets out the calculation method for the outstanding loan and its interest rate. The CJEU for the first time elaborated on the meaning of a notion that contractual terms have to be drafted in "*plain and intelligible*" language in order to be transparent.[26] To determine

21 CJEU 16 July 1998, case C-210/96, ECLI:EU:C:1998:369 (*Gut Springenheide*).

22 See e.g. Directive 2005/29/EC of 11 May 2005 concerning unfair business-to-consumer commercial practices in the internal market, *OJ* 2005, L 149/22 ("UCPD"). UCPD, Article 7 Para. 1, Article 8.

23 CJEU 6 July 1995, case C-470/93, ECLI:EU:C:1995:224 (*Mars GmbH*).

24 Ibid, para. 24.

25 CJEU 30 April 2014, case C-26/13, ECLI:EU:C:2014:282 (*Kásler*). For argumentation why the average consumer benchmark should not be extended to other areas of European consumer law see, e.g., B. Duivenvoorde, *The Consumer Benchmarks in the Unfair Commercial Practices Directive*, PhD thesis defended at the University of Amsterdam, in Amsterdam on 3 July 2014, p. 222–224.

26 See more on the principle of transparency: C. Leone (footnote 4), p. 312–325.

whether consumers received transparent information, a national court first needs to establish whether an average consumer, a reasonably well-informed, observant and circumspect consumer, will be aware of the difference between the selling and buying exchange rates of a currency. Next, the court needs to consider whether an average consumer could predict the influence of that difference on the costs of the loan she would need to repay.[27] While the credit provider has a duty to draft contractual terms not only in a grammatically correct way but also in an understandable language, the consumer needs to have a basic understanding of the financial market and has to be able to apply these terms to her financial situation, as a reasonably well-informed consumer should be able to do. This signifies that the possibility of the consumers' passive behaviour, e.g., the low likelihood of the consumer actually reading and understanding the financial terms of the contract, should not influence the outcome of the unfairness test.

Moreover, not all consumers who conclude a particular contract will benefit from European consumer law protection measures, but only these who will then actually invoke them. For example, the Consumer Sales Directive grants European consumers a right to claim remedies when the goods they have purchased prove to be non-conforming the agreement.[28] Consumers have then a free choice of the remedy, but in order to obtain it, they have to request it first from the trader. This was well-illustrated by the judgment of the CJEU in the case *Duarte Hueros*.[29] Ms Duarte Hueros purchased a car with a sliding roof that proved to be leaking when it rained. The defect could not be repaired, the car dealer refused to replace the non-conforming car with another one, therefore, Ms Duarte Hueros claimed termination of the sales contract in a Spanish court. Since the Spanish court considered the defect at hand a minor one, it refused the claim for a termination of the contract and did not see a possibility to grant the last remedy remaining to the consumer – price reduction. The consumer, namely, had not claimed price reduction as an alternative remedy from the court. The CJEU recognised here the importance of the consumer being able to claim her remedies in the case of non-conformity.[30] At the same time, however, the CJEU did not oblige the national courts to *ex officio* expand the consumer's claim to all possible remedies that could be due to her.[31] It is clear that the consumer has to, therefore, actively pursue her rights in order to benefit from them, even if certain procedural benefits (such as an *ex officio* control of unfair contract terms[32]) may be granted to her by European consumer law. Of course, in order

27 CJEU (footnote 25), *Kásler*, para. 74.

28 Article 3 Consumer Sales Directive.

29 CJEU 3 October 2013, Case C-32/12, ECLI:EU:C:2013:637 (*Duarte Hueros*).

30 Ibid, para. 41–42.

31 Ibid, para. 43.

32 The Unfair Contract Terms Directive (Council Directive 93/13/EEC of 5 April 1993 on unfair terms in consumer contracts, *OJ* 1993, L 095/29) is one of a few both substantive and procedural European consumer protection measures that seems to aim at protecting passive consumers. That is to say, consumers who were unaware of their rights and, therefore, did not try to claim them. The CJEU repeatedly outlined the need to protect consumers who may not be aware of the unfairness of a given contractual term and who may, therefore, not claim this unfairness in front of a national court. See e.g. CJEU 26 October 2006, case C-168/06, ECLI:EU:C:2006:675 (*Mostaza Claro*), para. 26, 38; CJEU 4 June 2009, case C-243/08, ECLI:EU:C:2009:350 (*Pannon*), para. 25; CJEU 6 October 2009, case C-40/08,

to fully understand her rights and to make appropriate claims, it is important that the mandatory disclosure reaches the consumer first, so that she can consult it and familiarise herself with her rights at the right moment.

The above-presented analysis clearly points to a pre-dominant trend to protect active consumers in substantive European consumer law. That is to say consumers who make use of the information and invoke legal measures provided to them. The question remains whether consumers also need to be active in obtaining the pre-contractual and contractual information or whether they may remain passive and await this information to reach them.

III. The Distance Selling Directive & the *Content Services* judgment: protecting passive consumers

Pursuant to Article 4 of the DSD a trader who used any means of distance communication to conclude a contract with a consumer had to provide the consumer with certain pre-contractual information, as well as with a confirmation of a concluded contract (Article 5 DSD). The confirmation did not have to be issued if the pre-contractual information had already been given to the consumer in writing or on a durable medium. These two provisions aimed to facilitate the consumer's retention of the information. If the consumer is able to store the contractual information received either prior to or after the conclusion of the contract, then when she has a need to consult this information she will be able to recall contractual terms and conditions and check, e.g., whether the trader properly fulfilled all his obligations.[33] Additionally, if the consumer receives this information already prior to the contract's conclusion, then she has a better opportunity to assess the contract's value for her and to compare the trader's offer with other offers.[34]

In the *Content Services* case the question arose how to interpret the wording used in the two above-mentioned provisions of the DSD. That is to say, whether a consumer could remain completely passive and await the receipt of the information given to her by the trader or whether the trader could expect that the consumer would, at least partially, participate in obtaining the information, as well. Specifically, this issue surfaced due to the possibility to use hyperlinks on an online trader's main website that would send consumers to another webpage displaying and storing the mandatory pre-contractual and contractual information. As a result of this practice, even when the trader has

ECLI:EU:C:2009:615 (*Asturcom Telecomunicaciones*), para. 30–31. National courts grant this protection to European consumers through the *ex officio* mechanism, which means that national courts may step in and invoke unfairness of a given contractual term without the consumer mentioning it. However, even this protection does not extend as far as to protect completely passive European consumers. In the *Asturcom* case (CJEU 6 October 2009, case C-40/08, ECLI:EU:C:2009:615 (*Asturcom Telecomunicaciones*), para. 47) the CJEU clearly requires national courts to compensate for consumers' procedural omissions, however, this obligation does not extend as far as to oblige them to "*make up fully for the total inertia on the part of the consumer*".

33 P. Mankowski (footnote 5), p. 782–783, 787.

34 T. Wilhelmsson, 'European Fair Trading Law', in: G. Howells, H.-W. Micklitz, T. Wilhelmsson (eds.), *European Fair Trading Law*, Ashgate: Aldershot, 2006, chapter 5, s (c) (ii); S. Grundmann, 'The EU Consumer Rights Directive', *Uniform Law Review*, vol. 18, 2013, p. 109.

provided this information online, it could still not reach consumers, since they may not find themselves on the webpage containing all the mandatory information if they do not click on the hyperlink. Therefore, the trader by using a hyperlink requests the consumer to undertake a certain action: to click on the hyperlink. Moreover, traders often layer up their disclosures, which means that a hyperlink on the trader's main website would be likely to send the consumer to a webpage with part of the disclosure, and there the consumer may find more hyperlinks to websites containing more mandatory disclosures.[35] It seems reasonable to assume that the likelihood that the consumer will read each subsequent disclosure, 'hidden' behind yet another click, diminishes with every successive step/click. The conclusion of the contract is not prevented if a consumer does not access the information available to her through the hyperlink. This is consistent with the approach to offline disclosures, where it is not required for the trader to ascertain that the consumer has read the disclosure but only to provide the consumer with an opportunity to read it.[36] However, it remains debatable, whether by placing a disclosure on a different website and linking to it through a use of a hyperlink the trader actually provided the opportunity to read the mandatory information to the consumer.

The trader, Content Services, offered access to free or trial versions of various software to those internet users who would register to use their services. To register with Content Services, consumers had to fill in a registration form and tick a box on it that confirmed their acceptance of the company's standard terms and conditions together with the consumers' waiver of their right of withdrawal. The information on the consumers' right of withdrawal was, however, placed on a different webpage to which Content Services referred to by means of a hyperlink.[37] Since the consumer could not access the service without ticking the box, it meant that all clients of Content Services had to waive their right of withdrawal. Some consumers were likely to waive their right of withdrawal without realising what right they were waiving and what the consequences thereof could be. Furthermore, even after a consumer had registered with Content Services, in the confirmation email sent by the trader with her password and username, there was no specific notice of the consumer's right of withdrawal and its waiver. Instead, again, the email contained only a hyperlink to the website with the information about this right and its significance.[38] Only in the invoice, issued shortly after the confirmation e-mail was sent to a consumer, to claim the payment of the 12-months subscription fee for the service, the consumer received information about her right to withdraw from the contract and the fact that she had already waived it.[39]

35 This practice has even been recommended to American traders by the Federal Trade Commission in its guidelines for effective disclosures in digital advertising, see: FTC, '.com Disclosures', March 2013, available at www.ftc.gov/sites/default/files/attachments/press-releases/ftc-staff-revises-online-advertising-disclosure-guidelines/130312dotcomdisclosures.pdf last accessed online on 14 January 2015, p. 10–13.

36 P. van Wijck, J. Theeuwes, 'Protection against Unfair Contracts: An Economic Analysis of European Regulation', *European Journal of Law and Economics*, vol. 9, 2000, p. 79, 85.

37 CJEU (footnote 10), *Content Services*, para. 18.

38 CJEU (footnote 10), *Content Services*, para. 20.

39 CJEU (footnote 10), *Content Services*, para. 21.

The Austrian court invested with this case asked the CJEU whether just by placing information about the right of withdrawal on a website, which consumers could access through a hyperlink, the trader fulfilled both his pre-contractual information duties, as well as the obligation to provide the consumer with the confirmation of this information. What draws attention to the judgment is that the CJEU clearly states, for the first time while interpreting substantive European consumer law, that the DSD aimed at protecting passive consumers.[40] The Court deduced this from the wording of Article 5 DSD, which mentioned that consumers must "receive" confirmation of and "be given" pre-contractual information. The CJEU's interpretation is mainly based on the meaning of these words in everyday language, however, it also considers the context, in which these words are used, as well as the Directive's aim.[41] The notions "receive" and "be given" refer to a process of transmission, in which it is unnecessary for the information's recipient to take any particular action to obtain this information, pursuant to the CJEU. The Court states then that if a consumer is required to click on a hyperlink to obtain information, she needs to undertake an activity and, therefore, it cannot be said that the information "was given" or was "received" by her.[42] The CJEU explicitly indicates the difference between the wording used in Articles 4 and 5 DSD, observing that in the first provision the European legislator preferred to use a more neutral notion pursuant to which the consumer is to be "provided" with the relevant information.[43] Article 5 DSD, instead, uses a notion indicating a preference for the trader's active behaviour and allowing for a passive conduct of consumers.[44] Unfortunately, the CJEU does not address the issue why the European legislator would choose to expect an active behaviour of consumers with regard to obtaining pre-contractual information but not in respect of receiving confirmation of that information after the contract's conclusion. The Court does not examine either whether, in general, encompassing passive consumers within the scope of protection of the DSD fits in the broader *consumer acquis*.[45]

The Court interprets provisions of the DSD as, at least partially, aiming to protect passive consumers in the substantive European consumer law. This is of special significance for this research, since as it has been argued in the previous paragraph, European substantive consumer law generally focuses on protecting active consumers. Considering the high costs of compliance with providing consumers with mandated disclosures for traders, it would not have come as a surprise if the Court decided to limit the scope of consumers who are to receive such disclosure to active consumers. With this judgment the Court introduced, however, a new standard for consideration when elaborating on the notion of European consumers. Therefore, what is important to reflect on is whether broadening of the scope of this notion could be justified due to specific

40 CJEU (footnote 10), *Content Services*, para. 35.
41 CJEU (footnote 10), *Content Services*, para. 32.
42 CJEU (footnote 10), *Content Services*, para. 33.
43 CJEU (footnote 10), *Content Services*, para. 35.
44 See also C. Goanţa, 'Information Duties in the Internet Era: Case note on *Content Services LTD v. Bundesarbeitskammer*', *European Review of Private Law*, vol. 21, 2013, p. 648.
45 On the idea of lack of "cross-directive" interpretation by the CJEU see also C. Goanţa (footnote 44), p. 650.

characteristics of online trade. For example, such justification could be found if consumers were more prone to passive behaviour and more likely to conclude contracts they would later regret online rather than offline. The attitudes of online consumers to disclosures will further be discussed in paragraph 5 to review whether they could provide a justification for a different approach to the scope of consumer protection. First, in the following paragraph, the new formal requirements that have been introduced in the CRD are illustrated in order to examine whether they continue to protect passive conduct of online consumers or whether they deviate from the standards set in the DSD, as explained in the *Content Services* judgment.

IV. CRD: new online disclosure rules

Article 8 of the CRD sets the formal requirements for conclusion of consumer distance selling contracts. Its paragraph 1 replaces Article 4 of the DSD and its paragraph 7 – Article 5 of the DSD. When we compare all these provisions some significant differences in their wording become clear.

While Article 4 of the DSD used, pursuant to the CJEU, a neutral wording that pre-contractual information needs to be "provided" to consumers, Article 8(1) of the CRD states that the trader has to "give" information to consumers or "make it available" to them. We may wonder whether the European legislator, in recognition of the CJEU's interpretation in the *Content Services* judgment of the notion "to provide information" as a neutral one, purposefully decided to alter the focus group of this provision: from active to passive consumers. This assumption could be supported by the shift of focus in the provision from the consumers' right to information to the traders' obligation to inform. Former law shed spotlight on the consumer's right to be "provided" with information, while the new provision changes the perspective and highlights instead the trader's obligation to "give" information or to "make it available". At the first glance this seems to follow the reasoning of the CJEU expressed in the *Content Services* judgment. That is to say, at least the first part of this provision indicates the need to protect passive consumers by requesting active conduct of the trader, for him to "give" the information to a consumer. Unfortunately, the second part of this provision introduces an ambiguity to this evaluation. While the new notion of the trader having to "give" information to consumers should have greater implications for the trader than the old notion of consumers having to be "provided" with information, the same cannot be said about the second new notion of "making information available" to consumers. The CJEU has not elaborated on the meaning of this last notion and it begs a question why the European legislator would decide to introduce yet another wording on the formal requirements for providing information to consumers, one without a harmonised meaning in the EU. The fact that the European legislator did not stop at the first notion of the trader having to "give" information to the consumer but also gave him a possibility to "make information available" could suggest that under some circumstances passive consumers should be excluded from the scope of the CRD's protection.[46] It remains, however, to be seen how

46 J. Luzak, 'Online Consumer Contracts', *ERA Forum*, vol. 15, 2014, p. 386–387.

the national and European courts will interpret this provision and under what circumstances will they consider the information as perhaps not "given" but still "made available" to consumers.

On the other hand, while Article 5 of the DSD required that the consumer "received" the confirmation of the contractual information, unless it has already been "given" to her, Article 8(7) of the CRD now introduces the trader's obligation to "provide" consumers with this confirmation. If the trader has already "provided" the pre-contractual information to the consumer on a durable medium, he does not have to separately deliver its confirmation. The change of the wording in this provision is even more confusing in light of the *Content Services* judgment, where the Court specifically interpreted the notion of "providing" information as a neutral one.[47] The European legislator in the guidelines accompanying the adoption of the CRD clarifies that the choice to use a neutral notion in this provision was an intentional one and explains that it has introduced it with the full awareness of the CJEU's judgment in the *Content Services* case.[48] This could imply that the European legislator aimed at introducing more trader-friendly formal requirements that could better accommodate conclusion of online contracts in the future by limiting the scope of their recipients to active consumers. After all, ensuring that the mandated disclosure have reached every online customer of a given trader, also completely passive ones, might make disclosures more complex, require additional technology to be used, etc. Placing too complicated and not adjusted to modern technology formal requirements for provision of consumer information could hinder online trade, e.g., if it delayed provision of services that consumers expect to have access to immediately. Under such circumstances consumers may begin to consider concluding such contracts with other online traders, not bound by the CRD rules. This could cause harm to the internal market of the EU.

While the European legislator might have intended to halt the proliferation of the CJEU's interpretation of the above-discussed provisions with a deliberate change of wording introduced in Article 8 of the CRD, the national legislators seem more reluctant to abandon this construction. In the Netherlands the formal requirements of Article 8 of the CRD are implemented in Article 6:230v of the Dutch Civil Code.[49] Interestingly, the Explanatory Memorandum to the new Dutch law still relies on the interpretation given to Article 5 of the DSD by the CJEU while discussing the implementation of Article 8 of the CRD. That is to say, it highlights the need to provide consumers with the confirmation of contractual information, drawing attention to the fact that consumers need to possess a copy of contractual provisions for their purview. The word used by the Dutch legislator to define the traders' obligation to provide pre-contractual information and its confirmation to the consumer is "*verstrekken*", which could either mean to "give" or to

47 See, however, for interpreting the notion of 'providing' information as requiring an active behaviour of the trader rather than forming a neutral obligation: S. Grundmann (footnote 34), p. 111.

48 European Commission, DG Justice document, June 2014, available at http://ec.europa.eu/justice/consumer-marketing/files/crd_guidance_en.pdf, last accessed online on 14 January 2015, p. 36–37.

49 Memorie van implementatie van de Richtlijn consumentenrechten, available at www.rijksoverheid.nl/documenten-en-publicaties/rapporten/2013/02/01/memorie-van-implementatie-van-de-richtlijn-consumentenrechten.html, last accessed online on 14 January 2015, Transporteringstabel.

"provide" information.[50] The Memorandum refers, however, to the *Content Services* judgment and states that only when a trader makes a disclosure to a consumer it would be effective. Consequently, the Dutch legislator clarifies that if a trader uses a hyperlink to disclose mandatory information online to consumers this practice will not be considered a compliant, effective one. It seems, therefore, that without waiting for the CJEU to interpret the scope of application of Article 8 of the CRD the Dutch legislator decided to uphold the passive consumers' protection as established in the *Content Services* judgment.[51]

In English law the CRD was implemented through the Consumer Contracts (Information, Cancellation and Additional Charges) Regulations 2013 (hereafter, the "Regulations 2013").[52] The formal requirements of Article 8 of the CRD are laid down in Articles 13 and 16 of the Regulations 2013. In the Implementing Guidance to the new law the English legislator clarifies that it requires an action on the side of the trader when the latter provides consumers with information. The trader needs to either "send" the information to consumers or "place" it on the website, which wording reflects the wording of Article 8 of the CRD. However, also the English legislator explicitly states that the trader may not settle for just providing consumers with mandatory information through the use of a hyperlink to another website that contains this information. Especially, if this website is under the control of the trader, which means he may change its content at any time.[53] This latter argument may, however, be based more on the consumer's need to have a possibility to store the information than on how she receives it.

Even if the European legislator tried to give a broader meaning to the formal requirements for mandatory consumer disclosures, requiring some activity on the side of the consumer to obtain this information, the national legislators may not follow this new path so easily. That is to say, as long as the CJEU does not interpret the European legislator's intentions in adopting Article 8 of the CRD as encompassing within its protective scope only active consumers, the national legislators and courts could follow the *Content Services* approach. The narrow interpretation of the formal requirements for online disclosures may, however, prove problematic for online traders who could find it difficult to comply therewith in the evolving modern technology world. Not to mention it may negatively impact the European traders' capability to compete against traders from outside the EU since it could significantly raise their costs of providing online consumers with mandated disclosures. Moreover, such a narrow interpretation would deviate from the general trend of protecting active consumers in substantive European consumer law, as outlined in paragraph 2. The following paragraph examines, therefore,

50 This follows the Dutch text of the CRD, Article 8.

51 Implementatiewet Richtlijn consumentenrechten, *Kamerstukken II* 2012/2013, 33520, No. 3, p. 33.

52 The Consumer Contracts (Information, Cancellation and Additional Charges) Regulations 2013, No. 3134, available at https://www.gov.uk/government/uploads/system/uploads/attachment_data/file/265898/consumer-contracts-information-cancellation-and-additional-payments-regulations-2013.pdf, last accessed online on 14 January 2015.

53 Department for Business Innovation and Skills, Consumer Contracts (information, cancellation and additional charges regulations), Implementing Guidance, December 2013, p. 15–17. See also: P. Mankowski (footnote 5), p. 787; S. Grundmann (footnote 34), p. 111.

whether behavioural studies on the attitudes of internet users to disclosures show differences in the consumers' approach to disclosures online and offline. If the assumption that it is more difficult to draw consumers attention to disclosures online rather than offline held true, the introduction of additional protection for passive online consumers should be actively pursued by the European legislator aiming at attracting more consumers to online trade.

V. Internet users' attitudes to disclosures

While the precise interpretation and scope of application of the new Article 8 of the CRD is yet unknown, the question remains whether it would be desirable to encompass within its protection also passive consumers. As it has been mentioned above, the CJEU did that in the *Content Services* case, but some authors have already argued that this was a mistake.[54] One of the raised arguments is that while online consumers have to be active and click on a hyperlink added to an e-mail to receive their mandatory disclosure, consumers concluding offline distance transactions may also be required to be active to obtain their mandatory information. As an example may serve a situation, in which a consumer receives a letter from a trader with a disclosure enclosed in it.[55] To reach the disclosure the consumer needs to open an envelope, therefore, also exhibit some activity. This comparison contrasts the use of two different methods of distance communication, as a result of which contracts may be concluded online or through mail. In both these situations consumers may have an enhanced need for receiving additional disclosure, considering they are concluding a distance selling contract and may need to compensate for lack of information as to the goods' quality or lack of trust in the transaction's success.[56] However, this comparison does not seem to be the most fitting. Nowadays, consumers receive many spam e-mails with unnecessary and often also ridiculous information. For this reason many e-mail inboxes have spam filters installed and immediately direct any dubious e-mails there.[57] Most often these would be e-mails that come from a new e-mail address, e.g., from the new trader that the consumer just got in touch with. Additionally, e-mails which contain suspicious hyperlinks or attachments are likely to be diverted to the spam inbox, as well. The consumer may, therefore, never experience the online version of an envelope in her hands that she could decide whether

54 See e.g.: C. Goanţa (footnote 44), p. 650–653.

55 See also C. Goanţa (footnote 44), p. 652.

56 See e.g. footnote 6.

57 See e.g. D. Hendricks, 'Reaching Spam-Savvy Consumers by Email Is Harder Than Ever', *Forbes*, 2 June 2014, available at www.forbes.com/sites/drewhendricks/2014/02/06/reaching-spam-savvy-consumers-by-email-is-harder-than-ever/, last accessed online on 14 January 2015. It could be argued that it would be the active consumers that would have sophisticated spam filters installed, if these would not come pre-installed in the purchased computer hardware, since activity would be required to install them on consumer's computer. However, the division between protection granted to active and passive consumers in the substantive European consumer law as applied in this paper refers to any activities that consumers would need to take to obtain information and to use their rights instead of this information being provided to them and their rights being recognised *ex officio*.

to open, since not every consumer reviews her spam inbox and its content nor could be expected to do so.[58]

Researchers often claim that consumers are unlikely to benefit from any mandatory online disclosures since they are either incapable of processing the information revealed to them or not interested in even attempting to process this information.[59] In this paper it is important to consider the first step that could lead to consumers' understanding of the (pre-)contractual information, namely, when consumers notice disclosures and whether the requirements for gaining their attention differ online and offline. After all, as mentioned in the introduction, while mandated disclosures might have failed in their goal to better inform consumers, they could still provide consumers with useful information on the transaction and its conditions. For this, the disclosure needs only to reach the consumer in a format that would allow for storing of this information and, therefore, it is important to consider when consumers would notice disclosures. If there is a difference in consumer approach to disclosures online and offline, this could explain why the European legislator may want to set different standards for consumer protection in the CRD than in other substantive European consumer law measures. Researchers of consumer behaviour have identified five main reasons why consumers do not notice or do not pay attention to disclosures: when the disclosure is not personally relevant; when the consumer was already familiar with the disclosure; when the consumer was distracted from the disclosure; when the trader did not ensure to capture sufficient attention of the consumer; when the consumer has become desensitised to the disclosure after repeated exposure to it.[60]

Since the disclosure's content would be similar for online and offline distance selling transactions, the first two factors should not contribute to a difference between the levels of attention consumers pay to disclosures in these two different environments. However, we could imagine that the type and the amount of distractions that consumers would face online and offline would differ. In general, consumers tend to pay attention selectively to the information that is provided to them.[61] This means that while they focus on certain information, they ignore some other information. Especially when consumers are confronted with a large amount of information at once and they need to analyse it in a

58 This reasoning would continue to apply also to consumers receiving an e-mail with an attached file in a.pdf format containing the disclosure instead of with an e-mail containing a hyperlink that directs the consumer to the disclosure. See also: C. Goanţa (footnote 44), p. 652.

59 O. Ben-Shahar and C. E. Schneider (footnote 1), p. 7–13; G.R. Milne and M. J. Culnan, 'Strategies for Reducing Online Privacy Risks: Why Consumers Read (or Don't Read) Online Privacy Notices', *Journal of Interactive Marketing*, vol. 18, 2004, p. 17, 19, 23–25; S. Furnell and A. Phippen, 'Online Privacy: A Matter of Policy?', *Computer Fraud and Society*, August 2012, p. 14–15; I. Pollach, 'A Typology of Communicative Strategies in Online Privacy Policies: Ethics, Power and Informed Consent', *Journal of Business Ethics*, vol. 62, 2005, p. 223.

60 D. Albarracin, J. B. Cohen, G. T. Kumkale, 'When Communications Collide with Recipients' Actions: Effects of Post-Message Behavior on Intentions to Follow the Message Recommendation', *Personality and Social Psychology Bulletin*, vol. 29, 2003, p. 834–845; T. Hansen (footnote 15), p. 420–437; D. W. Stewart, I. M. Martin, 'Intended and Unintended Consequences of Warning Messages: A Review and Synthesis of Empirical Research', *Journal of Public Policy and Marketing*, vol. 13 (1), Spring 1994, p. 5.

61 T. Hansen (footnote 15), p. 420–437; D. Zillman, J. Bryant, *Selective Exposure to Communication*, Hillsdale, NJ: Lawrence Erlbaum Associates, 1985.

short time, they might need to make trade-offs as to which information they will follow more closely and which they will not spend much of their energy and time on.[62] A lot of research on online disclosures focuses on the topic of how to attract consumers' attention to them, which shows that – whether online or offline – consumers may ignore certain displayed information and special marketing techniques may be needed to encourage consumers to notice certain information.[63] However, due to the increased availability and constant presence of online advertisements consumers may suffer more distractions online than offline, that could further inhibit their memory and data-processing capabilities when they are to notice and read even a simple disclosure (or perform an otherwise easy task[64]). This last research may point to the need to protect passive consumers online more than offline, however, more empirical data would need to be gathered to fully support this statement.

Additional complication arises when we consider how traders draw consumers attention to disclosures. The online environment may offer traders more varied options with regard to increasing the attractiveness of the disclosure's display than the offline world. For example, online traders may play around with the disclosure's design, position, colour, font, etc. in order to increase the internet users' chance of actually noticing and reading it.[65] The options of an offline trader are not only more limited in this respect, but also less flexible, since he will not be able to easily change an already printed design. However, in both cases similar rules apply: the disclosure's font should not be smaller than the font of any other information that is being conveyed alongside it; the disclosure's content should be concise in order to be comprehensive; the information should not be hidden but rather prominently displayed.[66] As I have mentioned previously, it can be problematic to disclose mandatory information to consumers through the use of a hyperlink, which would lead to the information opening in a separate Internet window. After all, this may require the consumer to pay even more attention to what is happening on her computer screen and for her to take an action to receive this information. However, some authors have argued that the disclosure's display would be more clear and, therefore, more approachable to internet users if it occurs in a separate window.[67] In such a case, the hyperlink should be prominently displayed and the importance of the internet users clicking on it should be clearly communicated to them.[68] While the consumer may be

62 L. A. Morris, M. B. Mazis, D. Brinberg, 'Risk Disclosures in Televised Prescription Drug Advertising to Consumers', *Journal of Public Policy and Marketing*, vol. 8 (1), 1989, p. 64–80.

63 G.R. Milne and M. J. Culnan (footnote 59), p. 17, 19, 25; S. Harridge-March (footnote 7), p. 754–755; J. Wirtz, M. O. Lwin, J. D. Williams, 'Causes and Consequences of Consumer Online Privacy Concern', *International Journal of Service Industry Management,* vol. 18, 2007, p. 341.

64 B. J. Sagarin, A. Britt, J. D. Heider, S. E. Wood, J. E. Lynch, 'Bartering Our Attention: The Distraction and Persuasion Effects of On-line Advertisements', *Cognitive Technology*, vol. 8, 2003, p. 4–17.

65 G.R. Milne and M. J. Culnan (footnote 59), p. 17, 19, 25; S. Harridge-March (footnote 7), p. 754–755; J. Wirtz (footnote 63), p. 341.

66 G.R. Milne and M. J. Culnan (footnote 59), p. 23.

67 R. Jones and D. Tahri, 'EU Law Requirements to Provide Information to Website Visitors', *Computer Law and Security Report*, vol. 26, 2010, p. 620.

68 L. van Wel and L. Royakkers, 'Ethical Issues in Web Data Mining', *Ethics and Information Technology,* vol. 6, 2004, p. 134.

more distracted from the information online rather than offline due to the large amount of ever-present online advertisement, an online trader seems to have more techniques and tricks available to him to draw consumer's attention to the disclosure.

The remaining factor that may influence the consumers' attention to disclosures is the consumers' potential desensitisation to disclosures due to the repeated exposure to them.[69] Some research suggests that as long as online disclosures would vary, consumers would be less likely to get desensitised to them, since the single-message overexposure would thus be prevented.[70] However, other research suggests standardisation of online disclosures in order to facilitate consumers' understanding of the disclosed message.[71] It is logical to assume that the possibility of overexposure would be bigger online, especially if online trade continues to grow and consumers more often find themselves concluding online contracts. Due to the mandatory nature of the CRD's information requirements every online trader will have to provide consumers with the same, extensive list of information. However, the evidence from behavioural studies is not conclusive as to the effects of overexposure. Therefore, it is hard to estimate whether the dangers of overexposure would hinder consumers' attention to online disclosures and how precisely these could be overcome.

Despite a few potential differences between consumers' attention to disclosures online and offline, more empirical research is needed in order to conclude that consumers have more difficulties noticing and paying attention to disclosures online rather than offline. It certainly could be easier to attract consumers' attention due to various disclosure methods that are at the disposal of online traders, their flexibility. Still, there is a big risk online of overwhelming consumers with many different disclosures, particularly if every online trader has to repeat the same information. Whether this would lead to consumers becoming better informed with mandatory disclosures or rather becoming desensitised to them remains to be seen. In any case, so far, the behavioural studies do not indicate the need to treat online consumers differently than offline consumers, e.g., by protecting passive and not only active online consumers.

VI. Conclusion

Despite some arguments presented in the previous paragraph as to why the internet users' attention to disclosures could be limited in comparison to that of offline consumers, it is difficult to assess whether these differences should stimulate the European legislator to introduce the passive consumers' protection in online transactions. At the moment,

69 W. Magat, W. K. Viscusi, J. Huber, 'Consumer Processing of Hazard Warning Information', *Journal of Risk and Uncertainty*, vol. 1, 1988, p. 201–232.

70 R. N. Mayer, K. R. Smith, D. L. Scammon, 'Evaluating the Impact of Alcohol Warning Labels', *Advances in Consumer Research*, vol. 18, 1991, p. 706–714.

71 C. Castro, F. J. Tornay, T. Horberry, C. Martínez, A. Gale, F. J. Martos, 'Worded and Symbolic Traffic Stimuli Analysis Using Repetition Priming and Semantic Priming Effects', *Advances in Psychology Research*, vol. 53, 2007, p. 39–40; J.A. Luzak, 'Privacy Notice for Dummies? Towards European Guidelines on How to Give 'Clear and Comprehensive Information' on the Cookies' Use in order to Protect the Internet Users' Right to Online Privacy', *Journal of Consumer Policy*, vol. 37, 2014, p. 547–559.

there is still no sufficient empirical research proving the existence of special needs of online consumers with regard to providing them with mandatory information. Additionally, even if online consumers were more difficult to reach through mandatory disclosures, the legislators should first establish whether there are any less intrusive formal requirements that could be adopted to improve the disclosures' visibility to online consumers, diminishing, therefore, the consumers' weak transactional position. Only following the failure of such measures, should the European legislator consider whether to broaden the scope of application of substantive European consumer law, such as formal requirements on mandated disclosures, to passive consumers in the case of online transactions. After all, this last solution deeply influences the balance between the parties' rights and obligations in a consumer online transaction and other, more proportional measures could be more appropriate to protect consumers.[72]

It would be a complex process to establish whether online disclosures are less likely to be noticed by consumers than offline disclosures, to what extent and what measures could remedy this situation. This may be the reason why the European legislator did not take a specific stand on this issue while drafting Article 8 of the CRD and instead used mixed-meaning notions that require national courts to protect at times only active, but at other times also passive consumers. Whether the CJEU will interpret this provision in accordance with its point of view expressed in the *Content Services* judgment remains to be seen. In the meantime, considering the interpretation given to Article 8 of the CRD in the Netherlands and in the UK, at least on national levels passive consumers online could continue to enjoy the protection against online traders hiding mandatory disclosures behind various hyperlinks.

[72] W. Kerber, 'Soft Paternalismus und Verbraucherpolitik', *List Forum für Wirtschafs- und Finanzpolitik*, vol. 40 (2), 2014, p. 282.

G.J.P. (Gerard)
de Vries*

IS THE GENERAL PRE-CONTRACTUAL EU NOTIFICATION DUTY OF TRADERS TO PROVIDE CONSUMERS WITH INFORMATION WITH RESPECT TO THE MAIN CHARACTERISTICS OF THE GOODS OR SERVICES TO BE SUPPLIED IN KEEPING WITH THE SYSTEMS OF PRIVATE LAW OF THE MEMBER STATES AND CONSISTENT WITH THE *ACQUIS COMMUNAUTAIRE*?

I. Introduction

Pre-contractual notification duties of traders have become hot with EU legislators, especially vis-à-vis consumers. This may for instance be concluded from the *Draft Common Frame of Reference* (*DCFR*), the *Consumer Rights Directive* (*CRD*) and the – recently withdrawn[1] – proposal for a Regulation concerning an optional *Common European Sales Law* (*CESL*).

With respect to the pre-contractual Notification duties of traders contained in these and other EU instruments, questions with respect to their consistency with the systems of national law of the Member states of the EU have been raised before. Notification duties under EU law are for instance reputed for their lengthiness[2] and it has been submitted the German legislator left them for this reason outside of the *Bürgerliches Gesetzbuch* and transposed them into a special national regulation, the so-called '*Verordnung uber Informations- und Nachweispflichten nach Bürgerlichem Recht*'.[3] In this contribution I intend to focus on the question whether the most important Notification duty incumbent on traders – their duty to provide the other party, especially

* G.J.P. de Vries is associate professor of private law at the University of Amsterdam.

1 Cf. the Work Programme for 2015 sent by the EU Commission to the European Parliament on 16 December 2014. The reason given for this withdrawal is yet another proposal, the 'Modified proposal in order to fully unleash the potential of e-commerce in the Digital Single Market' (see COM(2015)192def. about this latter proposal).

2 A.H. Eidenmüller e.a speak with respect of the Notification duties contained in the *DCFR* of 'the informational flood ordered by the DCFR' ('*die in DCFR angeordnete Informationsflut*'), *Der Gemeinsahme Referenzrahmen für das Europäische Privatrecht*, Juristenzeitung 2008, p. 535. See also C. Cauffmann, M.G. Faure and T. Hartlief, *Harmonisatie van het consumentencontractenrecht in Europa: consequenties voor Nederland*, Den Haag WODC 2009, p. 108 ff.

3 H. Kötz, *Vertragsrecht*, Tübingen: Mohr Siebeck 2009, No. 39.

if it is a consumer, with information with respect to the main characteristics of the goods or services to be supplied – is *intrinsically* in keeping with the systems of private law of the Member States. What I especially will look down into is whether this Notification duty is intrinsically concurrent with what in most systems of private law of the Member States is deemed to be a point of departure derived from the postulate of private autonomy, namely that parties engaging into negotiations are in this process primarily *themselves* responsible for gathering information that may be relevant to them.[4]

This question with respect to the concurrence of Notification duties with national law systems does not appear out of the blue: in her monograph on the rise of Information and Notification duties in Europe in the last century in general and their effect on traditional concepts such as vices of consent, R. Sefton-Green does not rule out the possibility that these duties 'are going to swallow the older more traditional concepts, such as mistake and fraud.'[5]

In order to evaluate this consistency I will not look into the private law-systems of áll EU Member States, but only into those of France, Germany, the Netherlands and England. This collection of law-systems may be considered to be representative both in that it includes the largest national private law systems within the EU – without excluding the smaller ones – and both Civil and Common Law-systems.

I also intend to deal with the question whether the before-mentioned duty of traders to provide the other party, especially if it is a consumer, with information with respect to the main characteristics of the goods or services to be supplied is intrinsically consistent with existing EU law, the *acquis communautaire*.

Let us first take stock of what the above-mentioned EU instruments actually have to say about the duty of traders to provide the other party with information with respect to the main characteristics of the goods or services to be supplied and of the remedies they provide for in case a trader fails to comply with this duty.

4 Cf. for instance A.H. Eidenmüller e.a. who conclude with respect to the Information and Notification duties in the *DCFR* that its rule that a party 'has to notify the other party extensively contradicts both the rule in the systems of national law of the Member States that a party is itself responsible for the information it gathers and its postulate of private autonomy' (o.c., p. 544 ff.). See also K.J.O. Jansen, *Informatieplichten, Over kennis en verantwoordelijkheid in contractenrecht en buitencontractueel aansprakelijkheidsrecht*, Deventer: Kluwer 2012, thesis Leiden University 2012, p. 83 ff.

5 R. Sefton-Green, Mistake, Fraud and Duties to Inform in European Contract Law, Cambridge: University Press 2005, p. 29.

II. The EU Notification duty of traders to provide the other party with information with respect to the main characteristics of the goods or services to be supplied

The *Draft Common Frame of Reference (DCFR)*, encompassing 'Principles, Definitions and Model Rules of European Private Law', advises EU legislators by way of 'Model Rules' to impose on traders ('businesses') the general Notification duties to:

- 'disclose to another person such information concerning the goods, other assets or services to be supplied as the other person can reasonably expect' (Article II.-3:101 *DCFR*);
- 'in the case of transactions that place the consumer at a significant informational disadvantage (…) to provide clear information about the main characteristics of any goods, other assets or services to be supplied' (Article II. -3:103 *DCFR*).

Whereas Article II. -3:103 *DCFR* only advises a Notification duty for those traders who conclude contracts 'that place the consumer at a significant informational disadvantage' – e.g. a distance contracts or an off premises contract –, the advice contained in Article II. -3:101 *DCFR* is broader in scope since it applies:

- to áll kinds of contracts;
- not only when the other party is a consumer, but also when the other party is also a trader, although this Notification duty is then limited to those cases where 'the failure to provide information would deviate from good commercial practice' (Article II.-3:101 (2) *DCFR*).

This general Notification duty contained in Article II.-3:101 *DCFR* is, however, more limited than the one that is only applicable to distance contract and off premises contracts in that the trader is only obliged to disclose to another person such information concerning the goods, other assets or services to be supplied 'as the other person can reasonably expect' (Article II.-3:101 *DCFR*).

Since Article II.-3:101 *DCFR* according to its Comments 'ties in with the provisions on non-conformity in Book IV.A, Chapter 2, Section 3 (Conformity of the goods) and in the Consumer Sales Directive 1999/44/EG)'[6] , it will does nót come as a surprise that Article II.-3:109 (2) *DCFR* on 'Remedies for breach of Information duties' provides that if, in case of such a breach, a contract has been concluded, 'the business has such obligations under the contract as the other has reasonably expected as a consequence of the absence or incorrectness of the information. Remedies provided under Book III, Chapter 3 apply to

6 Principles, Definitions and Model Rules of European Private Law, Draft Common Frame of Reference (DCFR), Full Edition, Edited by Christian von Bar and Eric Clive, Munich: Sellier European Law Publishers, 2008, Volume I, Comment on Article II.- 3:101 DCFR sub D. 'Relationship to other provisions', p. 202.

non-performance of these obligations'. These remedies for non-performance of an obligation comprise the rights of the other person to: enforce performance, terminate the contract, reduce the price, claim damages on the basis of the so-called 'expectation interest' and also interest. Since the remedies provided by Article II.-3:109 *DCFR* are, according to its 4th paragraph, 'without prejudice to any remedy which may be available under Article II.-7:201 *DCFR* (Mistake)' and this latter Article even holds a special provision for a Mistake resulting from the breach of a Notification duty – 'a party may avoid a contract for mistake if the other party caused the contract to be concluded in mistake by failing to comply with a pre-contractual information duty' (Article II.-7:201 (1) (b) (iii) *DCFR* (Mistake) -, the breach of the Notification duty in question may also be remedied by the right of other party to avoid the contract for Mistake.

The *Consumer Rights Directive* (*CRD*) imposes the following Notification duties on traders vis-à- vis consumers:

- 'before the consumer is bound by a contract other than a distance or off-premises contract (...) the trader shall provide the consumer with the following information in a clear and comprehensible manner, if that information is not already apparent from the context: the main characteristics of the goods or services, to the extent appropriate to the medium and to the goods or services' (Article 5(1)(a) *CRD*);
- in case the trader concludes a distance or an off-premises contract 'before the consumer is bound (...) the trader shall provide the consumer with the following information in a clear and comprehensible way: the main characteristics of the goods or services, to the extent appropriate to the medium and to the goods and services' (Article 6(1)(a) *CRD*).

The Notification duties the Directive on Consumer Rights imposes on traders resemble their counterparts in the *DCFR* in that the general Notification duty contained in Article 5(1)(a) *CRD* applying to contracts between traders and consumers in general is more limited than the one that is only applicable to distance contract and off premises contracts, since traders are only obliged to provide the consumer with information with respect to the main characteristics of the goods or services 'if that information is not already apparent from the context' (Article 5(1)(a) *CRD*). It should, however, also be noted that the *CRD* is thus much more strict on the trader than the *DCFR*: the consumer may no longer only expect the information he 'can reasonably expect' (*DCFR*), but may expect all the information that is 'not already apparent from the context' (*CRD*).

There is nothing in the *CRD* itself to be found in the way of remedies on account of a breach by a trader of either of these general Notification duties. In view of the obligation of Member States to 'ensure that adequate and effective means exist to ensure compliance with this Directive' (Article 23 *CRD*), legislative bodies and the judiciary of these States are, however, most likely to introduce remedies including the above-mentioned remedies of private law recommended by the *DCFR*.[7]

7 And so they do: under Dutch law for instance breaches of the above-mentioned Notification duty of traders concluding a distance or off-premises contract to inform the consumer about the main

The – recently withdrawn – proposal for a Regulation concerning an optional *Common European Sales Law* (*CESL*) also intends to impose Notification duties on traders vis-à-vis consumers with respect to the main characteristics of the goods, digital content or related services to be supplied and they resemble those of the *DCFR* and the *CRD*:

- in contracts other than distance and off-premises contracts a trader has a to provide that information in a clear and comprehensible manner before the contract is concluded only if that information is not already apparent from the context (Article 20(1)(a) Annex I to the *CESL*);
- a trader concluding a distance or off-premises contract has a duty to provide that information *tout court* in a clear and comprehensible way before the contract is concluded (Article 13(1)(a) Annex I to the *CESL*)

This proposal for a *CESL* resembles the *DCFR* in that it imposes on traders also a Notification duty to disclose the main characteristics of the goods or services vis-à-vis other traders, but this duty is, much in the way recommended by Article II.-3:101 *DCFR*, limited to information 'which the suppliers has or can be expected to have and which it would be contrary to good faith and fair dealing not to disclose to the other party' (Article 23(1) Annex I to the *CESL*).

This proposal for a *CESL* resembles the *CRD* in that the general Notification duty contained in Article 20 paragraph 1 under (a) Annex I to the *CESL*) applying to contracts between traders and consumers in general is more limited than the one that is only applicable to distance contract and off premises contracts. It also resembles the *CRD*, but differs from the *DCFR* in that traders are not just obliged to provide the consumer with information the latter 'can reasonably expect', but with all the information that 'is not already apparent from the context'.

In keeping with the provision in the *CESL* to the effect that 'only the Common European Sales Law shall govern the matters addressed in its rules' (Article 11 *CESL*), this EU instrument also provides for remedies for a breach by traders of their Notification duties. The party to whom incorrect or misleading information has been supplied and who reasonably relied on that information in concluding the contract:

- has a right to damages for any loss caused thereby (Article 29(1) Annex I to the *CESL*);
- may avoid the contract for vices of consent: for Mistake if the trader 'knew or could be expected to have known of the mistake and caused the contract to be concluded in mistake by not pointing out the relevant information, provided that good faith and fair dealing would have required a party aware of the mistake to point it out'

characteristics of the goods of services (Article 6 paragraph 1 sub (a) *CRD*) constitute a 'misleading commercial practice' by way of 'misleading omission' (Article 6:193f sub b jo Article 6:193d *Burgerlijk Wetboek*) and so do breaches of other Notification duties in the *CRD*, which omission will award consumers recourse to the remedy of avoidance of their contracts with the trader in case it was concluded as a result of this omission (Article 6:193f (3) *Burgerlijk Wetboek*).

(Article 48(1)(b) (iii) jo Article 29(3) Annex I to the *CESL*) or for Fraud if the trader 'has induced the conclusion of the contract by fraudulent misrepresentation, whether by words or conduct, of fraudulent non-disclosure of any information which good faith and fair dealing, or any pre-contractual information duty, required that party to disclose' (Article 49(1) jo Article 29(3) Annex I to the *CESL*).

One may conclude then from this brief overview of EU instruments that:

- EU law imposes or intends to impose on traders pre-contractual Notification duties with respect to the main characteristics of the goods and services to be supplied, especially vis-à-vis consumers, a breach of which will grant consumers remedies based on both non-performance of an obligation and on vices of consent;
- the pre-contractual Notification duty applying to contracts between traders and consumers in general is more limited than the one applicable only to distance contract and off premises contracts, since traders are in general only obliged to provide the consumer with information with respect to the main characteristics of the goods or services 'if that information is not already apparent from the context' (*CRD* and *CESL*), whereas the latter Notification duty is incumbent on traders regardless of what is apparent from the context;
- the pre-contractual Notification duty applying to contracts between traders and consumers in general has, however, a tendency to become much more strict on the trader over time: whereas the consumer in the *DCFR* was still only entitled to expect the information he 'can reasonably expect', he is under the *CRD* and *CECL* entitled to expect all the information that is 'not already apparent from the context';

III. Why address the questions whether the general EU Notification duty of traders to provide consumers with information with respect to the main characteristics of the goods or services to be supplied is in keeping with the systems of private law of the Member States and consistent with the acquis communautaire?

In view of the fact that the effectiveness of Notification duties vis-à-vis consumers has been put into question from a behavioural point of view, one may as to the first-mentioned conclusion above with respect to these EU instruments one may be tempted to wonder why the European Union attaches importance at all to duties of traders to notify consumers: consumers seldom read/understand the information they are provided with[8] and the before-mentioned lengthiness of EU Notification duties imposes on traders may even pose the risk that it enables them to hide from consumers exactly thát particular bit of information that is relevant to them: are consumers that are swamped by information, not only the more readily prone to overlook the relevant bit of it? It is, however, also a fact

8 F. Marotta-Wurgler, *Does Disclosure Matter?*, Law and Economics Research Paper Series, Working Paper No. 10-53, November 2010 and, with respect to information about 'cookies and J.A. Luzak, 'Privacy Notice for Dummies?', *Journal of Consumer Policy* (2014), p. 547.

of life that behavioural insights like the one in question, hardly ever prevent national or EU legislators from imposing new Notification duties – in the process also obliging them to discharge these duties 'in a clear and comprehensible manner' – and the *CRD* and the – recently withdrawn – proposal for a *CESL* are only recent examples of this tendency.[9] Therefore I will leave the matter of the ineffectiveness of these Notification duties aside here.

I have also decided to narrow the question with respect to the consistency of these duties with the systems of private law of the Member States and with the *acquis communautaire* down to the general EU Notification duty of traders to provide consumers with information with respect to the main characteristics of the goods or services to be supplied. As far as their consistency with the systems of private law of the Member States is concerned, it is obvious that the specific Notification duty of traders in distance and off-premises contracts to provide the consumer with information with respect to the main characteristics of the goods and services to be supplied regardless of what is apparent from the context (cf. Article II.-3:103 *DCFR*, Article 6(1)(a) *CRD* and Article 13(1)(a) Annex I to the *CESL*) – which exempts consumers *a priori* from ány responsibility for gathering information about these goods and services – would at first sight have made a better candidate, since it is clearly nót in keeping with national private law systems of the Member States of the European Union. It is also obvious, however, that this discrepancy can as a rule be justified by the fact that distance and off-premises contracts place consumers, as Article II.-3:103 *DCFR* puts it with accuracy, 'at a significant informational disadvantage'.[10]

I will therefore focus only on the general EU Notification duty of traders applying to all contracts between traders and consumers to provide the latter with information with respect to the main characteristics of the goods or services if that information is not already apparent from the context and try to ascertain whether this general EU Notification duty is intrinsically consistent with the systems of private law of the Member States of the EU and with the *acquis communautaire*.

9 Cf. M.B.M. Loos with respect to the *CRD* in: *Consumentenkoop*, Mon. BW nr B65b, par. 17, Deventer: Kluwer 2014.

10 One may, however, doubt whether this justification is sufficient in those cases where it was in fact the consumer who took the initiative to conclude a distance or off-premises contract. When for instance an off- premises contract has been concluded at the initiative of the consumer at his home the Notification duty contained in Article 6(1)(a) *CRD* to the effect that 'before the consumer is bound (...) the trader shall provide the consumer with the following information in a clear and comprehensible way: the main characteristics of the goods or services, to the extent appropriate to the medium and to the goods and services' is also applicable to this situation and the same is true for the similar Notification duty in Article 13(1)(a) Annex I to the CESL.

IV. Is the general EU Notification duty of traders to provide consumers with information with respect to the main characteristics of the goods or services to be supplied in keeping with the systems of private law of the Member States?

The way the EU deals with the duty of traders to notify the other party has already met with criticism in literature before. I will set out by establishing what triggered it and assess this criticism and will then give my own answer to the above-mentioned question.

This criticism was mainly directed at the following Comment in the *DCFR* on the provision in Article II.-7:201(1) on 'Mistake known to the other party' in where 'the other party caused the contract to be concluded in mistake by leaving the mistaken party in error, contrary to good faith and fair dealing, when the other party knew or could reasonably be expected to have known of the mistake' (Article II.-7:201(1)(b)(ii) *DCFR*): 'It is true that some legal systems within the EU as a general rule do allow a party to remain silent about important information, even if aware that it would influence the other's decision. That may be appropriate in certain cases, for example when the knowledgeable party has only gained the knowledge at considerable expense, or in highly competitive situations (see Illustration 2 below), but as a blanket rule it is not appropriate. It does not accord with either commercial morality or what contracting parties will normally expect of each other. Unless there is a good reason for allowing the party to remain silent, silence is incompatible with good faith and will entitle the other party to avoid the contract under this Article.'[11]

It was notably this sweeping statement concluding the above-quoted Comment on the provision for 'Mistake known to the other party' in Article II.-7:201(1)(b (ii) *DCFR* that provoked the following criticisms:

- The *DCFR* 'opens the way to dismantle private autonomy' and 'is especially dangerous since it chooses as a point of departure that the all-encompassing Notification of the other party is the rule and the responsibility of the parties engaging into negotiations for gathering information that is relevant to them as the exception (…). This rule/exception-relationship contradicts the legal situation in the European law systems and the fact systems of private law are based on freedom.'[12]
- 'One may wonder whether this idea (that 'Silence is incompatible with good faith'; GdV) is actually based on a *communis opinio* in Europe.'[13]

11 Principles, Definitions and Model Rules of European Private Law, Draft Common Frame of Reference (DCFR), Full Edition, Edited by Christian von Bar and Eric Clive, Munich: Sellier European Law Publishers, 2008, Volume I, Comment on Article II.-7:201 DCFR sub E. 'Mistake known to other party', p. 460.

12 A.H. Eidenmüller e.a., o.c., p. 549 resp. p. 544 ff.

13 K.J.O. Jansen, o.c., p. 83.

It is in my opinion quite right to criticise this conclusion as a sweeping statement, but only as a slip of the pen. It simply contradicts the black letter rule of Article II.-7:201(1)(b)(ii) *DCFR* that it is supposed to comment on, since the latter stipulates that the mistaken party has only recourse to this ground of mistake 'if the other party caused the contract to be concluded in mistake by leaving the mistaken party in error contrary o good faith and fair dealing' (Article II.-7:201(1)(b)(ii) *DCFR*. This ground for recourse to mistake is not only very familiar to Civil Law-systems[14] but even a classical one: it was already dealt with by M.T. Cicero where he brought up the grains salesman travelling to hunger-stricken Rhodos with his ship filled to the brim with grains, wondering whether this salesman should be obliged to tell its hungry inhabitants that more ships filled with grains were on their way to the island.[15] Although the answer to this question may still be debated up to these days[16], the requirements Article II.-7:201(1)(b (ii) *DCFR* mentions for recourse to this 'Mistake known to the other party' reflect by and large the following requirements for recourse to this ground for mistake in Civil Law-systems derived from German[17] and from Dutch law[18]:

- the other party is a knowledgeable party or should have known about the facts;
- it knew about their relevance to the mistaken party;
- it knew of the mistake of the other party or could reasonably be expected to have known of it;
- it caused the contract to be concluded in mistake by leaving the mistaken party in error;
- it did so contrary to good faith and fair dealing or to societal usages to the effect that the knowledgeable party should notify the other one.

One may then conclude that despite of the sweeping statement in the Comments on Article II.-7:201(1)(b)(ii) *DCFR* that 'unless there is a good reason for allowing the party to remain silent, silence is incompatible with good faith and will entitle the other party to avoid the contract under this Article'[19], the way this provision in the *DCFR* itself deals with 'Mistake known to the other party' is similar to Civil Law-systems and may even be said to be 'classical'.

14 As we will see later on, a pre-contractual duty to disclose information to the other party has been rejected under English law.

15 M.T. Cicero, *De Officiis*, III, 50 ff.

16 See for more information on this subject K.J.O. Jansen, o.c., p. 15 ff.

17 Cf. Staudinger/Loosschelder/Olzen, *Kommentar zum Bürgerlichen Gesetzbuch*, Buch 2 *Recht der Schuldverhältnisse*, Berlin: Sellier-De Gruyter 2015, par. 241 BGB, Rn 447, *Münchener Kommentar zum Bürgerlichen Gesetzbuch, Band 2, Schuldrecht, Allgemeiner Teil*, Munich: C.H. Beck 2012, par. 241–432, Roth, par. 241 BGB, Rn 123 ff. and Bamberger/Roth/Holger Sutschet, *Kommentar zum Bürgerlichen Gesetzbuch*, München: C.H. Beck 2007, par. 241, Rn 4.

18 Cf. Asser/Hartkamp andSieburgh, 6-III, *Verbintenissenrecht, Algemeen overeenkomstenrecht*, Deventer: Kluwer 2014, nr 230 ff. and Asser-Hijma, 7-I*, *Bijzondere overeenkomsten, Koop en ruil*, Deventer: Kluwer 2013, No. 233.

19 *Principles, Definitions and Model Rules of European Private Law, Draft Common Frame of Reference (DCFR)*, Full Edition, Edited by Christian von Bar and Eric Clive, l.c.

As has already been mentioned above, Article II.-7:201 *DCFR* on Avoidance for Mistake also holds a special remedy for a 'Mistake resulting from the breach of a pre-contractual Notification duty': 'A party may avoid a contract for mistake if the other party caused the contract to be concluded in mistake by failing to comply with a pre-contractual information duty' (Article II.-7:201(1)(b)(iii) *DCFR*).

It is this newly concocted special provision in the *DCFR* for a 'Mistake resulting from the breach of a pre-contractual Notification duty' that in my opinion deserves much more attention. It reads as follows: 'A party may avoid a contract for mistake if the other party caused the contract to be concluded in mistake by failing to comply with a pre-contractual information duty' (Article II.-7:201(1)(b)(iii) *DCFR*)? Does this provision that also applies to the general Notification duty in question of traders to provide consumers with information with respect to the main characteristics of the goods or services if that information is not already apparent from the context, fit in with the law-systems of the Member States of the EU?

This latter question is much more relevant, since this special provision in the *DCFR* for a 'Mistake resulting from the breach of a pre-contractual Notification duty' (Article II.-7:201(1)(b) (iii) *DCFR*) simply does away with all the before-mentioned requirements for recourse to 'Mistake known to the other party' (Article II.-7:201(1)(b)(ii) *DCFR*) which, as we have seen, so duly reflect the requirements stipulated by Civil Law systems! One should realise that the application of this general EU Notification duty of traders to provide consumers with information with respect to the main characteristics of the goods or services to be supplied does nót depend on the knowledge of traders as to these main characteristic, since they are already obliged to provide consumers with this information 'if that information is not already apparent from the context.' Therefore situations very different from the one of grains salesman brought up by M.T. Cicero will also fall within the scope of a 'Mistake for the breach of a pre-contractual duty' or within the scope of another remedy for such a breach: one might for instance think of a garage proprietor that has sold and delivered to a consumer a 10-year old used car that turns out to pull up too slowly for the high speed that is necessary to merge fluently with the on-going traffic on highways. One can see at a glance that none of the above-mentioned requirements for recourse to 'Mistake known to the other party' has to be met for this new provision on 'Mistake for the breach of a pre-contractual duty' to apply: provided this defect in a characteristics of the car that may be said to be a main one, is not already apparent from the context, a garage proprietor that does nót know about this defect will also be obliged to inform the consumer about it, and since 'a knowledgeable party' is thus nót a requirement for recourse to this new remedy, nóne of the other above-mentioned requirements for it – that the knowledgeable party knew of the mistake or could reasonably be expected to have known of it; that it knew about their relevance to the mistaken party; that it caused the contract to be concluded in mistake by leaving the mistaken party in error; that it did so contrary to good faith and fair dealing or to societal usages to the effect that the knowledgeable party should notify the other one – will have to be met with.

It remains to be seen, however, how the systems of private law of the Member States of the EU deal with informational duties of traders and especially how they would have dealt with their pre-contractual duty in question to provide consumers with information with respect to the main characteristics of the goods or services to be supplied. As has been mentioned above, I will take a look into the law-systems of France, Germany, the Netherlands and England.[20]

It is a well-known fact that none of these law systems imposes such a general Notification duty *expressis verbis* on traders. This does, however, not imply that these law systems may not do so implicitly, as French law will exemplify.

Under *French* law the judiciary applies to traders on account of their '*qualification professionnelle*' presumptions to their detriment when the other party invokes fraud (Article 1116 *Code civil: 'dol')* or a claim based on a hidden lack of conformity (Article 1641 ff. *Code civil: 'vice caché'*), especially when this other party is a consumer:

- as a result of the application of the principle of good faith and fair dealing ('*bonne foi*') to the time preceding the conclusion of the contract[21], traders are frequently presumed by judges to have induced the contract by fraudulent non-disclosure of information which this principle required them to disclose (so-called '*réticence dolosive*'), especially when the other party is a consumer[22], thus facilitating the right of the latter to avoid the contract on account of Fraud and to claim for damages based on tort (Article 1382 *Code civil: 'faute'*);
- professional sellers are even irrefutably presumed to have known of the hidden lack of conformity in the goods they have delivered[23], so the other party will have recourse to the remedies based upon this non-performance.

Since disclosing the other party information about the goods, other assets or other services to be provided before the conclusion of the contract is the only appropriate way for traders to escape from these readily available remedies[24], French law may be said to have accepted, although implicitly, the general pre-contractual Notification duty in question.

As far as pre-contractual Notification duties are concerned, German law has become more complicated since the law of obligations in the very liberal *Bürgerliches Gesetzbuch* that came into force in 1900, has been reformed in 2002 ('*Schuldrechtsreform*'). Those engaging in negotiations about a contract to be concluded between them, thereby enter according to

20 I am indebted to K.J.O. Jansen for the information on this subject gathered in his above-mentioned, well thought-out thesis.

21 J. Ghestin, *Traité de droit civil, La formation du contrat*, Paris: LGDJ 1993, No. 262.

22 J. Ghestin, o.c., nr 571.

23 J. Ghestin, o.c., nr 624.

24 This is for instance true for sellers who according to French law are nót able evade the above-mentioned presumptions by contracting for disclaimers or for limitations of their liability (cf. ECJ Alsthom Atlantique/Sulzer, C-339/89).

German law into a legal relationship (§311(2) *Bürgerliches Gesetzbuch: 'Schuldverhältnis'*) that may impose on them the general duty 'to look after the rights, the legal goods and the interests of the other party' (§241(2) *Bürgerliches Gesetzbuch*) and it is by virtue of this general duty that the German judiciary has imposed pre-contractual Notification duties on parties.[25] In case of a breach of such a pre-contractual Notification duty the other party has a claim for damages on account of non-performance of an obligation (§280(1) *Bürgerliches Gesetzbuch*) or for restoration of the situation that would have existed had the Notification duty been correctly fulfilled (§249(1) *Bürgerliches Gesetzbuch*).

It should be noted, however, that these duties are only imposed in exceptional cases where there is a specific reason to do so, but that as a rule they only come into play if the following general requirements (*allgemeine Voraussetzungen*) have been met:

- the other party is a knowledgeable party or should have known about the facts;
- it knew about their relevance to the mistaken party;
- it knew of the mistake of the other party or could reasonably be expected to have known of it;
- it caused the contract to be concluded in mistake by leaving the mistaken party in error;
- it did so contrary to good faith and fair dealing (*'Treu und Glauben'*).[26]

Thus, German law, despite its recent creation of a legal relationship (§311(2) BGB: *'Schuldverhältnis')* between those engaging in negotiations that may impose on them the general duty 'to look after the rights, the legal goods and the interests of the other party' (§241(2) BGB), may nót be said to be in keeping the general EU pre-contractual Notification duty of traders to provide consumers with information with respect to the main characteristics of the goods or services to be supplied.

Dutch law resembles German law in that according to the judiciary the principle of good faith and fair dealing (*'redelijkheid en billijkheid')* also applies to the time preceding the conclusion of the contract, but the first and foremost conclusion it draws from this application is that those engaging into negotiations about a contract are bound to take measures to prevent themselves from concluding a contract in mistake, notably measures to inform themselves.[27]

Although this first and foremost duty of a possibly mistaken party to inform oneself may be overridden by the pre-contractual duty of the other party to disclose information, based on Article 6:228(1)(b) *Burgerlijk Wetboek* on Mistake[28], this pre-contractual Notification duty comes into play only if the following requirements have been fulfilled:

25 K.J.O. Jansen, o.c., p. 58.

26 Cf. Staudinger/Loosschelder/Olzen, l.c., MünchKomm BGB/Roth, l.c. and Bamberger/Roth/Holger Sutschet l.c.

27 Cf. Hoge Raad 15 November 1957, *Nederlandse Jurisprudentie* 1958, 67 (Baris/Riezenkamp).

28 Cf. notably Hoge Raad 30 November 1973, *Nederlandse Jurisprudentie* 1974, 97 (Van der Beek/Van Dartel), Hoge Raad 10 April 1998, *Nederlandse Jurisprudentie* 1998, 666 (Offringa/Vinck en Van

- the other party is a knowledgeable party or should have known about the facts;
- it knew about their relevance to the mistaken party;
- it knew of the mistake of the other party or could reasonably be expected to have known of it;
- it caused the contract to be concluded in mistake by leaving the mistaken party in error;
- it did so contrary to societal usages to the effect that the knowledgeable party should notify the other one.[29]

Under *English* law, that bluntly rejects any duty to carry on negotiations in good faith[30], a general pre-contractual duty to disclose information to the other party has also been bluntly rejected:

- 'Ordinarily the failure to disclose a material fact which might influence the mind of a prudent contractor does not give the right to avoid the contract';[31]
- 'There is no legal obligation on the vendor to inform the purchaser that he is under a mistake not induced by the act of the vendor.'[32]

It is only by way of rare exception that such a duty has been accepted in English law, namely if:

- a lack of Notification constitutes Misrepresentation, which is only rarely applied in cases of reticence by a knowledgeable party;[33]
- Notification would have prevented the seller in the course of a business from violating the – statutory – implied term that goods supplied to a buyer that has made known a particular purpose for which the goods are being bought, are reasonably fit for that purpose except where the circumstances show that the buyer does not rely, or that it is unreasonable for him to rely, on the skill or the judgment of the seller (Section 14 (3) Sale of Goods Act).

With respect to the question whether the general EU Notification duty of traders to provide consumers with information with respect to the main characteristics of the goods or services to be supplied is in keeping with the law systems of Member States of the EU, one may conclude from this brief survey that, with the exception of French law that implicitly accepts this pre-contractual duty, these law systems reject such a general duty. This conclusion is self-evident as for law systems that reject any duty of persons entering into negations with one another to carry these on in good faith, such as the English one. It is, however more remarkable that even law systems that accept such a

Rosberg) and Hoge Raad 21 December 1990, *Nederlandse Jurisprudentie* 1991, 251 (Van Geest/ Nederlof).

29 Cf. Asser/Hartkamp and Sieburgh, l.c. and Asser-Hijma, 7-I*, l.c.

30 Walford v Miles [1957] 2 AC 128, p. 138.

31 Bell v Lever Brothers [1932] AC 161, p. 227.

32 Cf. Smith v Hughes (1871), LR 6 QB 597, p. 607.

33 Cf. E. McKendrick, Contract Law, London: Palgrave MacMillan 2013, p. 276.

duty, such as the Dutch one, or the German law system that creates a legal relationship (‘*Schuldverhältnis*’) between them *expressis verbis*, reject a general duty of traders to provide consumers with information with respect to the main characteristics of the goods or services to be supplied.

V. Is the general EU Notification duty of traders to provide consumers with information with respect to the main characteristics of the goods or services to be supplied consistent with the *acquis communautaire*?

The other question with respect to the general EU Notification duty of traders to provide consumers with information with respect to the main characteristics of the goods or services to be supplied concerns its consistency with the acquis communautaire.

EU legislation, like all legislation, may be expected to be consistent in itself. Legal provisions should not contradict one another or, if they do so, be presented in a clear rule/exception-relationship to one another. In this respect the question arises whether the general EU Notification duty of traders to provide consumers with information with respect to the main characteristics of the goods or services to be supplied is consistent with EU Directive 1999/44/EC on certain aspects of the sale of consumer goods and associated guarantees and therefore with the acquis communautaire. Article 2 (3) of this Directive on ‘Conformity with the contract’ provides: There shall be deemed not to be a lack of conformity for the purposes of this Article if, at the time the contract was concluded, the consumer was aware, or could not reasonably be unaware of, the lack of conformity (…)’.

What does this provision bring along in the above-mentioned case where a garage proprietor that has sold and delivered to a consumer a used car that turns out to pull up too slowly for the high speed that is necessary to merge fluently with the on-going traffic on highways, a character is of the car the proprietor did not know about. The garage proprietor might defend himself against any claim of the consumer based on non-conformity by stating that ‘at the time the contract was concluded (…) could not reasonably be unaware of the lack of conformity (…) (Article 2(3) of the EU Directive 1999/44/EC).’ As we have seen above before the newly introduced general EU Notification duty of traders in question to provide consumers with information with respect to the main characteristics of the goods or services to be supplied cuts of this line of defence. One may therefore conclude that the EU Notification duty of traders in question is inconsistent with part of the *acquis communautaire*.

VI. Conclusion

With respect to the questions whether the recently introduced general pre-contractual EU Notification duty of traders to provide consumers with information with respect to the main characteristics of the goods or services to be supplied is in keeping with the systems of private law of the Member States and consistent with the *acquis communautaire*, the following conclusions may be drawn:

- it is nót in keeping with most of the systems of private law of the Member States: although French law may be said to have accepted this pre-contractual Notification duty, although implicitly, this duty is not in keeping with the law systems of Germany, the Netherlands and England that all reject such a general duty;
- it is inconsistent with Article 2 (3) of the EU Directive 1999/44/EC and thus with at least part of the *acquis communautaire*.

Mark T. Kawakami
and Catalina
Goanta*

EVEN LAWYERS ARE CONSUMERS: PERCEIVING BUSINESS ATTITUDES IN ONLINE CONTRACTS

I. Introduction

When lawyers research EU consumer law, they generally tend to focus on interpreting applicable rules and discussing case law.[1] Using the subject of withdrawal rights, which will be the main topic of this paper, we can see that there is an abundance of literature that covers rules and cases, answering questions such as whether the right to withdraw is efficient (and/or necessary), or whether the EU should stay the course with their maximum harmonisation of mandatory withdrawal rights.[2] Furthermore, there are countless articles that purport to analyse mandatory withdrawal rights from the consumers' perspective by looking into behavioural economics or by taking into consideration consumer psychology.[3] Our primary focus in this contribution, on the other hand, is to argue that the mere existence of these types of literature might mislead some to believe that the interests of the consumers have thoroughly been discussed, considered, and incorporated into the existing conversation.

* Maastricht University, We would like to thank Jiangqiu Ge for his invaluable assistance in helping us understand Chinese consumer law and Jasmine Styles for her editing work.

1 *See* for instance J. Dickie, 'Consumer Confidence and the EC Directive on Distance Contracts', *Journal of Consumer Policy* 21 (1998): 217–229; M. Loos, 'Consumer Sales Law in the Proposal for a Consumer Rights Directive', *European Review of Private Law* 18(1) (2010): 15–55; S. Whittaker, 'Unfair Contract Terms and Consumer Guarantees: the Proposal for a Directive on Consumer Rights and the Significance of 'Full Harmonisation'', *European Review of Contract Law* 5(3) (2009): 223–247. J.A. Luzak, 'To Withdraw or Not to Withdraw? Evaluation of the Mandatory Right of Withdrawal in Consumer Distance Selling Contracts Taking into Account its Behavioural Effects on Consumers', *Journal of Consumer Policy* (2014) 37:91–111, at p. 91 (noting that the paper aims to take 'the point of view of consumer's interests' by relying not just on behavioural economics, but on consumer psychology).

2 C. Mak, 'Fundamental Rights and the European Regulation of iConsumer Contracts' *Journal of Consumer Policy* 31 (2008): 425–439; N. Reich and A. Halfmeier 'Consumer Protection in the Global Village: Recent Developments in German and European Union Law', *Dickinson Law Review* 106 (2001–2002): 111–138; P. Rott, 'Harmonising Different Rights of Withdrawal: Can German Law Serve as an Example for EC Consumer Law?', *German Law Journal* 7(12) (2006): 1109–1136.

3 O. Ben-Shahar and E.A. Posner, 'The Right to Withdraw in Contract Law', *The Journal of Legal Studies* 40(1) (2011): 115–148; P. Rekaiti and R. van den Burgh, 'Cooling-Off Periods in the Consumer Laws of the EC Member States. A Comparative Law and Economics Approach', *Journal of Consumer Policy* 23 (2000): 371–407; J.A. Luzak, *supra* note 1, at p. 1 (noting that the paper aims to take 'the point of view of consumer's interests' by relying not just on behavioural economics, but on consumer psychology).

While the aforementioned contributions do indeed offer unique and interdisciplinary approaches for the determination of whether the mandatory right to withdraw is in the best interest of consumers, many – if not most – of the existing research fails to actually step into the shoes of a consumer.[4] In other words, much of the existing literature discusses withdrawal rights from the viewpoint of academics (and perhaps understandably so), rather than incorporating actual consumer experiences into the analyses.[5] In this sense, the academic world might have the theoretical overview as to how law is being applied, but legal knowledge can be considered a transaction cost that not all businesses are willing to support. This potentially creates a gap between the theoretical analysis of the law and factual reality. Such a gap between perception and reality could even prove to be detrimental if it skews the way in which businesses perceive the impact of new regulations. Rather than attempting to answer the question of the 'likely effect'[6] of mandatory withdrawal rights on consumers (as some have already attempted), this research will go beyond mere speculation and documents some *actual* experiences that consumers had when exercising their withdrawal rights. Our motivation behind this research was our concern about the apparent disconnect that exists between how we, as academics, debate the pros and cons of withdrawal rights vis-a-vis how we, as consumers, exercise withdrawal rights in our daily lives. It is our working hypothesis that once we climb down from the ivory tower and attempt to return an item that we purchased online, there is a world of previously unaddressed frustrations that can only be experienced by consumers. After all, everyone is a consumer, even the lawyers amongst us.

This paper consequently wishes to answer the following question: 'What standard of consumer protection do businesses *actually* offer to consumers in online contracts?' In order to answer this question, this contribution looked at internet contracts by conducting a personal experiment in three European jurisdictions: England, the Netherlands and Romania. For every jurisdiction, we determined the e-store that had the largest market share in the sale of information technology products. We then ordered the same product (an Apple 'Magic Mouse') from all identified e-stores and subsequently exercised our withdrawal rights. The European perspective on mandatory withdrawal rights was then compared to Japanese and United States (New York) law in order to determine the protection granted to consumers in online sales, and the nature of this protection (mandatory/optional/insurance).

With regards to the structure of this paper, the European Union will be our starting point: Section 2 will discuss the Consumer Rights Directive (CRD),[7] which entered into force in June 2014. This Section will address the current obligations of traders in online contracts (information duties and withdrawal rights). Section 3 will outline our

4 This is, admittedly, a difficult group to categorise into one generic sum, but alas.

5 Likely due to the fact that as academics, we have been taught to stay away from relying on anecdotes in order to reach any meaningful conclusions.

6 J.A. Luzak, *supra* note 1, at p. 1 (noting that the paper aims to take 'the point of view of consumer's interests' by taking into consideration the impact right of withdrawal 'is likely to have on consumers').

7 Directive 2011/83/EU on consumer rights.

methodology and discuss the results of the purchasing experiences in the aforementioned jurisdictions. While the details of the methodology will be elaborated below, suffice it to state here that the objective of this experiment was to gain valuable, first-hand experience as consumers, which provides new insight into how businesses actually attempt to comply with their duties, as imposed by European consumer protection standards. A comparative compliance tool will also be applied to the three European e-stores to highlight business practices in the light of the CRD. In this Section, we will also introduce two non-European e-stores to see if and how different perspectives on withdrawal rights affect the consumer's purchasing experience. Section 4 will then address a classification of withdrawal models based on our findings, and lastly, Section 5 will bring together our observations on the experiment and Section 6 will put forth our conclusions. Overall, this paper aims to make a fresh contribution to the discussion regarding consumer protection in internet contracts.

II. The Consumer Rights Directive – A brief overview

As mentioned above, the CRD entered into force on 13 June 2014. In a nutshell, its adoption back in 2011 aimed at enhancing consumer protection with regard to doorstep/distance selling. Its goal is to strengthen the internal market and achieve a high level of consumer protection by fully harmonising the areas of consumer contract law the internal market rests on.[8] In doing so, the CRD moved away from the minimum harmonisation policy that had governed the Doorstep Selling Directive (DSD),[9] and introduced maximum harmonisation in doorstep/distance contracts, keeping in line with what is perceived to be a wider EU policy.[10]

Whether maximum harmonisation is more desirable to minimum harmonisation, how this policy came into being and the reasons justifying it are beyond the scope of this paper. As far as this research is concerned, any rules adopted by a legislator reflect a rather paternalistic approach to the protection of consumers. Individuals are vulnerable when dealing with businesses, and they need the state to adopt and enforce mandatory rules on consumer protection.

8 Proposal for a Directive of the European Parliament and of the Council on Consumer Rights, COM(2008) 614 final, 8.10.2008, at p. 6; *see* also M.T. Kawakami, 'Adjusting EU Consumer Protection Mechanisms to the Needs of Private Actors: Collaborative Consumer Protection and the *Ex Ante* Avoidance of Conflict', *European Review of Private Law* 21(5 and6) (2013): 1255–1276, at p. 1259; J. Smits, 'Full Harmonization of Consumer Law? A Critique of the Draft Directive on Consumer Rights', European Review of Private Law 20(1) (2010): 5–14, at p. 6.

9 Directive 97/7/EC on the protection of consumers in respect of distance contracts.

10 E. Hondius, 'The Proposal for a Directive on Consumer Rights: The Emperor's New Clothes?', *European Review of Private Law* 19(2) (2011): 163–166, at p. 164. For an overview of the CRD, *see* also M. Hesselink, 'The Consumer Rights Directive and the CFR: Two Worlds Apart?', *European Review of Contract Law* 5(3) (2009): 290–303; E. Hall, G. Howells and J. Watson, 'The Consumer Rights Directive – An Assessment of its Contribution to the Development of European Consumer Contract Law', *European Review of Contract Law* 8(2) (2012): 139–166; C. Twigg-Flesner and D. Metcalfe, 'The Proposed Consumer Rights Directive – Less Haste, More Thought?', *European Review of Contract Law* 5(3) (2009): 368–391.

Figure 1. CRD drafting procedure according to eurlex.eu

Nothing proves this point better than the way in which the CRD addresses consumer protection. While the CRD is a technological, policy and legal update of the DSD, the reasons why consumers need to be protected in internet contracts stayed the same – making contracts 'in the dark' puts them in a situation prone to abuse.[11] What is more, the Commission increasingly sees this vulnerability as diminishing consumer confidence, and thus as a limitation of all cross-border transactions the internal market has the potential for. In this respect, Recital 5 of the CRD reads:

> 'The cross-border potential of distance selling, which should be one of the main tangible results of the internal market, is not fully exploited. Compared with the significant growth of domestic distance sales over the last few years, the growth in cross-border distance sales has been limited [...]'

The EU legislator has sought to empower consumers in doorstep/distance contracts by creating rules on two central aspects: information duties and withdrawal rights. This was the case for the DSD and continues to be the case for the CRD. However, while the CRD followed the structure of earlier regulation, its provisions are much more detailed.[12] Information duties in the DSD used to be governed by Article 4 ('Prior information') and Article 5 ('Written confirmation of information'), totalling 514 words. The CRD deals with the same matter in Arts. 6 ('Information requirements for distance and off-premises contracts') and 8 ('Formal requirements for distance contracts') in 1790 words. Similarly, the DSD tackled withdrawal rights in Article 6 ('Right of withdrawal') and Article 7

11 J. Dickie, *supra* note 1, at p. 217; G. Borges, and B. Irlenbusch. 'Fairness Crowded Out by Law: An Experimental Study on Withdrawal Rights', *Journal of Institutional and Theoretical Economics* 163 (2007): 84–101, at p. 85; K. Henderson and A. Poulter, 'The Distance Selling Directive: Points for Future Revision', *International Review of Law Computers and Technology* 16(3) (2002): 289–300, at p. 289; E. Mik, 'Mistaken Identity, Identity Theft and Problems of Remote Authentication in E-Commerce', *Computer Law and Security Review* 28(4) (2012): 396–402, at p. 397; P. Rekaiti and R. van den Bergh, 'Cooling-Off Periods in the Consumer Laws of the EC Member States. A Comparative Law and Economics Approach', *Journal of Consumer Policy* 23 (2000): 371–407, at p. 373. Also, Horst Eidenmüller states that '[t]he optional character of withdrawal rights corresponds to the potential impairment of the consumer's will formation, in the sense of his or her intention to be bound, as the basis of the withdrawal right. Something might have been wrong with this will formation process, but we do not know for sure', in H. Eidenmüller, 'Why Withdrawal Rights?', *European Review of Contract Law* 7(1) (2011): 1–24, at p. 5.

12 For a more in-depth comparison between the DSD and the CRD, *see* J. Luzak, 'Online Consumer Contracts', *Centre for the Study of European Contract Law Working Paper Series* No. 2014–08.

('Performance'), in 759 words overall. The equivalent content is now seen in Article 9 ('Right of withdrawal'), Article 10 ('Omission of information on the right of withdrawal'), Article 11 ('Exercise of the right of withdrawal'), Article 12 ('Effects of withdrawal'), Article 13 ('Obligations of the trader in the event of withdrawal'), Article 14 ('Obligations of the consumer in the event of withdrawal'), Article 15 ('Effects of the exercise of the right of withdrawal on ancillary contracts') and Article 16 ('Exceptions from the right of withdrawal'), encompassing 2038 words.[13]

Figure 2. Partial comparative word count DSD/CRD

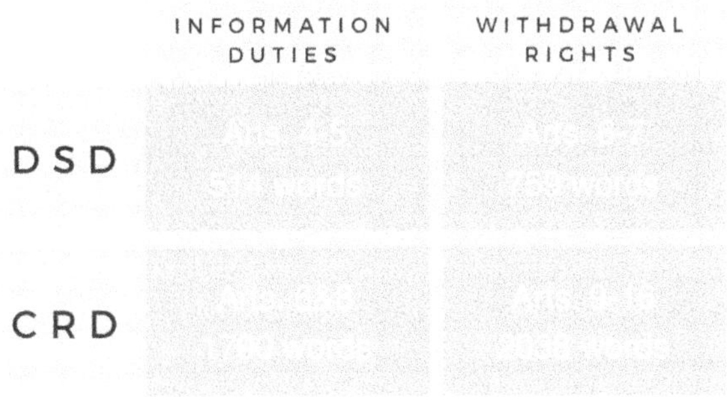

We will now briefly look into the aforementioned articles to better understand consumer protection as it currently stands.

First, in the area of information duties, Article 6(1) establishes a list of detailed information that the trader needs to provide to the consumer in a clear and comprehensible manner, including: characteristics of the goods/services, identity of the seller, contact details (e.g. physical address, phone number, e-mail address, etc.), the total price of the goods/services, arrangements for payment/delivery/performance, conditions for an eventual right of withdrawal, express mention that a withdrawal right might not be applicable, the applicability of any return costs, reminder for the existence of a legal guarantee, potential after-sale customer assistance, potential codes of conduct, and the possibility of out-of-court redress. Though this may already seem like a lot, these details only partly reflect the 20 sub-paragraphs of Article 6(1). In addition, Article 8 complements the communication of prior information, either by establishing its format (Article 8(1)), or by signalling an obligation to confirm the information as well (Article 8(7)). If the consumer has already been provided with information regarding the transaction in a way which is '[...] appropriate to the means of distance communication used in plain and intelligible language',[14] and a durable medium has

13 This calculation is based on the overall number of words in the indicated articles. Some of the selected articles might make specific references to doorstep selling as well (e.g. Article 9(3) CRD), but these references are minor in comparison with the overall text, thus in spite of this aspect, the argument according to which CRD has lengthier rules than the DSD still holds.

14 Article 8(1) CRD.

been used in doing so, the trader is released from the obligation to confirm this information.[15]

Second, as far as withdrawal rights are concerned, Article 9(1) establishes the 14 day withdrawal period, starting from the day of the conclusion of the contract (in the case of service contracts – Article 9.2(a)), or from the day on which the consumer acquires physical possession of the goods (in the case of sales contracts – Article 9.2(b)). Article 10(1) specifies that in cases where the trader failed to provide the consumer with the information on the right of withdrawal, the withdrawal period only expires 12 months from the end of the initial withdrawal period. Article 11(1) mentions that the withdrawal right can be exercised by way of notifying the trader about the decision to withdraw before the expiry of the given period. In determining when notification becomes effective, Article 11(2) further relies on the dispatch theory: only the moment when the notification is sent must fall within the withdrawal period. Article 12 governs the effects of withdrawal and clarifies that once the right of withdrawal is exercised, parties terminate their obligations to perform the contract.[16] Once withdrawal has taken place, the trader must reimburse the payments made using the same means of payment, unless special agreements are made (Article 13(1–2)), and may do so only after receiving back the goods or being supplied with evidence in this sense (Article 13(3)). According to Article 14(1), the consumer must send the goods back within a period that must not exceed another 14 days from the moment the decision to withdraw was communicated. Consumers must only bear the direct cost of returning the goods. If the trader agreed to bear them, or if he failed to inform the consumer that the consumer must cover these costs, then it is up to the trader to bear them. The consumer may be held liable for diminishing the value of the goods if this resulted from circumstances other than handling the goods in order to establish their nature, characteristics and functioning (Article 14(2)). Moreover, ancillary contracts are considered to be equally terminated by

15 Unlike the DSD, the CRD actually defines what a 'durable medium' is in Article 2(10): 'means any instrument which enables the consumer or the trader to store information addressed personally to him in a way accessible for future reference for a period of time adequate for the purposes of the information and which allows the unchanged reproduction of the information stored'. While this is the same definition as the Court of Justice of the European Union (CJEU) used in *Content Services*, it does not solve the technological limitations the Court established in this case. *See* Case C-49/11, *Content Services Ltd v* Bundesarbeitskammer [2012] CJEU. *See* also Opinion of Advocate General Mengozzi, Case C-49/11, *Content Services Ltd v* Bundesarbeitskammer [2012] CJEU; Case E-4/09 *Inconsult Anstalt v* Finanzmarktaufsicht [2010] EFTA Court Report; C. Goanta, 'Information Duties in the Internet Era: Case Note on Content Services Ltd v. *Bundesarbeitskammer*', *European Review of Private Law* 21(2) (2013): 643–659.

16 Article 12 also mentions in sub-paragraph b) that where an offer was made by the consumer, the right of withdrawal will terminate the obligations of the parties to conclude a contract. The wording of this sub-paragraph is dubious at best. First, because the verb 'to terminate' is used to explain the effects of withdrawal, which shows that withdrawing from the contract is somewhat affiliated with contractual termination/rescission. Second, because this sub-paragraph refers to a situation in which a contract was never concluded, in which case withdrawal can be easily mistaken with the withdrawal of the offer (e.g. German law already has a problem in this respect – P. Rott, 'Harmonising Different Rights of Withdrawal: Can German Law Serve as an Example for EC Consumer Law?', *German Law Journal* 7(12) (2006): 1009–1136, at p. 1112.

virtue of the effect of the right to withdraw (Article 15). Finally, Article 16 sets forth several exceptions from the right of withdrawal, including: service contracts if the service has been fully performed or the consumer, acknowledging the loss of his withdrawal right upon full performance by the trader,[17] assented to the beginning of these services; contracts for the supply of personalised goods; contracts for the supply of goods that deteriorate rapidly; contracts for the supply of sealed goods which have been unsealed and cannot be returned for health and hygiene reasons.

According to Article 28 CRD, Member States had the obligation to transpose the Directive by 13 December 2013.[18] At this point, looking into the national transpositions of the CRD could provide us with greater insight into how Member States have considered accommodating the new provisions.[19] However, we rely on the assumption that all the provisions mentioned above are maximum harmonisation rules.[20] In addition, according to the supremacy principle, national legislation needs to be applied in the light of the CRD.[21]

III. Shopping as lawyers

3.1. Explaining the methodology

This research collected actual consumer experiences to see how consumers may exercise withdrawal rights, and charted experiences across various jurisdictions (some that offer *mandatory* withdrawal rights and some that do not). This project offers some *real* insight into what it means to exercise withdrawal rights and hopefully, we will be able to illustrate

17 The same exception is also valid in the case of contracts for the supply of digital content (Article 16(m)) CRD.

18 Article 28 CRD also states that the transposing laws, regulations and administrative provisions adopted at national level would be applicable as of 13 June 2014, the date of the entry into force of the Directive.

19 For the Netherlands, *see Wijziging van Boek 6 en Boek 7 van het Burgerlijk Wetboek, de Wet handhaving consumentenbescherming en enige andere wetten in verband met de implementatie van richtlijn* 2011/83/EU, *Staatsblad* no. 140/03.04.2014; *see* also J. Luzak and V. Mak, 'The Consumer Rights Directive', *Centre for the Study of European Contract Law Working Paper Series* No. 2013-01. For Romania, *see Ordonanța de Urgență a Guvernului No. 34/2014 privind drepturile consumatorului în cadrul contractelor încheiate cu profesioniștii, precum și pentru modificarea și completarea unor acte normative, Monitorul Oficial al României* no. 427/11.06.2014. For the United Kingdom, *see* Consumer Contracts Regulations (Information, Cancellation and Additional Charges) Regulations 2013; *see also* P. Giliker, 'The Transposition of the Consumer Rights Directive into UK Law: Implementing a Maximum Harmonization Directive', *European Review of Private Law* 23(1) (2015): 5-28.

20 The exceptions to the maximum harmonisation nature of these rules are Article 8(6): 'Where a distance contract is to be concluded by telephone, Member States may provide that the trader has to confirm the offer to the consumer who is bound only once he has signed the offer or has sent his written consent. Member States may also provide that such confirmations have to be made on a durable medium', and Article 9(3): 'The Member States shall not prohibit the contracting parties from performing their contractual obligations during the withdrawal period. Nevertheless, in the case of off- premises contracts, Member States may maintain existing national legislation prohibiting the trader from collecting the payment from the consumer during the given period after the conclusion of the contract'. None of these articles are, however, relevant to online contracts.

21 *See* Case 6-64, *Flaminio Costa v E.N.E.L.* [1964].

how consumers are benefiting from mandatory withdrawal rights or, in the alternative, coping without them.

In our attempt to understand these aspects, we selected five jurisdictions: the Netherlands, Romania, the United Kingdom, Japan, and the United States (New York). There are two main reasons that explain our selection. First, supporters of legal diversity often highlight the importance of local preferences,[22] and we wanted to ensure a diverse representation of business practices. Second, this research was carried out not just in the EU Member States where the right to withdraw is mandatory, but also in jurisdictions where such a right is either default or optional. This allowed us to compare regimes with different withdraw rights.

We then went on to choosing the websites we would make purchases on: bol.com (the Netherlands), eMag.ro (Romania), Amazon.co.uk (the United Kingdom), rakuten.jp (Japan), and amazon.com (the United States-NY). The companies behind these websites were selected for reason of their very high national market shares in online trade (see Fig. 3 below). Given the size of the respective market shares, we assumed that these business practices account for a large chunk of consumer transactions, to which the same standard rules and business practices apply.

Figure 3. Total revenue for selected business in 2013 – independent research

Total revenue for 2013	
amazon.co.uk	£4.5 bn
bol.com	€680 m
eMAG	€200 m
amazon.com	$74 bln
Rakuten	$4.9 bln

22 W. Bull et al., 'Who Does What in Consumer Law: A Search for Criteria for Centralized Lawmaking', in B. Akkermans et al., *Who Does What? On the Allocation of Regulatory Competences in European Private Law*, (Intersentia, 2015), at p. 98.

As to the type of product we decided to purchase, we chose to focus on consumer hardware, namely an Apple Magic Mouse. While the ranking of consumer hardware sales may vary depending on the website/market research consultancy making the classification, one thing is certain: buying computer parts on the internet is quite popular.[23]

The last step of our experiment consisted of gathering the general terms and conditions employed by the respective traders, as well as the e-mail communication that was received after the purchases were made. This data will represent the focal point of the analysis in the next subsection, which follows our experiences with each jurisdiction. We added a small comparative compliance tool to the European countries sub-sections, since we could also determine how business practices apply European consumer policy on the basis of the collected information. For this reason, we created a compliance table based on CRD information duties, as the website itself, the general terms and the e-mails are the means often used for the communication of prior information.[24] Since information duties are a particularity of the CRD, we did not use this tool for Japan and New York, where the focus was exclusively on withdrawal rights.

At this point, an important choice we made in the research process needs highlighting. The experiments we conducted entailed purchasing an item nationally, and not cross-border. This is because we wanted to focus on the particularities of the selected businesses, some of which (e.g. eMag.ro) do not sell cross-border. While there might be some mystery shopping data already available from cross-border transactions, this is indeed a topic that we have left for future observations.[25]

All in all, the modest aim of this piece of research is to test how consumer experiences across different jurisdictions compare with various academic articles, which attempted to predict 'likely effects' of mandatory withdrawal rights on consumers. In essence, this research picks up the baton left for us by Luzak who 'call[ed] upon researchers to conduct more empirical studies focused specifically on the influence of the right of withdrawal on consumers...'[26] Moreover, while this research does not as such measure the *effect* of

23 *See* for instance the classification made by commerce website Insider Monkey. Available at: www.insidermonkey.com/blog/the-10-best-selling-products-online-330887/. *See also* the market study made by Walker Sands. Available at: www.marketingprofs.com/charts/2013/12195/online-shopping-trends-most-popular-categories-top-purchase-drivers (both sources last accessed on 25 August 2015).

24 Analyzing general terms is not uncommon. *See* for instance F. Marotta-Wurgler, 'Are 'Pay Now, Terms Later' Contracts Worse for Buyers? Evidence from Software License Agreements', *Journal of Legal Studies* 38 (2009): 5–10; M. Loos and J. Luzak, 'Wanted: A Bigger Stick. On Unfair Terms in Consumer Contracts with Online Service Providers (January 8, 2015). *Centre for the Study of European Contract Law Working Paper Series* No. 2015–01.

25 ECC-NET, 'Online Cross-Border Mystery Shopping – State of the E-Union', (2011); Consumentenbond, '*Webwinkels overtreden massaal de wet*'. Available at www.consumentenbond.nl/actueel/nieuws/2015/webwinkels-overtreden-massaal-de-wet/?cid=ext_twitterweek35wijzerwebwinkelenwebwinkelsnb (last accessed on 25 August 2015).

26 J.A. Luzak, *supra* note 1, at p. 2 (limiting the application of her contribution by noting that 'it is impossible to precisely measure such an effect, it is feasible to draw general conclusions and to estimate

withdrawal rights, we also strived to account for the other more practical features of the withdrawal experience that are often left out of academic analysis. Below are the findings of our exciting project.[27]

3.2. *An analysis of consumer experiences*

3.3.1. The Netherlands

Purchasing a product from bol.com was a remarkably efficient experience. The website required the creation of an account in order to purchase products from it. Once the order was placed, we received an e-mail confirming the purchase, which also included information the trader was supposed to provide the consumer with. Fig. 4 shows an overview of how bol.com fulfilled these particular information duties stemming from the CRD.

Figure 4. bol.com compliance with CRD[28]

	BOL.COM	E-MAIL	STANDARD TERMS
Characteristics	✓	✓	N/A
Identity	✓	✓	✓
Contact details	✓	✓	✓
Total price	✓	✓	✓
Withdrawal conditions	✓	✓	✓
Payment & delivery	✓	✓	✓
Consumer costs	N/A	N/A	✓
Withdrawal N/A	N/A	N/A	✓
Guarantee reminder	✗	✗	✓
Durable medium	✗	✓ ✗	✓ ✗
Restrictions (delivery & payment)	✓	✓	✓

the overall effect of the right of withdrawal on the consumer welfare taking into account findings on what contributes to consumers' happiness and what lets them avoid feelings of regret.').

27 All print screens and photos collected during this process are on the record with the authors and available upon request.

28 The 'Withdrawal N/A (not available)' category stands for situations in which withdrawal rights are exempted; in this case, we specified that information on whether withdrawal rights are not offered was not applicable, since the purchased product benefitted from this right in all circumstances.

As can be seen from this overview, bol.com is very CRD-friendly. The existence of a clear return procedure and form, explained step by step using attractive icons, made withdrawal exceptionally easy and uneventful. An interesting and rather practical approach that bol.com took in communicating information to the consumer is the creation of FAQs. For instance, on the website itself, bol.com addressed the conditions applicable to withdrawal rights in its FAQs, whereas on the page displaying a specific product it only signalled the existence of a 30 day withdrawal right in a short sentence. The information provided on the website greatly overlapped with the details which are confirmed by e-mail. The general terms and conditions were all- encompassing. Although it may be claimed that general terms are not the 'go-to' source of information for the average consumer, when it comes to information duties, there is no specific prohibition for the use of standard terms to inform the consumer.

This was the case with one of the two issues regarding the information provided on the website and in the confirmation e-mails. Article 6(1) CRD asks the trader to provide the consumer with 'a reminder of the existence of a legal guarantee of conformity for goods'. This requirement spans consumer goods and associated guarantees, as governed by the Consumer Sales Directive.[29] Neither the website (on the Magic Mouse page) nor the confirmation e-mail made reference to legal guarantees. However, Article 12 of the *Algemene Voorwaarden Thuiswinkel* mentioned the legal rights of consumers in relation to extra guarantees.[30] The second issue dealt with the durable medium discussion. According to the Court of Justice in *Content Services*, '[w]here a medium allows the consumer to store the information which has been addressed to him personally, ensures that its content is not altered and that the information is accessible for an adequate period, and gives consumers the possibility to reproduce it unchanged, that medium must be regarded as 'durable' within the meaning of that provision.'[31] The website itself does not fit the conditions enumerated by the Court. Neither does the situation in which the trader sends the consumer a link to his own website, since the trader could, in principle, always alter the information available in the accounts it hosts. Moreover, standard terms may be considered durable when printed, but their online versions suffer from the same problem mentioned above.

With respect to withdrawal rights, bol.com extended the withdrawal period from 14 to 30 days, offering the same conditions for this protection as those mandated by the CRD.[32] In spite of the mandatory harmonisation nature of the CRD, it is Member States who may not impose a lower or higher standard of consumer protection. Companies may, if they so will, apply other terms to this protection, provided that these terms do not conflict with the CRD.

29 Directive 1999/44/EC on certain aspects of the sale of consumer goods and associated guarantees.

30 Article 12(2) reads: '*Een door de ondernemer, diens toeleverancier, fabrikant of importeur verstrekte extra garantie beperkt nimmer de wettelijke rechten en vorderingen die de consument op grond van de overeenkomst tegenover de ondernemer kan doen gelden indien de ondernemer is tekortgeschoten in de nakoming van zijn deel van de overeenkomst*'.

31 Case C-49/11, *Content Services Ltd v Bundesarbeitskammer* [2012], para. 43.

32 Article 6 of the *Algemene Voorwaarden Thuiswinkel*.

3.3.2. Romania

Purchasing a Magic Mouse from eMag.ro and subsequently withdrawing from the contract was also a success. It was interesting to notice that the company had not yet fully adapted to the CRD, both in terms of information duties but also withdrawal rights. A general withdrawal right of 30 days was given to consumers, as with bol.com; however, this right was subject to limitations going beyond the requirements of the CRD, and moreover, did not apply to all products. One example of such a limitation was the mention that '[i]f you purchase more products of the same kind and wish to return all of them, only one of them may be unsealed, while the rest are only accepted back if they sealed.'[33] According to the CRD, it is only possible to deny a right of withdrawal in the cases covered by Article 16 (e.g. in the case of 'sealed audio or sealed video recordings or sealed computer software which were unsealed after delivery'). Otherwise, according to Article 14(2) CRD, '[t]he consumer shall only be liable for any diminished value of the goods resulting from the handling of the goods other than what is necessary to establish the nature, characteristics and functioning of the goods.' This article does not specify that if more goods of the same type are ordered, only one of them can be inspected. After all, even when purchasing five Magic Mouse devices at the same time, it is not unreasonable to consider that a consumer might want to inspect all of them. It must be mentioned at this point that all the five Magic Mouse devices – including the one from eMag.ro – came in generic cardboard boxes, and not in their original Apple packaging. This shows that in practice, businesses protect themselves from whatever losses might be incurred if a consumer unwraps a good and then sends it back. In other words, the risk of not being able to re-sell that item is lowered through re-packaging practices such as the ones just mentioned. This being said, not allowing a consumer to unseal a good is a requirement that does not have any equivalent in the CRD and thus conflicts with the Directive's standard of consumer protection.

To complicate matters further, eMag.ro also mentioned that '[t]he 30-day withdrawal right does not affect the 14 day withdrawal right offered in distance selling.'[34] This seemed to be more of a disclaimer than the notification of a voluntary withdrawal policy. While on the one hand giving consumers more time to change their mind might seem to be in their interest, on the other hand, such an extended right does not comply with the conditions governing the 14 days withdrawal period, in which case consumers are worse off.

33 The original text reads: '*Daca ai cumparat mai multe produse de acelasi fel si vrei sa le returnezi pe toate, doar unul dintre produse poate fi desigilat, restul de produse le putem accepta doar daca sunt sigilate.*'

34 The original text reads: '*Serviciul '30 de zile drept de retur' nu afecteaza in niciun fel drepturile legale de retur in 14 zile, in cazul comertului la distanta. Vezi aici mai multe detalii despre dreptul la retragere.*'

Figure 5. eMag.ro compliance with CRD

	EMAG.RO	E-MAIL	STANDARD TERMS
Characteristics	✓	✓	N/A
Identity	✓	✓	✓
Contact details	✓	✓	✓
Total price	✓	✓	✗
Withdrawal conditions	✓	✗	✓
Payment & delivery	✓	✓	✓
Consumer costs	✓	✓	✗
Withdrawal N/A	N/A	N/A	✓
Guarantee reminder	✗	✗	✗
Durable medium	✗	✓ ✗	✓ ✗
Restrictions (delivery & payment)	✓	✓	✓

In terms of information duty pitfalls, eMag.ro had more problems than bol.com. First, the general terms did not make any reference whatsoever to the way in which the price was determined and which costs must be borne by the consumer upon withdrawal. What is more, the confirmation e-mails and the separate bill issued to the user account made no reference to the withdrawal right. Second, while guarantees were mentioned in the confirmation e-mail as well as in the user account, none of the texts appeared to refer to legal guarantees. Even the standard terms were silent on this category of legal rights. Third, the same problem with durable medium existed as for bol.com.

3.3.3. The United Kingdom

The Amazon.co.uk experience started out very similarly to the bol.com purchase. The vast experience in online trade Amazon has accumulated throughout the years has led to very professional and well-designed consumer support services. Just like with the other two websites, a consumer needs a personal account, from where information regarding past purchases and other details can be retrieved. Amazon.co.uk was the website that sent the most e-mails to confirm the purchase and announce the delivery: a total of four e-mails were issued on these matters.[35] However, when time came to

35 By comparison, eMag.ro sent three e-mails, and bol.com sent two e-mails to confirm the purchase.

return the good, we chose the option to have the good picked up from a given individual address. This was a service the value of which was to be deducted from the refund amount. The pick-up service did not manage to retrieve the package upon the first try, and neither was it able to do so upon the second attempt. Each time, this meant we had to call Customer Service. One positive aspect was the fact that the telephone call made to Customer Service was interrupted in order for Customer Service to call back. This way, consumers do not have to pay for a lengthy telephonic conversation. Each of the two times we contacted Customer Service we were called back from what was presumably a call centre outside of the UK, and perhaps even outside of Europe. This created certain communication burdens, and while each time we were assured the pick-up service would come to retrieve the Magic Mouse on a specific date, this failed to happen. For this reason, the Magic Mouse was never returned to Amazon.co.uk. However, for items that do not make it back to Amazon, or for items with no withdrawal possibility, there is always an option to 'Sell' or 'Trade-In the item', which Amazon can offer because of its marketplace.[36] A marketplace is a platform where not only B2C but also C2C (also known as 'peer-to-peer') commerce takes place.

Figure 6. Amazon.co.uk compliance with CRD

	EMAG.RO	E-MAIL	STANDARD TERMS
Characteristics	✓	✓	N/A
Identity	✓	✓	✓
Contact details	✓	✓	✓
Total price	✓	✓	✗
Withdrawal conditions	✓	✗	✓
Payment & delivery	✓	✓	✓
Consumer costs	✓	✓	✗
Withdrawal N/A	N/A	N/A	✓
Guarantee reminder	✗	✗	✗
Durable medium	✗	✓ ✗	✓ ✗
Restrictions (delivery & payment)	✓	✓	✓

As to pitfalls in CRD compliance, Amazon.co.uk had almost the same features as bol.com. The one difference is that just like eMag.ro, Amazon.co.uk did not seem to

36 Bol.com has its own marketplace as well, but eMag.ro does not.

acknowledge a specific statutory guarantee right. It only referred to so-called 'warranty repairs',[37] which are commercial guarantees, and its Conditions of Sale actually named its voluntary withdrawal right a 'guarantee'.[38] Just like eMag.ro and bol.com, Amazon.co.uk offered a return period of 30 days, but unlike the Romanian e-store, it made a clear distinction between the statutory and voluntary periods.

3.3.4. Japan

The Japanese prescription of withdrawal rights for consumers with regards to online purchases is *incredibly* different from that of the EU. It is worth clarifying at the onset that cooling off periods *do* exist in Japan. As a matter of fact, Japan first introduced the concept of a cooling off period in 1976 (even before China), when they promulgated the Act on Doorstop Selling [訪問販売法].[39] This regulation on doorstop selling was subsequently absorbed into the Act on Specified Commercial Transaction [特定商取引法], which is the relevant law today that generally deals with consumer protection, doorstep selling, distance selling, etc.[40] The Act initially provided consumers with a cooling off period of 4 days to return goods if there was, at the time of the contract, some element of undue pressure or influence (i.e. doorstep selling, aggressive telemarketing, etc.). In 1984, amendments to the Act extended the cooling off period from 4 days to 7 days, and then again in 1991, when yet another amendment to the Act extended the cooling off period from 7 days to 8 days (which is the prescribed cooling off period in Japan today).[41]

Although the duration of the cooling off period was extended periodically since the Act's first inception, what remained unchanged throughout the decades was Japan's insistence on not extending the right of withdrawal to consumers making online purchases.[42] Whereas in the EU or across the sea in China, regulations that prescribe *mandatory* withdrawal rights enable consumers to generally return goods that they purchased online 'without justification' or 'without giving any reason', in Japan, this particular

37 It may be the case that we simply did not find the page on the website where legal guarantees are mentioned. We thus assume that the average consumer would have even more problems retrieving this information.

38 Article 2 of the Conditions of Sale reads: 'Without prejudice to your statutory rights, Amazon provides you with the following voluntary returns guarantee: All products from the Amazon sites can be returned within 30 days of receipt of the products to Amazon if the products are complete and are in an unused and undamaged condition. For shrink-wrapped and/or sealed data media (for example CDs, audio cassettes, VHS videos, DVDs, PC and video games and software) this means that we only take back the products in the unopened shrink wrap film or with an undamaged seal. The products are to be returned via our Returns Support Centre. This voluntary returns guarantee does not apply to digital products or software which are not supplied on a tangible medium (e.g. on a CD or DVD).'

39 Pronounced '*houmonhanbaihou*'.

40 Pronounced '*tokuteishoutorihikihou*'.

41 Act on Specified Commercial Transaction Articles 9, 24 and 48.

42 For what it is worth, Japan's Justice Ministry's Legislative Council subcommittee made a proposal to amend various parts of the Japanese Civil Code this year (2015) to address issues on consumer protection.

right to withdrawal from online purchases is not guaranteed by the law. The reasoning behind Japan's refusal to do so is that unlike doorstop selling, telemarketing or other more aggressive sales tactics, online shopping does not pressure the consumer to make unwanted purchases, thus reducing the need to protect them in such situations, especially at the expense of the Japanese retailers.[43]

Due to this fact, if a Japanese consumer buys a hand bag online from a Japanese retailer that does not voluntarily offer withdrawal rights, that consumer does not have an enforceable right that is guaranteed by the law to return the bag for a refund (even if it is returned within 8 days). In other words, while many businesses offer individual return policies, there is no *mandatory* withdrawal right that would allow a Japanese consumer to return that bag for a refund. What it comes down to is that Japan's withdrawal right regime is the *optional* withdrawal right regime.

Because Japan employs the *optional* model, not all sellers offer a return policy. When searching for the Apple Magic Mouse from Japan's largest online retailer, Rakuten.jp, we observed that there were Magic Mouse devices on sale that came with withdraw rights and those that did not. Moreover, similarly to Amazon, Rakuten is an online marketplace where a plethora of sellers can list items that they want to sell on its massive online marketplace, all offering different return policies. The most notable aspect about Rakuten's online marketplace – besides the sheer number of items that are on sale – was the fact that depending on which seller you ordered from, there were different return policies: Some sellers specified that 'no returns' were allowed, while others offered a cooling off period of 8 days.

The mouse with 'no returns' was priced at ¥8,800 [roughly € 64], whereas the mouse that came with an 8-day withdrawal right was ¥11,000 [roughly € 80]. While this is only one example, it demonstrates that in a jurisdiction with no *mandatory* withdrawal rights, choices like these are available to the consumers. If a consumer knew for certain that he was not going to return the mouse, he had the opportunity to save roughly € 16.[44] The main takeaway from the Japanese experience was the allure of this € 16. More generally, the fact that *optional* withdrawal rights would give a consumer € 16 on possible savings, which could make a consumer prefer this system of optional withdraw rights vis-à-vis the mandatory system where the savings might otherwise be unavailable. There is more opportunity to find something cheaper, albeit by taking a bit more risk, in an *optional* model jurisdiction. The decision whether to take that risk or not is ultimately up to the

43 The EU, at least, justifies granting withdrawal rights to its citizens in the belief that it will increase cross border trade and strengthen the internal market, which is an issue that Japan is not particularly concerned with.

44 Consumers, even in mandatory withdrawal right regimes, are not immune from this type of a dilemma: For example, when they reserve a flight a few months ahead of their trip and the airlines provide them with the option to 'insure' their trip in the event that they want to cancel or modify their trips later. At lease from personal experience, whenever a consumer decides not to buy the insurance of the 'trip protection' is usually when it becomes necessary for them to change their flights.

consumer, which is the very essence of 'consumer autonomy' and principal behind freedom of contract. In light of these concerns, the new question that arose was whether a consumer would have paid € 16 in order to avoid the process of sorting out which product offered what kind of withdrawal rights.[45]

In addition to the € 16 savings, there was another noteworthy issue in the return process: Exercising the consumer's withdrawal right in an *optional* withdrawal right regime like Japan – was quite laborious given that in such a jurisdiction, most sellers are not generally accustomed to handling such claims. The process of returning the mouse through Rakuten (or in our case, to a seller who placed the Magic Mouse for sale on the Rakuten market place) had a very interesting return process: first, because our return was not due to a defect, we only had 8 days to notify the seller about the return, rather than the 14 days we would have had had there been a defect. Second, the return policy required the consumer to actually call the seller to notify them of the return. Upon calling the seller, we were placed on hold and subsequently informed that the person in charge of handling returns was out and that he was unable to handle our request at the time. The person who answered the phone took our information and told us that we should expect a call back soon. The call from the other person, the person 'in charge of handling returns', came a few hours later. The person in charge informed us that we would be able to return the mouse. The man was very polite and apologised for the entire ordeal. We did not have the heart to tell him that the Magic Mouse was purchased for the sole purpose of returning it and that there was no need for him to apologise.

3.3.5. United States (New York)

In the United States, the protection offered – at least at the Federal level – is clearly less than what is offered by its European counterparts. Sellers generally have 'no legal obligation to take back conforming goods that do not satisfy the buyers – unless agreed to do so by contract.'[46] There are a few notable exceptions such as the Federal Trade Commission's[47] 16 CFR Part 429, which in relevant part offers a '3-day cooling-off period for certain goods that are purchased away from the seller's permanent place of business.'[48] This means that the duration of the cooling-off period along with the substantive protection offered by the US federal law is more meagre compared to that of the EU. Although the likes of Ben-Shahar and Posner suggest that there are ways in which the US attempts to cope with this

45 This can be tied into the so called 'insurance model'.

46 O. Ben-Shahar and E.A. Posner, *supra* note 3, at p. 115, 139 (noting that '[t]he common law of contract in the United States does not recognise a right to withdraw' and while there are no legal obligations, many sellers do still provide withdrawal rights voluntarily); In California, '[s]ellers are not required by law to accept returned items unless they are defective.'

47 The agency that primarily deals with e-commerce in the US.

48 16 CFR Part 429 (2008); *see* also, O. Ben-Shahar and E.A. Posner, 'The Right to Withdraw in Contract Law', *The Journal of Legal Studies* 40(1) (2011): 115–148, 116 (providing doorstep selling as an example of this type of a contract).

lack of protection,[49] comparatively speaking, the protections offered by US federal law do not necessarily boost consumer confidence when it comes to online shopping.

As to the protections offered at the state level, a quick survey illustrates that some states offer more consumer protection, above and beyond what is offered by the FTC. For example, the state of New York offers 'consumers the right to return unused and undamaged goods within 30 days[50] unless the store conspicuously posts a different return policy.'[51] This right to withdraw in New York is not limited to distance or off-premises contracts like in the EU, but extends to 'on-premises sales' as well.[52] The catch with this provision, however, is that the seller can quash this withdrawal right if he makes the consumer aware of its specific return policy (or the lack thereof) at the time of the purchase. In a manner akin to the red hand rule in the UK, this rule allows consumers to be aware of the repercussions (i.e. no cancellations or refunds permitted) and that way, at least the consumers will have a clear idea of what they are getting themselves into.

The rules are similar in other states such as in California, where sellers are also free not to permit any returns so long as their refund policies are 'conspicuously displayed' in areas such as by the cash register or on the sales counter.[53] The seller who fails to present this information or have it displayed on their webpage for the consumer's viewing 'shall be liable to the buyer for the amount of the purchase' so long as the buyer 'returns, or attempts to return, the purchased goods on or before the 30th day after their purchase.'[54]

While some states like New York and California provide consumer protection that are on a par with that of the EU, if not slightly better, given that the consumer protection laws are not harmonised in the United States, it follows that some states have less protection than others. For example, states such as Texas and Georgia – just to name a few – only offer the most minimal levels of consumer protection, which is the implementation of the aforementioned FTC rule – 16 CFR Part 429 – that equips the consumers with the 3 day cooling-off period for sales made at facilities other than the seller's place of business, including but not limited to the customer's residence or similar door-to-door sales situations.[55] In other words, outside of this federally mandated

49 O. Ben-Shahar and E.A. Posner, *supra* note 3, at p. 142 (giving the examples that 'under the Uniform Commercial Code, the buyer has a right to reject delivered goods (Section 2–601) and a right to revoke acceptance of delivery (Section 2–608)' if the goods delivered goods are nonconforming.

50 Prior to December 2010, this was 20 days.

51 New York Code, General Business, Section 218–2; *see also*, O. Ben-Shahar and E.A. Posner, *supra* note 3, at p. 116 (providing doorstep selling as an example of this type of a contract).

52 New York Code, General Business, Section 218–2; *see also*, O. Ben-Shahar and E.A. Posner, *supra* note 3, at p. 143.

53 California Civil Code §1723(a). There are similar exceptions listed in §1723(b) to these provisions such as exceptions for 'as is', 'no returns accepted', 'all sales final' or custom contracts that contain similar language indicating to the consumer about the nature of the sale.

54 California Civil Code §1723(c)(1).

55 Texas Business and Commercial Code §601.002 (Applicability of Chapter) and §601.051 (Consumer's Right to Cancel) stating that §601 only applies for solicitation and sales that take place other than the

protection, consumers are on their own and must rely on the sellers to offer a specific refund policy.

Although there are various differences between consumer protection schemes offered in the states as briefly illustrated above, American consumers generally appear not to be concerned by such differences. This is likely due to the fact that even though state and federal laws generally do not require businesses to offer the right to withdraw for consumers to return goods purchased online, many businesses do so anyway on a voluntary basis. What this suggests is that consumers are not looking at what the law says, but rather at what the businesses are saying. For example, an average consumer in New York will probably not have any idea what New York Code §218–2 says, but he will most likely know that Walmart allows returns or exchanges within 90 days, whether the purchase took place at the store or on-line.[56] If a good number of businesses voluntarily go above and beyond what the law is offering,[57] practically speaking, the law loses some of its relevance, at least in the eyes of the consumer in a jurisdiction where withdraw rights are not mandatory.[58] This was substantiated, at least during our empirical research when we ordered the Apple Magic Mouse through Amazon.com. Rather than looking at whether the online seller was following the relevant state and federal law, which again, the average consumer is likely oblivious to, we – as consumers – looked only at the specific refund policy offered by Amazon and/or by the sellers that listed their products on the Amazon marketplace. While there was less reliance on the law, it would be difficult to argue that as a result, the consumers felt less protected. This is likely because in reality, they were protected not by what the consumer protection regulations required them, but by the binding nature of a contact between two private parties.

What was more fascinating while shopping on Amazon was that we had the option of buying the mouse from a seller located not just within the US from sellers based in New York, New Jersey, or California, but from European countries like Germany, France and Ireland as well. Depending on which seller we selected from, there were different return and refund policies available, similar to our experience on Rakuten. While most sellers simply used the Amazon Product Policy,[59] which generally offered 30 days for returns, depending on the type of a product sold, sellers were permitted to impose additional requirements for returns.[60] For example, our seller who was based in New York, offered

merchant's place of business and only in such cases can a consumer 'cancel transaction not later than midnight of the third business day after the date the consumer signs an agreement or offer to purchase.'

56 *See* the Walmart Returns Center. Available at http://help.walmart.com/app/answers/detail/a_id/190/~/walmart-returns-center (last accessed on 25 August 2015).

57 Hypothetically, for the sake of increasing profits by enhancing customer satisfaction.

58 Even in a jurisdiction where the right to withdraw is not mandatory, the law does serve a valid purpose (i.e. it creates a commonly accepted practice).

59 *See* the Amazon Customer Help. Available at: www.amazon.com/gp/help/customer/display.html?ie=UTF8 andnodeId=15015721 (last accessed on 25 August 2015).

60 There were different return policies for automotive items, baby items, cell phones, collectables, coins, computers, fine art, games and software downloads, gift cards, hazardous materials, independent design items, jewelry and watches, live plants, insects, groceries, wine, pre-paid phone cards and televisions.

30 days to return the product, which was Amazon's standard policy, but our seller imposed an additional requirement that required us to contact them in order to get a Return Merchandise Authorization (RMA), which involved filling out a questionnaire about why we were returning the items: 'Packages will not be accepted without this RMA number and will be returned to you via the designated carrier. To obtain an RMA, please contact us through Amazon's Request Link.' This first-hand account goes to show that while the substantive protections might be there in the US, there are procedural hurdles that may discourage consumers from actually putting in the effort to return the goods.

IV. Back to theory: A(nother) classification of withdrawal rights

Before diving into describing the various consumer experiences when exercising their right to withdraw in various jurisdictions, it is important to categorise the various regimes of withdraw rights at the onset. For the purposes of this research, we identified three general models of withdraw rights: a) mandatory rights, b) default/optional rights and c) insurance-like rights.

4.1. Mandatory withdrawal rights

In most EU jurisdictions, the CRD accomplishes its objective given that the withdrawal rights are guaranteed and consumers can return goods within the contours of the Directive (and the MS transposition thereof): 'Implementation of the mandatory right of withdrawal could be justified by the need to protect irrational consumers from the effects of their less-fortunate choices. This paternalistic approach is often quoted as a justification of special rights granted to consumers in European contract law.'[61] The EU is not the only place where mandatory rules can be found. China's newly amended Consumer Protection Code [中华人民共和国消费者权益保护法][62] similarly to that of the EU offers the mandatory model offer withdrawal rights to consumers for online purchases, although China only offers a cooling off period of 7 days compared to the EU's 14 days.[63] More importantly, Article 9 of the EU's Consumer Rights Directive allows consumers to return most goods purchased online 'without giving any reason', and similarly in China, a consumer can return most goods purchased online 'without justification'[64] in accordance with Article 25 of the newly amended Chinese Consumer Protection Code. Prior to the amendment, the Chinese Consumer Protection Code back in 1993 did not mention withdrawal rights, thus the consumers could not rely on cooling off periods to escape their contracts. The right to withdraw in China first emerged in 2003 at a very local level with the promulgation of Regulations of Shanghai Municipality on the

61 J.A. Luzak, *supra* note 1, at p. 14 (citing to Gomez 2003, at p. 3 and Mak, at p. 3).

62 Pronounced '*zhōnghuá rénmín gònghéguó xiāofèi zhě quányì bǎohù fǎ*' for those motivated readers.

63 There are other differences as well (i.e. the Chinese law does not obligate the trader to inform the consumer about their right to withdrawal, etc.).

64 In Chinese, it is stated as follows: '且无需說明理由'.

Protection of Consumers' Rights and Interests [上海市消費者权益保护条例].[65] This was the Regulation that first introduced the cooling off period to protect consumers in Shanghai from (mostly) doorstep sellers that pressured consumers into buying something that they did not particularly need or want. The 2013 Amendment [2013修正][66] of the Chinese Consumer Protection Code expanded this protection offered by withdrawal rights nation-wide via the aforementioned Article 25 (thus giving the consumers a 7 day withdrawal period for distant purchases, which includes purchases made over the telephone, online, etc.).[67]

In a jurisdiction with the mandatory model, such as Member States within the EU, China, etc. withdrawal rights are mandated by law and distance sellers must provide consumers with the right to withdraw from the online contract (Arts. 9–16 CRD). In theory, the right to withdraw generally serves as a 'cooling-off instrument, which allows consumers to reign in their emotions and assess more objectively the transaction they had concluded', which supposedly makes 'consumers more willing to enter into transactions' because they can simply take back their mistakes after having made them.[68] The underlying presumption of many existing literature argues for mandatory withdrawal rights on the assumption that the consumers are uninformed, indifferent or dumb. Put more euphemistically, consumers are – at the very least – 'emotional' and tend to 'make cognitive errors.'[69] Therefore, governments and laws must make consumer protection measures mandatory for their sake. If this assumption is indeed true, then why do we limit the application of withdrawal rights to distant contracts? Academics argue that consumers are better equipped to determine the value of the goods with hands-on inspection available with on-premise shopping, but if we assume that we are 'emotional' creatures susceptible to making cognitive errors, should this consumer protection not extend to on-premise contracts as well?[70]

4.2. *Default/optional withdrawal rights*

In a jurisdiction with the default/optional model, such as states within the US, Japan, etc., the law generally does not require businesses to offer consumers withdraw rights.[71] Under this model, the law might provide a right to withdraw for the consumer, but also

65 Pronounced '*Shanghaishi Xiaofeizhe Quanyi Baohu Tiaoli.*'

66 The Amendment went into effect on 15 March 2014.

67 The Regulations of Shanghai Municipality on the Protection of Consumers' Rights and Interests, not to be confused with the Chinese Consumer Protection Code, was also amended in 20 November 2014 and went into force earlier this year on 15 March 2015. The date, 15th of March, holds a special place in China as it is the Consumer Protection Day.

68 J.A. Luzak, *supra* note 1, at p. 4.

69 Ibid., at p. 5.

70 Ibid., at p. 12 (stating that '[t]here is no empirical evidence that suggests that consumers concluding distance selling contracts are likely to be more susceptible to be led by their emotions than if they purchase goods or services in a store.').

71 At least in the US, there is one major exception to this general rule that will be elaborated upon in later sections.

allows the businesses to opt-out of it, so long as certain conditions are met (i.e. so long as the seller makes clear to the consumer at the time of the contact that returns are not permitted).

4.3. *Insurance-like withdrawal rights*

The last model, which could also be considered as a subcategory of a default/optional model, is the insurance model, where the law does not mandate businesses to offer withdrawal rights to consumers, but instead, gives the consumers the possibility to buy added protection (i.e. cancellation insurance), which effectively allows the consumers to buy 'withdrawal rights' as if they were insurance. By allowing consumer to either opt-in or opt-out of withdrawal rights, 'give[s] consumers the choice whether to opt into a transaction with or without the right of withdrawal'.[72] One noteworthy difference between the default/optional model and the insurance model at its core is the fact that with the latter, the consumers will know exactly how much they are paying for the right to withdraw, whereas in the default/optional model (or in the mandatory model for that matter), the price increase that the sellers impose in exchange for giving the consumers the right to withdraw is unknown to the consumer. This is of course assuming that the right to withdraw does not come for free. While *mandatory* withdrawal rights reduce party autonomy and the opportunity for consumers to haggle for a cheaper price, this model allows for price differentiation.[73]

Figure 7. Prices and rights in selected e-stores

Country	Website	Price	Return policy
Netherlands	bol.com	€69,00	30 days cooling-off period
Romania	emag.ro	€80,00	right to return acknowledged but not defined/ 30 days return right
UK	amazon.co.uk	€58,64 [on discount from €73)	14 days cancellation right/30 days explicit voluntary returns guarantee (different policies for Marketplace)
Japan	rakuten.jp	+WR €80 -WR €64	8 days return (different policies for Rakuten Marketplace)
US	amazon.com	€58	30 days return (different policies for Marketplace)

72 O. Bar-Gill and O. Ben-Shahar, 'Regulatory Techniques in Consumer Protection: A Critique of the Common European Sales Law', *NYU Law and Economics Research Paper Series* 12(12) (2012), at pp. 19–20; J.A. Luzak, *supra* note 1, at p. 31; H. Eidenmüller, *supra* note 11, at p. 12.

73 Based on the assumption that traders that are compelled to refund consumers will likely increase the price charged to the consumers.

V. Reflecting on our own consumer experiences

5.1. Do mandatory withdrawal rights make things easier for consumers? Some comparative remarks

The goal of this paper, as noted in the beginning, was to describe withdrawal rights from a more consumer-based perspective, rather than from the point of an academic. From this admittedly anecdotal perspective, Section 3 presented an account of our online purchases from five different jurisdictions. Then, Section 4 labelled the offered protection according to a three-tier classification of withdrawal models. What follows now will be some general thoughts on this classification, proceeded by highlights of some key aspects of the withdrawal experience often left out from academic discussions. We must acknowledge at this point that we do not seek to use the five purchasing experiences described in this research to draw broad and far-reaching conclusions.

While the EU system of mandatory withdrawal rights is – without a doubt – a lot easier to deal with once the consumer has been put in a position where they want to withdraw, there are lingering doubts as to whether the nature of the withdrawal right (mandatory, optional or insurance) really changes the behaviour of the consumers *ex ante*. In other words, consumers might not really look at the return policy until they actually want to return something so to an average consumer, it really does not matter what the jurisdiction's position is on withdraw rights. Moreover, the maximum amount of time to practically withdraw from the contract can legally take up to 28 days, allowing for consumers to legally 'procrastinate'.[74]

In theory, in a jurisdiction where withdrawal rights are not mandatory, a business' offer to provide the consumers with such rights voluntarily is a stronger signal of trust and confidence to the consumers relative to a jurisdiction where everyone offers them. However, in practice, in an *optional* withdrawal right regime like Japan, where consumers are required to do a bit more research to compare and contrast not just the products themselves, but their return policies, shopping became somewhat of an inconvenience at best and a nuisance at worst.

What is more important than the model of the withdrawal right, we propose, is not the nature of the withdrawal right in itself, but for the consumers to be made aware of the nature of the return policy prior to the purchase as illustrated by the state laws of New York and California. In this regard, the CRD serves a valid purpose in informing the consumers that the withdrawal right for distant purchases is 14 days.

While it could be said that consumers are weak, this characterisation could be controversial in particular circles, given that there are many consumers, at least in the

[74] J.A. Luzak, *supra* note 1, at p. 24.

United States, that exploit and abuse their right to withdraw. For example, what some might consider a victimless crime is 'wardrobe renting', which is a practice that a consumer buys something, uses it once and then returns it for a full refund: 'Criminals trying to get refunds on stolen merchandise and customers engaged in practices like 'wardrobing' cost retailers an estimated $9.1 billion in return fraud last year...'[75] While this exorbitant amount includes more serious case such as seeking 'returns for items purchased with fraudulent payment like stolen our counterfeit gift cards, wardrobing – where customers typically purchase a dress for a party or a big-screen television for the Super Bowl and return the item after it has been used – accounted for 62 percent [of cases].'[76] This growing trend could be an argument against jurisdictions requiring every web shop to offer their consumers a right to withdrawal.

In addition, new apps make it incredibly easy for consumers to visualise the product they are buying. One of the most revolutionary examples in this sense does not deal with electronics, but with make-up. The L'Oreal Make-Up Genius is a state-of-the-art virtual make-up tester that shows consumers – mostly female – how a specific shade of lipstick or a certain type of blush would look on them.[77] While consumers who order these products at home might not necessarily benefit from a withdrawal right because of the nature of such products (Article 16(e) CRD), the point to be made is that it is a matter of time until such apps are available for a wider range of products (e.g. clothes). What is more, as Microsoft develops its revolutionary HoloLens, virtual reality is going to have an immense impact on online consumer decision-making, and may turn out to be a great solution for some online shopping problems.[78]

5.2. *What about practical matters?*

Looking at the EU, the CRD is a package of rules that absolutely fails to take into account *how* they should be communicated to consumers. What is clear is that Article 6 that entails information duties will be provided in a 'clear and comprehensible manner'. What is also clear is that Article 8(7) requires the confirmation of information on a durable medium. Nevertheless, what is not known for sure is whether displaying *all* the required information on a website is clear and comprehensible in itself to start with. E-stores also need to catch the eyes of consumers and attract them to buy. On the other hand, what benefit does a consumer derive out of having to dig through every page of the website to make sure all necessary information is accessed? Even the most aware consumers could have a hard time understanding what rights are applicable to them by virtue of the law or by virtue of voluntary promises made by the sellers. From this

[75] J.C. Shearman, 'Return Fraud Cost 9.1 Billion in 2013', *National Retail Federation* (1 January 2014). Available at: https://nrf.com/news/return-fraud-cost-91-billion-2013 (last accessed 21 November 2014).

[76] Ibid.

[77] *See* the L'Oreal website for more details about the app. Available at: www.lorealparis.ca/_en/_ca/brands/makeup-genius/ (last accessed on 25 August 2015).

[78] *See* the Microsoft website for more details about the HoloLens. Available at: https://www.microsoft.com/microsoft-hololens/en-us (last accessed on 25 August 2015).

perspective, information duties are rather paradoxical, especially in the lengthy format prescribed by the CRD.

Moreover, the durable medium requirement remains a mystery. In *Content Services*, a link to a website under the control of the trader was deemed not to be a durable medium.[79] And yet, this seems to be the practice of all three European e-stores we visited. It is true that some websites require the creation of a personal account, however, the Content Services website operated exactly in the same way, and yet that was not sufficient to comply with the law.

Moreover, online contracts cannot exist in isolation from the other obligations a trader has in on-premise contracts as well. In the EU, one of these obligations is the legal guarantee, as required by the Consumer Sales Directive. However, overlaps between these obligations (e.g. Article 6(l) CRD) can be confusing both for the trader as well as for the consumer. The trader will normally operate with commercial guarantees, as was clearly seen on all three European websites, since these platforms distribute goods and very rarely produce them (e.g. the Amazon Kindle). Since the businesses behind the websites will most likely obtain their own commercial guarantees from other distributors or directly from producers, it is understandable that they will not focus on solving defective goods claims under the legal guarantee, regardless of whether the protection standards of the legal and commercial guarantee might overlap.

Logistical aspects of business practices have simply not been addressed by EU legislation beyond the creation of a standard withdrawal form, and a rather similar situation exists in Japan and New York. It can indeed be argued that these are procedural steps outside the scope of substantive law. However, the content of the Directive leaves the impression that these more practical aspects were not even acknowledged by the design of the CRD. For this reason, businesses try to come up with whatever solutions they have access to, provided that these solutions contribute to making transactions more efficient. Examples of this are the FAQs page (thereby reducing the number of questions by e-mail or phone call), withdrawal forms with catchy doodles that make it easy to understand how to return goods, or self-adhesive postal stickers which sometimes even cover transportation costs (e.g. bol.com). Amazon.co.uk took a very creative approach and tried to provide consumers with a venue to get rid of goods even if they cannot return them – the sell or swap policy. According to this option, consumers can use the Amazon marketplace to sell the good or barter it for another item. While it might depend on the nature of the product, the very idea that the consumers might not be at a loss even if they do not have a withdrawal right can be a strong argument against the view that mandatory withdrawal rights are necessary.

The features dealt with above are just a few examples of transactional details that are not included in policy or academic discussions relating to withdrawal rights. Future research should consider similar aspects of online contracts especially because, just as we

79 Case C-49/11, *Content Services Ltd v* Bundesarbeitskammer [2012], para. 43.

mentioned earlier, technology can help solve some of the problems both businesses and consumers might deal with when engaging in internet transactions. An example in this sense could be the creation of third party platforms operating consumer accounts where individuals could find information regarding the particular rights offered to them by specific traders. In our view, future research over how these technical solutions should look like could lead to practical proposals that businesses and consumer can directly benefit from.

VI. Conclusion

The objective of this contribution was not to advocate for one particular model of withdrawal right over another as *the* model that best protects consumers. The purpose of our modest research was merely to discuss various consumer experiences in an attempt to narrow the gap between how academics perceive withdrawal rights and how consumers actually experience them. In order to do so, we researched five jurisdictions as consumers by actually ordering Apple's Magic Mouse from the largest e-stores in the Netherlands, Romania, the United Kingdom, Japan and the United States (New York), with the sole purpose of returning them and exercising our withdrawal rights. Once the withdrawal occurred, we collected all of the web information along with details sent to us by e-mail and we analysed our experiences.

For the European countries in particular, we used a comparative compliance table to identify how the websites reflected the new requirements of the CRD. The compliance table consisted of ticking information duties as mandated by Article 6(1) CRD. While all three European e-stores fulfilled most of their obligations in this respect, there were problems with the requirement of notifying the existence of a legal guarantee, and the provision of information on a durable medium.

In a nutshell, our online experiences with bol.com, eMag.ro and Amazon.co.uk were positive: We felt 'protected' knowing that we were entitled to our withdrawal rights and that the companies were required by law to ensure them. Given that this sense of empowerment could only exist when consumers are actually aware of their rights, the experience of different consumers will surely be mixed *ceteris paribus*. Otherwise, the information overload that occurs as a result of the traders being obliged to inform consumers might act against this awareness.

Our observation from online shopping outside of the EU, in jurisdictions where withdrawal rights for online shopping were not mandated by the government, was that consumers still felt – more or less – safe, empowered, and protected. The catch was that in order to feel that way required a bit more effort on the consumer's part (i.e. making sure that we bought from a seller that offered returns) and, at times, taking more of risks (i.e. deciding whether or not to buy goods from sellers that did not offer refunds because they were cheaper than those that did). In addition, we observed that even in jurisdictions like the US, where the level of consumer protection ensured by the federal government and the states were not as high as that of the EU, we still felt that we were entitled to a return regardless of online or in-store shopping because a great majority of sellers, including but not limited to Amazon, Wal Mart, K-Mart, Target, and Costco just to name a few all offer 30 – 90 day returns as their company policy, even if not mandated by the government to do so.

These experiences inspired the creation of a classification of withdrawal rights into: (i) mandatory rights; (ii) default/optional rights; and (iii) insurance rights. Our conclusions are unsurprisingly mixed, as all withdrawal models seem to face issues, both in theory as well as in practice. In sum, the observation that mandatory withdrawal rights are not necessary in order for consumers to feel protected possibly because most major companies end up offering refunds any way, goes to substantiate our hypothesis that mandatory withdrawal rights, as promoted by the EU, is not the only way to ensure consumer protection, nor is it the 'best' way of doing so.

One last take away from this experiment was to discuss the features of online shopping outside of the academic debate. For example, finding information on a website, logistical support offered by traders, the use of personal accounts registered on the traders' website, and any other business practices aimed at making withdrawal more transaction-friendly. From this perspective, we consider that European law makes no contribution to simplifying the procedures affiliated with the exercise of withdrawal rights, but that the non-European systems did not really have any solutions for this either.

IUS COMMUNE EUROPAEUM

A peer-reviewed book series in which the common foundations of the legal systems of the Member States of the European Union are the central focus.

The *Ius Commune Europaeum* series includes horizontal comparative legal studies as well as studies on the effect of treaties within the national legal systems. All the classic fields of law are covered. The books are published in various European languages under the auspices of METRO, the Institute for Transnational Legal Research at Maastricht University.

Recently published:
Volume 128: *Tradition, Codification and Unification. Comparative – Historical Essays on Developments in Civil Law*, J.M. Milo, J.H.A. Lokin and J.M. Smits
Volume 129: *Nobody's Perfect. Comparative Essays on Appeals and Other Means of Recourse Against Judicial Decisions in Civil matters*, A. Uzelac and C.H. van Rhee (eds.)
Volume 130: *Legal Aid in the Low Countries*, B. Hubeau and A. Terlouw (eds.)
Volume 131: *State Aid and Public Procurement in the European Union*, S. Schoenmaekers, W. Devroe and N. Philipsen (eds.)
Volume 132: *Property Law Perspectives III*, A. Apers, S. Bouly et al. (eds.)
Volume 133: *Multi-Party Redress Mechanisms in Europe: Squeaking Mice?*, V. Harsági and C.H. van Rhee (eds.)
Volume 134: *Europe at the Edge of Pluralism*, D. Gozdecka and M. Kmak
Volume 135: *Cooperative Agreements between Public Authorities. The Influence of CJEU Case Law on National Legal Systems*, K. Wauters
Volume 136: *Common Core, PECL and DCFR: Could They Change Shipping and Transport Law?*, W. Verheyen, F.G.M. Smeele and M.A.I.H. Hoeks
Volume 137: *Who does What? On the Allocation of Competences in European Private Law*, B. Akkermans, J. Hage, N. Kornet and J.M. Smits
Volume 138: *The Nature of Mutual Recognition in European Law*. W. van Ballegooij
Volume 139: *Evidence in Contemporary Civil Procedure. Fundamental Issues in a Comparative Perspective*, C.H. van Rhee and A. Uzelac (eds.)
Volume 140: *The Effect of D&O Insurance on Managerial Risk Taking*, Maximilian K.P. Gaber

www.ingramcontent.com/pod-product-compliance
Ingram Content Group UK Ltd.
Pitfield, Milton Keynes, MK11 3LW, UK
UKHW051927100926
8556IPUK00022B/1421

9 781780 683539